GL ...ON

Theory and Practice

Third Edition

Edited by Eleonore Kofman
and Gillian Youngs

continuum

NEW YORK • LONDON

2008

The Continuum International Publishing Group Inc
80 Maiden Lane, New York, NY 10038

The Continuum International Publishing Group Ltd
The Tower Building, 11 York Road, London SE1 7NX
www.continuumbooks.com

Printed in the United States of America

 Library of Congress Cataloging-in-Publication Data

Globalization : theory and practice / edited by Eleonore Kofman and Gillian Youngs. – 3rd ed.
        p. cm.
 Includes bibliographical references and index.
 ISBN-13: 978-0-8264-9364-4 (hardcover : alk. paper)
 ISBN-10: 0-8264-9364-5 (hardcover : alk. paper)
 ISBN-13: 978-0-8264-9365-1 (pbk. : alk. paper)
 ISBN-10: 0-8264-9365-3 (pbk. : alk. paper) 1. Globalization. I. Kofman, Eleonore. II. Youngs, Gillian, 1956- III. Title.

 JZ1318.G67916 2008
 303.48′2—dc22

                              2007036214

Contents

PART 5   Knowledge and Technologies

Contributors

Jon Binnie is Reader in the Department of Environmental and Geographical Science at Manchester Metropolitan University. His main research interests are geographies of sexuality; citizenship and governance; and cosmopolitanism and everyday life. He is coeditor of *Cosmopolitan Urbanism* (Routledge, 2006) and author of *The Globalization of Sexuality* (Sage, 2004).

Philip G. Cerny is Professor of Global Political Economy in the Division of Global Affairs, Rutgers University – Newark (New Jersey, USA) and is also Professor Emeritus of Government at the University of Manchester (UK). His most recent publications are the coedited *Internalizing Globalization: The Rise of Neoliberalism and the Erosion of National Models of Capitalism* (Macmillan, 2005), 'Dilemmas of Operationalizing Hegemony', in M. Haugaard and H. Lentner, eds., *Hegemony and Power: Consensus and Coercion in Contemporary Politics* (Lexington Books, 2006), and 'Restructuring the State in a Globalizing World: Capital Accumulation, Tangled Hierarchies and the Search for a New Spatio-Temporal Fix', *Review of International Political Economy* (October 2006).

Simon Dalby is Professor of Geography and Political Economy at Carleton University in Ottawa, where he teaches courses on environment and geopolitics. He has degrees from Trinity College Dublin, the University of Victoria and from Simon Fraser University in Vancouver. He is coeditor of *Rethinking Geopolitics* (Routledge, 1998) and of *The Geopolitics Reader* (Routledge, 1998; 2nd ed., 2006) and author of *Environmental Security* (University of Minnesota Press, 2002).

Chris Farrands is Principal Lecturer in International Relations at Nottingham Trent University, where he teaches and researches contemporary theory of international relations and international political economy. He is the author of around 70 papers and articles in these areas in journals, including *Global Society*, *Journal of Common Market Studies*, *Theoria*, and *Alternatives*, as well as a number of single or coauthored books, the most recent concerned with technology and global political economy.

Dr Gerhard Fuchs, University of Stuttgart, Institute for Social Sciences, focuses his research on information and communications technologies, innovation and regional economic restructuring. Recent publications include his work as coeditor with H.-J. Braczyk and H.-G. Wolf in *Multimedia and Regional Economic Restructuring* (Routledge, 1999), editor of *Biotechnology in Comparative Perspective. Industry. Development and Regional Concentration* (Routledge, 2003), and coeditor with Philip Shapira of *Rethinking Regional Innovation* (Springer, 2005).

Richard J. Harknett is Faculty Chair of the Charles Phelps Taft Research Center at the University of Cincinnati. He is author of *Lenses of Analysis: A Visual Framework for the Study of International Politics* (W.W. Norton, 2001) and coeditor of *The Absolute Weapon Revisited: Nuclear Arms and the Emerging International Order* (University of Michigan, 2001). His research on international security dynamics has been published in such journals as *Security Studies, Parameters, The Berkeley Press Forum, Orbis, National Security Studies Quarterly* as well as several edited volumes.

Ahmet Icduygu is Professor of International Relations at Koc University. He has a particular interest in immigration, irregular and transit migration, citizenship and civil society. He has written numerous articles on these issues and is coeditor of *Citizenship in a Global World: European Questions and Turkish Experiences* (Routledge, 2005).

Eleonore Kofman is Professor of Gender, Migration and Citizenship at Middlesex University, UK and Review Editor of the journal *Political Geography*. She has written extensively on feminist political geography and on gendered migrations in Europe. She is the coauthor of *Gender and Migration in Europe: Employment, Welfare and Politics* (Routledge, 2000) and coeditor of *Mapping Women Making Politics: Feminist Perspectives on Political Geography* (Routledge, 2004).

Emma Mawdsley lectures in Geography at the University of Cambridge and is a Fellow of Newnham College. She is particularly interested in the interface between development studies and political geography, and has worked on non-secessionist regionalism in India and how that relates to issues of environment, gender and development, and on the transnational community of NGOs. She is currently working on middle-class environmentalism in India and contemporary relations between India and Africa.

Hélène Pellerin is Associate Professor at the School of Political Studies at the University of Ottawa. She has published several articles and book chapters on the regulation of migration in the context of regional integration, and of globalization. She is coediting with Christina Gabriel *Governing International Labour Migration* (Routledge, 2008).

V. Spike Peterson is Professor in the Department of Political Science at the University of Arizona. She coauthored (with Anne Sisson Runyan) *Global Gender Issues* (1993, 1999). Her most recent book, *A Critical Rewriting of Global Political Economy: Integrating Reproductive, Productive and Virtual Economies* (Routledge 2003), examines intersections of ethnicity/ race, class, gender and national hierarchies in GPE. Her current research investigates informalization and 'coping, combat, and criminal economies' in conflict zones.

Jan Jindy Pettman is Emeritus Professor of the Australian National University, and Visiting Fellow in Gender, Sexuality and Culture at ANU. She is the author of *Worlding Women: A Feminist International Politics* (Routledge, 1996) and a founding editor of the *International Feminist Journal of Politics*. Her current research focuses on transnational feminist organizing, and feminist critiques of war, identity and peace.

Gina Porter is Senior Research Fellow in Anthropology at Durham University, UK. Her recent research has focused principally on rural access, market institutions and social networks (including those at the NGO-state interface) in West Africa. She is currently leading a three-country research study of children's mobility employing a child-centred approach.

Anne Sisson Runyan is Professor of Women's Studies and Head of the Department of Women's Studies at the University of Cincinatti. The author of many publications in the areas of feminist international relations and political economy, her current projects include the third edition of *Global Gender Issues* (coauthored with V. Spike Peterson), the second edition of *Gender and Global Restructuring: Sightings, Sites, and Resistances* (coedited with Marianne H. Marchand), a monograph on transnational feminisms as world feminist politics, and a coedited collection on women's human rights, citizenships and identities in a North American context.

Banu Senay is PhD Scholar at the Centre for Research on Social Inclusion at Macquarie University. Her PhD research project explores the production of knowledge about Turkishness among the Turkish community in Sydney through transnationalism from above and below. Her research interests include citizenship, transnationalism, diasporic and migrant communities.

Tracy Simmons is a lecturer in the Department of Media and Communication at the University of Leicester, UK. A key research interest is concerned with sexuality and immigration, which was the subject of her doctoral thesis examining UK immigration provision for same-sex couples.

Tracey Skelton is Professor of Critical Geographies at Loughborough University. Her research within the Caribbean focuses on Montserrat, in particular the social and cultural impacts of the volcanic disaster. She does research on young people's geographies and is the Viewpoints Editor for *Children's Geographies*. From mid-2007 she has been working in the Department of Geography at the National University of Singapore, where she is blending her research on global processes and small island communities with geographies of children and young people.

David Slater is Professor of Social and Political Geography at Loughborough University, UK. His latest book is *Geopolitics and the Post-Colonial* (Blackwell, Oxford, 2004), and his current research focuses on imperiality and the geopolitics of memory.

Roy Smith is Co-Director of the Centre for Asia-Pacific Studies and Principal Lecturer in the Department of International Studies, Nottingham Trent University. His primary area of research is the small island states of the Pacific. Publications include *Diseases of*

Globalization: Socioeconomic Change and Health, coauthored with Chris McMurray (Earthscan, 2001) and articles in *Security Dialogue* and the *International Journal of Politics and Ethics*.

Jill Steans is Senior Lecturer in International Relations Theory at the University of Birmingham. Her research interests are in the fields of gender and international relations theory and international political economy. She is the author of *Gender and International Relations: Issues, Debates and Future Directions* (Polity Press, 2nd ed., 2006) and coauthor of *International Relations: Perspectives and Themes* (Longman, 2005).

Peter J. Taylor is Professor of Geography at Loughborough University and Director of the Globalization and World Cities (GaWC) Research Network, a virtual centre for cities in globalization (www.lboro.ac.uk/gawc). His latest books are *World City Network: A Global Urban Analysis* (Routledge, 2004), *Cities in Globalization: Practices, Policies and Theories* (Routledge, 2006), coedited with Ben Derudder, and *Political Geography: World-Economy, Nation-State, Locality* (Pearson, 5th ed., 2006), coauthored with Colin Flint.

Janet Townsend is Senior Research Investigator in the School of Geography, Politics and Sociology at the University of Newcastle, UK. Her research has been chiefly in low-income countries, first with pioneers settling the rainforests of Latin America, later with women in the rainforests, with women's self-empowerment and, more recently, with nongovernment organizations working in 'development', again in low-income countries.

Marc Williams is Professor of International Relations, University of New South Wales, Sydney, Australia. His current research focuses on trade politics, sustainable consumption, and the politics of genetically modified food. He is coauthor, with Robert O'Brien, Anne Marie Goetz and Jan Aart Scholte, of *Contesting Global Governance: Multilateral Economic Institutions and Global Social Movements* (Cambridge University Press, 2000), and coauthor, with Robert O'Brien of *Global Political Economy: Evolution and Dynamics* (Palgrave, 2nd ed., 2007).

Gillian Youngs is Senior Lecturer in the Department of Media and Communication at Leicester University, UK. Her main research interests are globalization, diverse issues of inequality including gender, the politics and economics of information and communication technologies (ICTs), and the impact of the 'war on terror'. She serves on the editorial boards of *International Feminist Journal of Politics* (which she cofounded), *Political Geography*, *Journal of Global Ethics*, and *Development*. Her publications include *Global Political Economy in the Information Age: Power and Inequality* (Routledge, 2007), *International Relations in a Global Age: A Conceptual Challenge* (Polity, 1999), and the edited collection, *Political Economy, Power and the Body: Global Perspectives* (Macmillan, 2000). In addition to journal articles and chapters in academic publications, she has contributed to diverse policy-related processes and publications in her areas of expertise both in the UK and internationally, including different sections of UNESCO and a range of NGOs.

Preface

Gillian Youngs and Eleonore Kofman

Globalization became a core-connecting concept in the early stages of the twenty-first century. From its lowly status as a primarily academic term in the latter part of the twentieth century, it rose to pervade all ranges of professional and cultural realms: business, the economy, politics, culture and the arts, the media, to name but a few. The scepticism that surrounded the introduction of the term in academia a decade or more ago when the first edition of this volume was published (1996) has been overtaken by a commonplace use of the term that can hardly ever have been expected. The problems voiced in that volume about its lack of specificity endure, but are now dwarfed by an apparent general embrace of it in virtually every domain of human endeavour. Does such a development make a collection such as this more or less relevant? Obviously that is a question best answered by readers. But it is worth reflecting on it from the editors' point of view with regard to this third edition.

Clearly globalization as a field of study now has its own history. It may be relatively new, but it has passed quite quickly from purely an academic or expert area of concern to one that is part of everyday discourse. One aspect of this progression, if it can be regarded as such, is its relevance as much to individuals as to major institutions, to the ways in which they think about the actions and justifications of their governments, the functioning (or not) of their economies, their work destinies and consumption habits, their concerns about the environment, new and changing migration patterns, and so on. So perhaps this volume might attract more interest from a general readership than its first two editions. It certainly appears at a time when globalization is well and truly outside the academic box and thus open to more mass scrutiny than ever before.

It is interesting to note the old and the new in this edition in that context. The collection continues to foreground questions of North and South and global gender inequalities, indicating a sense that these are still key areas in need of greater attention and wider critical understanding. Its focus on power maps the enduring political and military hegemony of the US as a defining characteristic of contemporary globalization, but also points to a new era of complex hegemony with the rise of powerful economies, notably China. The 'new' enlarged Europe and growing membership of former eastern bloc countries is part of this picture, as are the diverse security impacts of the so-called 'war on terror'.

This edition addresses the continuing move of environmental issues up the global agenda and global governance issues associated with the contrasting conflicts of interest in evidence there, especially between growing and rich economies. Patterns of production, consumption and investment continue to shape the tensions between those economies and stability across them. Technology and trade-related intellectual property rights (TRIPS) remain central to power and inequality across these areas, and the new section introduced in the second volume on this area has been updated. The growth and impact of information and communications technologies (ICTs) across, as much as within, national borders and their role in development is part of this picture. Global connectivity comes increasingly through virtual links as much as through the more familiar material ones.

New areas covered include sexuality, illustrating the extent to which globalization is a concept as much mobilized in relation to identity and cultural issues as at the more grand structural levels of international politics and the economy. 'We are all global now' has become the cry of the man or woman in the street or the rural village as much as the big corporation or major investor. Perhaps globalization is becoming a more democratic concept or at least one that has many more meanings to many more people and institutions (civil society as well as commercial, governmental or intergovernmental).

This edition retains the volume's roots in international relations and geography scholarship, but also reflects how they are linking with wide fields and areas of interest such as business, cultural and communications studies, signalling shifts in research frameworks associated with material developments related to globalization. Our aim is to maintain a critical edge in thinking through these developments and the complex ways in which individuals and groups, states and economies, are differentially advantaged and disadvantaged by them.

Acknowledgments

Eleonore Kofman and Gillian Youngs are grateful to the contributors for their continued interest in, and enthusiasm for, this project. They also thank colleagues near and far and their students who inspire their work.

An earlier version of chapter 4 was published as D. Slater. (2006) 'Imperial powers and democratic imaginations', *Third World Quarterly*, 27 (8), pp. 1369–86. An earlier version of chapter 7 was published as J. G. Townsend, R. Porter and E. E. Mawdsley. (2002) 'The role of the transnational community of non-governmental organizations: governance or poverty reduction?' *Journal of International Development*, 14 (6), pp. 829–39. We are grateful for permission to publish the versions that appear in this volume.

Part 1

Globalization, Political Economy and Political Geography

CHAPTER 1

Complex Hegemony and Twenty-first Century Globalization

Gillian Youngs

Globalization has taken on major new patterns in the first decade of the twenty-first century, making real much that was heralded by early debates about the phenomenon. This is in other words a kind of 'coming of age' of globalization, and is part of this fresh power dynamics that signal a new era of complex hegemony (Youngs, 2007: 127–42). The purpose of this chapter is to explore this picture of 'old' and 'new' and, equally important, to map some of the influential connections between them. This picture makes clear the fundamental fact that even if we adhere to what might be termed a short history of globalization[1], there is indeed a history to be mapped. Such a short history relates to the latter part, say thirty years, of the twentieth century to the present day, and is the main focus of this chapter.

Two main arguments are developed, the first concerning the spatial reach of globalization, and its 'coming of age' as an East-West phenomenon, notably with the rise of China as in the first instance a major economic power. The second associated argument is that from a stage of globalization as arguably primarily Westernization and/or Americanization (see, for example, Slater and Taylor, 1999), we have now moved into a stage of complex hegemony where certainly economic (and most likely political and cultural) influence will increasingly be located in the East (China) as much as in the West. I examine how these interconnected developments represent historic shifts in globalization that deeply inform how its new patterns will develop in the future.

They also inform how we might review the short history of globalization to pay more attention, for instance, to the geographical disagregation of the 'West' to include Japan (part of the triad of power with the USA and the EU (see Strange, 1994, 1997). This disagregation reminds us that the 'West' was (and is) a description related to power and political economy, Japan being defined as much (and perhaps more) by its integration into the dominant Western political economy, including its trading and monetary regimes, as by its geographical location. With the economic growth of China, we now have at least a dual focus in the 'East' with major distinctions between Japan and China, the latter being a relative newcomer to, and only at the stage of growing (while still highly significant) integration into, the global (liberal) economic system. The distinctions between Japan and China are political and economic, with the former, broadly speaking, in the liberal democratic camp, and the latter continuing as a communist authoritarian state with market characteristics.

s new stage of complex hegemony can only be understood in depth
political economy that reminds us of the inevitable ties between the ways
, govern and regulate ourselves as human communities (local, national
ai) and the resources through which we enact and secure such governance. The
complexity of contemporary hegemony is far from neat. It does not locate the main share
of political, economic and cultural influence in one or a few closely linked locations. It is in
such ways much more challenging in terms of theory and practice (e.g., policy) than the
early stages of the short history of globalization may have seemed to be (although may not
necessarily have been). I maintain that it requires a much more 'global' perspective and one
that is nuanced in recognizing asymmetric balances of political, economic and cultural
power even between the major players.

The 'coming of age' of globalization: East meets West

The twentieth century marked the passing from the Pax Britannica to the Pax Americana
(Cox, 1981), the establishment and assertion of US hegemony (Strange, 1994), including its
strategic roles in the two world wars (1914–18 and 1939–45), and, some would argue, its
ultimate triumph in the collapse of the Soviet Union communist bloc at the end of the 1980s
(for a range of assessments on these areas related to globalization, see, for example: Kennedy,
1989; Agnew and Corbridge, 1995; Clark, 1997; Slater and Taylor, 1999). Towards the end
of the twentieth century, there were three notable strands of debate. The first related to
whether US hegemony endured directly or indirectly. Those who favoured the former emphasized, for example, American military and associated technological dominance and
concentrations of US institutional and corporate power in the global economy (see, for
example, Strange, 1994 and 1997). The rise and decline of American hegemony debate, in
certain ways, linked notions of direct and indirect power. It included discussion of the ongoing structural influence of the US through the neoliberal ideology steering the institutional
architecture of the global political economy, including the International Monetary Fund
(IMF), World Bank and more recently, World Trade Organization (WTO).

The internationalizaton/liberalization/freer trade (and, in the 1980s and beyond, dereg-
ulation/privatization) principles defining the post-1945 Bretton Woods and General Agreement on Tariffs and Trade (GATT) financial and trading system, and reflecting strongly US
and Western interests, persisted, despite the 1970s collapse of the gold/dollar standard.
'Hegemonic stability theory' and 'after hegemony' debates placed major focus on institutional (regime) influence (see, in particular, Keohane 1984, 1986 and 1989; Baldwin, 1993).
These firmly featured the state-centric logic of the discipline of international relations dominant theory of realism, and its more political-economy-oriented extension neorealism, and
some critiques of them (Youngs, 1999).

Notions of an indirect persistence of US hegemony are most closely linked to the development of globalization perspectives. Whether in the original post–Cold War 'new world
order' guise or that of the by now famous and infamous 'end of history' thesis of Francis
Fukuyama (1992), the emphasis was on the global triumph of capitalism and its associated
liberal political and economic principles (Little, 1995; Youngs, 1996). The implications of
the 'end of history' approach were that liberal ideology and the social and individual development and freedoms it offered were the most universally applicable, proven and available
way forward at the global level.

This current stage of complex hegemony both supports the 'end of history' thesis's emphasis on the global triumph of capitalism and its associated liberal political and economic principles, and contests them. This support and contestation is witnessed in the notable example of China as both a rising economic giant on the global stage but a state defined by communist politics albeit in increasingly market-oriented form. While Fukuyama's thesis celebrates what it sees as the interconnection between liberal democratic freedoms in political and economic guises, China is explicitly maintaining distinctions between such political and economic freedoms by actively inhibiting the former while facilitating to some degree the latter. China's experimentation with, and modification of, capitalism at both national and international levels is at one and the same time an affirmation of the global success of liberal political economic principles and a denial of the inevitability (certainly at least in the immediate and short term) of liberal economy's dependence on liberal politics in any grand sense at the national level.

China's growing economic status means that globalization is a truly global geographic phenomenon for the first time, stretching from East to West, with, of course, as has always been the case, significant gaps and huge unevenness in between, including within China itself. The scale and speed of China's economic boom has been truly breathtaking (see, for example, Youngs, 2007: 96–97). Its growth rate in gross domestic product (GDP) terms – averaging almost 8 per cent in the twenty years to 2003 – was described as 'spectacular', equally so the growth in its share of world trade from less than 1 percent in 1979 to around 6 percent by 2003 (Prasad and Rumbaugh, 2004: 1). Its integration as a leading growth economy globally was equally notable, with it following the USA and the UK as the third largest recipient of Foreign Direct Investment (FDI) by 2004 (UNCTAD, 2005: ix), and by 2003 being the third largest importer of developing countries' exports after the United States and European Union.

The rapid development and diversification of China's economy has been part of this picture, with shifts in its exports towards higher-end electronics and other goods from textiles and light manufacturing, a feature between the early 1990s and early 2000s (Rumbaugh and Blancher, 2004: 7). The World Bank (2007a: 3–4) has emphasized the regional as well as the global dimensions of China's influence, pointing out, for example, that it has proved a fast-growing market for components and other inputs from other East Asian economies. This has resulted in 'a new division of labour, with pan-Asian production networks centred on China as a final integrator of products for export to the outside world, and a rapid rise in intra-regional trade in production inputs' (4).

In spring 2007 the World Bank forecast GDP growth for the year in China at 10.4 per cent and a current account surplus of almost 11 percent of GDP (World Bank, 2007b: 1). The growth continued to be industry-led, fuelled by external trade and investment, China's stock markets were reported to be 'booming' and export growth to the EU and developing world 'surging' (1). As already the world's third-largest trading nation, China was anticipated by the Organisation for Economic Co-operation and Development (OECD) to account for 10 percent of all trade by 2010.[2] By the end of 2006, China's foreign reserves passed \$1 trillion and its current account surplus was estimated to have overtaken Japan's to be the world's largest (World Bank 2007a: 3, 39).

China's rapid establishment of itself as a leading economic player was all too obvious and most global attention was fixed on this. But I would agree with Will Hutton's emphasis on the wider political implications of this growing power.

ew factor in global politics and economics, and its rulers and people
s the single most important financier of the United States' enormous
t is the world's second largest importer of oil. Before 2010, it will be
gest exporter of goods. It is, comfortably, the world's second largest
military power. . . . A new great power is in the making. (Hutton, 2007a. See also
Hutton, 2007b)

All the indications are that the story of the twenty-first century will be substantially about
the nature and impact of China as a 'great power'. Learning about the economic dimensions
of this story is well underway as globalization 'comes of age' as a truly East-West phenomenon, but learning about the political (and cultural) dimensions is likely to feature
among the biggest challenges of globalization in the coming years.

So, I would argue, there is much to contest a simple 'end of history' perspective on
contemporary globalization. Indeed, quite the reverse, in that a whole new phase of world
history is unravelling, where new economic powers (notably China but also India) are drivers
from Asia rather than the West. The diverse political implications of such growing power
are far from evident as yet.

There are several aspects of this situation that are worth touching on before I go on to
look at the complex hegemony that is beginning to characterize this stage of globalization.
The first relates to the familiar debates about whether globalization challenges the authority of states or is, in part at least, an expression of such authority, albeit perhaps in new
(and sometimes global) forms (Strange, 1997). The rise of China contributes, I would
argue, to both sides of this debate in different ways. In so doing, it demonstrates the contradictory forces of globalization in action, and, equally importantly, the dynamism that is
at its heart, including pressures on, and changes in, relationships between political and
economic processes.

I have argued (Youngs, 2007: 134) that while we talk about China's rise, this is perhaps
too state-centred a perspective on what has actually happened. Clearly China's economic
growth has been a matter of state policy and productivity and wealth generation by that
country's people. But, it is also worth noting that the Chinese economic miracle has been
substantially fuelled through the latter part of the twentieth century and the beginning of
the twenty-first century by the direction to it of the bulk of FDI from rich economies. It is,
arguably, as much a miracle of globalization as it is an internal economic transformation
(see, for example, Youngs, 1997). Both are clearly important and interrelated. They indicate
that the story of China's success should be told as much in terms of globalization (or global
political economy) as of an individual country. We could think about this as in part a transformation of Western hegemony in the era of globalization into a story of markets as much
as states.

There are complicated political-economic contradictions and tensions in this picture,
for part of China's state power is clear in its adherence to a distinctive path through globalization, including a duality of politics. It is holding firm to a communist line in relation
to its internal (state) politics, while engaging with and building its growing power in a contrasting liberal global political economy. Its global market success is being built in large part
on state control and direction. Commentators such as Will Hutton (2007b) do not see this
as a long-term possibility, positing that the tensions between the liberal and the communist
sides are likely to result in pressure towards the former.

For Hutton (2007a), an 'enlightenment infrastructure' consisting of 'an independent public realm that includes free intellectual inquiry, free trade unions and independent audit' represents 'in both the West and East . . . the essential underpinning of a healthy society'. So akin to the 'end of history' framing of the inevitable intertwining of liberal politics and economics, Hutton foresees the duality of Chinese politics as ultimately unsustainable. His 'guess is that sometime in the mid to late 2010s, the growing Chinese middle class will want to hold Chinese officials and politicians to account for how they spend their taxes and for their political choices' (Hutton 2007a). Clearly we don't know exactly what will happen yet, but I tend to agree with Hutton's (2007a) conclusion that 'China's route to becoming a world economic power is not going to proceed as a simple extrapolation of current trends'.

I have made some related points about the Internet and its role in China's development, where China's contradictory positions over the market and internal politics are being played out daily (Youngs, 2007: 133). While promoting information and communications technologies (ICTs) and Internet use as part of its economic development, China is simultaneously exerting its state control as rigidly and extensively as possible to inhibit knowledge sharing and political exchange and connection online about democracy. In both technological and communications senses, the Internet represents a powerful arena in which the neoliberal principles of free exchange (politically and culturally as much as economically) are being expressed and enacted. In other words, we can think of such principles as being embedded within the fundamental nature and workings of technologies such as the Internet. While this ideological dimension can be undermined by forms of control exerted by countries, such as China[3], it may be that its intrinsic techno-political influence can persist in some ways despite this.

Complex hegemony: the new stage of globalization

The globalization unfolding in the first decade of the twenty-first century therefore offers a more complex picture of power than the earlier stage of late-twentieth-century globalization. While the height of US and Western power remains a major consideration economically, politically and culturally, what we might think of as the 'pure' stage of Americanization and Westernization as globalization is now accompanied by the rise of China in the East and its growing global influence. This influence is most evident economically, but its increasing political and cultural impact in the world is likely to be a feature of the decades to come. This time of complex hegemony requires a broad East-West geographical perspective, and a sense of how the dominant neoliberal ideology of globalization to date may be challenged and modified by China's efforts to separate liberal politics and economics, and to reject the former and to shape the latter to its own needs and goals.

One problem in these developments is the relative lack of knowledge about China's path compared to the neoliberal principles and agenda that have been writ large in globalization up to now. As a communist state operating on the basis of substantial state control and direction, transparency is far from high on the political agenda in China either internally or externally. So it may well be that some key processes of globalization in the coming years will be much less evident or subject to scrutiny in advance or as they are underway than they have been previously. If we take China's growing power seriously as a rapidly changing force for globalization, then detecting and understanding the nature of aspects of that change may well be one of the major challenges for those in the neoliberal camp. While undergoing and facilitating massive economic change due to globalization, China has worked to maintain political continuity. The contrast across the economic and political dimensions of China has been stressed as particularly strong. 'Globalization has brought about sea changes to every aspect of economic and social life in China. Nevertheless, the Chinese state appears to have remained in its traditional Leninist form' (Zheng, 2004: 1). One result of this scenario can be argued as a bringing back of the centrality of the state to debates about the future of globalization, now that we have such starkly different forms of state (the USA and China) wielding power and influence albeit of different kinds at this stage.

On the economic side, China's rapid industrialization and modernization has introduced a whole new historical model in economic capitalism that is distinct from the long, slow, stage-by-stage industrial development in Europe and America. In simple terms there is a sense in which everything is happening at once in China, so, to some degree, there is a collapsing of the familiar framework of historical stages of industrial development into one where multiple forms of economic transition are taking place in parallel. China represents not just a traditional industrial miracle in terms of speed of development but also a rapidly rising 'new economy' in terms of ICTs.

'China's globalization is driven not only by foreign investment and trade, but also by the rapid development of an information society' (Zheng, 2004: 7). ICTs have been a significant part of the success story of major economic growth in China and India, resulting in 'new' and 'old' (traditional industrial) economic developments running to some extent side by side. This phenomenon has severely disrupted old-fashioned and simplified hierarchical notions of developed and developing economies on the technological front, resulting in an increasingly hybrid picture of economic innovation across them. UNCTAD (2006: 57) reported that FDI in China's manufacturing sector had been shifting towards more advanced technologies, with, for example, foreign transnational corporations (TNCs) investing $1 billion in China's integrated circuit industry in 2005.

The notion of 'leapfrogging' in this context, where developing economies can harness the possibilities of ICTs to speed up their growth and benefit from the global economy, is a new focus in the study of the global economy, most notably because of the contrasting examples of China and India.[4] This is another area where the complexity of power distribution in globalization, especially in terms of dynamic growth, is bound to attract increasing attention. A major hegemonic characteristic of globalization in the late twentieth century, of technological advances and ownership concentrated in the triad (the USA, Japan and the EU), continues.[5] UNCTAD statistics (2006: xviii), for example, made it clear that the triad continued to dominate in the sphere of TNCs, being home to 85 of the world's top 100 TNCs in 2004. Five countries (France, Germany, Japan, the UK and the USA) accounted for 73 of the top 100 firms, while 53 were from the EU (xviii).

But equally another aspect of the 'coming of age' of the current period of globalization is the growing role of developing country TNCs, with China at the forefront of these advances. In 2004, according to UNCTAD, five companies from developing economies featured in the top 100 TNCs: Hutchison Whampoa (Hong Kong, China), Petronas (Malaysia), Singtel (Singapore), Samsung Electronics (the Republic of Korea) and CITIC Group (China) (xviii). Of the top 100 TNCs from developing countries, 77 were headquartered in Asia, and the rest were evenly distributed between Africa and Latin America (xviii). China saw a sixfold increase in outward investments in 2005 amounting to $11 billion (5).

The World Bank (2007b: 1) identified a rebalancing of the economy in 'a shift in production from industry towards services' as a key economic challenge for China.

UNCTAD (2006: 57) reported that already in 2005 foreign banks and financial institutions invested about $12 billion in China's banking industry compared to $3 billion in 2004. This was yet another sign of rapid change. And the East-West picture of flows was highlighted by the news breaking in late July 2007 at the time of writing that 'the China Development Bank sent shockwaves round the City [of London] when it paid more than £1 bn to take a stake in Barclays' as 'part of a deal that will furnish Barclays with extra cash to buy ABN, the Dutch financial institution that is the target of a bidding war between Barclays and a consortium led by the Royal Bank of Scotland' (*Observer*, 2007: 4).[6] The language of the media coverage signalled the significant change that such outward investment by China represented in the overall picture of globalization. One analyst says:

> It's an extraordinary turn of events: Communist China helping a Western bank buy a continental competitor. This gives globalisation a new twist. The amount that the Chinese bank is paying is relatively small, but it throws the spotlight on foreign state-owned institutions and companies that are *gobbling*[7] up British firms with increasing frequency (*Observer*, 2007: 4; emphasis added).

Another feature of China's outward investment is the sourcing of the raw materials to fuel its economic miracle. 'FDI to access natural resources is very important for Chinese and Indian TNCs, as well as those from a number of other developing countries, because the security of supply of raw materials is deemed essential for their rapidly growing economies' (UNCTAD, 2006: 161). So, the latest stages of globalization increasingly feature the diverse roles of outward as well as inward investment. This is quite a 'twist' as the media commentary above suggests, when the outward economic influence of China, notably as a strategic investor, is of growing importance alongside its attractions as a host for investment and a boom marketplace.

It can be assumed that China's influence within the global economy will continue to expand, possibly very quickly, and possibly in many ways that may as yet be unanticipated. What may be even less clear are the implications for any growing political and cultural influence that China may have in the near future, either directly or indirectly associated with its economic power, or not as the case may be. In the current developing scenario of complex hegemony the linkages between shifting economic, political and cultural power are more challenging to map than they have been to date in the era of US hegemony. One distinguishing characteristic of the period of US hegemony has been the combined economic, political and cultural influence of the hegemon (for relevant debates see Slater and Taylor, 1999). And, even though China is already making huge inroads economically, we cannot yet know how closely, or in what ways, its growing global power will mirror such a combination of economic, political and cultural influence. Indeed we cannot know what the weighting across these three areas will be, what timings any developments may follow, and their implications. These are all obviously vital aspects to consider in contemporary and future debates about globalization.

There is no suggestion that the era of US hegemony is over yet. Its technological military might and global role, as demonstrated notably in the recent Iraq war and its aftermath, and the 'war on terror', are prime considerations here.[8] So are its continuing and historically embedded leadership roles and influence in key global political and economic institutions, and the clout of its giant transnational corporations and their global brands. Such factors, and there are of course many more that can be listed in relation to the ongoing unilateral power of the USA, bring us back to debates around the 'end of history' thesis. They give pause for thought about the kind of hegemonic influence communist China could have in a world where American and Western neoliberalism has defined the major frameworks of globalization.

Of course such terms can be challenged and it could be argued that China's hybrid communist market-oriented model is already doing this to some degree. The limits on it include its engagement in the neoliberal institutional framework of globalization. Marc Lanteigne (2005) argues that we need to take this engagement into detailed consideration when looking at the rise of China.

> China's opening to international institutions since the late 1980s is a crucial component in its multilateral approach to foreign policy and to the advancement of state power. What separates China from other states, and indeed previous global powers, is that not only is it 'growing up' within a milieu of international institutions far more developed than ever before, but more importantly, it is doing so while making active use of these institutions to promote the country's development of global power status. (Lanteigne, 2005: 1)

I would agree with Lanteigne's sense of the need for an expanded perspective on China in the coming years. 'It will be necessary to the study of China's evolving role in the world to look beyond material capabilities and power politics to gain further knowledge of how China cooperates with the international system' (Lanteigne, 2005: 172). One area of such cooperation that is high on the global agenda relates to sustainability and environmental issues (see also the chapter by Dalby in this volume) where China's massive economic growth has significantly exacerbated both its own and global problems. The environmental toll of its rapid development is constantly highlighted as one of China's toughest challenges, with it now containing 20 of the world's 30 most polluted cities (World Bank, 2007a: 3). Inequality gaps driven by rural/urban divides are another core issue for China, as they are in India and across the globe (see Youngs, 2007). Despite significant reductions in its poverty levels, China still had at the end of 2006 an estimated 8 per cent of the Chinese population, 105 million people, living on less than a dollar a day, the second largest number of poor in the world after India (World Bank, 2007a: 9).

Conclusion: the future of globalization

The discussion in this chapter suggests that globalization is moving into a dramatic new phase with many conceptual and substantive challenges especially related to great power dynamics and shifting patterns of hegemony. From my perspective this is probably the most exciting stage of globalization studies since their early days when this volume was first published in 1996. In just over a decade, globalization has moved from being a phenomenon primarily concerned with Western and especially US power in the global political economy and the dominant, increasingly institutionalized neoliberal patterns of global governance, trade and investment associated with it. Now we have the rise of China as a major growth economy and the potential of its expanding political and cultural influence in Asia and across the globe. I have argued that much is as yet unknown about that potential and how and when it may be manifested.

What we do know is that China as a rising great power does not simply map onto the historically established and dominant neoliberal shape of globalization. It remains a communist state harnessing the benefits of the capitalist global economy while attempting to constrain the impact on its centralized and illiberal style of government. It represents a new model in two important ways. The first is in disrupting the linkages between liberal economy and liberal politics, capturing and modifying the former to its own needs and denying the latter in favour of its own communist approach. Second, its speed of development offers a duality of 'old' and 'new' economies, of traditional manufacturing industrialization alongside high-tech information society, ICT-driven growth. It is not following the familiar stage-by-stage development that the whole of Western understanding of the history of political economy is based on.

The new shape of East-West globalization is as exciting and daunting and full of unknowns as the early days of globalization studies, and the implication of many of the points that I have raised is that we will increasingly need to look East as well as West for the knowledge and understanding we will need for the future, in theory as well as in practice. The role of ICTs in the growth of economies like China and India indicate that this need for eastward attention will include focus on the area of innovation, up to now so heavily steered by the West in the global economy. It is unlikely that we will long be able to assume that innovation will continue to be dominated solely by the triad of the USA, Japan and Europe. Other players will increasingly come onto the field.

This new phase of globalization is already seeing more prominence given to issues that were already well-established features of the global economy. Notable among these are environmental problems, at least in part as a result of industrial capitalism. Also, growing inequality gaps (both within and across states) fuelled substantially by rural/urban divides. We could hope that the extent of these shared problems across East-West globalization might help to generate more collective political will towards solutions to them, and also that innovations in political economy will increasingly be steered towards such solutions, as much if not more than their traditional orientation towards continued expansion of capitalist production and consumption. There are no guarantees of course, but there should be new possibilities.

Notes

1. There has been much debate about how globalization should be viewed in historical terms. For simplicity's sake we might look at this in terms of either a long or short view, with argument over periodizations for both. See, for example, Clark (1997) and Scholte (2005: chapter 3).
2. OECD's regional activities with China accessed online 24 July 2007 at http://www.oecd.org/document/16/0,3343,en_36335986_36339083_36449360_1_1_1_1,00.html.
3. Of course China is not alone in heavy censorship of the Internet. Other regimes opposed to (Western) democratic traditions of free speech such as Saudi Arabia have adopted such policies (see Youngs, 2007: 132–33; see also on associated issues Everard, 2000, and Amnesty International's campaign on the Internet and human rights, http://web.amnesty.org/pages/internet-index-eng, accessed online 25 July 2007).
4. See my discussion of both China and India and ICTs in Youngs (2007). Outsourcing has been among the key factors in the Indian case.

5. For a historical perspective, see, for example, Jones (2005).
6. Ultimately, the RBS-led consortium, not Barclays, triumphed in the ABN Amro takeover (see Financial Times, 2007).
7. The levels of private equity investment were another area gaining particular attention in the UK at this time. UNCTAD (2006: 18–19) pointed out that globally cross-border mergers and acquisitions (M&As) by private equity funds, hedge funds and other similar investors, were rising and reached a record $135 billion in 2005, accounting for as much as 19 per cent of total cross-border M&As. Statistics presented by International Financial Services London (IFSL) indicated that the UK's global share of private equity funds had risen from 10 per cent in 2004 to 30 per cent in 2006. Around 85 per cent of UK funds were raised to finance buyouts, with nearly three-quarters of funds coming from over-seas. At 2.2 per cent of gross domestic product (GDP), the UK had a higher ratio of investments and funds raised than any other country. A record $365 billion of private equity was reported by IFSL to have been invested globally in 2006, up nearly three times on the previous year (see IFSL, 2007a and b). The controversy surrounding this kind of investment, including its relation to tax breaks, was the subject of an examination by an all-party Commons Treasury committee in the UK (*The Guardian*, 2007). UNCTAD (2006: 19) commented on the global picture: '. . . the role of private equity in foreign acquisitions is particularly strongly debated when they invest in firms in distress. In a number of cases, private equity funds have been accused of putting companies up for resale within a short time period after squeezing profits out of them and laying off workers, or of slicing up and destroying companies. Sometimes they have been referred to as "heartless asset strippers", provoking a public outcry.' Transparency problems are part of the concerns over private equity investments. As IFSL (2007b: 1) explained: 'Categories of private equity investment include all types of venture investing, buyout investing and special situations. It should be stressed that any analysis of the private equity market is handicapped by a lack of readily available information.'
8. See the discussion on related points in Lanteigne (2005: 4–5).

References

Agnew, J. and Corbridge, S. (1995) *Mastering Space: Hegemony, Territory and International Political Economy*, London, Routledge.

Baldwin, D. A. (ed.) (1993) *Neorealism and Neoliberalism: The Contemporary Debate*, Transnational Corporations and the Transnationalization, Columbia University Press.

Clark, I. (1997) *Globalization and Fragmentation*, Oxford, Oxford University Press.

Cox, R. W. (1981) 'Social forces, states and world orders: beyond international relations theory', *Millennium: Journal of International Studies*, 10, 127–55.

Financial Times (2007) 'Companies – UK: Victory formally declared in ABN tussle', October 9, accessed online December 31, 2007 at http://search.ft.com/ftArticle?sortBy=gadatearticle&queryText=RBS+completes+takeover+of+ABN&y=5&aje=true&x=12&id=071009000036&ct=0

Fukuyama, F. (1992) *The End of History and the Last Man*, London, Penguin.

The Guardian (2007) 'MPs seek inquiry into private equity tax breaks', July 30, p. 21.

Hutton, W. (2007a) 'New China. New crisis', *Observer*, January 7, accessed online 25 July 2007 at http://observer.guardian.co.uk/review/story/0,,1984044,00.html.

———. (2007b) *The Writing on the Wall: China and the West in the 21ˢᵗ Century*, New York, Little Brown.

International Financial Services London (IFSL) (2007a) Press release. 'UK share of private equity funds raised triples in past two years to nearly a third of global total', 27 July, accessed online on 30 July 2007 at http://www.ifsl.org.uk.

International Financial Services London (IFSL) (2007b) *'Private Equity 2007'*, London, IFSL, accessed online on 30 July 2007 at http://www.ifsl.org.uk/uploads/CBS_Private_Equity_2007.pdf.

Jones, G. (2005) 'Multinationals from the 1930s to the 1980s' in A. D. Chandler Jr., B. Mazlish (eds), *Leviathans. Multinational Corporations and the New Global History*, Cambridge, Cambridge University Press, pp. 81–103.

Kennedy, P. (1989) *The Rise and Fall of the Great Powers: Economic Change and Military Conflict from 1500–2000*, London, Fontana.

Keohane, R. O. (1984) *After Hegemony: Cooperation and Discord in the World Political Economy*, Princeton, NJ, Princeton University Press.

Keohane, R. O. (ed) (1986) *Neorealism and Its Critics*, New York, Columbia University Press.

Keohane, R. O. (1989) *International Institutions and State Power*, Boulder, CO, Westview Press.

Lanteigne, M. (2005) *China and International Institutions: Alternate Paths to Global Power*, London, Routledge.

Little, R. (1995) 'International relations and the triumph of capitalism' in K. Booth and S. Smith (eds) *International Relations Theory Today*, Cambridge, Polity, pp. 62–89.

Observer (Business and Media Section) (2007) 'China takes great leap forward into Western markets', July 29, pp. 4–5.

Prasad, E. and Rumbaugh, T. (2004) 'Overview' in E. Prasad (ed), *China's Growth and Integration into the World Economy: Prospects and Challenges*, Washington, DC, International Monetary Fund, pp. 1–4. Accessed online 23 July 2007 at http://www.imf.org/external/pubs/ft/op/232/op232.pdf.

Rumbaugh, T. and Blancher, N. (2004) 'International trade and the challenges of WTO accession' in E. Prasad (ed), *China's Growth and Integration into the World Economy: Prospects and Challenges*, Washington, DC, International Monetary Fund, pp. 5–13. Accessed online 23 July 2007 at http://www.imf.org/external/pubs/ft/op/232/op232.pdf.

Slater, D. and Taylor, P. J. (eds) (1999) *The American Century*, Oxford, Blackwell.

Strange, S. (1994) *States and Markets*, 2nd ed., London, Pinter.

———. (1997) *Retreat of the State*, Cambridge, Cambridge University Press.

United Nations Conference on Trade and Development (UNCTAD) (2005) *World Investment Report 2005: Transnational Corporations and the Transnationalization of R & D*, New York, United Nations.

United Nations Conference on Trade and Development (UNCTAD) (2006) *World Investment Report 2006: FDI from Developing and Transition Economies: Implications for Development*, New York, United Nations.

World Bank (2007a) *East Asia and Pacific Update: 10 Years After the Crisis*, April 2007, accessed online 24 July 2007, at http://siteresources.worldbank.org/INTEAPHALFYEARLYUPDATE/Resources/5501921175629375615/EAPUpdate-April2007-fullreport.pdf.

World Bank (2007b) *Quarterly Update*, Beijing: World Bank Office. Accessed online 23 July 2007 at http://siteresources.worldbank.org/CHINAEXTN/Resources/318949-1121421890573/china_05_07.pdf.

Youngs, G. (1996) 'Dangers of discourse: the case of globalization' in E. Kofman and G. Youngs (eds) *Globalization: Theory and Practice*, London, Pinter, pp. 58–71.

———. (1997) 'Political economy, sovereignty and borders' in L. Brace and J. Hoffman (eds), *Reclaiming Sovereignty*, London, Pinter, pp. 117–33.

———. (1999) *International Relations in a Global Age: A Conceptual Challenge*, Cambridge, Polity.

———. (2007) *Global Political Economy in the Information Age: Power and Inequality*, London, Routledge.

Zheng, W. (2004) *Globalization and State Transformation in China*, Cambridge, Cambridge University Press.

CHAPTER 2

Political Geography and Globalization in the Twenty-first Century

Eleonore Kofman

Globalization in the making

In *Making Political Geography*, John Agnew (2002) traced the intellectual genealogy of the field of political geography since its emergence as an aid to statescraft and imperial endeavour at the end of the nineteenth century. This earlier *fin de siècle* coincided, in the eyes of one of political geography's founding fathers, Halford Mackinder (Mayhew, 2000), with the closure of the world map. For imperial powers the completion of terrestrial occupation represented a new level of global consciousness and the need to think strategically about threats to the existing distribution of power. Imperial globalization generated by British commerce, conquest and colonization had the important effects of bringing previously unconnected regions together into a system, albeit a highly uneven one of exchange and movement and constructing a global picture of geography, which went beyond the elites (Ballyntyne, 2001: 195).

Universal visions were also pursued by dissident geographers critical of state power and imperial exploitation, such as Peter Kropotkin (1842–1921) and Elisée Reclus (1830–1905). Reclus voyaged around the world in the many tomes of his *Geographie Universelle*. He argued that it was becoming increasingly meaningless to speak of the history of a particular country, which was being dissolved by Europeanization, and that the most ardent patriot was becoming a 'citizen of the world'. Reclus wrote in much detail about global capitalist expansion and imperialism at a time when Marx limited his analysis to the development of capitalism in Britain:

> Over the great world market capital is accumulating inordinately and, in disregarding all the old frontiers, tries to make the mass of producers for its own profit and to secure for itself all the consumers in the world, whether they be wild and barbaric or civilised. (Lacoste, 1987: 14)

However, during the twentieth century political geography adopted a state-centric approach. What I therefore want to do in this chapter is to look at the re-emergence of global perspectives towards the end of the twentieth century and the ways in which political geography has made a contribution to a more complex understanding of globalization as contradictory and complex processes, operating within and beyond the state and often generating an unruly world (Herod et al., 1998). In particular, such perspectives contrast with the exaggerated claims of a borderless and deterritorialized world, all too frequently espoused in the 1990s. This chapter is not intended as a comprehensive survey of geographical concepts (borders, scales, territoriality) (Kelly, 1999) or of imperialism and neo-liberal globalization (see Slater, this volume; Sparke, 2004; 2006). Rather, the objective is more limited. I first examine the challenge to state-centric approaches and the emergence of global perspectives at the end of the twentieth century and claims of a borderless and deterritorialized world, usually propounded by economists and cyber scholars. However, changing geopolitics post 11 September 2001, the hardening of many borders and the strengthened security state have undermined this vision. I then explore some of the recent discussions of bordering and complex interactions between scales including the global, the latter building upon relational geographies which bring together actors, institutional arrangements and structures.

The challenge to state-centric approaches

For a variety of reasons which I shall not enter into in this chapter, political geography declined in the decades after the Second World War until it was revived in the mid-1970s (Agnew, 2002). Regional and state-centric approaches (Taylor, 1996) dominated the discipline until the 1980s, when the primacy of the state as a unit of analysis began to be subjected to a growing critique. Peter Taylor's geographical exposition (1989) of Wallerstein's work within a materialist political geography framework acknowledged geography's earlier interest in the global and the centrality of the world system in structuring capital accumulation. Three key aspects contributed to what Agnew and Corbridge (1995) called the territorial trap: (1) national units are fixed units of securing sovereign space; (2) there is a clear distinction between domestic and international; and (3) the territorial state exists prior to and is a container of society (83–84). The nation-state as a particular scale reflecting the interplay of economic, social and political forces had rather to be situated within a historical dynamic of an unfolding global panorama and distinctive forms of order and rivalry. Taylor (1996) had identified state-centric politics and theory as major causes of social science orthodoxy. However, several commentators queried the actual degree of change in the world resulting from globalization (Agnew, 1996) and considered that global theories could become equally constraining (Gamble, 1996).

    Global perspectives also rose more to the fore in the 1990s through the development of critical geopolitics (O'Tuathail and Dalby, 1998; O'Tuathail, 1996) which emerged forcefully after the end of the Cold War. Critical geopolitics can be conceptualised as the analysis of political discourses and representations of global spaces (Dodds, 2001), especially by politicians, statescraft intellectuals and the media. Though its remit has been the global arena, critical geopolitics has gazed on the world from the vantage of the West and has largely neglected critical scholarship from other continents (Dodds and Atkinson, 2000; Dodds, 2001; Skelton, this volume). The omission of the Other of geopolitical discourses and their strategies of resistance have been taken into account to some extent in an endeavour to broaden the remit of critical geopolitics (Dalby, 1998; Routledge, 1998). However, the re-writing of geopolitics to include social divisions, such as class, gender

(Hyndman, 2004; Kofman, 1996; Dowler and Sharp, 2001), race, ethnicity and age, and the political agency of those written out of geopolitical scripts, has been slow.

Together these diverse critiques of dominant notions of the relationship between political order and territoriality have sought to question an analysis of the state as the primary unit and container of society (Taylor, 1995). By ceasing to take the state and its boundaries for granted, these perspectives opened up discussion of the salience of other scales of economic, social and political processes, their relativization and co-constitution.

Henri Lefebvre (1978, 2003), whose writings have heavily influenced a number of radical geographers such as Agnew (Agnew and Corbridge, 1995), Brenner (1997, 2004), Harvey (1989) and Smith (1984) in their interpretation of globalization, presciently discerned in the 1970s the contradictory and complex relationships between the state, capital and globalization and the diversity of scales through which this worked itself out. Lefebvre (1978) saw that

> the global emerges paradoxically on the horizon as partially realised possibilities, induced and produced, but also fought against and counteracted by modernizing forces. It both breaks the obstacles and frontiers as well as attracting that which opposes it. We know the ways in which the State simultaneously globalises and opposes these processes (p. 415).... The State is not eternal. It is breaking up through its contradictions, split between that which spills over externally and internally; it is historic and of its time.... This State will not allow itself to disappear or be overtaken without resistance. Maybe the global will become so in the course of a world crisis or after that? (p. 422)

As an abstract space, the global may appear to be homogeneous (Kirsch, 1995), but in reality it is not. A calculative logic (Elden, 2005) and fragmentation, differentiation and hierarchization of spaces may be applied to the planet (Lefebvre, 1991). Unlike Lefebvre's rich and probing analysis of contradictory processes in the historical production of different kinds of spatiality at a variety of scales, a number of writers (Ohmae, 1995; O'Brien, 1992; Castells, 1996b/2000) had been seduced by the allure and simplicity of a world without borders and places. Furthermore, much of the rhetoric of the redundancy of geography and a borderless world has been based on the changing role of the state, especially its permeability by global processes, and a technological interpretation of economic and social change.

Redundant geography in a borderless world?

In specifying an end state or what a fully globalized world would be like, Waters (2001) envisaged that

> territoriality will disappear as an organizing principle of social and cultural life; it will be a society without borders and spatial boundaries ... we can expect relationships between people in disparate locations to be formed as easily as relationships between people in proximate ones. (p. 5)

Waters was influenced by Robertson (1992) and especially Giddens (1990) in his notion of spatial distantiation and the intensification of worldwide social relations stretched between localities. The supposed ease of relating to distant others is equated with loss of territoriality. The fact that communities and localities are now shaped by global processes, and are an integral part of global connections, would appear to mean that borders no longer matter in social life, and for many are easily transcended by key economic actors (O'Brien, 1992; Ohmae, 1995).

Others, for example Scholte (1996b), postulate a dichotomy between a non-spatialised global world and lower levels in which place and territorialities still play a part. Thus

> global space is placeless, distanceless and borderless – and in this sense 'suprana-tional'. In global relations, people are connected with one another pretty much irrespective of their territorial position.... Global relations thus form non-, extra-, post-, supra-territorial aspects of the world system. In the global domain, territorial boundaries present no particular impediment and distance is covered in effectively no time. (1996a: 1968)

This partial vision of a deterritorialized globe constructs an undifferentiated world without significant places, dominated by spaces of flows which do not require maintenance, that is a global space that is produced and reproduced immaculately. Yet the circulation of flows requires substantial fixed infrastructure (Harvey, 1982; 2000), and institutional arrange-ments and legal rules, which have increasingly been concentrated in global cities (Sassen, 2000b). The global and the local are also treated as a zero-sum game of deterritorialized global space in opposition to territorialized smaller scales below the level of the state. Castells (1996b), for example, leaves us with two disconnected universes, that of the managerial elites, masters and beneficiaries of the information economy and network society, who exist in the timeless time of spaces of flows, and the rest of the population, including many of those in the developed world, who live in places, these being defined in the most traditional terms as a locale whose form, function and meaning are self-contained within the boundaries of physical contiguity (see Massey, 1995, for a critique). Not surprisingly, the upshot is a structural schizophrenia between the two spatial logics (Castells, 1996b: 428).

For the proponents of the demise of territorialization, deterritorialization signifies the transcendence of fixed, physical borders, that is a reductive interpretation of the meaning of territory which equates to an a-territorial world. Sack (1986) defined territoriality more broadly as 'spatial strategy which can be employed to affect, influence or control resources and people, by controlling territory'. The bounding of territory reflects power relations produced under specific conditions (Storey, 2001). Though a crucial element of the power and reach of the state (Mann, 1985), territoriality is not restricted to any particular scale or political agents (Lacoste, 1987) but ranges from personal spaces to the global (Wastl-Walter and Staeheli, 2004). Such strategic thinking does not disappear in spaces of flows; it simply becomes reconfigured and more complex (Paasi, 1999). For O'Tuathail (1998), globaliza-tion evokes

> challenges posed to the status of territory and our territorially embedded under-standings of geography, governance and geopolitics, states, places and the social sciences by planetary communication networks and globalizing tendencies. But it is not about the disappearance of terrritoriality for the problematic of deterritorialization is also the problematic of reterritorialization; it is not the pres-ence or absence of state territoriality but its changing, power and meaning in

ship to postmodern technological constellations, speed machines and global
capitalism. (p. 82)

Cn.   olitics, or politics of speed and time, networks that are able to overcome spatial
obstacles, and emerging transnational problems might yield a fuller understanding of contemporary geopolitics than simple territory and distance. American leaders throughout the
twentieth century had imagined their post-colonial imperium as a victory over geography
(Smith, 2003), though the framework through which it operated differed. This shift could
be seen in the difference between the modern and postmodern geopolitical imaginations
exemplifed by the Bush and Clinton administrations (O'Tuathail, 1999). The second Bush
administration, however, has signalled a return to an overtly state-security-centred geopolitics dividing the world into friend and foe of the United States (Bush, 2001).

The first Bush administration of the early 1990s interpreted world politics within a
framework of territorial nation-states and strategic categories. The Clinton administration,
on the other hand, recognised a changing world dominated by geo-economics and geo-
finance, incorporating global issues and environmental problems that referred to themes of
deterritorialized threats and global dangers. These threats frequently operated through
transnational networks, for example organized crime in drugs, weapons and human smuggling that have expanded in what Castells (1996a) calls perverse forms of capitalism (drugs,
weapons, money laundering, human trafficking). Yet, as with the space of financial flows,
these transnational networks need people in places to enable the circulation of illicit goods
and those people denied the right to global mobility. Even though such circulations encompass a multitude of states, they pass through particular territories and use certain routes.

The election of George Bush Jr. in 2000, the events of 11 September 2001 (Dalby, 2003)
and the invasion of Afghanistan and Iraq (O'Tuathail, 2003) disrupted the geopolitics of the
1990s and led to a re-evaluation of the relationship between the workings of neo-liberalism
and American imperialism (Harvey, 2003; see Slater, this volume; Sparke, 2004). The attack
against America gave it the justification to extend its geopolitical reach in its war on terrorism
in order to bolster its hegemony (Arrighi, 2005) in an increasingly competitive world.
However, its military interventions have weakened its economic position (Harvey, 2003)
and have unmasked its neo-liberal globalization project. The increasing American trade and
budget deficits are undermining and making vulnerable its economic hegemony which its
geopolitical calculus had set off during the Cold War (Agnew, 2005)[1].

Not only has accumulation occurred through dispossession of resources (Harvey, 2003)
but the very core of state security has been privatized (Klein, 2003; Scahill, 2007) as part of
the rise of a highly profitable disaster capitalism (Klein, 2007). In mid-2007, there were 630
companies in Iraq working on contracts for the US government, with 180,000 employees
who outnumbered the 160,000 official troops. A major difference is that the casualties of
the private companies are not included in official figures and their actions are largely beyond
accountability (Scahill, 2007).

As Sparke (2004) notes, the argument for interventionism by the neo-conservatives was
made on grounds of connecting disconnected parts of the globe in which barriers to movement of goods, capital and people, which were maintained by recalcitrant or rogue states,
could be finally dismantled. In particular, the US and its allies have sought to reshape the
whole of the Middle East, including the US's old enemy, Iran, which it has attempted to
block economically. Ironically this has served to increase the presence in the region of
Russia and China, to whom Iran has turned (Bakhtiar, 2007).

More generally, the fallout from 11 September 2001 has strengthened the security state through reinforced borders, including e-borders, and internal surveillance. Increasingly the world is presented in Manichean terms in the 'war against terrorism' in which the world is divided into good and evil and where poor countries in particular become vulnerable to punitive expeditions (Hannah, 2005). In this endeavour, the leader presents himself as a virtuous male (Young, 2003) avenging the nation's virility (Hannah, 2005) and protecting his citizens against aliens, whether they be fearsome outsiders or alien insiders. A strategy of containment and penal borders, the most extreme being Guantanamo Bay, is deployed towards groups depicted as threats to sovereignty and national identity. Borders of different kinds create a security perimeter of a bounded space and limit a more 'relational, cosmopolitan, and dynamic geographical notion of place' (Hyndman, 2005: 566). What had been soft borders, such as that between Canada and the US, have been hardened so that US citizens must now show passports to cross the border (see Runyan in this volume). Both the hardening of physical borders in many regions and the earlier discourse of a borderless world have contributed to a renaissance of studies on borders, boundaries and bordering, territorial and non-territorial, and as processes of group inclusion and exclusion (Newman, 2006).

Rethinking borders and territory

Paasi (1999) has sought to broaden the conceptualization of boundaries and territory, suggesting we consider three aspects. The first is boundaries as knowledge, narratives and institutions in which states continue to play a key role in place making not merely at the border but in a variety of institutional arrangements such as education and the media. The second is boundaries and the construction of identity whereby boundaries produce exclusions and inclusions as well as mediating relationships between groups and communities. Foreign policy provides a good example of the use of boundaries in this context. The third is boundaries and power where boundaries embody norms, values and legal codes. Territorial and non-territorial aspects may combine.

The relationship between territorial and non-territorial borders can be illustrated through developments in the European Union, and especially pertaining to its management of migration. Geddes (2005) argues that the emphasis by the European Union on projecting its external territorial borders has to do with regulating and reducing unwanted flows of migrants and asylum seekers and needs to be considered with non-territorial borders such as organizational and conceptual borders. Furthermore, its external borders are not only about dividing inside from outside but also about creating spaces to be governed, as in its European Neighbourhood Policy (Rumford, 2006), and where borders may be seen as increasingly fuzzy and liable to change in the future (Newman, 2006). External territorial borders may be emphasised so as to maintain organizational borders which establish the limits of political community. The latter refer to those sites where membership conditions for migrant newcomers, including access to the labour market, the welfare state and national citizenship, are specified (Geddes, 2005: 789) and which vary according to type of migrant (e.g., highly skilled, irregular, asylum seeker). Conceptual borders, which are more abstract and centred on notions of belonging and community, can be linked with transnational, national or sub-national communities (Geddes, 2005: 790). In the wake of the critique of multiculturalism in many European states and bombings in cities such as Madrid (2003) and London (2005), debates on national identity and dominant values have come to the fore (Kofman, 2005; see Icduygu and Senay, this volume).

As with the incorporation of new institutional actors in providing security and military capacity, a raft of measures, such as carrier sanctions and visas, have pushed controls further down the line (Guiraudan and Lahav, 2000) and led to the formation of privatised intermediary arrangements for handling cross-border operations (Sassen, 1999). At the same time, states may be pushing out their borders beyond the contiguous territory of the state, for example through the reinforcement of visa controls in consulate offices throughout the world. These diverse developments are thus creating new locations and interaction between institutional actors of flexible bordering.

Many of the more sophisticated attempts to understand the multiplicity of spaces, scales, networks and institutional actors in relation to Europeanization and global processes have emanated from a relational geography (see Taylor, this volume). Yeung (2005: 38) defines it as 'the ways in which socio-spatial relations of actors are intertwined in broader structures and processes of. . . . change at various geographical scales . . . connecting actors and structures through horizontal and vertical power relations'. Relational thinking seeks to go beyond binary and exclusionary terms, such as the local and global which are often endowed with properties in opposition to each other (Roberts, 2004).

For a number of economic and political geographers, world capitalism at the end of the twentieth century could not be contained within the national scale and consequently generated territorial reorganizations as it bypassed its traditional sites in a period of Fordist production (Brenner, 1997, 1999a, b; Smith, 1993, 1997; Swyngedouw, 1997). Brenner (1999b) links processes of deterritorialization and reterritorialization dialectically such that there is an interplay between the drive to space-time compression and the continual production and reconfiguration of fixed spatial configurations. The most significant modes of reorganization and competition are the restructuring of urban spaces, especially the concentration of economic power and strategic command in world cities (Sassen, 2000a), regional and local restructuring (Cox, 1997) below the state, and macro regional bodies such as the European Union.

Others have pushed the analysis of the configuration of scale to smaller units, such as the household. Such studies have sought to embrace processes other than production, namely social reproduction and consumption which are crucial to the reproduction of capital and social life (Marston, 2000; see Petersen, this volume). Households and families have played a central part in feminist geography as a site of biological and social reproduction, labour power (paid and unpaid) and living space (Mitchell et al., 2003) and have increasingly become dependent in the South on the remittances of migrant women (Sassen, 2000a; Pettman, this volume).

Relational thinking is also about interconnections between discrete phenomena and how they recombine across space and time to create new assemblages (Sassen, 2006: 5)[2]. For Sassen, globalization has destabilized particular scalar assemblages which have been reassembled in new configurations around three building blocks of territory, authority and rights across space and time. This analysis enables one to see more clearly what elements of a national state are undergoing denationalization and how they become relodged within a novel globalizing logic. Most significantly, the global and the national and mobility and fixity are not mutually exclusive. Too often, globalization is confined to global processes or what

Sassen (2006: 4) calls 'endogeneity trap' which can be explained simply as a tendency towards growing interdependence. Hence we fail to recognise the ways in which the global may be embedded in the national and emerge from transformations within the nation-state. To understand the historical antecedents of the current neoliberal globalization, Sassen (2006: 168–71) suggests we delve into the earlier redistribution of power inside the state, for example the growing power of the executive in the 1970s and 1980s which manifested itself earliest in the United States and was a consequence of both national and international politics as well as constitutive of those changes.

States are also enablers of globalization while national states organise the tension between globalization and other scales in their own ways (for Japan see Yamazaki, 2002) in a continual pursuit of a spatial fix between the abstract moments of global accumulation and concrete material moments (Jessop, 1999). The state, composed of a heterogeneous ensemble through which social and political struggles are worked out, itself promotes internationalization, especially by certain dominant factions.

Another type of relationship between the local and the global is provided by local political activists, who though embedded in states, participate in and shape global issues and global change. Social movements in particular often work at the margins of political spaces and are able to jump logics and scales (Staeheli, 1994). Rape, for example, which had been a domestic issue, was propelled onto the international scene through the International War Crimes Tribunal for the former Yugoslavia and recognised as a weapon of war and a crime against humanity (Hyndman, 2004).

Conclusion

Political geography has been interested in the making of the world since the nineteenth century when its complete appropriation was thought to demand new geographies. At the beginning of this century, empire and imperial endeavours within the context of neoliberal globalization and increasing competition between the leading, but overstretched, hegemonic power and the European Union and Asia pose challenges for social-science understandings of spatial reconfigurations. At the same time the inherited scales of economic and political activities (local, state, macro regional and world) are being refashioned and connected in new ways. Fresh theorizations and approaches have grappled with the way that flows and places intersect and the complex assemblages that connect institutional practices, actors and structures across space and time. There has been a shift away from the local and the global as exclusionary categories and growing awareness of the multiplicity of borders, territorial strategies pursued at different scales and the complex interconnections between the global and other scales, especially the state.

Nonetheless, despite the shift that relational approaches have brought to our understanding of global processes, particular narratives, subjects and spaces are privileged whilst others are silenced. The political geographies of the previous turn of the century did this (Gilmartin and Kofman, 2004); we are in danger of repeating the same mistakes. The valorized narratives of today include financial flows, transnational corporations and the elite who circulate at the global scale and shape those sites of strategic importance and dominance in the global economy. The narrative of eviction (Sassen, 2000a) covers heterogeneous groups, spaces and practices. There are certainly attempts to include the geopolitics of those who do not write its scripts or who are not written into them, such as indigenous peoples, migrants, anti-liberal globalization protesters, and women in the charting of neo-liberalism, imperialism and security. Women, for example, have demonstrated that they can jump scales (Staeheli, 1994) and forge global alliances (Runyan, Steans, this volume) with relatively few resources. The actors, willing and unwilling, in processes of globalization are not just those at the apex of the power-geometry. Those left out of its accounts both constitute counter geographies of globalization and are integral to its formal and informal processes and practice.

Notes

1. Agnew rejects the term 'empire' which he associates with centralized rule and organization as a description of American power but prefers the term 'hegemony' as a loose description of dominant economic, cultural and political practices connected with a networked geography of power. However, many writers, including Hardt and Negri (2000), deploy this term to refer to a more networked and diffuse power structure.
2. Sassen insists she is using the concept in a purely descriptive sense unlike Deleuze and Guattari (1987: 504–5) for whom it is a contingent ensemble of practices and things that can be differentiated and that can be aligned along the axes of territoriality and deterritorialization in which particular mixes of technical and administrative practices 'extract and give intelligibility to new spaces by decoding and encoding milieux'.

References

Agnew, J. (1987) *Place and Politics: The Geographical Mediation of State and society,* London, Allen and Unwin.

———. (1996) 'Spacelessness versus timeless space in state-centred social science', *Environment and Planning A,* 28, 1929–32.

———. (2002) *Making Political Geography,* London, Arnold.

———. (2003) 'American hegemony into American empire? Lessons from the invasion of Iraq', *Antipode,* 35, 871–85.

———. (2005) *Hegemony: The New Stage of Global Power,* Philadelphia, Temple University Press.

Agnew, J. and Corbridge, S. (1995) *Mastering Space: Hegemony, Territory and International Political Economy,* London, Routledge.

Anderson, B. (2002) *Reproductive Labour and Migration,* ESRC Transnational Communities, WPTC-02-01.

Arrighi, G. (2005) 'Hegemeony unravelling –1', *New Left Review,* 32, 45–69.

Bakhtiar, A. (2007) 'The plan for economic strangulation of Iran', *Global Geopolitics Net,* 3 February, http://globalgeopolitics.net/article/0203%20Bakthar%20-%20Plan.htm.

Ballyntyne, T. (2001) *Orientalism and Race: Aryanism in the British Empire,* Basingstoke, Palgrave.

Brenner, N. (1997) 'Global, fragmented, hierarchical: Henri Lefebvre's geographies of globalization', *Public Culture,* 24, 135–67.

———. (1999a) 'Globalisation as reterritorialisation: the re-scaling of urban governance in the European Union', *Urban Studies,* 36 (3), 431–51.

———. (1999b) 'Beyond state-centrism? Space, territoriality and geographical scale in globalization studies', *Theory and Society,* 28 (1), 39–78.

————. (2004) *New State Spaces: Urban Governance and the Rescaling of Statehood*, Oxford, Oxford University Press.

Bush, G. W. (2001) 'Address to a joint session of Congress and the American people' 20 September, http://www.whitehouse.gov/news/releases/2001/09.

Castells, M. (1996a) 'The net and the self: Working notes for a critical theory of the informational society', *Critique of Anthropology*, 16 (1), 9–38.

————. (1996b) *The Rise of the Network Society*, Oxford, Blackwell.

Cox, K. (1997) *Spaces of Globalization: Reasserting the Power of the Local*, New York, Guilford Press.

Dalby, S. (1998) 'Introduction: Geopolitics, knowledge and power at the end of the century' in G. O' Tuathail, S. Dalby and P. Routledge (eds), *The Geopolitics Reader*, London, Routledge, pp. 179–87.

————. (2003) 'Calling 9/11: geopolitics, security and America's new war', *Geopolitics*, 8, 61–86.

Deleuze, G. and Guattari, F. (1987) *A Thousand Plateaus: Capitalism and Schizophrenia*, Minneapolis, University of Minneapolis Press.

Dodds, K. (2001) 'Political geography III: critical geopolitics after ten years', *Progress in Human Geography*, 25 (3), 469–84.

Dowler, L. and Sharp, J. (2001) 'A feminist geopolitics?', *Space and Polity*, 5 (3), 165–76.

Flint, C. (2002) 'Political geography: globalization, metapolitical geographies and everyday life', *Progress in Human Geography*, 26 (3), 391–400.

Gamble, A. (1996) 'Embedded statism', *Environment and Planning A*, 28, 1933–36.

Geddes, M. (2005) 'Europe's border relationship and international migration relations', *Journal of Common Market Studies*, 43 (4), 787–806.

Giddens, A. (1990) *The Consequences of Modernity*. Cambridge, Polity.

Gilmartin, M. and Kofman, E. (2004) 'Geopolitics, Empire and Imperialism', in L. Staeheli, E. Kofman and L. Peake (eds) *Feminist Perspectives in Political Geography*, New York, Routledge. pp. 113–25.

Guiraudon, V. and Lahav, G. (2000) 'A reappraisal of the state sovereignty debate: The case of migration control', *Comparative Political Studies*, 33 (2), 163–95.

Hannah, M. (2005) 'Virility and violation in the US "war on terrorism"' in L. Nelson and J. Saeger (eds.), *Companion to Feminist Geography*, Oxford, Blackwell Publishing, pp. 550–64.

Hardt, M. and Negri, A. (2000) *Empire*, Cambridge, Harvard University Press.

Harvey, D. (1982) *The Limits to Capital*, Oxford, Oxford University Press.

————. (1989) *The Condition of Postmodernity: An Enquiry into the Origins of Cultural Change*, Oxford, Blackwell.

————. (2000) *Spaces of Hope*, Edinburgh, Edinburgh University Press.

————. (2003) *The New Imperialism*, Oxford, Oxford n University Press.

Herod, A., Tuathail, G. and Roberts, S. (eds) (1998) *An Unruly World: Globalization, Governance and Geography*, London, Routledge.

Hyndman, J. (2004) 'Mind the gap: bridging feminist and political geography through geopolitics', *Political Geography*, 23, 307–22.

————. (2005) 'Feminist geopolitics and September 11' in L. Nelson and J. Saeger (eds), *Companion to Feminist Geography*, Oxford, Blackwell Publishing, pp. 565–77.

Jessop, R. (1999) 'Reflections on globalization and its illogics' in K. Olds, P. Dickens, P. Kelly, L. Kong and H. Wai-chung Yeung (eds), *Globalisation and the Asia-Pacific. Contested Territories*, London, Routledge, pp. 19–38.

————. (2005) 'The political economy of scale and European governance', *Tijdschrift voor Economische en Sociale Geografie*, 96, 225–30.

Kelly, P. (1999) 'The geographies and politics of globalization', *Progress in Human Geography*, 23 (3), 379–400.

Kirsch, S. (1995) 'The incredible shrinking world?', Technology and the production of space', *Environment and Planning D. Society and Space*, 13, 529–55.

Klein, N. (2003) 'Privatisation in disguise? *The Nation*, 15 April.

————. (2007) *The Shock Doctrine: The Rise of Disaster Capitalism*, New York, Holt and Co.

Kofman, E. (1996) 'Gender relations, feminism and geopolitics: problematic closures and opening strategies' in E. Kofman and G. Youngs (eds), *Globalization: Theory and Practice,* London, Pinter, pp. 209–24.

———. (2005) 'Migration, citizenship and the reassertion of the nation-state in Europe', *Citizenship Studies,* 9 (6), 453–67.

Lacoste, Y. (1987) 'Geographers, action and politics' in P. Girot and E. Kofman (ed. and trans.), *International Geopolitical Analysis,* London, Croom Helm, pp. 1–9.

Lefebvre, H. (1978) *De L'Etat. Les contradictions de l'Etat moderne,* Paris, Union Générale d'Editions (extract from chap. 17 'Worldwide Experience' translated in S. Elden, E. Lebas and E. Kofman (eds), (2003) *Henri Lefebvre: Selected Writings,* London, Continuum.

———. (1991) *Production of Space,* Oxford, Blackwell.

Marston, S. (2000) 'The social construction of scale', *Progress in Human Geography,* 24 (2), 19–42.

Massey, D. (1993) 'Power-geometry and a progressive sense of place' in J. Bird et al., *Mapping the Futures: Local Cultures, Global Change,* London, Routledge, pp. 59–69.

———. (1995) 'Conceptualization of place' in D. Massey and P. Jess (eds.), *A Place in the World,* Oxford, Oxford University Press/Open University, pp. 45–86.

Mayhew, R. (2000) 'Halford Mackinder's "new" political geography and the geographical tradition', *Political Geography,* 19, 771–91.

Mitchell, K., Marston, S. and Katz, C. (2003) 'Introduction: Life's work: An introduction, review and critique', *Antipode,* 35 (3): 415–42.

Newman, D. (2006) 'The lines that continue to separate us: borders in our 'borderless' world', *Progress in Human Geography,* 30, 143–61.

O'Brien, R. (1992) *Global Financial Integration. The End of Geography,* London, Pinter.

Ohame, K. (1995) *The End of the Nation-state,* New York, Free Press.

O Tuathail, G. (1995) 'Political geography I: history, gender and world order amidst crises of global governance', *Progress in Human Geography,* 19 (2), 260–72.

———. (1996) *Critical Geopolitics,* London, Routledge.

———. (1998) 'Political geography IIII: dealing with deterritorialization', *Progress in Human Geography,* 22 (1), 82–93.

———. (1999) 'De-territorialised threats and global dangers: geopolitics and risk society' in D. Newman (ed.), *Boundaries, Territory and Postmodernity.* London, Frank Cass, pp. 17–31.

O Tuathail, G. and Dalby, S. (1998) *Rethinking Geopolitics,* London, Routledge.

O Tuathail, G., Dalby, S. and Routledge, P. (eds) (1998) *The Geopolitics Reader,* London, Routledge.

Paasi, A. (1999) 'Boundaries as social processes: territoriality in the world of flows', in D. Newman (ed.), *Boundaries, Territory and Postmodernity,* London, Frank Cass, pp. 69–88.

Parker, G. (1996) 'Globalization and geopolitical world orders', in E. Kofman and G. Youngs (eds), *Globalization: Theory and Practice,* London, Pinter, pp. 72–80.

Roberts, S. (2004) 'Gendered globalization' in L. Staeheli, E. Kofman and L. Peake (eds), *Mapping Women, Making Politics: Feminist Perspectives on Political Geography,* New York and London, Routledge, pp. 127–40.

Robertson, R. (1992) *Globalization,* London, Sage.

Routledge, P. (1998) 'Introduction: Anti-geopolitics' in O Tuathail, G., Dalby, S. and Routledge, P. (eds), *The Geopolitics Reader,* London, Routledge, pp. 245–55.

Sack, R. (1986) *Human Territoriality: Its Theory and History,* Cambridge, Cambridge University Press.

Sassen, S. (1999) 'Servicing the global economy: Reconfigured states and private agents' in K. Olds, P. Dicken, P.Kelly, L. Kong and H. Wai-chung Yeung (eds), *Globalisation and the Asia-Pacific: Contested Territories,* London, Routledge, pp. 149–62.

———. (2000a) 'Women's burden: countergeographies of globalization and the feminization of survival', *Journal of International Affairs,* 53 (2): 503–24.

———. (2000b) *The Global City: New York, London, Tokyo,* Princeton, NJ, Princeton University Press.

————. (2006) *Territory, Authority, Rights: From Medieval to Global Assemblages*, Princeton, NJ, Princeton University Press.

Scahill, J. (2007) 'A very private war' *The Guardian G2*, 1 August, pp. 4–9.

Scholte, J. A. (1996a) 'What are the new spaces?' *Environment and Planning A*, 28, 1965–69.

————. (1996b) 'Towards a critical theory of globalization' in E. Kofman and G. Youngs (eds), *Globalization: Theory and Practice*, London, Pinter, pp. 43–57.

Smith, N. (1984) *Uneven Development: Nature, Capital and the Production of Space*, Oxford, Blackwell.

————. (1993) 'Homeless/global: scaling places' in J. Bird et al., *Mapping the Futures: Local Cultures, Global Change*, London, Routledge, pp. 87–119.

————. (1996) 'Spaces of vulnerability: the space of flows and the politics of space', *Critique of Anthropology*, 16, 63–77.

————. (1997) 'The satanic geographies of globalization: uneven development in the 1990s', *Public Culture*, 10 (1), 169–89.

————. (2003) *American Empire: Roosevelt's Geographer and the Prelude to Globalization*, Berkeley, CA, University of California Press.

Sparke, M. (2004) 'Political geography: political geographies of globalization (1) – dominance', *Progress in Human Geography*, 28 (6), 777–94.

————. (2006) 'Political geography: political geographies of globalization (2) – governance', *Progress in Human Geography*, 30 (3), 357–72.

Staeheli, L. (1994) 'Empowering political struggle: spaces and scales of resistance', *Political Geography*, 13 (5), 387–91.

Storey, D. (2001) *Territory: The Claiming of Space*, Harlow, UK, Pearson Education Ltd.

Swyngedouw, E. (1997) 'Neither global nor local: "glocalization" and the politics of scale' in Cox, K. (1997) *Spaces of Globalization: Reasserting the Power of the Local*, New York, Guilford Press, pp. 137–66.

Taylor, P. (1984) 'Introduction: geographical scale and political geography' in P. Taylor and J. House (eds), *Political Geography: Recent Advances and Future Directions*, London, Croom Helm, pp. 1–7.

————. (1989) *Political Geography: World-Economy, nation-state, Locality*, 2nd ed., London, Longman.

————. (1995) 'Beyond containers: internationality, interstateness, interterritoriality', *Progress in Human Geography*, 19(1), 1–15.

————. (1996) 'Statism and the social sciences: opening up to new spaces', *Environment and Planning A*, 28, 1917–28.

————. (1999) 'Places, spaces and Macy's: place, space tensions in the political geography of modernities', *Progress in Human Geography*, 23, 7–26.

Wastl-Walter, D. and Staeheli, L. (2004) 'Territory, territoriality and boundaries' in L. Staeheli, E. Kofman and L. Peake (eds), *Mapping Women, Making Politics: Feminist Perspectives onPpolitical Geography*, New York and London, Routledge, pp. 141–52.

Waters, M. (2001) *Globalization*, 2nd ed., London, Routledge.

Yamazaki, T. (2002) 'Is Japan leaking Globalisation, reterritorialisation and identity in the Asia-Pacific context', *Geopolitics*, 7 (1).

Yeung, H. W. (1998) 'Capital, state and space: contesting the borderless world', *Transactions of theIBG*, 23, 291–309.

————. (2005) 'Rethinking relational economic geography', *Transactions of the IBG*, 30, 37–51.

Young, I. (2003) 'The logic of masculinist protection: reflections on the current security state', *Signs*, 29 (1), 1–25.

Part 2

North-South Debates

CHAPTER 3

Geographies of Global Environmental Security

Simon Dalby

Global environment

One of the first sociologists of globalization to use the term widely, Roland Robertson (1992), defined it as including some sense of the 'compression' of global politics and the emergence of a subjective identity of living on a single relatively small planet. In the early 1990s this theme was prominent in the discussions leading up to and at the 'Earth Summit' where 'global' issues were debated in the full glare of the world's media in Rio de Janeiro in June 1992. The environmental dimensions of globalization highlight the emergence of the conceptualization of the 'globe' as humanity's home, a quality of 'globality' where state political boundaries seem less important (Yearley, 1996). This sense of the global suggests a common fate, a shared home and some necessity to get along in what the 1990s Commission on Global Governance (1995) simply called 'Our Global Neighbourhood'. But environmental discussions also suggest that this neighbourhood is threatened and in danger. Given the disruptions caused by such changes a whole discourse of 'environmental security' (Barnett, 2001) has emerged as scholars, activists and policy-makers try to grapple with these changes. They specify new universal dangers and disruptions, drawing on and emphasizing precisely this theme of *the global*.

The invocation of the globe as endangered is a powerful rhetorical device and was used in numerous attempts to mobilize support for global political change in the 1990s (Karliner, 1997; Sachs, 1999). Questions of corporate control over genetic heritage were increasingly raised in debates over tropical rain-forest preservation. The global trade in toxic waste, and the lack of regulations of production processes in many of the Southern states, raised social justice and health-impact concerns in many places (O'Neill, 1998). The ability of states to effectively regulate technologically sophisticated industries was also in doubt, raising profound questions about global governance and the transfer of power to unelected officials and unaccountable corporate employees (Clapp, 1998). In response to these matters many international environmental movements sprang up and were instrumental in bringing states to the negotiating table at the Earth Summit in Rio de Janeiro in 1992, and at the lengthy negotiations that eventually produced the Kyoto protocol on climate change (Wapner, 1996). International discussions and regime formation now supposedly constrain states to comply with international agreements, although as the debate about the Kyoto protocol on climate change makes clear, treaties are not enough to force states or corporations to change.

There are complex geographies operating in these matters, geographies that need to be thought through carefully. The threat from *global* actions is seen by many as the source of numerous environmental dangers in specific places, where habitat disruption endangers species and where modern economies encroach on ecosystems and aboriginal landscapes, simultaneously threatening cultures and their ecologies (Mander and Goldsmith, 1996). The destruction of rain forests has been linked directly to the campaigns to protect aboriginal peoples for the simple reason that many indigenous peoples live in the forests that loggers are cutting down. Aboriginal peoples are also living on lands used by corporations for mines, wells and pipelines to extract resources for use in economies and cities far from aboriginal lands (Gedicks, 2001). Understanding forest destruction as a global process, especially because of the trans-national trade in timber, suggests that globalization directly endangers peoples in many specific places while simultaneously endangering everyone through the indirect effects of atmospheric and climate change (Marchak, 1995). In these terms the environment is a problem of global proportions that could be considered to include all the facets of globalization: novelty, scale, challenges to conventional understandings, the need for political innovation beyond the scale of the nation-state, dramatic cultural change and economics as the driving force.

But how novel are these environmental developments? Might they be better understood in terms of a very long-term human pattern of displacement of aboriginal peoples by more technologically capable and violent agricultural populations in their search for land and other resources (Diamond, 1997)? Global environmental problems might also be understood in terms of the centuries-long process of European expansion and associated environmental disruptions (Crosby, 1986). Globalization then is simply the latest phase in a long history of urbanization, industrialization and the displacement of rural and traditional peoples to provide the raw materials, and recently the recreational spaces, for urban dwellers. If so, then some of the other assumptions about both the novelty of globalization, and the geographical premises of autonomous spatially separate cultures that are supposedly challenged by globalization, may also be up for conceptual critique (Dalby, 2005). So too are Malthusian fears of peasants in the South either cutting down rainforests or invading the North in search of food and jobs.

What is undoubtedly novel, and has become much clearer in the years since the initial debates about globalization in the 1990s, is the recognition of the global economy as a new 'forcing mechanism' in the biosphere. The global economy, and its use of fossil fuels, is changing the composition of the earth's air, reducing the number of species living and changing the patterns of plant and animal life. It is introducing new chemical elements such as chlorofluorocarbons into the biosphere. The sum total of these processes is now so large that earth-system scientists are saying we live in a new geological era, one commonly simply called the Anthropocene (Schellnhuber, et al., 2005).

But while the planetary conditions for life are being changed, their effects on human societies are far from evenly spread; global environmental change is not a matter of life changing in similar ways for everyone. This too has become clearer in recent years as the matter of who benefits and who loses in environmental change is discussed and the interconnectedness of the global economy makes it clear that some win and some lose in situations of rapid change (O'Brien and Leichenko, 2003). As the rest of this chapter

shows, thinking about environment and about globalization requires p
the geographical formulations in the arguments about both.

Whose globalization? Whose security?

Claims that global social, political and economic processes on a planet affect humanity *in general* should make anyone aware of the geographical diversity of the human condition highly suspicious. General claims that global environmental degradation is occurring frequently lead to assumptions that it must therefore be happening in each and every case. But as the case of supposed desertification in Namibia makes clear, this may have much more to do with ideological agendas than with any detailed scientific analysis of a particular case (Sullivan, 2000). Questions about what is being invoked as a threat, by whom, in what context, for what political purpose, are essential to any analysis of environmental security (Barnett, 2001). In particular, the economic processes of globalization are directly challenging traditional structures of livelihood security, because of changing production processes and rapidly shifting global labour markets. To advocates of the neoliberal economic and political agendas of globalization, it is precisely these processes that promise greater wealth and hence, so they argue, greater human security for all (Westbrook, 2004).

But economic security for some enhances the economic disparities that are the cause of human insecurities for so many others. This point was an important part of the argument for what subsequently became the human security agenda. The United Nations *Human Development Report* of 1994, the crucial text in formulating this agenda, suggested that the ratio of income shares between the poorest 20 per cent and richest 20 per cent of the world population grew from 30:1 to 60:1 between 1960 and 1991 (UNDP, 1994). The trend to greater inequality has continued since. Affluence for some is undoubtedly increasing, indeed the overall percentage of the world population outside the UN category of absolute poverty might also be decreasing, but these processes are often at the expense of further impoverishment of those displaced or marginalized by the processes of economic change. These people are often not part of the statistical calculus of progress used to legitimate current models of economic growth, despite the arguments of activists at the Earth Summit in Rio de Janeiro in 1992. Since then it has been clear that these matters need to be taken seriously (Chatterjee and Finger, 1994).

Insecurity is heightened through the dismantling of institutions that provide some protection from the vagaries of international markets. It doesn't matter whether this happens due to formal policies of structural adjustment, or as state responses to international market and financial pressures and conditionalities on macro-economic policies, the poor end up with fewer protections. Such considerations raise the most important questions about the specification of the term 'globalization'. Viewed as a global process of enlarging the scope of international markets, the technocratic view of global problems suggests further *development* and the further deployment of technical expertise. In Jan Aart Scholte's (1996: 51) terms:

> Tacitly if not explicitly, liberal orthodoxy treats the market, electoral democracy, growth, national solidarity and scientific reason as timeless virtues with universal applicability. The discourse effectively rules out the possibility that capitalism, individualism, industrialism, consumerism, the nationality principle and rationalism

might be causes rather than cures to global problems. To this degree, liberalism is ideological, a form of knowledge that obscures disempowerment and thereby serves, often quite unintentionally, to sustain unfreedoms with false promises.

If the expansion of modernity, and the acceleration of global processes of development, are seen as the solution to numerous global problems, then anything that stands in the way of them is viewed as a threat to the political order of modernity. On the other hand, that economy is precisely what is setting in motion environmental changes that will have dramatic effects on climate in particular, and in turn make numerous people more vulnerable to storms, floods and droughts, and in so far as these phenomena disrupt the production and distribution of food and other essentials, also to famines. These are clearly matters of concern to those who worry about international security, and indeed in the 1990s there was a considerable scholarly debate about global environmental threats to security and the possibilities of various scarcities leading to violent conflict (Homer-Dixon, 1999).

Environmental insecurity

One of the great dangers of invoking environmental threats is that such arguments will revive traditional Malthusian fears of population growth and resource shortages. Despite the focus on the global dimensions of these matters, these arguments frequently focus only on the local and supposedly indigenous causes of insecurity. They, the poor who live far from where such arguments are formulated, are irresponsible, having too many babies, cutting down rainforests, polluting rivers, causing erosion and many other 'environmental' calamities. An especially high-profile articulation of these matters was published in Robert Kaplan's influential article 'The Coming Anarchy' in the *Atlantic Monthly* magazine in February 1994. Here collapsing states, environmental degradation, surging population growth, deforestation and disease were woven together in an alarmist prediction of imminent chaos that would shape the national security agenda for the United States and much of the rest of the world for the twenty-first century.

This was a powerfully stated argument that chaos 'over there' in the wild zones of the South would spill over into the metropolitan zones of postmodern prosperity, a threat that presumably needs among other things the shoring up of defences to prevent the anarchy spreading. The discussion about globalization and security since 1994 has been heavily influenced by these two lines of argument. But it is very important to note that the Malthusian argument is mostly about indigenous causes in the South supposedly setting in motion threats to the North (Dalby, 2002).

The *population question* is frequently linked directly to a geographical understanding of these matters that specifies the problem as one in the South that will have deleterious spill-over impacts on the North, and needs Northern intervention and management precisely for these reasons (Hartmann et al., 2005). Michael Thompson's (1998) scathing critique of Malthusian environmental-security thinking shows clearly that much of this approach is premised on a false ethnocentric assumption of the 'ignorant fecund peasant' as the root of 'Third World' troubles. The 'ignorant fecund peasant' model of overpopulation leading to environmental crisis that is so popular with Northern environmentalists is inaccurate, not least because of the gross over-generalizations about peasant behaviour, but more importantly because of the overlooked intricacies of rural political ecologies, as well as the disruptions of traditional livelihoods by global trade.

Viewed by those who are supposedly the population threat, that is by the numerous humans in the South rendered insecure by the accelerations of global economic activity, globalization often looks very different from the rosy picture painted by the advocates of neoliberal versions of modernization. The appropriation of environmental resources in the South by consumers in the North can be understood in the terms of 'eco-imperialism' (Shiva, 1994). The example of Japanese corporate connections with the destruction of Southeast Asian forests is just one notable case (Dauvergne, 1997). These processes can also be understood in terms of the North appropriating the South's 'environmental space' both by disrupting ecosystems as a result of its resource extractions and by overloading atmospheric and oceanic environmental 'sinks' (Sachs et al., 1998).

Rather than a threat to the North, current processes in the South might more adequately be understood as the historical product of continued Northern dominance of the global economy (Dalby, 2003). The *global* problems of ozone holes and climate change are global only in some senses, and caused directly by only part of humanity, and maybe the part least vulnerable to coming disruptions. The key point is that this is a matter for the North to address most directly. The South has other concerns as a consequence of its colonial history of resource appropriations and the more recent models of development that perpetuate these patterns. Focusing on population as a security threat obscures these important social processes.

Despite the obvious acceleration of processes of degradation in the last few decades, the disruptions of 'environmental space' caused by Northern consumption have specific geographies with a much longer history than the recent claims to globalized environmental novelty encompass. The re-emergence of explicit discussions of empire in recent years has made all this substantially easier to see. The patterns of extraction of resources from the South, and the intervention by powerful Northern states in many places to ensure the continued supply of key resources, and the profits that go with them, to the metropoles of the global economy is a long story of empire and imperial power (Dalby, 2004). All of which requires a more comprehensive understanding of security for the twenty-first century than that provided by Malthusian geopolitics.

Human security

The debate about human security which has gradually superseded many of the 1990s Malthusian fears draws much more heavily on geographical understandings of global interconnections. This reformulation of security has itself been stimulated by the processes of globalization and the vulnerabilities that it produces. Human security was proposed by the UNDP (1994) as an overarching concept to capture the reformulation of security needed to deal with numerous threats and vulnerabilities in the 1990s and to shift the focus from narrow preoccupations with national security understood primarily in military terms. The focus should be on people's lives and dignity not on weapons; on changes that undermine livelihood and social arrangements in addition to direct physical threats to safety. Environmental concerns are prominent among the new threats to human security. The UNDP's (1994) concept of global environmental degradation includes:

- air pollution that drifts across national frontiers
- chlorofluorocarbons that remain a problem in terms of stratospheric ozone depletion
- greenhouse gases that may cause climate changes and sea level increases with disastrous impacts in some coastal states
- biological diversity reduction with potential global consequences
- coastal marine pollution which reduces global fish catches.

To deal with these difficulties requires all sorts of policy innovations and a recognition of the importance of understanding the global processes that link economic and ecological processes with the livelihoods and safety of people in specific places. Crucial in all this discussion of human security is an insistence that the new security agenda is more about threats that come from 'the actions of millions of people rather than aggression by a few nations' (UNDP, 1994: 34).

Michael Renner (1996), of the Worldwatch Institute in Washington, used the United Nations' concept of human security to investigate the global connections between environmental problems and social conflict. Pointing to the growing inequities in the global political economy, he suggests that these are related in various ways to both conflict and degradation. More specifically, Renner (1996: 17) argues: 'It is becoming clear that humanity is facing a triple security crisis: societies everywhere have to contend with the effects of environmental decline, the repercussions of social inequities and stress, and the dangers arising out of an unchecked arms proliferation that is a direct legacy of the cold war period'.

Ancient concerns about human security 'are now magnified by the unprecedented scale of environmental degradation, by the presence of immense poverty in the midst of extraordinary wealth, and by the fact that social, economic, and environmental challenges are no longer limited to particular communities and nations' (Renner, 1996: 18). Political violence is often widespread in places where war is not officially occurring. But political fragmentation, fuelled by the proliferation of weapons, is only one half of the story (Hampson, 2002). The other half is the accelerating processes of globalization that are interconnecting the world's economies and cultures in ways that often operate to undercut traditional economies and challenge the sustainability of agricultural and survival practices. Wars in the South are now frequently about who will control the revenue from the extraction of resources for sale on the global market (Le Billon, 2005).

The crucial point about rejecting the simplistic and inaccurate assumptions of neo-Malthusian thinking is that the processes that are causing many contemporary insecurities are not solely driven by local endogenous factors, although their most obvious manifestations may be in specific environments (Williams, 1995). The processes of accelerating global interconnection that globalization as a concept tries to encapsulate explain much more than the geopolitically inadequate formulations of Malthusianism, which continue to assume that difficulties are driven solely by local autonomous processes of over-population (Peluso and Watts, 2001). To understand the forces setting populations in motion as unconnected to the processes of development is to miss a crucial dimension of the contemporary human condition. It is also to miss the important point that state elites are frequently guilty of manipulating and even creating crises to extend control or enhance their abilities to extract wealth from rural areas, or the additional point that states are sometimes simply incapable of coping with the complex disruptions that come with development (Kahl, 2006).

The historical patterns of commodification, overexploitation and domestication of resources in the expansion of commercial economies are not new. Neither are the population
disruptions and displacements that often result. Famines in the nineteenth century were
directly related to the spread of commercial agriculture and the world grain-trading system
(Davis, 2001). These displaced people may in turn damage marginal lands unsuited to agriculture, or swell the ranks of the poor in urban shantytowns and become a matter of concern
to environmentalists. The interconnections between globalization and environmental
degradation are crucial to Renner's (1996) argument, but the processes in motion are also
frequently those carried out by political and military elites. Modernization is about state
making (Scott, 1998). The enclosures and displacement of rural populations that are part
of the state-backed and -enforced expansion of commercial agriculture cause the displacement of many 'environmental refugees' (Gadgil and Guha, 1995). All of which leads to
complex situations requiring an understanding of displacement that connects people to the
specific environments and development activities occurring from whence they are displaced
(Najam, 2003).

On the largest scale, when these processes are not understood, or are ignored, these
people become the object of Malthusian security narratives on the crises of migration, and
invoke alarm claims as migrants apparently threaten the integrity of the nation to which
they flee (Tesfahuney, 1998; Shapiro, 1997). Renner's (1996) point is that rural land reform
and the construction of less unequal land-holding arrangements is often the key to improving environmental conditions and other facets of life in rural areas. But such initiatives often
run directly up against elites whose power and wealth rest on the unequal landholdings, and
who dominate the commercial sector of the agricultural economy (Peluso and Watts, 2001).
Where this concerns agricultural production for export, sometimes partly as a result of
internationally imposed economic conditionalities and structural adjustment policies, the
links between globalization and peasant struggles are especially direct.

Most recently some of these problems have been exacerbated by the sometimes bizarre
consequences of carbon emission trading systems. These sometimes lead to attempts to 'sink'
Northern carbon dioxide emissions that are causing climate change in trees in the South.
Northern corporations are getting into the plantation business as a way to make their operations 'carbon neutral'. Without clearly understanding, or apparently caring about either
local ecology or how local people use their environments, many of the mistakes of earlier
colonial administrations are being repeated. Those who pay the cost are those local people
whose lives and environments are disrupted, precisely the people who have not contributed
to the global climate-change problem (Development Dialogue, 2006).

Environmental security

It is now becoming clear that the largest causes of global change are the industrial production
systems of the global economy and the consumption habits of those with the wealth and
time to use all the technologies that this economy has made available (Lipschutz, 2004).
Such concerns in the South as cutting rain forests still matter, but in the long run it is the
massive use of fossil fuels that is changing the earth's atmosphere and setting in motion as
yet unknown changes in the biosphere (Flannery, 2005). This point too makes it very important to recognise that consumption in one part of the world may have indirect effects in

terms of both the supply of materials and the consequences of pollution elsewhere, a matter that involves complicated obligations across national boundaries (Mason, 2001).

Human activities are altering the atmosphere and many other facets of the global ecosystem (United Nations Environment Programme, 2002). Half the world's ice-free land has been transformed by human action, forests have dramatically declined. Half of the fresh water on the earth's surface is used by humans; major rivers now sometimes hardly reach their estuaries. More than a quarter of all the production of biological life in the oceans is removed by various fishing technologies. More nitrogen is now fixed by artificial means than by nature and more sulphur dioxide appears in the air as a result of human activity than natural processes.

All of which means that nature as humanity once knew it has been transformed; we now live in a new geological era called the Anthropocene. Environments are in some important ways now artificial, and if global climate change causes increased numbers and/or severity of tropical storms, hurricanes and typhoons then in part human activity is responsible. As the ice melts in the Arctic and livelihoods there are disrupted, so too the global economy is partly responsible for these changes (Dalby, 2003). Globalization is now an economic process and an ecological one too; seeing global environmental change and economic globalization as two sides of the same coin finally allows us to understand the contemporary human predicament in ways that are more appropriate to thinking intelligently about the future.

Crucially this means that we need to rethink how security is conceived. Clearly we can no longer specify threats in military terms, and whatever the long-term results of the so-called global war on terror, clearly many more people are vulnerable because of climate change than because of the activities of those resisting American and allied military power by the use of homemade bombs and machine guns. Neither can we formulate environment as something external to humanity that somehow threatens 'us' separate from that environment (Dalby, 2006). Neither do formulations that portray the populations of the South as a threat to the North, or a more general formulation of global security which effectively supports the current geopolitical divisions, stand up to scrutiny.

The interconnections between numerous facets of violence, vulnerability and change have to be worked into any analysis of these things (Worldwatch Institute, 2005). The discussion of human security is now being extended to make precisely these links between globalization and insecurity, understanding humanity and environment, as in some senses involved in a co-evolutionary process where human intelligence is part of what shapes the future (Pirages and DeGeest, 2004). Here too globalization and the sense of living in a compressed political space are complemented by increased recognition of the collapse of the distinction between natural and human places. Human and ecological matters are part and parcel of the same deliberations on the redefinition of security as one that encompasses the threats to human existence in diverse places rather than a more narrowly focused consideration of the perpetuation of state power (Dodds and Pippard, 2005). But this has to be understood as part of a global political economy that is in need of greening, so that the appropriate interconnections are clear (Clapp and Dauvergne, 2005).

Such formulations put the specific relations between places at the centre of a critique of globalization. They do so in a way that challenges arguments about novelty, interconnection and homogenization, and simultaneously the appropriateness of thinking of politics in terms of what happens within territorial states. Likewise, a discussion that divorces the global economy from its material context as part of the biosphere that it is now changing is also inadequate. Both environmental concerns and globalization challenge the contemporary spatial categories of political analysis, and powerfully suggest the necessity of more drastically rethinking the geographical categories of society, culture and identity and traditional formulations of environment.

Conversely, the focus on globalization and the more recent discussion of environmental threats in terms of climate change, and the need to formulate policies on the basis of a much more comprehensive understanding of human security, offers an opportunity to think beyond the geopolitical myopia of 1990s Malthusian threats or policy discussions focused only on states. Global environmental security focuses on the interconnectedness of the human condition in all its variety in different but connected places, rather than on the assumption of one humanity facing common threats. As such, the intellectual tools needed to confront our contemporary crisis have been helped recently by a more nuanced understanding of globalization, one nuanced in part by the recognition that geography matters. Globalization is not a matter of cultural or economic homogenization, but rather it is a matter of the acceleration of connections between peoples and places that have specific roles to play simultaneously in the global political economy and the ongoing transformation of the biosphere.

References

Barnett, J. (2001) *The Meaning of Environmental Security*, London, Zed.

Chatterjee, P. and Finger, M. (1994) *The Earth Brokers: Power, Politics and World Development*, New York, Routledge.

Clapp, J. (1998) 'The privatization of global environmental governance: ISO14000 and the developing world', *Global Governance*, 4, 295–316.

Clapp, J. and Dauvergne, P. (2005) *Paths to a Green World: The Political Economy of the Global Environment*, Cambridge, MA, MIT Press.

Commission on Global Governance (1995) *Our Global Neighbourhood*, Oxford, Oxford University Press.

Crosby, A. (1986) *Ecological Imperialism: The Biological Expansion of Europe 900–1900*, Cambridge, Cambridge University Press.

Dalby, S. (2002) *Environmental Security*, Minneapolis, University of Minnesota Press.

———. (2003) 'Geopolitical identities: arctic ecology and global consumption', *Geopolitics*, 8 (1), 181–203.

———. (2004) 'Ecological politics, violence, and the theme of empire', *Global Environmental Politics*, 4 (2), 1–11.

———. (2005) 'Political space: autonomy, liberalism and empire', *Alternatives: Global, Local, Political*, 30, 415–41.

———. (2006) 'Environmental security: ecology or international relations?' in P. Stoett and E. Laferrière (eds), *International Ecopolitical Theory: Critical Approaches*, Vancouver, University of British Columbia Press, pp. 17–33.

Dauvergne, P. (1997) *Shadows in the Forest: Japan and the Politics of Timber in South East Asia*, Cambridge, MA, MIT Press.

Davis, M. (2001) *Late Victorian Holocausts: El Nino Famines and the Making of the Third World*, London, Verso.

Development Dialogue (2006) 'Carbon trading: a critical conversation on climate change, privatisation and power', *Development Dialogue*, 46, http://www.dhf.uu.se/publications.html.

Diamond, J. (1997) *Guns, Germs and Steel: The Fates of Human Societies*, New York, Norton.

Dodds, F. and Pippard, T. (eds) (2005) *Human and Ecological Security: An Agenda for Change,* London, Earthscan.

Flannery, T. (2005) *The Weather Makers: How We Are Changing the Climate and What It Means for Life on Earth,* Toronto, Harper Collins.

Gadgil, M. and Guha, R. (1995) *Ecology and Equity: The Use and Abuse of Nature in Contemporary India,* London, Routledge.

Gedicks, A. (2001) *Resource Rebels: Native Challenges to Mining and Oil Corporations,* Boston, South End.

Hampson, F. O. (2002) *Madness in the Multitude: Human Security and World Disorder,* Toronto, Oxford University Press.

Hartmann, B., Subramaniam, B. and Zerner, C. (eds) (2005) *Making Threats: Biofears Environmental Anxieties,* Lanham, MD, Rowman and Littlefield.

Homer-Dixon, T. (1999) *Environment, Scarcity and Violence,* Princeton, NJ, Princeton University Press.

Kahl, C. H. (2006) *States, Scarcity and Civil Strife in the Developing World,* Princeton, NJ, Princeton University Press.

Kaplan, R. D. (1994) 'The coming anarchy', *The Atlantic Monthly,* 273 (2), 44–76.

Karliner, J. (1997) *The Corporate Planet,* San Francisco, Sierra Club.

Le Billon, P. (2005) *Fuelling War: Natural Resources and Armed Conflict,* London, Routledge.

Lipschutz, R. (2004) *Global Environmental Politics: Power, Perspectives and Practice,* Washington, DC, CQ Press.

Mander, J. and Goldsmith, E. (eds) (1996) *The Case Against the Global Economy, and for a Turn to the Local,* San Francisco, Sierra Club Books.

Marchak, P. (1995) *Logging the Globe,* Montreal and Kingston, McGill-Queens University Press.

Mason, M. (2001) 'Transnational environmental obligations: locating new spaces of accountability in a post-Westphalian global order', *Transactions of the Institute of British Geographers,* 26, 407–29.

Najam, A. (ed.) (2003) *Environment, Development and Human Security: Perspective from South Asia,* Lanham, MD, University Press of America.

O'Brien, K. and Leichenko, R. (2003) 'Winners and losers in the context of global change', *Annals of the Association of American Geographers,* 93, 89–103.

O'Neill, K. (1998) 'Out of the backyard: the problems of hazardous waste management at a global level', *Journal of Environment and Development,* 7, 138–63.

Peluso, N. and Watts, M. (eds) (2001) *Violent Environments,* Ithaca, Cornell University Press.

Pirages, D. C. and DeGeest, T. M. (2004) *Ecological Security: An Evolutionary Perspective on Globalization,* Lanham, MD, Rowman and Littlefield.

Renner, M. (1996) *Fighting for Survival: Environmental Decline, Social Conflict and the New Age of Insecurity,* New York, Norton.

Robertson, R. (1992) *Globalization: Social Theory and Global Culture,* London, Sage.

Sachs, W. (1999) *Planet Dialectics: Explorations in Environment and Development,* London, Zed.

Sachs, W., Loske, R. and Linz , M. (1998) *Greening the North: A Post-Industrial Blueprint for Ecology and Equity,* London, Zed.

Schellnhuber, H. J., Crutzen, P. J., Clark, W. C. and Hunt, J. (2005) 'Earth system analysis for sustainability', *Environment,* 47 (8), 11–25.

Scholte, J. A. (1996) 'Towards a critical theory of globalization' in E. Kofman and G. Youngs (eds), *Globalization: Theory and Practice,* London, Pinter.

Scott, J. C. (1998) *Seeing Like a State: How Certain Schemes to Improve the Human Condition Have Failed,* New Haven, CT, Yale University Press.

Shapiro, M. (1997) 'Narrating the nation, unwelcoming the stranger: anti-immigration policy in contemporary America', *Alternatives,* 22, 1–34.

Shiva, V. (1994) 'Conflicts of global ecology: environmental activism in a period of global reach', *Alternatives,* 19, 195–207.

Sullivan, S. (2000) 'Getting the science right, or introducing science in the first place' in P. Stott and S. Sullivan (eds), *Political Ecology: Science, Myth and Power*, London, Arnold.

Tesfahuney, M. (1998) 'Mobility, racism and geopolitics', *Political Geography*, 15, 499–515.

Thompson, M. (1998) 'The new world disorder: is environmental security the cure?', *Mountain Research and Development*, 18, 117–22.

United Nations Development Program (1994) *Human Development Report 1994*, New York, Oxford University Press.

United Nations Environment Program (2002) *Global Environmental Programme 3*, London, Earthscan.

Wapner, P. (1996) *Environmental Activism and World Civic Politics*, Albany, State University of New York.

Westbrook, D. A. (2004) *City of Gold: An Apology for Global Capitalism in a Time of Discontent*, New York, Routledge.

Williams, G. (1995) 'Modernizing Malthus: the World Bank, population control and the African environment' in J. Crush (ed.), *Power of Development*, London, Routledge.

Worldwatch Institute (2005) *State of the World 2005: Redefining Global Security*, New York, Norton.

Yearley, S. (1996) *Sociology, Environmentalism, Globalization: Reinventing the Globe*, London, Sage.

CHAPTER 4

Imperial Powers and Democratic Imaginations in a Global Era

David Slater

The analysis of global politics and the dynamics of North-South relations is increasingly marked by a sense of flux and fluidity. Whilst a concern for discussing the waning relevance of the 'three worlds of development' has given way to an emphasis on the relations between globalization and development, more recently there has been a re-focussing on questions of imperialism set in a context of a globalizing world. For Escobar (2004), for example, going beyond the third world can be seen against the rise of a new US-based form of imperial globality. At the same time, new forms of resistance as expressed by social movements and radical political leaders are raising issues about democracy and democratization that bring into question both neo-liberal versions of state and society and imperial power. In this context, the chapter discusses important facets of the interface between a resurgent imperialism and a contested terrain of democratic politics. There are three sections: in the first part relevant aspects of the contemporary literature on imperialism are critically considered with emphasis on the relationality of imperial power, the difference between imperiality and imperialism and the problem of the agents of power. The second section examines the particularities of the United States as an imperial democracy, which leads into a final discussion of the geopolitics of democratization. The mode of analysis is exploratory and given the extensive nature of the conceptual and political terrain, the themes dealt with are meant to open up dialogue and raise new questions for debate.

Conceptualizing imperialism today

As a way of beginning the first part of the analysis, it would seem useful to evaluate the forms in which key concepts have been defined and deployed. In this case, it is necessary to discuss the delineation of the term 'imperialism' especially as it has been used in the last few years to describe an apparently new phenomenon of globalizing power.[1] In fact, the apparent 'newness' of the phenomenon is frequently captured in the phrase the 'new imperialism' (Harvey, 2003a).

Harvey (2003a: 26), for example, stresses the point that he is defining '(
rialism', as both a 'distinctively political project on the part of actors whose
in command of a territory and a capacity to mobilize its human and natur.. ...
wards political, economic and military ends', whilst also imperialism is a diffuse political-
economic process in which command over the use of capital takes primacy (Harvey, 2003a:
26). The central idea is to posit the territorial and capitalist logics of power as distinct from
each other, whilst recognizing that the two logics intertwine in complex and contradictory
ways. Harvey notes for example, that whereas the Vietnam War or the invasion of Iraq could
hardly be solely explained in terms of the 'immediate requirements of capital accumulation',
conversely, it would be difficult to understand the general territorial strategy of containment
of the Soviet Union without taking into account the 'compelling need' felt on the part of US
business interests to keep as much of the world as possible open to capital accumulation
(Harvey, 2003a: 30). This sense of two intertwined but often dissonant logics finds a parallel
in the work of Arrighi (2005) and Callinicos (2003), and may be contrasted with a definition
given by Chalmers Johnson (2004) in his book on *The Sorrows of Empire*. Here, Johnson
suggests that the simplest definition of imperialism is the 'domination and exploitation of
weaker states by stronger ones', and he adds that imperialism is the 'root cause of one of the
worst maladies inflicted by Western civilization on the rest of the world – namely,
racism' (Johnson, 2004: 28–29).

What we have here are two perspectives: one which prioritizes a Marxist political economy framework, and another which privileges questions of culture and power. At the same
time, the perspective signalled by Johnson underlines the asymmetry in global power relations between weaker and stronger states. This approach can be seen as related to Said's
(1993: 8) suggestion that imperialism may be defined as the 'practice, the theory and attitudes
of a dominating metropolitan centre ruling a distant territory'. With these various takes on
imperialism,[2] it is possible to highlight a distinction between the conceptualization of imperialism as a specific system of rule and an emphasis on the unevenness of imperialist
relations in the sense that it is in the context of North-South relations rather than intra-West
relations (i.e., US-European relations) that the gravity and central significance of imperialism can be discerned. In an initial attempt to link the above-noted perspectives, I want to
suggest that the imperial relation may be thought of in terms of three interwoven elements
where the geopolitical context is formed by the North-South divide.

First, one can posit the existence of a geopolitics of *invasiveness* that is expressed through
strategies of appropriating resources and raw materials and/or securing strategic sites for
military bases, which are accompanied by the laying down of new patterns of infrastructure
and governmental regulation. Invasiveness, or processes of penetration of states, economies
and social orders (Panitch and Leys, 2004: vii), can be linked to what Harvey (2003a and
2003b) has called 'accumulation by dispossession' whereby the resources and wealth of
peripheral societies are continually extracted for the benefit of the imperial heartland (see,
for example, Boron, 2005: 118). But such penetration and invasiveness must not be seen as
only a matter of political economy since the phenomenon of invasiveness is also cultural,
political and psychological; it is in fact a multi-dimensional phenomenon whereby the determining decisions and practices are taken and deployed in the realm of the geopolitical.
For example, the violation of the sovereignty of a third world society is not only a question
of the transgression of international law, but more profoundly it reflects a negation of the

will and dignity of another people and another culture. Violations of sovereignty negate the autonomous right of peripheral societies to decide for themselves their own trajectories of political and cultural being (EZLN, 2005). In this sense, the imperial or more categorically the imperialist relation[3] is rooted in a power-over conception that reflects Western privilege and denial of the non-Western other's right to geopolitical autonomy. This aspect of imperialism has been sometimes neglected, and yet as Ahmad (2003) has recently reminded us, it is in the third world that the effects of imperialism are so clearly visible, a visibility that needs more attention than a mere signalling of the unevenness of imperialism.

Second, as a consequence of the invasiveness of imperialist projects, one has the *imposition* of the dominant values, modes of thinking and institutional practices of the imperial power on to the society that has been subjected to imperial penetration. This is sometimes established as part of a project of 'nation building' or geopolitical guidance, where the effective parameters of rule reflect a clear belief in the superiority of the imperial culture of institutionalization. Clearly, under colonialism such impositions were transparent and justified as part of a Western project of bringing 'civilization' to the non-Western other. In the contemporary era, and specifically in relation to Iraq, bringing democracy and neoliberalism, US-style, have been imposed as part of a project to redraw the geopolitical map of the Middle East (Achcar, 2004; Ali, 2003; Gregory, 2004; Ramadani, 2006), a project which has seen both resistance, especially in the Sunni triangle, and partial accommodation, especially in the Kurdish region of the country.

Whilst the violation of sovereignty can be more appropriately considered under the heading of invasiveness, the related imposition of cultural and governmental norms constitutes an effect of that violation, but here the process of geopolitical guidance can be better interpreted in terms of an imperial governmentality (Rajagopal, 2004). Such a governmentality may include the establishment of ground rules for democratic politics with an outcome that might not follow the imperialist's preferred route. Crucially, however, governmentality is concerned with installing new rules, codifications and institutional practices, which are anchored in a specific set of externally transferred rationalities concerning 'market-led' development and democracy, effective states, 'good governance', property rights, 'open economies' and so on. The imposition is thus a project for societal transformation that aims to leave behind an imperialized polity, which is 'owned' and run by indigenous leaders. Whether such projects can be successful is surely doubtful given the realities of their imposed nature, but in the final outcome much will depend on both the form, depth, extent and resilience of resistances to their power as well as on the efficacy of the domestic leaders who take on the externally designed political mantle, acting as introjecting agents of externally initiated authority. Again, in both instances, with resistance and accommodation, the primary significance of relationality is clearly evident. In addition, such situations are further complicated by the diverse kinds of resistance and accommodation and by the dynamic of change inherent in both processes. What is being emphasized here, therefore, is not only the role of process but crucially the complexities of the politics of the imperial encounter, including not only the limits of externally deployed power but also the unpredictable dynamics of internal situations which are affected by the clash of rival interests and competing discursive orientations.[4]

Third, it is important to stress that the imperial relation carries within it a lack of *respect* and *recognition* for the colonized or, expressed more broadly, imperialized society. Hence, the processes of penetration and imposition are viewed as being beneficial to the societies that are being brought into the orbit of imperial power. The posited superiorities of Western 'progress', 'modernization', 'democracy', 'development' and 'civilization' and so on are deployed to legitimize projects of enduring invasiveness that are characterized by a lack of recognition for the autonomy, dignity, sovereignty and cultural value of the imperialized society. Overall, there is a mission to Westernize the non-Western world, and resistances to such a mission, especially in their more militant forms, are seen as being deviant and irrational and in need of repression and cure.

This third element is often neglected by Western scholars, and yet it is rather crucial. Let us briefly refer to a resonant passage from Arundhati Roy's (2004) essay entitled 'Come September'. She writes, 'loss and losing . . . grief, failure, brokenness, numbness, uncertainty, fear, the death of feeling, the death of dreaming . . . the absolute, relentless, endless, habitual unfairness of the world . . . what does it mean to whole cultures, whole peoples who have learned to live with it as a constant companion?' (Roy, 2004: 20). What does loss mean to *whole cultures, whole peoples* of the global South who have seen their societies penetrated, worked over, re-structured, modernized and made more 'civilized'? What does it mean to experience a bloody military takeover, the overthrow of a democratically elected government, or the violent seizure and occupation of a people's land as has taken place in Afghanistan, Iraq and Palestine, with so many far-reaching social, economic, political and psychological consequences? The actual *violence* involved in such interventions is not infrequently ignored in accounts of imperial power, and yet, as Davis (2001), Mbembe (2001) and more recently Boggs (2005) remind us, it is an intrinsic part of colonial and imperial power. Equally, it is important to realize that the violence of intervention and the more visible horrors of an Abu Ghraib or a Guantánamo[5] are buttressed by an insidious and pervasive Western arrogance that posits the non-Western other as immanently inferior, albeit susceptible to advancement with the proper guidance.

Imperial relations, seen as the most acutely asymmetrical form of geopolitical encounter, can be discussed in terms of the three above-outlined features, but other issues need to be brought on to the analytical agenda. At this juncture, two questions can be posed. First, why might it be useful to distinguish imperiality from imperialism and second, how might we account for the imperialist drive in the current conjuncture?

In the specific context of global politics, imperialism may be broadly defined as the strategy, practice and advocacy of the penetrative power of a Western state over other predominantly non-Western societies, whose political sovereignty is thereby subverted. The word 'predominantly' is used here since I would argue that imperialism, or more specifically US imperialism, whilst having potentially dominating effects on other Western nation-states, is most clearly manifest in the context of West/non-West relations. Although it is abundantly clear that capitalist enterprises, or more specifically transnational corporations, exert far-reaching modes of power, including in their relation to the state, I would argue that it is the nation-state, as geopolitical pivot, and more specifically those key *agents of structuring influence* acting within its governmental apparatuses, that exert the central decision-making power. In other words, I would suggest that in the context of US imperialism, the decision-making power that brings an imperialist strategy into being is situated in the heart of the state (Panitch, 2000).

An imperialist strategy is thus essentially developed within the political space of the state, but this does not mean that imperialist ideas are only confined to this domain – they can be seen as being potentially sedimented in all the varying spheres of Western society and economy, and this is where the notion of imperiality can be useful. Imperiality can be defined as a composite term that infers the right, privilege and sentiment of being imperial or of defending ideas of Empire in which the geopolitical invasiveness of Western power is justified.[6] Thus, Western societies such as Britain, France and the US harbour imperial discourses that are rooted in the history of their geopolitical relations, so that an active strategy of imperialist expansion can be discursively sustained through a reliance on or direct appeal to the deeply rooted sense of imperial privilege. There can be a mutually sustaining process here whereby an active strategy of imperialism is supported by a reservoir of imperial sentiment which in turn is further reinforced by a reinvigorated imperialist strategy. Alternatively, where there has been an effective resistance, both internally and externally, as was the case during the Vietnam War, and especially during the later stages, the effects of imperiality are reduced, especially when the will of the imperial power has been defeated. However, much depends not only on the passage of time but crucially on the battle for ideas, or more specifically wars over geopolitical meaning, which are importantly characterized by struggles over what is remembered and what is consigned to oblivion. A current example of what is at stake here relates to the positive way the imperial past can be represented. For instance, in Britain, New Labour's Gordon Brown has recently suggested that, 'we should be proud . . . of the empire' and the 'days of Britain having to apologize for its colonial history are over' (quoted in Milne, 2005). Similarly, in France, legislation passed in 2005 concerning the regulation of the national curriculum includes an article that praises the contributions to civilization of French colonizers in Algeria, Morocco and Tunisia (Lemaire, 2006), re-echoing de Tocqueville's support for the civilizing mission of French colonialism.

Given this posited interrelation between imperialism and imperiality, how might we account for the current, post-9/11 resurgence of imperialism, especially as reflected in the renewed projection of US power and specifically the invasion of Iraq? Let us begin by briefly reviewing the different approaches to this question.

For David Harvey (2003a: 23–24), a confrontation with Iraq appeared inevitable and such a geopolitical thrust has to be linked to the strategic importance of oil: access to Iraqi and Middle East oil in general being in his view a 'crucial security issue for the United States, as it is for the global economy as a whole'. A similar perspective has been developed by Klare (2002) in his work on *Resource Wars*, and certainly the wealth of Iraq's oil resources needs to be taken into account as an important factor, but was it the determining factor that largely explains the drive to invade? For Stephen Gill (2004: 37–38), it is clear that whilst the war is directly linked to US policy on energy security, and its increased dependence upon foreign and especially Middle Eastern oil, it is necessary to probe deeper. The invasion was not only about removing Saddam Hussein from power and taking control of Iraqi oil, but it was also about reinforcing the US' long-term 'geopolitical position', involving both its military basing strategy and its commercial interests, including potential threats to dollar hegemony and its prerogative to pursue wars of impunity which has a long history. The significance of this element of historical and geopolitical continuity is further elaborated on by the San Francisco Bay area group called Retort (2005) who developed a detailed argument on contemporary US imperialism. Their key concepts are spectacle, capital and war.

In a similar vein to Gill, they suggest that whilst the American empire cannot forego oil, strategic and corporate oil interests cannot, of themselves, explain the US imperial mission. Rather, they go on, 'what the Iraq adventure represents is less a war for oil than a radical, punitive, "extra-economic" restructuring of the conditions necessary for expanding profitability – paving the way . . . for new rounds of American-led dispossession and capital accumulation'. This is discussed as a new form of what they call 'military neoliberalism' (Retort, 2005: 72), a phenomenon that they suggest is 'no more than primitive accumulation in (thin) disguise' (75), recalling Rosa Luxemburg's (1968: 454) notion that militarism is most appropriately viewed as a 'province of accumulation'. However, although there is no space here to go into a detailed consideration of the Retort text (for a recent review see Soper, 2006), it is important to indicate that the perspective that is developed is not as econcentric as it might first appear. The authors introduce a series of points that give considerable subtlety to their approach. When, for example, they state that primitive accumulation is essentially an exercise in violence, they go on to note, in answering their question concerning the circumstances that oblige the state to act in the way it has of late, that, *contra* Marx, these circumstances are rarely straightforwardly 'economic'; it is rather the *interweaving of compulsions* – spectacular, economic, geopolitical – that reveal the 'American empire's true character' (Retort, 2005: 77). Moreover, when they describe US imperialism, they stress the point that they are not talking of a 'smoothly gliding imperial machine, but rather a clumsy, lurching apparatus, responding contingently and by no means moving in a single direction' (81). Equally, they emphasize the 'relentless structural energy' of imperial power, whilst adding that although the empire's strategic apparatus may always be about to intervene militarily (permanent war), 'its levers must still be pulled' (102–3). Illustrating this idea they refer to the significance of 'ideological contingencies', whereby, for instance, zealots of various types may frequently gain the 'ear of the state' – these range, they go on, from the Zionists in the White House and the Pentagon (see, for example, Petras, 2005), to what they call the imperiously sociopathic, for example ' every ten years or so the US needs to pick up some crappy little country and throw it against the wall, just to show the world we mean business' (Retort, 2005: 102–3).

These so-called 'ideological contingencies' refer in this case to what I would call the actual *agents of power* (organized, for example, through the Project for a New American Century) working inside the imperial state with a myriad of links to the economy and civil society, and it is these agents of power that make decisions on how to act in the context of the interweaving of compulsions as the Retort group put it. This then is a cardinal interrelation – the working out of the interaction between the agents of power and the nature of the interweaving of compulsions. For example: how do these agents of power perceive the nature of these varied compulsions; what kinds of ideas inform their perceptions; how do their policies affect the place of the United States in the world? Furthermore, where do we place the 'spectacle' in this interlocking of agents and compulsions?

What happened on 11 September 2001 represented in one key sense a globally manifest puncturing of US power that required a response of reinvigorated force. Chomsky (2003) draws a parallel here with the enforcement style of a Mafia don. In this context, primary aspects of the 2002 National Security Strategy (White House, 2002) underlined the imperative of US exemplary action to demonstrate its reasserted power in the form of being prepared for permanent war, including the willingness to engage in preventive wars. The target had to be geopolitically significant, but also weak – Iraq and not North Korea. For Chomsky, Iraq was thus an ideal choice for exemplary action to establish the US doctrine of global rule by force as a new 'norm'. Equally, it has become clear that such exemplary action, a kind of *geopolitics of enforcement*, has Iraq as the first and not last target. In addition, it needs to be pointed out that in US strategy, enforcement is allied to a politics of justification rooted in notions of spreading freedom and democracy, as will be discussed below.

Several questions arise from the above-outlined points and these may be better contextualized by turning to the theme of US power itself – how, for example, do we account for the specificity of US imperialism?

On the geopolitics of imperial democracy

In 2002, US Vice President Dick Cheney argued that in Afghanistan, 'the world is seeing that America acts not to conquer but to liberate, and remains in friendship to help the people build a future of stability, self-determination and peace. We would act in that same spirit after a regime change in Iraq . . . our goal would be an Iraq that has territorial integrity, a government that is democratic and pluralistic, a nation where the human rights of every ethnic and religious group are recognized and respected' (quoted in Kelly, 2003: 347). Similarly in the National Security Strategy of September 2002, as well as in the recent strategy for 2006 (The White House, 2006), emphasis is placed on concepts of peace, democracy and freedom, so that, for example, America is defined as a 'great multi-ethnic democracy' that stands for the defence of liberty and justice in a world where the US must defend peace against the threats from terrorists and tyrants, and extend the peace by encouraging 'free and open societies on every continent' (White House, 2002: 1–3). What is visible in these short passages are major elements of the official representation of US power in the world, where, for instance, conquest becomes liberation, intervention is framed in terms of freedom, democracy, security and stability, and where the United States is defined as a plural, multi-ethnic home of global democracy. How is it possible to characterize such an imperial democracy as the United States – how may we view the specificity of its imperial power?

One response to this question is to suggest that unlike other Western powers, the imperiality of US power emerged out of a post-colonial anchorage, or in other words a project of imperial power gradually emerged out of an initial anti-colonial struggle for independence from British rule. This fact of emergence has given the United States a contradictory identity of being a 'post-colonial imperial power' with the determining emphasis falling on the 'imperial' (Slater, 2004a). The post-colonial essentially refers to the specificity of origin, and does not preclude the possibility of a coloniality of power as was exemplified in the case of the Philippines, or as is argued continues to apply to Puerto Rico (Pantojas-García, 2005). Such a paradoxical identity has two significant implications. First, one finds an affirmation of the legitimacy of the self-determination of peoples juxtaposed with a belief in the geopolitical destiny of the United States, a belief dating at least from the time of 'Manifest Destiny' and notions of 'benevolent assimilation' to the present wherein, as the Mexican political scientist Orozco (2005: 54) expresses it, the US sees itself as the 'first universal nation'. Historically, the contradiction between support for the rights of people to decide their own fate and a belief in the geopolitical destiny of 'America' (rather than José Martí's *nuestra América*; see Santos, 2001) has necessitated a discursive 'bridge'. This bridge has been formed through the invocation of a democratic mission that combines the national and international spheres. In order to transcend the contradiction between an identity based on the self-determination of peoples and another rooted in Empire, a horizon is created for other peoples who are encouraged to choose freedom and democracy, thereby embedding their own struggles within an Americanizing vision and practice.

Second, the primacy of self-determination provides a key to explaining the dichotomy frequently present in the discourses of US geopolitical intervention where a split is made between a concept of the people and a concept of the rulers. Given the historical differentiation of the New (American) World of freedom, progress and democracy from an Old (European) World of privilege and colonial power, support for anticolonial struggles has been accompanied by a separation between oppressed people and tyrannical rulers. For example, in the case of US hostility towards the Cuban Revolution, the Helms-Burton Act of 1996 makes a clear separation between the Cuban people who need supporting in their vulnerability and the Castro government which is seen as a tyrannical oppressor of its own people and a security threat to the international community (Slater, 2004b). Similar distinctions have been made in the contexts of interventions in Grenada (1983) and Panama (1989), and overall it can be suggested that geopolitical interventions have been couched in terms of a prominent concern for the rights of peoples that are being oppressed by unrepresentative and totalitarian regimes. The United States is thus represented as a benevolent guardian of the rights of a subordinated people. An imperial ethic of care is projected across frontiers to provide one form of legitimization for interventions. This particular ethic of care needs to be kept in mind as a constitutive feature of the imperial and although imperial power includes the capacity for force, equally it requires discourses of legitimization wherein ideas of care and guidance continue to play a leading role.

Geopolitical interventions have been a permanent feature of the landscape of North-South relations and can be viewed in terms of the interconnections between desire, will, capacity and legitimization. The will to intervene can be represented as a crystallization of a desire to expand, expressed for example in the notion of 'Manifest Destiny' (see, for example, Pratt, 1927), and such a will can only be made effective when the capacities – military, economic, political – to intervene are sufficiently developed. Will and capacity together provide a force, but their effectiveness is only secured as a hegemonic power through the deployment of a discourse of justification. A political will that focuses desire and is able to mobilize the levers of intervention seeks a hegemonic role through the ability to induce consent by providing leadership, whilst retaining the capacity to coerce.

The desire to intervene, to penetrate another society and help to re-order, re-adjust, modernize, develop, civilize, democratize that other society is an essential part of any imperial project. The geopolitical will is provided by changing agents of power working in and through the apparatuses of the imperial state, and the processes of legitimization for that will to power are produced within the state but also within civil society (see Joseph et al., 1998 and Salvatore, 2005). In the case of the United States and its relations with the societies of the global South and especially the Latin South, the processes of discursive legitimization have been particularly significant in supporting its power and hegemonic ambition. Specifically in this regard the aim of spreading or diffusing democracy, or a particular interpretation of democracy, has been and remains a crucial element in the process of justification of geopolitical power.[7]

The former national security advisor Zbigniew Brzezinski has discussed important aspects of the relation between imperial power and hegemony wherein democracy plays a key role. For Brzezinski (1997: 24), American supremacy can be seen in relation to its military prowess, its economic position as the locomotive of global growth, its leading role in cutting-edge areas of technological innovation and despite some crassness its unrivalled cultural appeal, but it is the combination of all four factors that makes America 'the only comprehensive global superpower'. In contrast to previous empires, the American global system emphasizes the technique of co-optation (as in the case of Germany, Japan and more recently Russia) and equally it relies heavily on the 'indirect exercise of influence on dependent foreign elites, while drawing much benefit from the appeal of its democratic principles and institutions' (Brzezinski, 1997: 25).

The appeal and impact of the democratic American political system has of course been accompanied by the growing attraction of what Brzezinski calls the American entrepreneurial economic model, which stresses global free trade and uninhibited competition. Hence, as the imitation of American ways gradually pervades the world, a more favourable setting for the exercise of an indirect and 'seemingly consensual American hegemony' is nurtured (Brzezinski, 1997: 27). However, it is also argued that America is too democratic at home to be autocratic abroad. The economic self-denial (i.e., defence spending) and human sacrifice (casualties among professional soldiers) which are required in the pursuit of power are seen as uncongenial to democratic instincts – 'democracy is inimical to imperial mobilization' (Brzezinski, 1997: 36). And yet, as Brzezinski subsequently has argued, it can be suggested that America today is both a globally hegemonic power and a democracy, and this poses the question of whether the outward projection of America's democracy is compatible with a 'quasi-imperial responsibility', since hegemonic power can defend or promote democracy if it is applied in a way which is sensitive to the rights of others, but it can also threaten democracy if there is a failure to distinguish between national security and the 'phantasms of self-induced social panic'(Brzezinski, 2004: 179. For a critical discussion of the last point, see, for example, Giroux, 2004).

Acutely present in the last passage is the question of democracy's 'inside' and 'outside'. Dominating power at home can lead to the erosion of the democratic ethos that helps to sustain the consensuality of hegemonic power just as the intensive deployment of what Nye (2002) has called 'hard power' can undermine the seductiveness of the democratic promise abroad. War and militarization, together with transgressions of international law, are inimical to the health of democratic politics in general, as well as being a source for the undermining of the American-made image of democracy for export. The suggestion that democracy might be for export gives us a link with the previously noted importance of capacities since US projects to diffuse its democratic way of life need some institutional supports.

In 1982, the Reagan administration announced that the United States would pursue a new programme to promote democracy around the world. It was called 'Project for Democracy' and it became institutionalized as the National Endowment for Democracy (NED) which has been funded by the US Congress. Congressional support for the NED has grown steadily during the last twenty years or so, so that in 2003, for example, both Senate and House resolutions commended the organization for its 'major contributions to the strengthening of democracy around the world'. Following 9/11, special funding has been provided for countries with 'substantial Muslim populations in the Middle East, Africa and Asia' and by 2003 core funding exceeded US$40 million for the first time, with an additional US$10 million being earmarked for specially mandated countries and regions

(Lowe, 2005). The efforts of the NED need, however, to be put next to the more important role played by USAID.

The United States Agency for International Development defines itself as the largest 'democracy donor', implementing US$1.2 billion of programmes in 2004. These programmes are developed in cooperation with the State Department, the National Security Council and US embassies. Echoing the National Security Strategy of 2002, USAID states that the United States is vigorously engaged in all corners of the globe, acting as a 'force for peace and prosperity' whilst adding that 'expanding the global community of democracies is a key objective of US foreign policy' (accessed 11/1/06, http://www.usaid.gov/our_work/ democracy_and_governance/). How then does USAID approach the workings of democratic politics in an actually existing 'corner of the globe' such as contemporary Bolivia? A recent USAID country strategic plan is revealing.

It is clearly stated that USAID's strategic approach is rooted in the US mission's goal of supporting and defending Bolivia's constitutional democracy as the 'best system for meeting legitimate citizen demands for justice, equity and accountability and for an opportunity to participate in shaping a sustainable future for the country' (USAID, 2005: 45). The report goes on to discuss 'conflict management and resolution' and notes that 'conflict is an inevitable and not necessarily always undesirable phenomenon in a diverse and complex society such as Bolivia's . . . and conflict can be an engine of positive change '. However, the report goes on, 'conflict all too often takes the form of aggressive and at times violent street confrontation between various groups and government authority . . . and . . . repeated Government capitulation to these extra-legal challenges legitimizes such methods . . . while undermining democracy by circumventing its official mediating institutions' (USAID, 2005: 45). Clearly one can see here a tension between the positive encouragement of institutionalized participation and the negative attitude towards a more populist perspective on participation linked to the role of social movements (for a critical discussion, see Lindsay, 2005). This dissonance raises a number of questions concerning democratic politics in the context of what Fukuyama (2006) has recently called the US' 'benevolent hegemony' in spreading democracy globally.[8]

Democratic politics in global times

Let us begin this final section of the paper by identifying and briefly discussing some important features of the diverse ambits of democracy.

First, democracy, as long as it is to remain vibrant, requires a process of democratization in the sense of the renewal of the forms of participation and the development of autonomy, as reflected in the will and capacity of citizens to be self-reflexive and critical of governmental authority. One can suggest that with the spread of democratic principles to the institutions of civil society, as well as the economy, that what Bobbio (1987) called the democratization of society can come to have equal weight to the democratization of the institutions of the state. These two potentially intertwined processes can be viewed as mutually sustaining, but at the same time such a 'double democratization' should not be seen in isolation from the existence of phenomena that limit democratization. Trends such as the accentuation of socio-economic inequalities, the denial of human rights, the growing shadow of state surveillance, the burgeoning global power of corporate capital, an increase in violence and a spreading sense of political apathy and cynicism towards existing democratic rule, all constitute sources for the corrosion of a democratic spirit.

Second, there is the issue of the contested meanings of democracy; the democratic is a classic example of a polysemic term being dependent on the different discourses that give the term its meaning. Concepts such as 'popular democracy', 'liberal democracy', 'radical democracy', 'social democracy', 'associational democracy', 'imperial democracy' and 'democratic totalitarianism' reflect the continuing attempt to ground a definition of democracy that will always remain contested. What needs to be underlined here is that it is a vision of 'liberal democracy' or 'market-led democracy' that has become hegemonic in an era of neoliberal globalization, so that what is in fact a specific form of democratic rule comes to be traditionally regarded as the only or most natural form for democracy to take.

Third, much of the current debate surrounding the need for democracy is characterized by an implicit belief in the desirability of an existing Western liberal democratic model of governance considered suitable for export and adoption in non-Western societies. Not infrequently, this goes together with an uncritical perspective on Western democracy itself. There tends to be a governing assumption that Western, or more specifically, US liberal democracy, has a universal validity acting as an already available democratic template that non-Western polities need to follow. Critiques of the Western universalism embedded in such visions tend to be overlooked, although such critical perspectives are to be found (see, for example, Dhaliwal, 1996; Doucet, 2005; Parekh, 1993; Rivera, 1990; Sheth, 1995).[9]

Fourth, there is another vision that emphasizes the radical indeterminacy of democratic politics and the openness of the political terrain on which democratic struggles take place (Lefort, 1988; Mouffe, 2000). Lefort (1988: 17), for instance, argued that *the* revolutionary feature of democracy was that the locus of power had become an '*empty place*' (emphasis added) since the exercise of power had become subject to the procedures of periodical redistributions. No one government or political force can permanently occupy that locus of power, hence the openness and indeterminacy of democratic politics in a new institutionalization of the social. Such a view can be linked to Laclau's (2001) suggestion that there is always an inherent ambiguity concerning the democratic process.[10]

Thus, for Laclau, on the one hand, democracy can be seen as the attempt to organize political space around the *universality* of the community with efforts to constitute a unity of *one* people. On the other hand, democracy has also been conceived of as an extension of a logic of equality to broader spheres of social relations – social and economic equality, racial equality, gender equality etc., so that here democracy involves respect for differences. The ambiguity of democracy can thus be formulated as requiring unity but only being thinkable through diversity (Laclau, 2001: 4).

But how do these varied points relate to the question of imperial democracy? In the context of global politics, the attempt to export and promote one vision of democracy as a unifying project across frontiers clashes with the logic of differences but in a way that is deeply rooted in nationalist discourses. In the formulations developed by Laclau, Lefort and Mouffe, there is an assumption that one is dealing with a territorially intact polity, that the conceptual terrain can be developed in accordance with a guiding assumption of territorial sovereignty. However, in the context of imperial powers, one needs to remember that the autonomy of other democratic experiments has been terminated by interventions organized by Washington (for example, Guatemala in 1954, Chile in 1973 and Nicaragua during the 1980s. See Slater, 2002). In this sense, the internal tension between the logic of unity and the logic of difference has been overshadowed by an imperial logic of incursion, followed by the imposition of a different set of political rules. In the example of the United States, it can be suggested that there is a logic of democracy for export and a logic of terminating intervention for other democratic processes that have offered a different political pathway. Furthermore, interventions which have led to the overthrow of dictatorial regimes, as in Iraq in 2003, ought not to lead us into forgetting the realities of Western support for military dictatorships in the global South throughout the twentieth century.[11] Nor, as Callinicos (2003: 24) reminds us, should we cast a blind eye to the fact that there are contemporary examples of support for non-democratic regimes, as shown in the case of the Bush administration's backing for the regime of Karimov in Uzbekistan, despite its numerous violations of human rights. Also the Pakistani regime of Musharraf, which receives US support, is scarcely to be considered a full-fledged democracy.

The imperative to 'democratize', just as the injunction to 'globalize', creates, as Dallmayr (2005) suggests, an asymmetry between those announcing the imperative and those subjected to it, between those who 'democratize' and those who are 'democratized'. Such an asymmetry has a long history, and Jeffersonian notions of both an 'empire of liberty' and an 'empire for liberty' represented an initial framing of the conflicting juxtaposition of emerging American imperial power – expressed for instance as the United States having a 'hemisphere to itself' – with a benevolent belief in America's mission to spread democracy and liberty to the rest of the world. This juxtaposition, which is also closely tied to the founding importance of the self-determination of peoples, is characterized by an inherent tension between strong anti-colonial sentiment and the projection of powers over peoples of the third world. Discourses of democracy are deployed in ways that are intended to transcend such dissonances and to justify the imperial relation, even though such a relation is frequently denied (for a critical review, see Cox, 2005).

What is also significant in this context is the idea that democracy – US style – is being called for, being invited by peoples yearning for freedom, so that more generally imperial power is being invited to spread its wings (Maier, 2005). Rather than democracy being imposed, it is suggested that the United States is responding to calls coming from other societies to be democratized so that through a kind of cellular multiplication a US model can become gradually introduced. The owners will be the peoples of other cultures who will find ways of adapting the US template to their own circumstances. As it is expressed in the National Security Strategy for 2006, 'it is the policy of the United States to seek and support democratic movements and institutions in every nation and culture' (White House, 2006: 1). What is on offer here is a kind of 'viral democracy' whereby the politics of guidance is merged into a politics of benign adaptation.[12] Nevertheless, at the same time, a specific form of democratic rule is being projected and alternative models that include a critique of US power and attempts to introduce connections with popular sovereignty and new forms of socialism are singled out for opprobrium, as is reflected in the commentary on Chávez: 'in Venezuela, a demagogue awash in oil money is undermining democracy and seeking to destabilize the region' (White House, 2006:15). This despite the fact that the Venezuelan leader has won more elections in the last seven years than any other Latin American leader.

In the post-9/11 period, the 'war on terror', with its attendant corrosion of civil liberties, denigration of human rights and overall insinuation of a politics of fear, has tended to undermine the effectiveness of a positive vision of the diffusion of American democracy. Both at home and abroad, market-based democracy as the universal model for the rest of the world has come to be associated more with a bellicose unilateralism than with a seductive system for political emulation and potential hegemony. Moreover, other democratic imaginations emanating from Latin America have been offering vibrant alternatives to the US model. Most notably, at the national level Hugo Chávez in Venezuela and Evo Morales in Bolivia have put on to the agenda critiques of US power in the Americas and are offering different visions of developing democratic polities more related to policies of redistribution, social justice, indigenous rights and national autonomy. Transnationally, the Hemispheric Social Alliance, which is a large coalition of civil society groups located throughout the Americas, has argued, for example, that the entire process of negotiating trade agreements should be democratized, just as the World Social Forums, originating in Porto Alegre, have similarly argued for a democratization of global organizations such as the WTO, World Bank and IMF (Doucet, 2005).[13]

Whilst imperial powers are being challenged, there is an amplification of democratic politics. In the context of US-Latin American relations, the mission to universalize a US model of democracy is being contested by a wide gamut of political forces and social movements. The promotion of democracy from above may be sustained by imperial sentiment at home, but it is actively called into question in a continent increasingly impatient with being framed as the passive recipient. For democracy to flourish, it has to be home grown and autonomously sustained, not exported as part of a legitimization of subordinating power.

When the imperial and the democratic are conjoined, a number of unresolvable contradictions emerge. As was noted above, the imperial relation entails processes of penetration, violation, imposition and ethnocentric universalism. Equally, such a relation requires legitimization to enhance its effectiveness, and in this context notions of promoting and sustaining a form of democratic politics assume their central relevance. Whilst imperial power requires a discourse of justification, the effectiveness of a democratic mantle is continually undermined by the subordinating practices of the actual deployment of such power. As a consequence, the interface between the imperial and the democratic is forever characterized by a dynamic series of tensions, which can only be resolved through a democratic geopolitics that challenges and transcends the imperial.

Notes

1. In this particular chapter, I shall concentrate on the meanings and debates surrounding the term 'imperialism'. Issues emerging out of the discussion of empire, especially connected to Hardt and Negri's (2000) book on the subject, will be taken up on another occasion.
2. For a relevant collection of essays on imperialism in the current era, see Panitch and Leys (2004).
3. The distinction between the imperial and the imperialist will be dealt with below.
4. As one example of the variegated responses to changing US–third world relations, the recently emerging cooperation between Evo Morales of Bolivia and Hugo Chávez of Venezuela, together with Fidel Castro's Cuba, a cooperation that includes a strongly critical position vis-à-vis US power, has provoked a wide range of responses from other Latin American governments and leaders. For example, the Brazilian President Luiz

Inácio Lula da Silva has recently commented that terms such as 'anti-imperialism' have lost their relevance – see *El País*, 25 de Mayo de 2006, p. 6, Madrid. Moreover, Alvaro Uribe of Colombia and Alejandro Toledo of Peru express clear pro-US views and distance themselves from the 'new left' leaders of Latin America.

5. For a useful overview of the use of torture from Algiers to Abu Ghraib, see, for example, Macmaster (2004).

6. This statement does not mean to imply that Western imperiality is the only form of imperiality, as the case of Japan demonstrates (see for example Buckley, 2000) but my focus in this analysis is on the West and specifically the United States.

7. For one supporter of the imperial mission, the United States needs to be able to 'impose democracy' in other parts of the world as a way of realizing its project of expanding power. See Ferguson (2005: 52).

8. One recent example of the role played by the US government in helping to create new institutions for the global spread and support for democracy concerns the UN Democracy Fund, which was established in June 2005 by the UN Secretary General Kofi Annan. President Bush provided the initiative for such a fund in 2004, declaring that 'because I believe the advance of liberty is the path to both a safer and better world, today I propose establishing a Democracy Fund within the United Nations'. For details see http://www.unfoundation.org/features/un_democracy_fund.asp (accessed on 27-April-2006).

9. In a similar vein, Amartya Sen has recently commented that it is illusory to assume that there is a strong, culturally specific relationship between the West and democracy. For Sen, democracy is 'government by discussion' and can be linked historically to 'traditions of public reasoning' which can be found in nearly all countries. Taken from a *Wall Street Journal* article from 27 March 2006 – see http://www.ccd21.org/news/sen_western_dem.htm.

10. It is important to signal the point here that in a recent publication, Laclau (2005: 166) indicates that in contrast to Lefort he would see the idea of an 'empty place' as a type of identity rather than a structural location.

11. As a specific example, the US School of the Americas, located at Fort Benning in Columbus, Georgia, has trained more than sixty thousand soldiers and police, mostly from Latin America, in counterinsurgency skills since it was founded in 1946. In a recent detailed investigation, Gill (2004) shows how the School's institutionalization of state-sponsored violence was a key pillar in the US' support for military rule in Latin America. So widely documented has been the participation of the School's graduates in torture, murder and political repression throughout Latin America that in 2001 the School officially changed its name to the Western Hemisphere Institute for Security Cooperation.

12. President Bush has expressed this idea quite clearly, noting that America's faith in freedom and democracy is now a seed upon the wind, taking root in many nations: 'our democratic faith is more than the creed of our country, it is the inborn hope of our humanity, an ideal we carry but do not own, a trust we bear and pass along' (quoted in Gardner, 2005: 25).

13. For a detailed discussion of the need for a democratic transformation of global institutions, see, for example, Patomaki and Teivainen (2004).

References

Achcar, G. (2004) 'U.S. imperial strategy in the Middle East', *Monthly Review*, 55, 23–36.

Ahmad, A. (2003) 'Imperialism of our time' in L. Panitch and C. Leys (eds), *Socialist Register 2004, The New Imperial Challenge*, London, Merlin Press, pp. 43–62.

Ali, T. (2003) 'Re-colonizing Iraq', *New Left Review*, 21, 5–19.

Arrighi, G. (2005) 'Hegemony unravelling', *New Left Review*, 32, 23–80.

Bobbio, N. (1987) *The Future of Democracy*, Cambridge, Polity Press.

Boggs, C. (2005) *Imperial Delusions*, Oxford, Rowman & Littlefield Publishers Inc.

Boron, A. A. (2005) *Empire and Imperialism*, London and New York, Zed Books.

Brzezinski, Z. (1997) *The Grand Chessboard*, New York, Basic Books.

———. (2004) *The Choice*, New York, Basic Books.

Buckley, S. (2000) 'Japan and East Asia' in H. Schwartz and S. Ray (eds), *A Companion to Postcolonial Studies*, Oxford, Blackwell, pp. 319–32.

Callinicos, A. (2003) *The New Mandarins of American Power*, Cambridge, Polity.

Chomsky, N. (2003) 'Truths and myths about the invasion of Iraq' in L. Panitch and C. Leys (eds), *The Socialist Register 2004, The New Imperial Challenge,* London, Merlin Press, pp. 114–24.

Cox, M. (2005) 'Empire by denial: the strange case of the United States', *International Affairs*, 81, 15–30.

Dallmayr, F. (2005) 'Mobilising global democracy', openDemocracy, http://www.opendemocracy.net/democracy-opening/global_3000.jsp, accessed 7 November 2005.

Davis, M. (2001) *Late Victorian Holocausts*, London and New York, Verso.

Dhaliwal, A. (1996) 'Can the subaltern vote? Radical democracy, discourses of representation and rights and the question of race' in D. Trend (ed.), *Radical Democracy*, London, Routledge, pp. 42–61.

Doucet, M. G. (2005) 'Territoriality and the democratic paradox: the Hemispheric Social Alliance and its Alternatives for the Americas', *Contemporary Political Theory*, 4, 275–95.

Escobar, A. (2004) 'Beyond the third world: imperial globality, global coloniality and anti-globalisation social movements', *Third World Quarterly*, 25, 207–30.

EZLN (2005) *Sixth Declaration of the Selva Lacandona*, http://www.ezln.org/documentos/2005/sexta1.en.htm, accessed 2 November 2005.

Ferguson, N. (2005) *Colossus*, London, Penguin Books.

Fukuyama, F. (2006) 'Neoconservatism has evolved into something I can no longer support', *The Guardian*, Feb. 22, 27.

Gardner, L. C. (2005) 'Present at the culmination: an empire of righteousness?' in L. C. Gardner and M. B. Young (eds), *The New American Empire*, New York and London, New Press, pp. 3–31.

Gill, L. (2004) *The School of the Americas*, Durham and London, Duke University Press.

Gill, S. (2004) 'The contradictions of US supremacy' in L. Panitch and C. Leys (eds), *The Socialist Register 2005, The Empire Reloaded,* London, Merlin Press, pp. 23–45.

Giroux, H. A. (2004) 'War on Terror – the militarising of public space and culture in the United States', *Third Text*, 18, 211–21.

Gregory, D. (2004) *The Colonial Present*, Oxford, Blackwell.

Hardt, M. and Negri, T. (2000) *Empire*, Cambridge, MA and London, Harvard University Press.

Harvey, D. (2003a) *The New Imperialism*, Oxford, Oxford University Press.

———. (2003b) 'The "new" imperialism: accumulation by dispossession' in L. Panitch and C. Leys (eds), *The Socialist Register 2004, The New Imperial Challenge*, London, Merlin Press, pp. 63–87.

Johnson, C. (2004) *The Sorrows of Empire*, London and New York, Verso.

Joseph, G. M., Legrand, C. C. and Salvatore, R. D. (eds) (1998) *Close Encounters of Empire*, Durham, Duke University Press.

Kelly, J. D. (2003) 'US power, after 9/11 and before it: if not empire, then what?', *Public Culture*, 15, 347–69.

Klare, M. T. (2002) *Resource Wars*, New York, Henry Holt & Co: Owl Books.

Laclau, E. (2001) 'Democracy and the question of power', *Constellations*, 8, 3–14.

——. (2005) *On Populist Reason*, London and New York, Verso.

Lefort, C. (1988) *Democracy and Political Theory*, Cambridge, Polity Press.

Lemaire, S. (2006) 'Debate sobre la historia colonial', *Le Monde Diplomatique*, edición española, año X no 123, enero, p. 32.

Lindsay, R. (2005) 'Exporting gas and importing democracy in Bolivia', *NACLA Report on the Americas*, 39, 5-11.

Lowe, D. (2005) 'Idea to reality: NED at 20', *National Endowment for Democracy*, Washington, DC, http://www.ned.org/about/nedhistory.html, accessed 18 February 2006.

Luxemburg, R. (1968) *The Accumulation of Capital*, New York, Monthly Review Press, first published in 1913.

Macmaster, N. (2004) 'Torture: from Algiers to Abu Ghraib', *Race and Class*, 46, 1–21.

Maier, C. S. (2005) 'Introduction: an American empire?: the problems of frontiers and peace in twenty-first-century politics' in L. C. Gardner and M. B. Young (eds), *The New American Empire*, New York and London, New Press, pp. xi–xix.

Mbembe, A. (2001) *On the Postcolony*, Berkeley, University of California Press.

Milne, S. (2005) 'Britain: imperial nostalgia', *Le Monde Diplomatique*, May, http://www.globalpolicy.org/empire/history/2005/05ukrom.htm, accessed 2 February 2006.

Mouffe, C. (2000) *The Democratic Paradox*, London and New York, Verso.

Nye, J. S. (2002) *The Paradox of American Power*, Oxford and New York, Oxford University Press.

Orozco, J. L. (2005) 'Para pensar la república pragmática' in J. L. Orozco and C. Pérez Espinoza (eds), *El Pensamiento Político y Geopolítico Norteamericano*, México, Fontamara, pp. 15–58.

Panitch, L. (2000) 'The new imperial state', *New Left Review*, 2, 5–20.

Panitch, L. and Leys, C. (2004) 'Preface' in L. Panitch and C. Leys (eds), *The Socialist Register 2005, The Empire Reloaded*, London, Merlin Press, pp. vii–ix.

Pantojas-García, E. (2005) 'The Puerto Rican paradox: colonialism revisited', *Latin American Research Review*, 40, 163–76.

Parekh, B. (1993) 'The cultural particularity of liberal democracy' in D. Held (ed.), *Prospects for Democracy*, Cambridge, Polity Press, pp. 156–75.

Patomaki, H. and Teivainen, T. (2004) *A Possible World – Democratic Transformation of Global Institutions*, London and New York, Zed Books.

Petras, J. (2005) 'The meaning of war: a heterodox perspective', *Journal of Contemporary Asia*, 35, 423–46.

Pratt, J. W. (1927) 'The origin of "Manifest Destiny"', *American Historical Review*, 32, 795–98.

Rajagopal, A. (2004) 'America and its others', *Interventions*, 6, 317–29.

Ramadani, S. (2006) 'Iraqi voices are drowned out in a blizzard of occupiers' spin', *The Guardian*, Wednesday, February 8, p. 32.

Retort (2005) Boal, I., Clark, T. J., Matthews, J. and Watts, M. *Afflicted Powers*, London and New York, Verso.

Rivera Cusicanqui, S. (1990) 'Liberal democracy and *Ayllu* democracy in Bolivia: the case of northern Potosí', *Journal of Development Studies*, 26, 97–121.

Roy, A. (2004) *The Ordinary Person's Guide to Empire*, London, Flamingo.

Said, E. W. (1993) *Culture and Imperialism*, London, Chatto and Windus.

Salvatore, R. (ed.) (2005) *Culturas Imperiales*, Rosario, Argentina, Beatriz Viterbo Editora.

Santos, de Souza B. (2001) '*Nuestra América:* reinventing a subaltern paradigm of recognition and redistribution', *Theory, Culture and Society*, 18, 185–217.

Sheth, J. P. (1995) 'Democracy and globalization in India: post-cold war discourse', *Annals of the American Political Science Association*, 540, 24–39.

Slater, D. (2002) 'Other domains of democratic theory: space, power and the politics of democratization', *Environment and Planning D: Society and Space*, 20, 255–76.

——. (2004a) *Geopolitics and the Post-Colonial*, Oxford, Blackwell.

———. (2004b) 'The gravity of imperial politics: some thoughts on power and representation', *The Arab World Geographer*, 7, 91–102.

Soper, K. (2006) 'The awfulness of the actual: counter-consumerism in a new age of war', *Radical Philosophy*, 135, 2–7.

USAID (2005) *USAID/Bolivia Country Strategic Plan 2005–2009*, http://pdf.dec.org/pdf_docs/ PDACD586.pdf, accessed 2 February 2006.

White House (2002) *The National Security Strategy of the United States of America*, September, Washington, DC.

White House (2006) *The National Security Strategy of the United States of America*, March, Washington, DC.

CHAPTER 5

Globalization, Cultures of Land, Home and Natural Hazard

The Case of Montserrat in the Caribbean

Tracey Skelton

Introduction

In the insecure world of the twenty-first century, the complexities and interconnections of global process and events that impact at the global level are under intense scrutiny. The anxieties about the impacts of natural hazards on the international market, global investors and insurance companies are often talked about in the same newspaper articles as the loss of life, the loss of property and the negative impact on the countries in which they take place (Blaikie et al., 1994; Bankoff et al., 2004; Pelling, 2003; Skelton, 2006). What happens to people, their socio-cultural lives and economic livelihoods are considered but seem to have little staying power as the international media move on, satellite-like, to other stories, other events.

Natural hazards and their aftermath often have a deleterious effect on the development trajectory of the places in which they take place. After the initial rush of aid and goodwill with the NGOs falling over themselves to be seen spending donated money, the long-term project of rebuilding cultures, communities and livelihoods is often left to the people themselves, with the state and the larger NGOs participating if there is the political will and the resources.

The cultural security of people is often a sound bedrock on which to build redevelopment; however culture is sometimes the forgotten piece in debates about development and the role of globalization. Nevertheless, culture, globalization and development intersect in a number of complex ways (Skelton, 1996a, 2003). There have been several texts (and key debates within development policy and practice) which have explored the interconnections between culture and development and strengthened the argument for a cultural perspective within all aspects of development processes (Connell, 2007; Radcliffe et al., 2005; Schech and Haggis, 2000, 2002; Skelton and Allen, 1998; Tucker, 1997). Such debates also connect with the concept of 'globalization from below.'

For the first edition of this book, I submitted a chapter entitled 'Globalization, culture and land: the case of the Caribbean' (Skelton, 1996a). There I used established concepts around the subject of globalization and interrogated them through the consideration of land, cultures of land and people's relationships with, and sentiments about, land. In the second edition (Skelton, 2003), my chapter was called 'Globalizing forces and natural disaster[1]: What can be the future for the small Caribbean island of Montserrat?' Both chapters, and this one, are attempts to tell a story from the margin, to develop a non-Western focus and provide lived and genuine examples of people's interrelationships with their land and their home place. The first chapter, which was the starting point of the following two, showed how such relationships placed local people in conflict with global forces, or certainly with forces more powerful than themselves. It was about the micro-scale of everyday lives on small islands in the Caribbean and illustrated the ways in which local and global discourses can be scales (and cultures) apart in the ways in which they conceptualize a 'commodity' such as land and understand the local meanings of home.

In the global framework, whether that be political or economic, discussed by world leaders or transnational corporations, land is a commodity for ownership, exchange and power. For many people resident on the small Caribbean islands, hence for many within the local framework, land has stronger cultural meanings and connects with notions of memory, ancestry, belonging and future continuity (Besson, 1987; Skelton, 1996b). This is not to deny that at the local scale and in the face of a range of global pressures land will become a commodity for exchange and economic wealth creation. However, as I demonstrate below, such a transformation in the conceptualization of land is very much a contested one at the micro social-spatial scale.

My central geographical focus in previous work on this subject (Skelton, 1996a, b), and for this collection, remains the Caribbean and specifically the island of Montserrat. This is the site of my empirical qualitative research that provides ethnographic perspectives of the island and Montserratians. Montserrat is one of six British Overseas Territories in the Caribbean. They were previously designated as British Dependent Territories Overseas, but since the enactment of the British Overseas Territories Act 2002 their name has been constitutionally changed. This act also reinstated British citizenship to the residents in the territories, something that was removed in the 1981 British Nationality Act. The island is administered, to all intents and purposes, by an elected government, headed by a chief minister. However, all foreign policy issues are dealt with by the British government, but usually in consultation with the Montserratian government. A governor is resident on the island as the Queen' and Her Majesty's Government's representative and is employed by the civil service.

Prior to the volcanic crisis, Montserrat was experiencing steady economic growth (GDP in 1994 was $132.13 million EC, about £33million) and had not received budgetary aid since 1981. It received just under £1 million annually in development aid from the British government and there were negotiations underway to reduce this in 1996. In 1995 the island was in budgetary surplus, despite the extensive damage caused by Hurricane Hugo in 1989, one of the strongest hurricanes to hit the region in twenty years. Unemployment rates were low; there was free education provided from five to sixteen, with most Montserratian children aged three and four in state nurseries. The majority of Montserratians owned their own homes and everyone had access to high-quality health care. Hence the island could be defined as a development success and certain sectors and individuals were benefiting from aspects of globalization. For example, offshore banks were, and remain, an important source of revenue and employment for the island.

In this chapter I bring my two earlier discussions about Montserrat, the complex relationships with land, and the on-going presence of a natural hazard up to date. I illustrate some of the micro-complexities of small-island living and the extreme vulnerability that inhabitants of small islands can face, while at the same time hanging on to memories and attachments to their 'small places'. I argue that this cultural attachment to land and place is all too often ignored by 'outsiders' who are invariably the authors of development polices, programmes and projects, which are constructed within a globalized framework and which provide little space for local cultural meanings. I demonstrate the ways in which, through the natural hazard of a continuing major volcanic eruption, ordinary Montserratians have been thrown into complex political and economic power relations at an international level through the continued colonial relationship with the British government. First, though, an update on the situation in Montserrat since my chapter in the second edition.

Montserrat's volcanic crisis: 1995 – present

Part of the discussions about globalization revolve around the ways in which things have speeded up, that there is a time-space compression, that things change faster and faster. With such increases in speed come uncertainty, insecurity and a sense that nothing stays the same. For the island of Montserrat and for Montserratians, both those on the island and those who constitute the wider diaspora (Philpott, 1973; Skelton, 2000), as well as the rest of the Caribbean (Ahmed, 2004; Byron, 2004; Hall and Benn, 2000; Payne and Sutton, 2001; Sheller, 2003; Skelton, 2004b; Watson, 2000), there have been dramatic changes and forced insecurity that no one could have imagined. Montserratians now reside with uncertainty as a way of life; it is part of a newly emerging culture as people continue to live with events of extreme unpredictability related not to globalization per se but rather to the natural environment. Nevertheless the vulnerability they experience, as a result of the natural hazard, is to some degree compounded by wider international and global processes. Montserrat is not alone in this as Possekel (1999: 3) points out: 'development achievements of the SIDS (small island developing states) in the Caribbean are constantly crushed by natural disasters'.

In 1995 the tiny island of Montserrat, just 39 square miles, experienced the start of a major volcanic crisis which constitutes the most serious event of this kind in the Caribbean since the 1920s. The initial eruptions began in July 1995 and the Soufrière Volcano remains highly unstable and active to this very day[2]. Two-thirds of the island are now inaccessible and covered in several layers of super-heated rock and magma formations. There are legal restrictions on movement into large sections of the island.

From late in 1995 onwards, Montserratians residing in the east, south and central parts of the island (the most populous sectors) and the capital town of Plymouth experienced a series of evacuations to makeshift shelters in the north of the island. Most people were spending their nights and days in schools and churches, coping with very difficult, cramped and often humiliating living conditions. By the end of 1996, the evacuations were permanent as more and more of the southern and eastern part of the island was destroyed by pyroclastic flows. Montserratians were 'sheltered' in groups of 20 to 22 in container-style metal boxes with windows and doors that let in little light and almost no air or breeze. Given Montserrat lies in the tropics, the temperature inside these 'shelters' was often unbearable as they became super-heated in the sun. The signs on the doors had the Overseas Development Agency[3] logo with the words 'A gift from the British people'. When I saw this as a researcher on the island, I felt both ashamed and angry[4]. As a British citizen I was being represented as part of a nation that provided metal containers as homes for people who had lost everything. As one of the richest nations in the world, was this all we could do? After 1997, things improved significantly as the Department for International Development (DfID) provided more funds and began, albeit far too slowly, a house-building process.

The first purpose-built evacuation housing (fifty properties in Davy Hill) were handed over to rent-paying tenants in November 1997, two years and four months since the crisis began. Other houses have been made available to people from 1998 onwards (see the discussion of Look Out village below). DfID has funded a range of infrastructure developments such as the conversion of a school into a general hospital, the building of clinics, a new police headquarters, prison, fire station, port facility, air strip, roads and government headquarters. Total ODA and then DfID disbursements to Montserrat from 1995 to the end of 2004, added up to £206, 430 (DfID, 2005) and were estimated at about £230 million in 2006 (Ian Young, Technical Co-operation Officer, TCO, personal communication, 2006).

In total, 74 per cent of Montserratian households have had to relocate (Montserrat Social Survey, 1997) and about 7,000 people have migrated off the island to neighbouring Caribbean islands, especially to Antigua, to the UK and in smaller numbers to Canada and the USA. In the latter two cases, to join relatives and communities established through previous waves of economic migrations (Philpott, 1973). Those relocating to the UK, Antigua and other British Territories in the region were assisted post-August 1997 by British government-funded transportation costs, settlement grants and in the case of arrival in the UK, a guarantee of some form of local authority housing. Some islanders returned home from the UK from 1999 onwards, many helped by the Assisted Return Passage Scheme, which began in May 1999 (Clay et al., 1999). A population which had reportedly dropped from just under 11,000 prior to July 1995, to 2, 850 in March 1998 was estimated to be about 4,500 in August 1999 and has stabilised around this figure (Clay et al., 1999: 8, DfID, 2005: 4). Nevertheless, economically and structurally the island is still 'heavily reliant upon DfID for the bulk of required investment across all sectors' (DfID, 2000). However, the contemporary emphasis is on 'reducing dependence' (DfID, 2005: 4).

The development process for Montserrat began in earnest in post-May 1997 when substantial funds were forthcoming from the newly elected Labour government. This government made international development a key priority in its policies and transformations of government ministerial structures. The international development budget was substantially increased as one of the immediate changes and Montserrat was a direct beneficiary of this shift in approach. However, the development processes taking place on the island are a product of complex negotiations between DfID and the government of Montserrat (GOM). The latter has been through some turbulent times, having, at one point, three chief ministers in as many years. While the constitution allows the governor to take control at times of crisis, on the whole there are protracted and difficult negotiations with DfID. What GOM and DfID want for the island and what they plan for the future is not always the same thing and while they argue and discuss, ordinary Montserratians wait. The GOM takes its election as evidence that the people support it and its policies; there is not a tradition of participatory consultation in Montserrat. DfID works through the GOM rather than directly with the people or any NGOs as it often does in other development contexts. Hence a local and an international political institution battle out their policies over the heads of ordinary Montserratians who are therefore rendered dependent and passive, not perceived as agents of their own destiny. When things go wrong, and many have since 1995, it is hard to find out who to blame – the local government or the development agency of the colonial power, individual politicians or the development workers flown in club class and housed in expatriate luxury homes with a swimming pool?[5]

Montserratians have few ways to express their opinions, to find a voice and be heard, in this complex power relationship, except for using the radio station, Radio Montserrat. This is the source of all the information from the Montserrat Volcanic Observatory (MVO) and so people have it within earshot all the time. Telephone debates are lively, angry and humorous. Montserratians demonstrate regularly that they are acutely aware of the complexities of the development process and also that they have clear ideas about the ways forward they want for their own development. If only DfID and GOM would create the space for listening, then a future development for Montserrat might be possible. It would certainly be one that involved and respected local people and their culture rather than a structure imposed from above. The lack of awareness of cultural practices that remain fundamentally important for Montserratians is illustrated below, where I return to my central theme of 'cultures of land'.

The deepening complexities of land and home

In June 1997 there was a major turning point in the relationship between Montserratian people, the government of Montserrat and the British government. It relates directly to the ways in which local people were being treated, the apparent disregard for cultural patterns, ways of life and people's attachment to their land and homes.

Many people from the eastern villages of the island had long earned or supplemented their incomes from farming and livestock rearing. For some, their daily lives were spent out on their land, tending crops and animals; others carried out gardening as a dietary and livelihood supplement. Many of these people adapted poorly to the claustrophobic and cramped conditions in the shelters and so they walked across many miles of thick bush to get back to their land in the east, several residing in what remained of their own homes. This was in direct contravention of GOM rules relating to entry into the evacuated zones. On 25 June 1997, an intense and sudden pyroclastic flow down Mosquito Ghaut caught many people in the eastern area unawares and nineteen people burned to death, several others were airlifted out of the area, many suffering from severe burns. These were the first, and until now, only casualties as a direct result of the volcanic crisis. An inquest into the deaths, published in early 1999, and reported by the BBC stated that:

> The authorities on the UK territory should have offered nine farmers new homes away from the volcano. Those who died were among a number who stayed around it, fearing they would have nowhere else to go.... In a report endorsed by the inquest jury, the island's coroner Rhys Burriss called the UK's response to the crisis 'unimaginative, grudging and tardy'. Warning that his conclusions 'do not make comfortable reading for the British Government', Mr Buriss said land should have been bought

on a safe section of the island to house farmers from the volcano area. But a joint statement from the UK's Department for International Development (DfID) and the Foreign Office said this was not possible. It said the farmers were told to leave the exclusion area a month before the eruption, and that government-owned land in the north of the island had been unsuitable for farming while private owners had been unwilling to lease land. (http://news.bbc.co.uk/1/hi/uk/253237.stm)

In this BBC report, and within the inquest report itself, land is identified as a clear factor in the so-called management of the volcanic crisis. Farmers wanted to be provided with land in order to continue to work and to sustain themselves and their households; others felt so strongly about their land that a kind of homesickness took them back even though they had been warned of the dangers. However, the GOM owned very little land in the north, although the British government still owned small plots of Crown Land dating back to the times of colonial plantocracy. It was these small plots of land that were used to site the shelters in different parts of the north, and one section of Crown Land was used for the first emergency housing development at Davy Hill. The joint response from DfID and the Foreign Office states that 'private owners have been unwilling to lease land' (personal communication from HMG Governor for Montserrat, 1998) in this case to farmers, but private owners have also been unwilling to sell land for development in the north.

It is important to look at this statement in more detail. On a research visit to Montserrat in 1998, I interviewed the governor of the island at the time, Anthony Abbot. In our discussion he reported to me that he simply could not understand why families who had always lived in the north were not willing to sell their land, even in cases where all the family members were living off island having migrated some years previously. In his eyes the land was just sitting there doing nothing and not being utilized in any way. What the governor, members of DfID and the Foreign Office clearly lacked was any degree of understanding of the cultural construction of land in the Caribbean in general, and in Montserrat in particular. They saw the land as a commodity to be sold. However for Montserratians, the land is a link with a past of struggle against slavery and the desire to *own* something of their own in direct contrast to the historical legacy of once being owned *themselves*. The land that became the free peoples' land in the Caribbean was established as 'family land', 'children's property' or 'generation property' (Besson, 1984; Clarke, 1953; Philpott, 1973; Skelton, 1996b).

Montserratians still maintain that the small plots of land handed down through past generations have the potential to be a place for the future generations of their own families. Family land is a permanent resource that must be kept within the family ready for anyone who might need it in the future. The land is bound up with cultural meanings that far surpass its physical capacity. The land is a symbol of freedom and a type of security that can be handed down. The people of the north of Montserrat were as firmly connected to the family land they still retained as the people from the stricken parts of Montserrat were to the land that had been destroyed or was no longer accessible. At a time of great upheaval, both physically (literally) and socially, attachments to land, to the past through that land and to some kind of security through to the future, became ever more important for the people of the north. The significance of family land was suddenly more important for them than it would have been before July 1995. Just as farmers I interviewed in 1992 in the central and eastern parts of the island clearly stated that they would never sell their land (Skelton, 1996b), so too the people of the north who owned land stated the same thing through the late 1990s and continue to do so.

Interestingly, although this refusal to sell their land among northern Montserratians was painful for the evacuees who desperately wanted a piece of land of their own to farm or even to try and build their own house upon, they understood the position of the northerners. The culture of family land is so strong in the island that even at a time of acute crisis evacuated Montserratians could identify with the northerners' attachment. The 'outsiders' with their global and neoliberal economic discourses could not. From their perspective the land was needed, the prices offered were good and attractive to people facing an economic crisis through job losses, and so it should be sold. The market should triumph and the development process for the north could begin. Intellectually and culturally they could not understand the Caribbean construction of family land. The northern Montserratians and the governor, DfID and the Foreign Office faced an impasse that the mighty development policies of the external players have not been able to resolve. In fact, their lack of cultural understanding and the determination to see the lands of the north through their own 'western' lenses, lost precious time and added to an atmosphere of delay and uncertainty. There was no real alternative developed to an emergency package and subsequent redevelopment programme that was not based on land ownership.

However, partial solutions have been reached. Land has been compulsorily purchased from an estate owner who had put the land up for sale back in 1992. Current development is taking place on this land, but it is still subject to a court case as the owner, Dr Lee, is contesting the compulsory purchase by the British government. He argues that he was paid too little and refuses to sell any of the remainder of his large estate along the North Road on the north east of the island (personal communications from Dr Lee, HMG's governor and the governor's press officer in 1998).

There is a new village developing called Look Out, the traditional name of this barren area blasted by the Atlantic salt-soaked winds. It was initially the site of blue containers, which functioned as makeshift schools for the island's children. This has subsequently been developed into a primary school (which celebrated its fifth birthday in 2006), a nursery and play areas. Across the road is the island's only purpose-built, non-religious community centre and a range of sheltered and live-in homes for elderly and mentally challenged people. The first housing phase at Look Out comprised fifty two-bedroomed homes placed squarely within the land plot (based on US suburban style planning). Few Montserratian families could fit into two-bedroomed homes; very few of them matched the presumed nuclear family structure. The fact that less than 30 per cent of Montserratian households matched this 'type' seemed to have been overlooked and caused problems throughout the time of housing allocation. It is yet another cultural misconception that caused problems for effective and meaningful development.

The positioning of the houses allowed little to no room for extensions (a traditional building practice on the island as the living space grew to accommodate changes in household structure). There was also little space for the kitchen gardening which people of the south and east had practised through generations. There is a prohibition on the keeping of livestock in the estate, which is something most Montserratian households have done as a source of extra revenue. These first fifty homes were awarded on a 'grace and favour' system (Ian Young, DfID TCO, personal communication, 2006). They were awarded, in 1998, to key personnel on the island who had to be encouraged to stay if there was to be any hope of re-building the island (teachers, key civil servants, nurses, police officers, customs and excise officers etc.). The houses were initially provided on a rental basis and some people have been able to take mortgages out to continue the Montserratian tradition of house ownership, although previously property would have been inherited and owned outright.

Subsequent housing programmes on Look Out have been problematic. Force 10 houses brought in from Australia are raised on stilts and oriented to look out to sea (Montserratian vernacular structures would have verandas facing into the road to allow social engagement with neighbours and the goings on of the community). These imported homes are not standing up well to the tropical climate and Atlantic sea blast. They are in constant need of repair and are proving costly for the Montserratian government who remain as the landlord. The majority of residents feel that they will not withstand a hurricane. In contrast, the CARICOM (Caribbean Community and Common Market) village houses, following a Cuban design, have concrete roofs and residents argue that they are the best houses in the new village. They also have the capacity to accommodate extensions and provide back garden spaces for cultivation (all details about the housing are based on interviews with residents, interviews with the governor's press officer, 1998, 2003 and 2004, the governor, Deborah Barnes Jones, 2005 and 2006 and DfID TCO, Ian Young from 2003 to 2006). There are more houses being built at Look Out, phase 3, as there are many islanders still in rental accommodation belonging to private landlords or in 'shelter housing' that provides more privacy than the 'container-type' shelters but are still classed as temporary dwelling. The Roman Catholic Church is planning to build a church in the village and there are plans for commercial areas. However, Look Out remains a non-vernacular village with a street plan resembling something more akin to the USA[6] than Montserrat, and lacks basic services such as shops, churches, a clinic, recreational activities and so forth.

GOM set a series of deadlines for land titles to be formally registered and beyond these dates the land will be deemed government property. Nevertheless the shortage of land remains a serious problem for the development of the north (GOM, 2000: 67). It is also extremely difficult for southern and eastern Montserratians to gain access to their own land. The majority of the population in Montserrat owned their own land and their own homes; relocated households who remain on island have become renters of housing[7]. This has had a major impact on senses of security and self-esteem. It is another part of the enormous loss Montserratians have had to face and live with on a daily basis. Alice illustrates it sadly:

> Take my place [home], all my youth I have been working and I tried to put aside and eventually made a house to live in until . . . you see . . . *all* what you have done, *all* that you have put away, *all* that you have, you can't enjoy nothing, you can't even get inside to lay down on the bed. It's a lot to bear, it's not an easy world. Nobody in England could understand it only *who* has passed through it and those who put your foot in my shoe and see if it fits or doesn't fit. (Interview in Antigua, 1998)

The Caribbean cultural belief and practice of family land is an extremely strong construction. Previously, I stated that in the face of globalization a "retreat to the local', a 'deglobalizing reaction', a response to 'fractured modernity' for many who live in the Caribbean involves a cultural relationship with the land (Skelton, 1996a, 324; 2003, 72). In this chapter I suggest that the presence of an ongoing natural hazard combined with external powers and local elites who make development decisions, the significance of a relationship with the land and a sense of home become extremely powerful for both those who still have their land, their homes and communities and for those who have lost them. This complex relationship with their land, home villages and communities is a profound and fundamental one for Montserratians. It is part of their cultural heritage and contemporary lived experience, and as such it should be recognized formally at the government and international level and enshrined in development policies and programmes. It is an important part of Montserratian culture and hence it inevitably plays a significant role in development whether DfID and GOM choose to recognize it as such or not. Currently, there is evidence that GOM and DfID have learned something from their mistakes where new homes were concerned. Look Out phase 3 homes are designed to meet more of the criteria required by Montserratian household structures. The plans for the Little Bay development, the next substantial re-development project on the island, have been part of a consultation process for a good amount of time. Interested parties from the commercial and public sector, those involved in community development and sports development, fisher people, farmers and so forth have played a part in commenting on the various drafts for the development. Whether the final version of Little Bay will meet the needs of the community and people with small businesses will have to be seen. With talks of a marina, apartments and attractive commercial enterprises I do wonder whether the designers have the Caribbean in mind or Cardiff Bay. Perhaps Little Bay will be a globalized mish mash which does not attract the money-spending holiday elite it is designed for nor meet the needs of local people for a community space, local fresh produce market and leisure, cultural and sporting facilities which they can afford access to.

Montserrat in a regional, international and global context: changes in the power relationships

In this section of the chapter, I want to provide a brief insight into the complex political and economic power relationships Montserrat and Montserratians have been thrown into through a continued colonial relationship with the UK and within the Caribbean regional context[8]. I have already explored some of the complexities of the more 'local'/ 'national' level through my discussion of the relationship between DfID and the Montserratian government. Montserrat's volcanic hazard and the loss of significant numbers of its population has placed the island and its people on a regional, international and global stage where it now performs the role of victim and dependent whereas previously it had, despite its small size, been a more active, independent[9] and agentic player.

At the regional level Montserrat had a rather unique position as a member of the Organisation of Eastern Caribbean States (OECS) (Lewis, 2002; Skelton, 2000). It was a full member of the OECS whereas two other British Overseas Territories, Anguilla and British Virgin Islands, only had associate status. Hence, Montserrat was still a colony yet participating in an organization at the same level of neighbouring independent states, although it was not allowed to act independently of the UK in the context of 'foreign policy' decisions or actions. Nevertheless, it had considerable autonomy on the domestic front in relation to economic policies and also through negotiations about how to 'cope with globalisation' (Lestrade, 2002: 109, although see Lewis (2002) and Fergus (2004) for more detailed discussions of the island's complex relationship with OECS). Montserrat, prior to the volcanic eruption was, therefore, closely connected with a regional organization, which was working collectively, although not always in harmonious agreement, to try and tackle the challenges of globalization. There was a considerable degree of common experience among the small islands that constitute the OECS. There was also a sense that a collective of small voices might be more audible, especially within the larger regional grouping, the Caribbean Community and Common Market (CARICOM), which tended to ignore the small island states (Lestrade, 2002).

After the start, and with the continuation, of the volcanic eruption, Montserrat became a neighbour in need. OECS states and other members of CARICOM extended help to displaced Montserratians who moved to their islands. They provided work permits and education and health services for the Montserratians. In the case of Nevis, where a significant little community of Montserratians relocated, an offer of free land was made as long as DfID, as part of its development budget, funded the building materials so that Montserratians could build their own houses. This would have been an example of facilitated grassroots development. DfID refused, saying that any funding for housing was to be located on Montserrat and that if Montserratians wanted to have access to housing they would have to return to Montserrat. The Nevisian authorities, churches and community groups who had developed the 'land for building' idea were stung by DfID's response, arguing that they had already done a great deal to support Montserratians on the island and were contributing to a release of pressure on resources back in Montserrat. Montserratians too were bitter about this response from 'the mother country' and felt that they were perceived as being 'less Montserratian', because they had left the island, than those who had remained.

CARICOM, like the OECS, is trying to find strategies to resist marginalisation by global economic development. All of the countries of the Caribbean, with the exception of the French Caribbean which are politically and economically part of mainland France, and Cuba which has followed a distinctive path to a different type of development, are in extremely vulnerable positions *vis à vis* globalization. However, the Caribbean is playing this game against some very big and powerful players. As the Caribbean is forced, through changes in the Lomé convention between itself and the European Union, to try and diversify its economies, particularly its agricultural economy (Ahmed, 2004, Clegg, 2004), it faces trade restrictions, tariff barriers and direct competition from the USA. This is most obvious in the case of bananas, where peasant-style production in the Caribbean struggles against US transnational corporations in Central America (Byron, 2004; Payne and Sutton, 2001). Recent US representation against the European/Caribbean trade preferences at the World Trade Organization is an example of two huge global players (the USA and WTO) fighting and effectively crushing the small Caribbean islands underfoot. Nevertheless, CARICOM as a collective of island and mainland Caribbean nations and territories played an important role in the negotiations around the establishment of the Free Trade Area of the Americas, FTAA (Byron, 2004). The FTAA would lock the Caribbean economies firmly into (and out of) trade agreements within the Americas rather than across the Atlantic with former and continuing European colonial powers. Where Montserrat might fit into such a regional orientation is currently unclear. At the moment, it is hardly producing anything which might contribute to FTAA trading relationships. Certainly there is no mention of these external relationships in DfID's (2005) most recent Country Policy Plan for Montserrat.

Hence, the Caribbean faces an extremely difficult and uncertain future as it is forced to forge a new regional attachment and identity (Gill, 2001; Worrel, 2001). Being forced into a particular regionalization results in very different processes and differential positions of power within the regional space; it is different to that of an 'elective' regional formation. The emphasis on the Caribbean establishing a wider regional identity is pushed forward by the European Union and the USA; it is not a genuine bottom-up initiative. The European Union and the North American Free Trade Area were configured around some degree of choice (although this might be subject to debate from the perspective of Mexico in NAFTA) and elements of equity between the parties. Being forced into a regional grouping, especially one in which key players feel they have little natural affinity, may inevitably lead to conflict, suspicion, exclusion and resentment. Caribbean relations at the regional scale might be stretched too far and leave the smaller region at the mercy of the larger one.

Conclusions: what can be the future for the small Caribbean island of Montserrat?

An alternative development future

In the 2000 Country Policy Plan (CPP), DfID stated that an important part of the future planning between itself and the government of Montserrat (GOM) 'will be to intensify efforts to attract more interest from the wider donor community, civil-society organizations (which may need strengthening), the private sector, and importantly, regional organisations such as the Caribbean Community Secretariat (CARICOM)' (DfID, 2000). While Montserrat remains a British colony and remains living alongside a major natural hazard, it is very hard to envisage where private-sector support might originate. With CARICOM facing its own battles against iniquitous global economic forces (as discussed above), it seems highly unlikely that it might be in a position to help Montserrat more than it already has. DfID's statements in the 1990/2000 – 2001/2002 CPP seem to echo more the 'development policy position' of the British government than a true reflection of the potential future for Montserrat. As I stated above, if DfID and GOM would create the space for listening to Montserratians, then a future development for Montserrat might be possible. It would certainly be one that involved and respected local people and their culture rather than a structure imposed from above. It might not be the kind of economic development envisaged through neoliberal economic discourses and it might not link the island into many global economic processes. However, it may be an alternative development which allows Montserratians to remain on their island, rebuild what matters to them and move towards sustainable practices, however small-scale that might be.

The most recent DfID CPP (Country Policy Plan) for 2004/05 – 2006/07 (published in 2005) highlights unsustainable dependence as a key challenge but also names others which connect more with the lived reality of the island. Hence "The Challenge" in the CPP is listed as follows:

- Reducing the island's unsustainable dependence
- Coping with a 'persistently active' volcano
- Maintaining high standards of governance

- Handling regional issues
- Supporting a small but vulnerable population
- Maintaining Montserrat's unique natural environment
- Developing local capacity and skills

The latter three challenges (combined with the second point) are a direct recognition of the everyday situation within Montserrat. Finally too, there has been the recognition that Montserratians (and recent migrants from Guyana, Jamaica and Dominica who have residence status) have the capacity to work towards their own development. DfID finally seems to be recognising the possible future value of development from below and the effective support of local skills and abilities.

A future on the regional and global stage?

Where would the proposed possible futures in relation to the Americas region leave a place like Montserrat? It is not an independent state, through its constitutional status (and democratic choice) it remains a colony of Britain. It continues to look eastward across the Atlantic rather than westward towards the Americas. Yet the plight of small places in the game of large players on a global stage is highly problematic. Indeed, small island developing states (SIDS) are extremely vulnerable in a global context and in the Caribbean this has been particularly well articulated by William Demas (late President of the Caribbean Development Bank and Secretary General of the CARICOM Secretariat). St. Rose (2001) summarizes Demas's analysis of the particular problems faced by small states as follows:

- A very small country can achieve transformation only with a high ratio of foreign trade to GDP
- Only large economies with varied resources and very large populations can achieve fully self-sustaining growth
- Small countries, even if their economies have undergone transformation, are placed in serious degrees of dependence in that the momentum of growth is not fully determined by decisions of domestic producers, consumers and the local government. (St. Rose, 2001: 111)

Nevertheless, although Demas (1997) talked of the problems facing the small islands of the Caribbean region, he *also* provided a framework for possible future development strategies the Caribbean could adopt through its own regional organizations to both survive and avoid re-colonization. For Demas, integration within the Caribbean was the way to resist the vulnerability small islands face (see also Patsy Lewis's discussion of 'surviving small size', 2002). There was a future beyond survival through his analysis of development economics. However, for integration to bring more than a version of economic development for some of the participants, I would argue that there have to be structures of mutual respect for participants – a smaller place should not necessarily be dominated by a larger one. Also, within proposals for integration, and development policies to emerge from this 'unity', there has to be a place for culture and a recognition that cultural practices, values and traditions have important roles to play in effective development for people at the grassroots. Montserrat is a small island and when this status is combined with a major natural hazard, as often happens in SIDS, then what was once one of the most economically and socially developed islands in the Caribbean rapidly became a totally dependent economy with little autonomy and poor representation at a range of scales. It remains to be seen how Montserrat can challenge both globalizing forces and natural hazards in a way that provides some degree of sustainability and security for its people. The future path is more likely to lie within Montserrat and the Caribbean region than connected to larger global players who at the most fundamental level have already demonstrated they do not understand the cultural structures which constitute everyday Montserratian life.

Notes

1. Since the time of writing that chapter, I have conducted research into the way 'disasters' are represented in the media (Skelton, 2006). Through my engagement with the 'hazards' and 'disasters' literature (Blaikie et al., 1994; Bankoff et al., 2004), I have realised that I used the term 'disaster' incorrectly, as though it is interchangeable with the term 'hazard'. In reality they mean quite different things. Hazards, are part of the natural and human-made world (for example, volcanoes and chemical spills respectively); disasters are not natural. Disasters are what might happen as a result of a hazard, but they are really a result of the socio-economic and political contexts and responses that are put into action (or not) as a result of a hazard event.

2. At the time of writing (the week beginning 27 November 2006), the Montserrat Volcano Observatory weekly report indicates that visual observations suggest dome growth continues towards the northeast. The two cracks observed in the curved back of the eastward-facing shear lobe on the dome summit appear to have propagated downwards through the lobe, dividing it into three distinct blocks. Rockfalls and small pyroclastic flows have continued, predominantly affecting a sector from southeast to northeast. A small pyroclastic flow was observed in the upper part of Tuitt's Ghaut on the morning of 27 November. The two large boulders located on the crater rim above Tuitt's Ghaut (and visible from Salem) have now gone and there are fresh deposits on the uppermost parts of Farrells Plain. Minor rockfall and pyroclastic flow activity has also begun to affect the northern part of the dome at the contact between the back of shear lobe and the older material behind Tyres Ghaut. Nevertheless, along the northwestern margins the dome remains confined by the crater wall. The seismic network recorded 298 rock fall signals, 83 long-period rockfall signals, 101 long period earthquakes and 2 volcano-tectonic earthquakes. The continued rockfall activity would suggest that dome growth rate is similar to the past 2–3 weeks. The alert level remains at 3 (level 5 would indicate a dome collapse).

3. The ODA was the development sector of the conservative government and existed until May 1997 when the Labour government was elected and the Agency was upgraded to a full ministry, the Department for International Development, with a significantly increased budget and staff.

4. I began my research on Montserrat and with Montserratians in 1986 when I spent a year living in the east of the island conducting research for my PhD, 'Women, men and power: gender relations in Montserrat' (unpublished PhD, Newcastle upon Tyne

University). I conducted further research visits to the island in 1990, 1992, 1997 and 1998. The 1998 research trip was funded by a small grant from the HSBC/RGS. Research interviews were conducted with Montserratians on Montserrat and those who had migrated to Antigua and Nevis. From 2003 onwards, each year I have taken twenty undergraduate geography students from the Department of Geography at Loughborough University. The field trip is a mutually beneficial experience. The students have the opportunity to engage with and learn from a wide range of Montserratians and migrants to the island from other CARICOM countries. They learn about complex geographical and development processes in situ. The money the students and Loughborough University spend during the two-week trip contributes a not insignificant amount of revenue for many islanders. We are the largest group currently visiting the island, which is struggling to re-establish its tourism economy.

5. This very visible difference between DfID contractors and consultants who stayed in the rather grand vacated villas owned by American, Canadian and British expatriates when Montserratians were struggling with the degradations of shelter dwelling was the cause of considerable resentment from 1997 through 2000 when the number of DfID staff on the island was at its highest. This is based on my own research and comments made by islanders and DfID consultants themselves combined with participant observation while on the island in 1997 and 1998.

6. This alien street and housing design (evident in the new Davy Hill village too) may have something to do with the fact that the US construction company Brown and Root, a subsidiary company of Halliburton, were awarded the contract by DfID (Clay et al., 1999).

7. Renting has also become a harsh and very expensive reality for people who have relocated to other islands, especially Antigua. In the UK Montserratians unable to find employment and who are living on state benefits are in receipt of housing benefit. However, this degree of dependency carries with it feelings of shame for people who could previously proudly claim that they owned their own home.

8. I am not suggesting here that all the problems Montserrat faces at a regional and global scale are as a result of it remaining a British colony. In fact, there is considerable evidence that being a colony cushions the tiny islands of the Caribbean from some of the ravages of globalization which countries like Jamaica and Antigua battle against alone (Skelton, 2004a). Also, as I have demonstrated elsewhere (Skelton, 2000), most Montserratians through democratic choice wish to remain a colony. Nevertheless, the contradictions and complexities that are part of Montserrat's colonial status are important parts of the equation.

9. There is an ambiguous meaning about the term 'independent' in relation to Montserrat. In this particular instance, I am using it in the sense of the island being able to represent itself, voice its opinions and perspectives, and having the capacity to enter debates as an equal player to the other participants. However, constitutionally Montserrat is not an independent nation as it remains a British colony, but the British Overseas Territories Act 2002 has given full British citizenship to the residents of the newly named 'overseas territories'.

References

Ahmed, B. (2004) 'The impact of globalisation on the Caribbean sugar and banana industries' in S. Courtman (ed.), *Beyond the Blood, the Beach and the Banana*, Kingston, Jamaica, Ian Randle, pp. 256–74.

Bankoff, G., Frerks, G. and Hilhorst (eds) (2004) *Mapping Vulnerability: Disasters, Development and People*, London, Earthscan.

Besson, J. (1984) 'Family land and Caribbean society: toward ethnography of Afro-Caribbean Peasantries' in E. Thomas-Hope (ed.), *Perspectives on Caribbean Regional Identity*, Liverpool, Liverpool University Press, pp. 57–83.

——. (1987) 'A paradox in Caribbean attitudes to land' in J. Besson and J. Momsen (eds), *Land and Development in the Caribbean*, London, Macmillan, pp. 13–45.

Blaikie, P., Cannon, T., Davis, I. and Wisner, B. (1994) *At Risk: Natural Hazards, People's Vulnerability and Disasters*, London, Routledge.

Byron, J. (2004) 'The Caribbean in a globalised world: responses to a changing international political economy' in T. Skelton (ed.), *Introduction to the Pan-Caribbean,* London, Arnold, pp. 72–96.

Clarke, E. (1953) 'Land tenure and the family in four communities in Jamaica', *Social and Economic Studies,* 1, 81–118.

Clay, E., Barrow, C., Benson, C., Dempster, J., Kokelaar, P., Pillai, N. and Seaman, J. (1999) 'An evaluation of HMG's response to the Montserrat volcanic emergency', vol. 2, Evaluation Report EV635, Department for International Development.

Clegg, P. (2004) 'The transatlantic banana war and the marginalisation of Caribbean trading interests' in S. Courtman (ed.), *Beyond the Blood, the Beach and the Banana*, Kingston, Jamaica, Ian Randle, pp. 242–55.

Connell, J. (2007) 'Islands, idylls and the detours of development', *Singapore Journal of Tropical Geography*, 28, 2, 116–135.

Department for International Development (DfID) (2000) *Montserrat: Country Policy Plan 1999/2000 – 2001/2002.*

——. (2005) *Montserrat: Country Policy Plan 2004/05 – 2006/07.*

Demas, W. (1997) *Critical Issues in Caribbean Development: West Indian Development and the Deepening and Widening of the Caribbean Community*, Kingston, Jamaica, Ian Randle.

Fergus, H. (2004) *Montserrat: History of a Caribbean Colony*, Basingstoke, Macmillan.

Gill, H. (2001) 'Going south: CARICOM and Latin America' in K.O. Hall (ed.), *The Caribbean Community: Beyond Survival,* Kingston, Jamaica, Ian Randle, pp. 555–63.

Government of Montserrat (2000) *Approved Physical Development Plan for North Montserrat 2000-2009*, Montserrat, Physical Planning Unit, Ministry of Agriculture, Land, Housing and the Environment.

Hall, K. and Benn, D. (2000) *Contending with Destiny: The Caribbean in the 21ˢᵗ Century*, Kingston, Jamaica, Ian Randle.

Lestrade, S. (2002) 'Some challenges facing the OECS in the context of globalization', in R. Ramsaran (ed.), *Caribbean Survival and the Global Challenge,* Kingston, Jamaica, Ian Randle. pp. 106–21.

Lewis, P. (2002) *Surviving Small Size: Regional Integration in Caribbean Ministates*, Barbados, University of the West Indies Press.

Montserrat Social Survey (1997) Statistics Department, Ministry of Finance and Economic Development, Montserrat.

Payne, A. and Sutton, P. (2001) *Charting Caribbean Development,* London, Macmillan Caribbean.

Pelling, M. (ed.) (2003) *Natural Disasters and Development in a Globalising World*, London, Routledge.

Philpott, S. (1973) *West Indian Migration: The Montserrat Case,* London, Athlone Press.

Possekel, A. K. (1999) *Living with the Unexpected: Linking Disaster Recovery to Sustainable Development in Montserrat,* Berlin, Springer.

Radcliffe, S. A., Andolina, R. and Laurie, N. (2005) 'Development and culture: transnational identity making in Latin America', *Political Geography*, 24, 678–702.

Schech, S. and Haggis, J. (2000) *Culture and Development: A Critical Introduction*, Oxford, Blackwell.

———. (2002) *Development: A Cultural Studies Reader*, Oxford, Blackwell.

Sheller, M. (2003) *Consuming the Caribbean*, London, Routledge.

Skelton, T. (1996a) 'Globalization, culture and land: the case of the Caribbean' in E. Kofman and G. Youngs (eds), *Globalization: Theory and Practice*, London, Cassell, pp. 318–28.

———. (1996b) '"Cultures of land"' in the Caribbean: a contribution to the debate on development and culture', *The European Journal of Development Research*, 8, 71–92.

———. (2000) 'Political uncertainties and natural disasters: Montserratian identity and colonial status', *Interventions: Journal of Post-colonial Theory*, 2, 103–17.

———. (2003) 'Globalizing forces and natural disaster: what can be the future for the small Caribbean island of Montserrat?' in E. Kofman and G. Youngs (eds), *Globalization: Theory and Practice*, London, Continuum, pp. 65–78.

———. (2004a) 'Issues of development in the Pan-Caribbean: overcoming crises and rising to challenges?' in T. Skelton (ed.), *Introduction to the Pan-Caribbean*, London, Arnold, pp. 42–71.

———. (ed.) (2004b) *Introduction to the Pan-Caribbean*, London, Arnold.

———. (2006) *Representations of the 'Asian Tsunami' in the British Media*, Asian MetaCentre Research Paper Series, No. 21, available online at: http://www.populationasia.org/Publications/RP/AMCRP21.pdf.

Skelton, T. and Allen, T. (eds) (1998) *Culture and Global Change*, London, Routledge.

St. Rose, M. (2001) 'Extract from Caribbean sovereignty: an interpretation' in K. O. Hall (ed.), *The Caribbean Community: Beyond Survival*, Kingston, Jamaica, Ian Randle, pp. 108–19.

Tucker, V. (ed.) (1997) *Cultural Perspectives on Development*, London, Frank Cass.

Watson, H. (2000) 'Global neoliberalism, the third technological revolution and global 2000: a perspective on issues affecting the Caribbean on the eve of the 21st century' in K. Hall and D. Benn (**eds**) *Contending with Destiny: The Caribbean in the 21st Century*, Kingston, Jamaica, Ian Randle, pp. 382–446.

Worrell, D. (2001) 'Economic integration with unequal partners', in K. O. Hall (ed.), *The Caribbean Community: Beyond Survival*, Kingston, Jamaica, Ian Randle, pp. 427–74.

CHAPTER 6

Global Civil Society and Global Politics

Marc Williams

Introduction

Changes in political, security and economic structures in the past two decades have given rise to speculation concerning the current nature and future trajectory of world politics. Central to this debate has been speculation concerning the nature of agency and political behaviour in the contemporary world order. Traditional international relations scholarship has been challenged by perspectives that seek agency beyond the confines of the sovereign state. Students of global politics have challenged the dominant state-centric paradigm in the study of international relations. The conventional approach to international relations focuses upon states as the primary actors. To a considerable extent this intellectual attempt to homogenize the analytical approach to international relations represents poor history and, consequently, inadequate theorization. It is in the context of a debate on the contemporary meaning of statehood and sovereignty that specific attention has been given to the role of global civil society. Of course, non-state actors have not suddenly erupted onto the international scene. As many observers have noted, transnational non-governmental organizations (NGOs) have long played a role in global affairs (Boli and Thomas, 1999). For example, religious organizations were particularly instrumental in the first modern transnational policy campaign in the nineteenth century to rid the world of slavery (Florini, 2001: 9). Indeed, the anti-slavery movement was a harbinger of later ethically and morally committed NGOs who engaged politically beyond state borders. Recent research has focused on global civil society and global governance (Muetzelfedt and Smith, 2002; O'Brien et al., 2000; Taylor, 2005), NGOs and human rights (Bell and Carrens, 2004; Steele and Amourex, 2005), the international women's movement (Joachim, 2003; Sen, 2003), NGOs and environmental governance (Ford, 2003; Humphreys, 2004) and civic actors in the global economy (Poitras, 2003; Williams, 2005).

This attention to global civil society arises in the wider context of debates on globalization. 'Globalization' remains a contested term even though it entered academic, policy-making and popular lexicons more than a decade ago. This reflects the profoundly political and unsettling nature of contemporary change. Globalization is a multidimensional affair covering economic, political, social, technological, ecological and cultural dimensions of social life. Arguably the phenomenon is better described by the term 'globalizations' instead of 'globalization' (Shaw, 2006). It contains both material and ideational/normative dimensions, and refers not simply to changes in material structures and processes but also to ideological and ethical issues. Therefore, conceptually we can define globalization as a set of processes that transform the state of being of the world, rather than being the state of being itself. It does not follow that the trajectory of diverse dimensions of globalization need necessarily be the same. In other words, globalizing tendencies in one dimension does not necessarily lead to equivalent change in another dimension. Nevertheless, for many analysts global politics has undergone significant transformation as a result of globalization. Globalization alters the context of economic, social and political problems, generates new concerns about the development and implementation of global agreements and is fundamentally linked to the structure of global governance.

This chapter explores one aspect of current global politics, and the focus on globalization through an analysis of the impact of global civil-society in world politics. The aim is not to test the significance of civil-society actors (CSAs) in global politics through an empirical assessment of the role of various CSAs in influencing political events. Rather, the goal is to assess the process whereby social movements, NGOs, transnational advocacy networks (TANs) and other civil-society groups have attempted to secure participation in relevant issue-areas in international relations. As such, this chapter considers the manner in which transformations in world politics have created a political space for representatives of civil society to play an enhanced role in international relations.

It examines the extent to which globalization is fulfilling its promise of creating a global community of interest and influence. In the first section of the chapter, I briefly interrogate the concept of global civil society. The existence of, and key characteristics of, global civil society remains contested. The second part of the chapter focuses on situating the emergence of global civil society in an evolving global political and economic system. The third part of the chapter explores the manner in which globalization is transforming global political space and the implications of this development for the activities of CSAs.

Global civil society?

While the term 'global civil society' has become an inescapable part of the landscape of political science and public policy over the past two decades, no agreement exists on its meaning (Corry, 2006). Indeed, there are some analysts who dispute the existence of the concept. Thus any discussion of the relationship between civil society and global politics has to pay some attention to these definitional and conceptual issues. Dispute over the meaning and relevance of global civil society as a concept can be traced to two sources.

First, debates concerning the meaning of global civil society inevitably reflect and replicate some of the debates over the meaning of the older concept of civil society. Civil society is a concept with a heritage traceable to the ancient world, with claims made for its usage in Aristotle and Cicero (Thomas, 1998). However, many analysts agree that contemporary usage really begins with the Enlightenment (Cohen and Arato, 1992; Kocka, 2004; Kumar, 1993). In the post-Enlightenment period, civil society has been conceived in a number of different ways by political theorists, and contemporary usage is indebted to diverse political traditions. Three historical conceptions of civil society have resonance for current debates. Those indebted to the English liberal theorist John Locke tend to focus on the relationship between political society, the rule of law and civil society (Cohen and Arato, 1992: 87–88; Kumar, 1993: 376). From this perspective, emphasis is given to the voluntary nature of civil society. The writings of the German philosopher Hegel introduced a close relationship between civil society and the state. For Hegel, civil society was one of three primary social institutions, alongside the state and the family (Cohen and Arato, 1992: 91–102; Kumar, 1993; 378–79). Those writers who trace their usage of the concept to the writings of the Italian Marxist Antonio Gramsci tend to focus on relations of coercion and domination. For Gramsci, civil society was the sphere in which consensus replaced coercion in the maintenance of hegemony (Kumar, 1993: 382–83; Nielsen, 1995).

Second, another level of contestation arises over the application of civil society to the global sphere, with many analysts declaring that such a term is either profoundly ambiguous (Amoore and Langley, 2004) or a misnomer. It has been argued that the term 'civil society' cannot simply be transferred from the national to the global level. The addition of the term 'global', it is claimed, significantly modifies the meaning of civil society to produce a new concept. That is, global civil society is something more than and different from civil society (Thomas, 1998: 49). Thomas argues that it is not valid to talk of a global civil society without a state. In other words, while features of civil society may inform global civil society, global civil society is also not civil society. This line of argument is rejected by those who claim the existence of an historic global civil society. Thus the concept is not new in the contemporary era. What is new is its density and thickness (Lipschutz, 1992: 390; Keane, 2001: 23). This defence of the long gestation of civil society is challenged by analysts who argue that global civil society only arose in response to the pressures of globalization (Coleman and Wayland, 2006).

Some authors reject the term 'global civil society' not because of its historical connections with the state but rather because they believe that it is an empirically inaccurate term. They prefer the term 'transnational civil society' to that of 'global' civil society. For these writers, global linkages among advocacy groups and other civic actors occur on a transnational rather than a global basis. The reality of cross-border civic action is best understood as engagements that are limited geographically and practically. Political activity is not only limited to a few geographical regions, but engagement on issues rarely extends across more than a few borders (Piper and Uhlin, 2004: 5; Keck and Sikkink, 1998: 12). On the other hand, analysts who emphasize the normative potential of civil society as an effective sphere of activity in the context of the globalization of economic, social and political arrangements (Anheier et al., 2001: 16; Falk, 1997; Kaldor, 2003: 142) insist on the term 'global civil society' since global denotes a mode of thinking rather than an empirical reality of form of organization. In other words, the relative density of civil-society networks in certain regions and the paucity of civic activity across national borders in other parts of the world is not a sufficiently compelling argument for the replacement of 'global' with 'transnational'. The concept of global civil society reflects the growth of a global sphere of social and political participation, composed of various actors that transgress national boundaries to engage in dialogue and debate with other actors, and indicates the beginnings of a global consciousness, which transnational civil society fails to capture. Furthermore, the latter term continues to emphasize the primacy of the level of the nation, and in doing so fails to capture the nature of global civic actors like women's movements which seek to provide alternate modes of representation separate to the state.

Whether global is replaced by transnational (Florini, 2001; Olesen, 2005) or international (Colas, 2001), we tend to find that when it comes to empirical research, analysts are investigating similar organizations. Instead of searching for a single, dominant meaning of the term, I will begin from the observation that important political concepts carry a variety of meanings (Williams, 2005: 347). The essentially contested nature of the core concepts utilized in political science (Lukes, 1974) is a starting point for analysis. It is in this sense that this chapter explores the concept of global civil society

While there is no single definition of civil society (or global civil society), the concept does not exist in a neutral or content-free form. Civil society is discursively linked to certain features of contemporary political practice and theorizing. In other words, it is embedded in a set of relational terms and shared assumptions. Central to contemporary discussions of civil society are references to democratic practice, sovereignty and statehood, and market relations. In terms of democracy, civil society is often perceived as a voluntary sphere in which individuals or groups can pursue a common aim. In this sense, membership in civil society is positively linked to democracy since a society of voluntary association indicates one in which the rule of law and consent is the norm. The current dominant conceptualization of civil society is as a third sphere separate from the state and market. In this reading, official state activity is distinct from private, voluntary associations. Although the boundaries between official or state activity and non-official or civil society activity are not always easily separated, the non-state character of civil society is an important feature of contemporary uses of the term. Civil society in this sense refers to a voluntary political space that is not part of the formal state apparatus, and is frequently portrayed as being 'below the state' (Wapner, 1996: 158). Equally important to the third sphere model is the separation of civic associations, often referred to as non-profit organizations, and market-based actors whose existence is dominated by the search for profit.

While there is a tendency to reify these definitions, the empirical reality is often at variance with simple distinctions between private versus public, and a sphere wholly separate from the state and the market. For example, the private character of civic associations is not, however, always easy to sustain in the real world. Moreover, the boundaries between official or state activity and non-official or civil-society activity and between market and non-market actors may not always be easy to demarcate and maintain. Many NGOs, for example, maintain close associations with states, and civic associations compete to provide services in fields such as development assistance and humanitarian relief in ways that can be very similar to the activities of market-based participants.

The emergence of global civil society

The emergence of global civil society is the result of interrelated changes at the domestic and global levels. Renewed attention to civil society is linked to structural transformation and the agency of CSAs. The rise in civic activism and concomitant academic and political attention to global civil society is attendant on three changes in the global political economy: technological innovation, economic integration and political change; and three changes in national polities: increased attention to civil society, the changing role of the state and a new discourse on governance.

Global structural change

Advances in communication and information technology have had a significant impact politically as global civic actors are better able to enhance communication within their organizations and to disseminate information to individuals and organizations in other jurisdictions; they are able to organize across boundaries and mobilize political resources to meet their agendas. The Internet, fax and e-mail ensure rapidity of communication and facilitate the distribution of information at relatively modest cost. Previously, the financial resources necessary to distribute information on such a large scale were held by governments, private firms and the media. The Internet allows local issues global attention and enables new forms of lobbying (Lai, 2004: 105). Moreover, the Internet supplements broadcast media and provides multiple channels of communication controlled by multiple actors, subject (at the moment) to limited regulatory control from central government.

Furthermore, cheap air travel facilitates the physical transportation of social movement activists. This freer flow of information increases the resources which civil society has at its disposal to highlight issues and abuses, garner public and media support and lobby governments and international organizations. It can be argued that the ability of NGOs to mobilize public pressure and opposition to government policies further erodes the distinction between domestic and foreign policy. For example, human rights activists through activities facilitating the flow of information further develop transnational norms. Chinese students used modern communications technologies during the protests and after the massacre in Tiananmen Square in 1989 to inform human rights activists around the world (Turner, 1998: 30). The availability of information regarding undemocratic transitions – such as actions against minorities and freedom of speech – has the potential to create an international environment where the costs of undemocratic conduct are high, as the Chinese government discovered subsequent to its brutal suppression of student activists in 1989. Not only does the Internet provide a means of disseminating information about previous or existing abuses, it provides a channel for the reporting of abuses and activities as they occur. Real-time accounts of events may well increase the speed of action, reaction and mobilization.

The idea of different societies linked by technology has been one of the main drivers of the concept of a 'global' civil society. The communications 'revolution' of Internet, fax and e-mail has created what Devetak and Higgott (1999: 491) term a 'global public sphere' in which social movements, NGOs, advocacy networks and other civil society groups are able to voice their opposition, organize protests and mobilizations, publicize abuse and atrocities and share information outside the realm of international institutions and states. Of course, this does not mean an all-inclusive sphere that reaches across the globe. The majority of civil society networking is concentrated in developed countries, or between urban spaces in different parts of the world, and inequalities in access to communications technology must be taken into consideration (Sassen, 2002: 217).

Processes of economic globalization have disrupted existing patterns of distribution and redistribution resulting in changing patterns of inequality, relocated economic decision-making and contributed to global financial crises. Increased engagement with these processes of economic integration by national and trans-border civic groups has been an important feature of global politics in the past two decades. Many CSAs are animated by fear that economic globalization leads to a loss of economic sovereignty, and a consequent increase in the power of global corporations. The triumph of neo-liberal economic policies at national and international levels has led to a backlash most notably expressed in terms of the so-called anti-globalization movement. Protests against further trade liberalization under World Trade Organization (WTO) auspices, World Bank and International Monetary Fund (IMF) economic policies have been a recurring feature of civic engagement at the global level. Financial crises in Argentina, Asia, Mexico, Russia and the consequent increase in poverty levels has led to increased transnational mobilization of civic actors. The anti-globalization movement and its varied institutional forms represent a significant but not the sole organizational form of civic action in response to the forces of economic globalization. While some groups remain broadly oppositional, others engage on a more reformist or supportive basis.

Some writers emphasize the importance of political change as a consequence of the end of the Cold War. The end of the Cold War removed the last ideological and material barriers to the forming of linkages across international borders, and the end of the ideological conflict that dominated the Cold War years was seen as enabling non-state actors all over the world the space and freedom to dissent and demand a new order. This does not mean the 'end of history', the absence of ideological conflicts or the construction of a world in which ideas and people travel freely. John Keane (2001: 23) has argued that global civil society emerged following 'the implosion of the Soviet-type communist systems that implied a new global order'. And Peter Marden has linked the end of the Cold War with the decline of sovereignty. He argues that the end of the Cold War 'provided the impetus for the expansion of civil society on a global scale. The phenomenon is linked to the "leaking away of sovereignty" from the state' (Marden, 1997: 148)

Changes in domestic politics

The revival of the concept of civil society in Europe and Latin America during the 1980s challenged the primacy of the state, and was a significant development in the emergence of a global civil society. Civil society developed simultaneously, though separately, in Eastern Europe and Latin America as citizens in both regions recognized that the term 'civil society' proved a useful concept in opposing non-democratic regimes. The role of social movements in the overthrow of communism in Eastern Europe signalled a new dawn for many activists and authors (Cohen and Arato, 1992; Keane, 2003; Kaldor, 2003: 50–77). Kaldor (1999: 749) argues that the use of civil society in these contexts carried 'an entirely new resonance, as a political aspiration and technique and not just as an analytical tool'. She contends that a deliberate engagement with the concept of civil society led to the emergence of new social networks in direct opposition to the state. The activities of Eastern European dissidents and Latin American human rights groups not only challenged the primacy of the state, it also broke the inextricable link between civil society and the state that had delimited the concept since the writings of Hegel.

The linkages between peace and human rights generated by the civic discontent of the 1980s Cold War totalitarian societies transformed civil society from an analytical construct to the activist realm. Furthermore, this activist engagement with transnational issues such as peace and human rights ensured that the focus of civic activity moved inescapably beyond the confines of the nation-state. The linkages between unions, religious organizations and human rights organizations in the movements against communism offered a glimpse of the potential for the re-emergence of civil society on a transnational or global scale.

The decline in welfare provisions consequent on the rise of the neoliberal state led to increased civic activity. Global civil society has developed simultaneously with the rise of neoliberalism. The neoliberal project impinges on national societies in ways which affect international relations. In the industrialized world, the neoliberal agenda resulted in the erosion of welfare rights that populations had previously taken as a given. It has been claimed that the decline of the Keynesian state created the conditions for 'change from below' as citizens recognize the necessity of using non-state associations in order to achieve political goals (Lipschutz, 1992: 419). In the developing world, neoliberal policies rolled back state protection and exposed many people to degrees of economic vulnerability they had never envisaged as possible. Structural adjustment resulted in the shrinking of the state especially in terms of the delivery of welfare services. This resulted in the non-profit sector increasing its provision of basic needs such as education and health as a result of diminished state provision. In addition to this expanded service delivery, there was a concomitant increase in advocacy in response to alienation and demand. This situation did not change significantly when radical neoliberal policies were replaced by the post–Washington Consensus in the late 1990s, since this new policy framework accorded an important role to civil society organizations in the construction of development policies and the provision of development services (Edwards, 2001: 2).

Moreover, the state has not withered away and still remains the actor with the greatest capacity to influence the course of political, economic and social life. Scholte (2000: 185) argues that regulation is moving away from a focus on the state in a new process of multi-layered governance in which new centres of authority have become increasingly influential. He contends that contemporary governance 'includes important local, sub-state regional, supra-state regional and trans-world operations alongside and intertwined with national arrangements' (Scholte, 2002: 287). This process of multi-layered governance encourages the development of global civil society and shapes global collective identities. Sources of power and authority beyond the state take many forms, including financial institutions, regional organizations such as the European Union and multilateral economic institutions like the World Trade Organization (WTO) (O'Brien et al., 2000: 8).

Good governance has emerged as a main legitimizing device in contemporary politics. The security dilemma as it was conceived during the Cold War conflict tended to privilege anti-democratic forces. The end of the Cold War has seen a renewed emphasis on democracy in the advanced industrial countries and most regions in the developing world. The so-called 'third wave of democracy' which began in the 1970s accelerated after the end of the Cold War to encompass all developing regions. And within Western liberal democracies there was renewed focus on the benefits of democratic arrangements in this period. Social movement organizing has benefited from this new climate, and increased emphasis on the key features of representative democracy. Most commentators contend that CSAs possess a number of common characteristics. Central to these organizations is a strong desire to expand and democratise civil society through an increase in the participation of citizens in democratic processes. Contemporary theory suggests that social movements and NGOs enhance democratic politics through their existence and mode of behaviour. Existing as they do in opposition to the state, they revitalize civil society (Cohen and Arato, 1992). Furthermore, the discourse of good governance (Clark, 2001: 20) has focused citizen attention on the failures of governmental agencies in meeting public needs. Heightened awareness of the inadequacy of official agencies leads to a rise in citizen mobilization. The growth of domestic civic associational activity rarely remains focused solely on the national sphere, given increased interdependence between national societies.

Contesting global politics: challenging the traditional boundaries of the political

In this section, I explore how political space is changing and how civic actors can use that space to achieve their goals. As previously discussed, globalization is a multi-dimensional process in which technological, economic, cultural and political processes are important. The political does not flow directly from functional transformation, since far from being simply a technical issue, globalization is an inherently political process driven by the ideology, choices and intentions of states, private firms and 'wider publics' (Cerny, 1999: 149). It is through the challenge that globalization poses to traditional conceptions of sovereignty that we begin to see the promise of global civil society. The extent to which we perceive an expanded, or indeed any, role for civic actors in world politics will depend on our assessment of the impact of globalization on sovereignty and state structures. For some, globalization effectively signals the demise of the sovereign state while others maintain the continuing relevance of the state.

Globalization and the state

The state system remains the central organizing device in the international system but material and ideational change has resulted in diminished autonomy for all states (with the possible exception of the United Sates). States have become more constrained both by market forces and through the delegation of some governance functions to global organizations. The process of economic globalization has resulted in a shift from a world of discrete national economies exercising a large (although never total) control of their economies to one in which domestic economies are increasingly open to market forces and economic interdependence. These developments were the result of technological change, developments in capitalist accumulation and political decisions. The state has been a leading player in these processes through liberalization and deregulation policies implemented either voluntarily in the advanced industrial world or largely involuntarily through structural adjustment programs in the developing world. Economic restructuring has had a fundamental impact on the interests of the state. The character and interests of the state have changed, and it has been transformed into competition state or even a quasienterprise association (Cerny, 1997: 251).

States exist within a changing global market. The opening up of national economies to world markets, deregulation and the removal of many protectionist policies has meant that competition among firms is now increasingly global. Moreover, the removal of most capital controls has led to an unprecedented increase in the expansion and integration of financial markets around the world. The world financial market has become increasingly autonomous, separated from the real economy, but its influence over the global economy has increased dramatically. The emergence of a global financial market has had a tremendous impact on the interaction between states and markets. The effectiveness of macroeconomic policies has been significantly reduced as major economic variables are strongly influenced by external macroeconomic trends. These developments have also been accompanied by new mechanisms for inter-state co-operation. The recognition that self-interest must sometimes be advanced collectively coupled with the emergence of new problems associated with globalization has led to the emergence of new forms of global governance. There has been growing state participation in international organizations and increasingly states have delegated greater power to these bodies. This is evident in the enhanced competence of the WTO compared with its predecessor, the General Agreement on Tariffs and Trade. Thus, the state has a limited capacity to control economic processes within its borders, and to meet the demands of the majority of its citizens. States continue to control territory, population flows and the most covert means of coercion, but those assets are of limited utility when currencies fluctuate, capital takes flight or trade deficits produce unemployment.

These material changes have also been accompanied by developments in what can be termed the ideology of governance. The ideological structure of the global order is a key determinant of how globalization reconstitutes the state. The dominance of neoliberal ideas has proved crucial in promoting market solutions at the expense of governmental intervention. The dominance of the language of neoclassical economics and the conception of the minimal state has promoted the market as ideology. In what can be termed the economization of politics, governance is increasingly thought of and evaluated in terms of effectiveness and efficiency. Questions about justice, equity and the common good have faded into the background (Devetak and Higgott, 1999).

A new politics?

This brief review of the impact of globalization on the state suggests the limitations of current conceptions of politics exclusively focused on the nation-state. In practical terms, the state has abandoned or redrawn the boundaries of its traditional concerns. On a normative level, it suggests the necessity of constructing political activity on a non-territorial basis. This necessitates a changing conception of political space. It has been argued that the modern state system embodies a concept of politics and the political which restricts political activity (Walker, 1988). Within the traditional paradigm, a sharp distinction exists between politics within the state and international politics. Key political terms such as 'authority' and 'legitimacy' have been developed to reflect this divide. The legal system, bureaucratic apparatus and control of the means of violence are all based on the acceptance of national self-determination and sovereignty. Moreover, this internal/external divide is reproduced domestically with the division between public and private areas of interest. This distinction between a private sphere of individual preference and economic exchange and a public one in which the functions of government are exercised results in a narrow conception of politics. Reducing politics to the activities of states and state institutions limits the possibilities of social movement activity. As Walker (1988: 678) has argued, liberal discourse through privileging state sovereignty entrenches a particular, exclusive understanding of political possibility.

To what extent is the rise of global civil society and the activities of social movements, NGOs and other civic actors transforming this traditional conception of politics? Proponents of global civil society have tended to answer this question in the affirmative. They argue that CSAs have been responding to twin challenges: the practical and normative lacunae created by the impact of globalization on the state. This process is not complete and not all global civic action is progressive. Nevertheless, we can begin to document ways in which an emerging global civil society and the actions of social movements and NGOs present opportunities for redefining political action in the contemporary world order.

If as a consequence of globalization 'the notion of place is informed by an understanding of space, with this term being understood socially rather than territorially' (Waterman, 1994: 66), then the literature on the diverse activities of transnational CSAs documents political practice developed across national boundaries, outside of formal institutions and across multiple domains. The political praxis of such organizations is signified by discursive diversity rather than the singular conceptions of politics in modernity. Second, growing recognition of ecological interdependence, increased information about human rights and widening access to media and information technology is making more people organize for global issues. Domestic and locally focussed groups are extending their mandates to incorporate global goals. The nature of many of the issues around which global civic actors mobilize – such as refugees, environment and human rights – are inescapably local, regional and global. This citizen-based activity is a direct challenge to the political and economic organization of the global system. In traditional political discourse, groups sought to influence specific policies of states and firms. But it has been argued that new social movements seek 'general transformation of public consciousness' (Turner, 1998: 30) and develop political strategies not exclusively oriented to the state.

Third, proponents argue that global civil society has led to the reconstruction of political meanings and altered political consciousness in changed national and international environments. This construction of alliances based on non-territorial identities generates a new space for political participation. The process of globalization is thus constitutive of an emergent global order supportive of a transnational, cosmopolitan community and inimical to national forms of organization and solutions to contemporary problems. The political practice of global civic actors is symptomatic of new ways of thinking about politics. Furthermore, the process of transnational interactions fostered by civic associations provides a non-class-based focus on issues surrounding identity, creates new streams of identification and activism and operates increasingly outside the parameters of established political systems developing and enriching democratic politics. In Habermas's terms, they act as defensive mobilizations against political and economic forces seeking the 'colonization of the lifeworld' (Cohen and Arato, 1992: 471–74).

Whether these activities are capable of developing enduring forms of political representation is not yet evident. Nevertheless, evidence suggests that global civil society can play an important role in delegitimizing discourses (Lynch, 1998: 151–58).

On the other hand, a number of writers have challenged the positive potential of global civil society. Critics suggest two reasons why global civil society has not significantly transformed world politics. The first line of argument concerns the continuing relevance of state power. It is argued that CSAs are embedded in structures of governance in which states and organizations of states (international governmental organizations) effectively maintain control over decision-making. Insofar as global governance is based on liberal values of 'democracy, human rights, the rule of law and markets' (Barnett and Duvall, 2005: 5–6), these values determine access to various structures and institutions of governance, shape the strategies of CSAs and constrain the political outcomes. Whether it is the neoliberal logic of development enshrined in the new constitutionalism (Gill, 2002) or liberal rights ideology underpinning human rights claims (Hopgood, 2000; Robinson, 2003), global civil society represents less of a challenge to statism and a force for a new democratic politics. The implications of this argument are further developed by Chandhoke (2002: 50) who argues that existing structures of power privileges some CSAs and marginalizes others. That is, reform-minded CSAs which support rather than challenge existing forms of governance are given access to decision-making whereas those groups with a more radical or rejectionist agenda are rendered relatively powerless. In a similar vein, Lipschutz (2005: 768) suggests that CSAs are 'deeply enmeshed with forms and practices of governmentality' and thus are not capable of challenging structural inequalities in world politics. Furthermore, while from the perspective of a reformist agenda CSAs do have the potential to influence key global institutions, the degree to which increased transparency and greater participation in organizations like the World Bank and IMF has affected the economic policymaking of these institutions is limited (O'Brien et al., 2000: 216). The legitimacy of governance programs is dependent on the role of CSAs. In other words, CSAs play essential roles in maintaining the effectiveness and legitimacy of governance programmes (Amoore and Langley, 2004: 97) through disseminating information, implementing policies or acting in a consultative role.

A second critique focuses on the democratic credentials of CSAs (Baker, 2002) and asserts that these organizations are ill-equipped to make positive contributions to democratic politics. Three sets of arguments have been developed with respect to the democratic deficit of CSAs (Collingwood, 2006). First, it is claimed that these organizations are inherently unrepresentative and unaccountable. That is, although they claim to speak for the poor, marginalized and in the global interest, they are inherently illegitimate and undemocratic structures. Second, critics point to the diversity within global civil society and the unequal power relations between, for example, groups from the North and the South. Third, critics contend that CSAs are often inefficient and ill-equipped to meet the challenges they undertake. Collingwood (2006: 454) has argued that these criticisms are misplaced because they are rooted in an analogy with domestic sources of legitimacy and 'do not take account of novel or atypical ways in which transnational NGOs can achieve legitimacy comparable to that of states'.

Conclusion

This chapter has explored the implications of the rise of global civil society for global politics. It began with the recognition that contemporary students of international relations have given increased attention to the role of global civil society. The chapter has argued that this heightened awareness of global civil society arises from recognition of the impact of globalization on the structures and processes of governance. While some scholars contend that contemporary international relations remain fundamentally unchanged, the arguments presented here suggest that globalization has profound implications for authority, legitimacy and order in the contemporary global system. One result of recent transformations has been a changed role for the state. I have not argued that the state has lost its relevance but rather that the state has been transformed, and it is in relation to this transformation that the goals and strategies of social movements must be understood.

Increased challenges by global civil society to established structures of governance are a response to material and ideational change. Social movements and NGOs are motivated by political and social concerns inadequately met by the state and market (Lipschutz, 1992: 407–9; Turner, 1998: 29). The changing character of sovereignty and the increased power of capital constitute the framework within which CSAs have expanded their transnational and global activities. Similarly, the process of globalization has disrupted traditional, long-established political structures and patterns of political behaviour. Although the concept of the global citizen misrepresents current developments, global civil society has developed forms of political representation that are multiple, non-exclusionary and antithetical to the status quo. The actions of representatives of global civil society have been at the forefront of the redefinition of the limits and possibilities of radical politics. This does not mean that global civil society is necessarily progressive or that the solutions proposed by global civil actors provide workable, or indeed just, solutions to problems of social justice, and the maintenance of order.

Analysts will differ in their evaluation of the transformative potential of civil society. While many writers claim global civil society as a progressive force and the activities of CSAs are viewed in a favourable light, others argue that global civil society fails to provide a critical challenge to prevailing structures of power. This debate partly reflects the diversity of CSAs and also often the value preference of the analyst. There is convincing evidence from a number of case studies that CSAs can create global norms and influence various international regimes. For example, the campaign to ban landmines is undoubtedly a success for global civil society activism (Price, 1998). It is also the case that to some extent global citizen action reaffirms existing power and authority relations. Whether a specific CSA is representative of increased democratization and its activities alleviate injustice is an empirical question. The diversity of global civil society prohibits any general conclusions concerning its beneficial (or for that matter harmful) impacts on world politics.

References

Amoore, L. and Langley, P. (2004) 'Ambiguities of global civil society', *Review of International Studies*, 30 (1), 89–110.

Anheier, H., Glasius, M. and Kaldor, M. (2001) 'Introducing global civil society' in H. Anheier, M. Glasius and M. Kaldor (eds), *Global Civil Society 2001*, Oxford, Oxford University Press, pp. 3–22.

Baker, G. (2002) 'Problems in the theorisation of global civil society', *Political Studies*, 50 (5), 928–43.

Barnett, M. and Duvall, R. (2005) 'Power in global governance' in M. Barnett and R. Duvall (eds), *Power in Global Governance*, Cambridge, Cambridge University Press, pp. 1–32.

Bell, D. and Carens, J. (2004) 'The ethical dilemmas of international human rights and humanitarian NGOs: reflections on a dialogue between practitioners and theorists', *Human Rights Quarterly*, 26 (2), 300–329.

Boli, J. and Thomas, G. M. (eds) (1999) *Constructing World Culture: International Nongovernmental Organizations since 1875*, Stanford, CA, Stanford University Press.

Cerny, P. (1997) 'Paradoxes of the competition state: the dynamics of political globalization', *Government and Opposition*, 32 (2), 251–74.

———. (1999) 'Globalising the political and politicising the global: concluding reflections on international political economy as a vocation', *New Political Economy*, 4 (1), 147–62.

Chandhoke, N. (2002) 'The limits of global civil society' in H. Anheier, M. Glasius and M. Kaldor (eds), *Global Civil Society 2002*, Oxford, Oxford University Press, pp. 35–53.

Clark, J. (2001) 'Ethical globalization: the dilemmas and challenges of internationalizing civil society' in M. Edwards and J. Gaventa (eds), *Global Citizen Action*, Boulder, CO, Lynne Rienner, pp. 17–28.

Cohen, J. L. and Arato, A. (1992) *Civil Society and Political Theory*, Cambridge, MA, MIT Press.

Colas, A. (2001) *International Civil Society*, Cambridge, Polity.

Coleman, W. and Wayland, S. (2006) 'The origins of global civil society and nonterritorial governance: some empirical reflections', *Global Governance*, 12 (3), 241–61.

Collingwood, V. (2006) 'Non-governmental organisations, power and legitimacy in international society', *Review of International Studies*, 32 (3), 439–54.

Corry, T. O. (2006) 'Global civil society and its discontents', *Voluntas*, 17 (4), 303–24.

Devetak, R and Higgott, R. (1999) 'Justice unbound? Globalisation, states and the transformation of the social bond', *International Affairs*, 75 (3), 483–98.

Edwards, M. (2001) 'Introduction' in M. Edwards and J. Gaventa (eds), *Global Citizen Action*, Boulder, CO, Lynne Rienner, pp. 1–14.

Falk, R. A. (1997) 'Resisting "globalization-from-above" through "globalization-from-below"', *New Political Economy*, 2 (1), 17–24.

Florini, A. M. (2001) 'Transnational civil society' in M. Edwards and J. Gaventa (eds), *Global Citizen Action*, Boulder, CO, Lynne Rienner, pp. 29–40.

Ford, L. H. (2003) 'Challenging global environmental governance: social movement agency and global civil society', *Global Environmental Politics*, 3 (2), 120–34.

Gill, S. (2002) 'Constitutionalizing inequality and the clash of globalizations', *International Studies Review*, 4 (2), 47–65.

Hopgood, S. (2000) 'Reading the small print in global civil society: the inexorable hegemony of the liberal self', *Millennium*, 29 (1), 1–25.

Humphreys, D. (2004) 'Redefining the issues: NGO influence on international forest negotiations', *Global Environmental Politics,*, 4 (2), 51–74.

Joachim, J. (2003) 'Framing issues and seizing opportunities: the UN, NGOs, and women's rights', *International Studies Quarterly*, 47 (2), 247–74.

Kaldor, M. (1999) 'The ideas of 1989: the origins of the concept of global civil society', *Transnational Law and Contemporary Problems*, 9 (2), 475–88.

———. (2003) *Global Civil Society: An Answer to War*, Cambridge, Polity.

Keane, J. (2001) 'Global civil society?' in H. Anheier, M. Glasius and M. Kaldor (eds), *Global Civil Society 2001*, Oxford, Oxford University Press, pp. 23–47.

———. (2003) *Global Civil Society*, Cambridge, Cambridge University Press.

Keck, M. and Sikkink, K. (1998) *Activists Beyond Borders: Advocacy Networks in International Politics*, Ithaca, NY, Cornell University Press.

Kocka, J. (2004) 'Civil society from a historical perspective', *European Review*, 12 (1), 65–79.

Kumar, K. (1993) 'Civil society: an inquiry into the usefulness of an historical term', *British Journal of Sociology*, 44 (3), 375–95.

Lai, O. (2004) 'Transnational activism and electronic communication: cyber-rainbow warriors in action' in N. Piper and A. Uhlin (eds), *Transnational Activism in Asia: Problems of Power and Democracy*, New York, Routledge, pp. 94–108.

Lipschutz, R. D. (1992) 'Reconstructing world politics: the emergence of global civil society', *Millennium*, 21 (3), 389–420.

———. (2005) 'Power, politics and global civil society', *Millennium*, 33 (3), 747–70.

Lukes, S. (1974) *Power: A Radical View*, London, Macmillan.

Lynch, C. (1998) 'Social movements and the problem of globalization', *Alternatives*, 23 (2), 149–73.

Marden, P. (1997) 'Geographies of dissent: globalization, identity and the nation', *Political Geography*, 16 (1), 37–64.

Muetzelfeldt, M. and Smith, G. (2002) 'Civil society and global governance: the possibilities for global citizenship', *Citizenship Studies*, 6 (1), 55–75.

Nielsen, K. (1995) 'Reconceptualizing civil society for now: some somewhat Gramscian turnings' in M. Walzer (ed.), *Toward a Global Civil society*, Providence and Oxford, Berghahn Books, pp. 41–67.

O'Brien, R. et al. (2000) *Contesting Global Governance: Multilateral Economic Institutions and Global Social Movements*, Cambridge, Cambridge University Press.

Olesen, T. (2005) 'Transnational publics: new spaces of social movement activism and the problem of global long-sightedness', *Current Sociology*, 53 (3), 419–40.

Piper, N. and Uhlin, A. (2004) 'New perspectives on transnational activism' in N. Piper and A. Uhlin (eds), *Transnational Activism in Asia*, London, Routledge, pp. 1–25.

Poitras, G. (2003) 'Resisting globalization: the politics of protest in the global economy', *International Politics*, 40 (3), 409–24.

Price, R. (1998) 'Reversing the gun sights: transnational civil society targets land mine', *International Organization*, 52 (3), 613–44.

Robinson, F. (2003) 'NGOs and the advancement of economic and social rights: philosophical and practical controversies', *International Relations*, 17 (1), 79–96.

Sassen, S. (2002) 'Global cities and diasporic networks: microsites in global civil society' in H. Anheier, M. Glasius, M. Kaldor (eds), *Global Civil Society 2002*, Oxford, Oxford University Press, pp. 217–38.

Scholte, J. A. (2000) *Globalization: A Critical Introduction*, London, Macmillan.

———. (2002), 'Civil society and democracy in global governance', *Global Governance*, 8 (13), 281–305.

Sen, P. (2003) 'Successes and challenges: understanding the global movement to end violence against women' in H. Anheier, M. Glasius and M. Kaldor (eds), *Global Civil Society 2003*, Oxford, Oxford University Press, pp. 119–47.

Shaw, T. (2006) 'Globalization: concepts, contributions, constraints, and controversies', paper presented to the 21st Century Trust/Parliamentary Association Conference 'Where is Globalization Heading?', Bangalore, India, May.

Steele, B. J. and Amourex, J. L. (2005) 'NGOs and monitoring genocide: the benefits and limits to human rights panopticism', *Millennium*, 43 (2), 403–32.

Taylor, P. J. (2005) 'New political geographies; global civil society and global governance through world city networks', *Political Geography*, 24 (6), 703–30.

Thomas, G. D. (1998) 'Civil society: historical uses versus global context', *International Politics*, 35 (2), 49–64.

Turner, S. (1998) 'Global civil society, anarchy and governance: assessing an emerging Paradigm', *Journal of Peace Research*, 35 (1), 25–42.

Walker, R. B. J. (1988) 'Social movements/world politics', *Millennium*, 23 (3), 669–700.

Wapner, P. (1996) *Environmental Activism and World Civic Politics*, Albany, State University of New York Press.

Waterman, P. (1994) 'Globalisation, civil society, solidarity (Part I)', *Transnational Associations*, 46 (2), 66–85.

Williams, M. (2005) 'Globalization and civil society' in J. Ravenhill (ed.), *Global Political Economy*, Oxford, Oxford University Press, pp. 344–69.

CHAPTER 7

Development Hegemonies and Local Outcomes

Women and NGOs in Low-Income Countries

Janet Townsend, Emma Mawdsley and Gina Porter

Introduction

Imperialism constantly reshapes itself (Hoogvelt, 2001). Non-governmental organizations (NGOs) in part mediate the latest version. We shall argue that even those NGOs whose mission is to fight imperialism must engage in dialogue with hegemonic institutions and discourses, and that the latest communications revolutions have facilitated the faster, deeper and wider spread of specific discourses and practices through NGOs working in 'development' in both North and South than ever before. We have explored the knowledge economy of the transnational community of 'development' NGOs with NGOs in Ghana, India, Mexico and Europe (Mawdsley et al., 2002; Townsend et al., 2002; Porter, 2003; Townsend and Townsend, 2004; Alikhan et al., 2006). We asked, how do ideas from different people, organizations and places gain currency and value among NGOs? How can small, southern NGOs get their ideas on to the agenda? Our findings would support Duffield's (2001) argument that 'the networks of international aid are part of an emerging system of global governance'. These networks, including those of NGOs, appear to focus more on rendering societies more governable than on the elimination of poverty.

This chapter outlines the place of NGOs within this changing system and begins to explore the use that poor women in low-income countries are making of them. We look first at the transnational, near-global community of development NGOs. Then we explore its part in global governance, and its role in exclusion and inclusion under the influence of 'new managerialism', emphasizing some unintended consequences of the changes. We ask what poor women have made of this geography, using selected examples from our project. Clearly the issues are complex and contradictory from local to global levels, but there are unexpected cross-cultural, transnational similarities arising from the changed role and nature of NGOs, and we argue that many women have brought about consequences unintended by the donors but welcome to themselves. Once again, 'homogeneity calls forth diversity, in which difference is pluralized, deployed and valorized' (Burawoy et al., 2000: 344). Finally, we note global changes and possible implications.

Our project began with questions raised in the South. First, in 1995, Janet Townsend asked a workshop of peasant women and staff of small, rural, feminist NGOs in Mexico what research they wanted academics to undertake, what work we could do that would be useful to them (Townsend et al., 1999; Zapata et al., 2002). They asked us to find out what NGOs were all about and how they themselves could get their own ideas on to the donors' agenda. Second, Fatima Alikhan, Professor of Geography in Osmania University, Hyderabad, India, collaborated in the project and asked us another question: why the 'solutions' to poverty were so similar all around the world in very different places. The UK Department for International Development (DfID) funded this research as 'Whose ideas?', 1999–2001, with the goals of exploring this knowledge economy, of establishing how some Southern NGOs do get their own ideas on to the agenda, and of publicizing these successes to other NGOs. For this research, we defined NGOs loosely as 'development' organizations (whether professional or grassroots), which employed full-time staff, as such staff are more often involved in the knowledge economy (Townsend, 1999). We interviewed in NGOs working with women and/or environmental issues and have published booklets for Southern NGOs, in Telugu, Kannada and English (for South India), in Hindi and English (for North India), in English (for Ghana) and in Spanish and English (for Mexico). (For copies in English, contact Janet Townsend at janet.townsend@ncl.ac.uk.) A book, *Knowledge, Power and Development Agendas* was written primarily for northern NGOs (Mawdsley et al., 2002). The organizations where we interviewed were all externally funded, whether by Northern 'partner' NGOs, by Northern donors or directly by their own states. Few had support from the private sector, although there is increasing pressure to secure income both from the private sector and from NGO clients, who are, of course, poor. We regard NGOs as distinct from social movements, NGOs tending to be professionally staffed and externally controlled by donors, social movements more radical, more locally rooted, more self-funded, more organic, more spontaneous. There is some overlap here, as some NGOs are socially and even politically active: this is, of course, a complex continuum.

The transnational community of NGOs

The global development NGO community is remarkably diverse, and reaches deep into nearly all lower income countries, even China (Cooper, 2006). It includes huge transnational NGOs like Oxfam International, and very large Southern NGOs like BRAC in Bangladesh, through to tiny, community-based organizations working in single villages. Some, in both North and South, have vast city offices with highly educated and professionalized staff, who travel abroad frequently and are relatively well paid, while others are made up of a few local people who only speak the regional language and move around by bus, bicycle or foot. Then there is the immense diversity of roles (often within the same organization): humanitarian and relief work; development work; welfare work; advocacy and lobbying; and activities in myriad specialist fields, from agricultural extension to empowerment.

The motivations for development work also vary enormously. Some individuals and organizations are driven by their personal, ethical and ideological convictions, such as socialism, feminist beliefs, Gandhianism or religion. Impelled by specific commitments and outlooks, some NGOs have very particular ideas and agendas that they wish to pursue. Many – perhaps most – NGOs today were set up in response to the massive opening up of funding opportunities in the 1970s and 1980s, and the desire of Northern institutions to bypass the state and work through supposedly more efficient 'third sector' organizations. Given their dependent origins, it is no surprise that the majority of these Southern organizations have been 'domesticated' to the goals and agendas of Northern organizations and agencies, and more broadly to the dominant neoliberal vision of the world. Here the market is pre-eminent, and the way to achieve 'development' is to integrate (or subdue) the poor and the marginal more securely into market relations and the monetary economy (the privatization of water resources is just one example of this).

In recent years, NGOs have been viewed as having an important role in this transformation, and in the process many have been established without any particular agenda other than the need to access funds and survive. For many, NGO work represents a middle-class office job, which is, perhaps, relatively secure and well paid compared to other available opportunities.

> NGOs still form a transnational community of talk in a world that is more intimately connected than ever before, a world of increasing non-place intimacies. (Townsend, 1999)

Other transnational communities that share ideas and practices within each community include the global business community, the BBC's World Service, the (illegal) narcotics industry, and even Al Qaeda. Like NGOs, all have been transformed by the cheapening and vast acceleration of communication – whether computer-based or physical travel.

Financially, more than US$10 billion a year or about a fifth of 'international aid' has been moving from the North to 'development' NGOs in the South, through governments, United Nations agencies, private foundations and INGOs (International NGOs) such as Oxfam. NGO staff in poor countries learn what the donors want and what the latest solutions are supposed to be. NGO staff, in rich countries and poor, work closely together, have shared interests and objectives and have together built up a community with a common vocabulary and ways of working, although current changes may alter this, as we shall see.

NGOs remain a highly contested phenomenon as to the nature of both their global, long-term and their more local, immediate roles and impacts. Over the world, James Petras (1997) argues, global capital attacks the powers of the nation-state from above, while NGOs function as a parallel strategy from below, as the community face of neoliberalism. For Michael Hardt and Antonio Negri (2000: 36), humanitarian NGOs, which are assumed to act on the basis of ethical or moral imperatives, 'are in effect (even if this runs counter to the intentions of participants) some of the most powerful pacific weapons of the new world order.' Some argue that NGOs legitimate foreign intervention and delegitimate or even destabilise the state. For Alex de Waal (1997) and Terje Tvedt (1998), long-term humanitarian relief discourages citizens in East Africa from demanding better famine prevention from the state, and thus inhibits the growth of democracy (although new 'sector wide approaches' may have signalled a turn back to the state). In the short term, tens of millions of the world's poor may be seeing a NGO as their best chance of survival or even improvement, but the accountability of the great majority of NGOs is still to their donors, not to their clients, which is a grave limitation. Our concern is with the immediate impact for the poor, and with how activist, independent NGOs could improve that impact with better access to the knowledge economy.

NGOs as a transmission belt

We argue that NGOs are a transmission channel both for donor fashions and for 'new managerialism'. Fatima Alikhan's question about the apparent irrelevance of geography to the reduction of poverty today resonated through our research as we found NGOs promoting vegetable gardens, microcredit and women's empowerment from Puebla Norte (Mexico) to Karnataka (India). For the Norwegian writer, Terje Tvedt (1998: 75), NGOs have become a donor-created and donor-led system, 'a transmission belt of a powerful language and of Western concepts of development', carrying resources and authority from the core to the periphery, and information and legitimization from periphery to core. For Tvedt, despite the extraordinary diversity of the NGO scene both within countries and around the world, NGOs are responsible for taking buzz-words to all corners of the globe, and bringing back to the privileged of the earth images of people, of needs, of realities that attract more funding and legitimization to donors and to NGOs. Our findings on the knowledge economy of NGOs support Tvedt's characterization. To a most disconcerting degree, we met far more similarities in the ways that NGOs in Ghana, India and Mexico talked about their Northern partners and donors than we could readily believe. The places are so different, the talk so similar.

Now that so much NGO funding comes from governments, multilateral donors or foundations, these donors are much freer to impose not only new standardizations and new forms of upward accountability but whole solutions to poverty, solutions that keep changing. In Mexico, a NGO known to Janet Townsend for seven years built very impressive skills in training women to develop successful group enterprises and a strong network with local NGOs across the country, but lost many of its attractions for donors when microcredit became the preferred solution to poverty. In India, Mexico and Ghana we heard similar stories. NGO staff told us, 'You can't conflict with the overall agenda' (Ghana), 'NGOs have to talk about the flavour of the month' (North India), and 'We have very few spaces where we can put forward the needs of our country' (Mexico). On a different note, which we turn to below, from a European NGO worker, we heard, 'We are so overwhelmed by managing the [project] process that we have little time for reflection or thinking on development ideas.'

New managerialism?

Practices as well as ideas recur from northern Ghana to Uttar Pradesh. There are some strange overlaps here, for again we met the same language in sharply different environments. There are unexpected repetitions between NGOs in Ghana, India, Mexico and villages around Durham (UK), and again between these and British university staff talking of their own working lives. Vandana Desai and Rob Imrie (1998) write of the 'new public management revolution' and its 'auditing culture', also called 'the new managerialism'. Under this, the USA and UK governments, amongst others, applied a selection of private sector techniques to their public sectors over the 1980s, and subsequently exported them, mainly through aid and foreign policy, to lower-income countries. Hence we see the resonances and the apparently common concerns in unlikely places (Townsend and Townsend, 2004). In the UK, NGOs and public services (hospitals, schools, police forces) are being increasingly audited for procedural efficiency and for cost cutting, rather than for the difference actually made. Performance indicators and the audit of processes rather than results have unintended consequences. John Clarke et al., eds. (2000) and many others are highly critical of these in the UK, as are Desai and Imrie (1998) for India.

Dr. G. Muniratnam, founder of RASS, a very successful south Indian NGO, and a former member of India's National Planning Commission, is scornful of the detail of donor requirements. To him and to us, most donors are too often more concerned with their own image than with either the misuse of money or making a difference with or for poor people. 'Many donors value documentation above the actual work. They are not bothered about the fieldwork. They are bothered about reports, writing in a *professional* manner. [I think] the system has to be developed so that it can't be misused. Physical verification will reveal the real truth in the field' (Dr. Muniratnam, RASS, interview, 1999).

Onora O'Neill (2002) writes of the UK's supposed crisis of public trust, arguing that the crisis is really of suspicion which we seek to offset with a more perfect accountability, involving new instruments for control, regulation, monitoring and enforcement. These are supposed to make the public sector more accountable to the public, but she argues that they really impose forms of central control. They may be seen as often '*distorting the proper aims of professional practice* (50). . . . In the end, the new culture of accountability provides incentives for arbitrary and unprofessional choices' (O'Neill, 2002: 50, 56). The same instruments, as we have seen, are applied to NGOs and comparable distortions follow.

A knowledge economy

According to our research in Ghana, India and Mexico, it seems that a majority of NGOs are acquiescent to the demands of donors, the development fashions and the new managerialism. Few attach more importance to their mission or the needs of their recipients than to these demands. A major claim of NGOs is that they 'listen to the poor' and learn from them, but many seem not to find time. Most Southern NGOs find it very hard to get their priorities on the agenda. We argue that these consequences go beyond what is needed for improved governability to the point where they impede the work that NGOs claim to do with or for the poor.

[S]tructures and processes that restrict independent-thinking and committed southern NGOs from having a more appropriate voice within the global development NGO community . . . include the unequal ways in which 'partnership' tends to work in practice; the effects of an over-bureaucratised 'report culture'; the priority placed on tracking rather than achieving change; the exclusions of language and communication technologies (ICTs); and the dominance of a minority of southern NGOs. All these help to promote 'information loops' – privileged circuits of information and knowledge, which some southern NGOs find much harder to penetrate than others.

It is not just that smaller, independent-thinking NGOs find it harder to *access* certain forms of information, but that they are also excluded from *adding* their perspectives, ideas and experiences. This seriously compromises the supposed rationale of creating/inventing locally appropriate strategies, and is one reason why waves of 'global' development fashions dominate the sector. (Mawdsley et al., 2002: 137)

Women and NGOs

There are nevertheless very positive examples of women gaining from both feminist and nonfeminist NGOs. At the end of the millennium, a fashion in the 'development' industry for bringing women together to work in groups for 'self-improvement', whether in income, education or empowerment, changed the daily lives, the life worlds, the activity space of millions of women. At the same time, neoliberal discourse brought great Western and 'global' institutional support for notions of citizenship and democracy. New forms of resistance and participation became possible, if still severely restricted. There are new spaces for action. 'Aid' through NGOs and states transmitted the fashion for women's groups as a solution to poverty to almost all low-income areas outside China. Women's groups are promoted as efficient, and governments may see them as potentially controlling women better and exploiting women more. But two very important processes have transformed women's knowledge exchange and often women's lives: the bringing together of women away from their men, and the creating of a space for women to set their own priorities.

For Diane Otto (1996: 134), 'the relations of domination and subordination at the micro, local levels of society make possible the global systems of inequalities in power'. It remains to be seen how far these real grassroots transformations can change the world. Positive outcomes can be found in a remarkable diversity of NGOs. The examples which follow are feminist, pragmatic and Gandhian respectively.

Mahila Samakhya, India

> Mahila Samakhya has its own inbuilt strategies: it's accountable to the grassroots, and that's non-negotiable. (Urvashi Raju, Mahila Samakhya, interviewee)

Mahila Samakhya is a programme of informal education for women's empowerment, designed by Indian feminists from their experiences of working with poor women, and now operating in 15,283 villages. They secured funding from the Dutch government from 1988 to 2002 and then from the Indian government. Problems may now be arising in some states (Sharma, 2006), but its reputation has been excellent. Mahila Samakhya tried to create an environment for women to learn at their own pace, set their own priorities and seek knowledge and information to make informed choices. This is so that they can address and deal with problems of isolation and lack of self-confidence, oppressive social customs and struggles for survival (Batliwala, 1996). In an environment of mutual support and trust, women learn to make decisions, assume leadership and evolve collective strategies to change their own destinies. Self-empowerment of women is seen as the critical precondition for their participation in the education process.

> What MS has shown is that we are really going against the dominant trend today, where basically they're saying women are best organized into self-help groups about microcredit. In a sense, MS is a counterpoise to that. . . . We are looking at an empowering process in a completely different sense from what everybody else is doing. We do not deliver any services. We do not deliver any tangible benefits. The data show that women do come together, not necessarily around money. No matter what the issue, we should be able to take them through a process of analysis, take

them through a process of thinking, understanding what it is, what it means to them as women, how it's going to impact their lives, what they can do. . . . A poor woman knowing something is not going to be able to do anything, but thirty women, yes, possibilities are there. And we have a lot of evidence of that, right from getting the teacher to come to school on time to ensuring that upper-caste men do not use derogatory terms with reference to lower-caste women. The self is important, it has to come from within, and that is the key. (Kameshwari, interview, 1999)

Even so, in Mahila Samakhya, Kameshwari, once a professor of history, complains that the majority of her time is spent on the paperwork.

Enterprise, Mexico

Enterprise (a pseudonym), in Mexico City, works with a network of partner NGOs that advise groups of women in setting up their own businesses, or in allied activities such as revolving credit. They have substantial experience of providing long-term support and training directly to women's groups, and now also support other NGOs that share their feminist, egalitarian ideology. All retain a deep commitment to women's autonomy and empowerment, which remain their goals, and to the creation of the collective spaces that they see as central to these processes. As one interviewee explained: 'Collective work is very important, not waiting for the *conquistadors*' [literally, the sixteenth-century Spanish conquerors].

Its partners regard Enterprise as a model and 'Hope' (another pseudonym) calls it a 'guardian angel'. (Hope has a decade of harsh but very successful experience in the rainforests of Chiapas). Enterprise secures, circulates and publishes information on funding sources and methods of work – proving that such sharing is possible. Personal relations and face-to-face encounters hold the network together, so that e-mail can handle the information. They are highly critical of the donor fashion for documentation, but welcome donor visits.

Janet: How can unsatisfactory NGOs be identified?
Marina (interviewee): By looking at the tangible results: the businesses. We can take donors to the work. We have audits. It's all very transparent: you can't invent the businesses. Audits are a headache, but they really help in presentation.'

RASS, India

RASS has a modified Gandhian vision. Dr. G. Muniratnam, the inspirational General Secretary, has, since 1981, built up work in 3,540 villages in southern Andhra Pradesh, and begun work in Tamil Nadu and Orissa.

RASS, in no way feminist, is an example of women users and women professionals finding out how to use NGOs. RASS's first successes were in welfare. RASS believes that development of women transforms the entire family, which might be seen as a patriarchal view, and so set up women's groups (Mahila Mandals). By 1989 (personal communication), Dr. Muniratnam felt that RASS's considerable success in welfare was a beginning but that people had to be better able to earn. Unexpectedly, the women's groups provided much of the answer to his worries when, in 1990, RASS began to encourage them to form Self-Help Groups (SHGs) for microcredit and savings. Now, in the twenty-first century, many of these poor women are self-empowered and self-confident and groups are becoming independent, while RASS has nearly 4,000 staff and a budget of £1 million a year.

RASS is based in Tirupati, a great centre for Hindu pilgrims to the temple of Balaji. It has an immense array of programmes, from continued sponsorship of children through a diploma in work with mental retardation, to a wide range of activities linked to SHGs, including improved milk-cow programmes, training for self-employment, savings-and-loan and microcredit. One key feature throughout has been a clarity of goals supported by a commitment to persuade partners and donors of the goals, weaving together all kinds of funding for all kinds of activities. The child sponsorship NGOs, for instance, found them-selves sponsoring not selected individuals but all the poorest children in a village, and being persuaded to fund initiatives that benefited the whole community, such as clean water. Sponsorship would build a crèche for the children of mothers working in the fields, and the building would serve also for non-formal education of children not in school and as the village community centre. 'Not only child. Child, family, community: an integrated approach' (Dr Muniratnam, interview 1999; a view not traditionally popular with child sponsorship NGOs). Similarly, a range of donors supporting microcredit found themselves making loans for consumption as well as production, which was anathema to some.

In 1989, Janet Townsend was struck by the fact that RASS had no middle-class women volunteers as 'fashionable' administrators or fundraisers (which was common at the time), or salaried middle-class women in the offices, but women *were* giving their skills unpaid as gynaecologists and teachers. Village crèches were run and staffed by the village women, but no woman then travelled between villages for RASS. A decade later, the women in RASS's SHGs were determined to give visitors a positive impression of their relationship with RASS (language barriers notwithstanding), and were very competent at doing so. In 1999, it was salaried women on the staff of RASS who took Janet to see the SHGs; one of them has a PhD in nutrition. And retired men, including vets, worked as volunteers. Women are not at the top of RASS, but they make some good use of it.

Towards a new architecture of aid

In the last decade, there have been increasing experiments in delivering aid once again to the state, and in encouraging the state to subcontract some public services to NGOs. In 2005, the Paris Declaration (World Bank, 2005) of the world's richer countries took this further, making a commitment to a new architecture of aid. In the interest of the Millennium De-velopment Goals, aid is to increase and to move increasingly to Southern governments, whose national development strategies and/or budgets will determine the funding they receive. The criteria are, in theory, internationally harmonized. Direct support to national governments is presented as the most effective form of aid (OECD, 2006). Northern NGOs may lose much of their role in transmitting funds to Southern NGOs. For the South, national public administration, measured by performance indicators of efficiency, is to be at the centre of Northern funding decisions. Southern NGOs may become simply implementers of government plans. They may come to be even more instruments of the state, tied to a single set of aims imposed externally and losing much of their independence, their diversity, their role in offering alternative spaces (Lönnqvist, 2006; Pratt, 2006). Poor people will have to find places within the new architecture and cope with yet another change in their difficult worlds.

Conclusion

The neoliberal project has transformed 'development' NGOs and given them a place in the latest form of imperialism. Over the last twenty years, NGOs have burgeoned in numbers and size, as donors have directed some aid to them rather than to the state. They used new technologies of communication to become a transnational community of talk, but this has itself become a transmission channel for development fashions and management practices under considerable donor control. NGOs in general became far more dependent on donors and their 'new managerialist' practices, which we would argue have many unintended and undesirable consequences in NGO work (Townsend et al., 2002; Townsend and Townsend, 2004). Insofar as donors consciously impose these changes, this would appear to be in the interest of governance rather than poverty reduction. We believe that some of these practices could be modified in the interests of the more needy without any reduction in the governability achieved. Accountability and transparency are entirely necessary, but (resonating with the views of Onora O'Neill in the UK) we argue that current practice tends not to achieve these goals, or does so in ways that damage both people and organizational goals. We suggest (Mawdsley et al., 2002) other ways in which the transnational NGO sector can be internally and externally monitored in less distorting *and* more effective ways.

We have explored the outcomes of this transformation for some women, and they are naturally complex and diverse. Many women's movements became 'NGO-ized' in the 1990s, as funding for NGOs expanded and significant material resources became available to implement new public policies. There have been real advances in policies and rights as some feminist ideas have become mainstream, in governments and societies. At the same time, 'mainstreaming' has too often led to very unfeminist institutionalization, and some feminists who went into traditionally male-dominated institutions in order to change them have become 'femocrats', or 'a new gender technocracy', while 'feminist NGOs' sometimes act like 'neo- rather than non-governmental organizations' (Álvarez, 1998: 307). Any overall balance has yet to be determined, but some women's NGOs (and women clients and staff of even some nonfeminist NGOs) are using one donor fashion, for women's groups, to liberate women. Some women's NGOs and clients do get ideas on to the agenda and do get funded to do the work they want to do, not merely the latest fashion.

The recommendation from our interviewee Kameshwari (Mahila Samakhya, Hyderabad, India) for getting more ideas on to the agenda is, 'All the donors these days talk a language of sharing. We need to give these words teeth.'

Acknowledgements

Thanks to the UK Department of International Development (DfID), which funded 'Whose ideas?' and 'NGOS and the State under the new forms of aid', and to Fatima Alikhan

(India), Elizabeth Ardafyio-Schandorf (Ghana), Saraswati Raju (India), Emma Zapata (Mexico), Peter Oakley, Brian Pratt, Sara Gibbs and Jon Taylor (of INTRAC, Oxford) for their collaboration.

DfID supports policies, programmes and projects to promote international development. It provided funds for this study as part of that objective, but the views and opinions expressed are those of the authors alone.

The authors wish every success to NGDO clients and to committed local NGOs in getting more of their priorities on to the agenda. Our deepest thanks to the NGO staff and key informants (recipients, officials and academics) who have made this research possible by being so generous with their knowledge.

References

Alikhan, F., Kyei, P., Mawdsley, E. E., Porter, G., Raju, S., Townsend, J. G. and Varma, R. (2006) *NGOs and the State in the Twenty-first Century: Ghana and India*, Oxford, INTRAC.

Álvarez, S. E. (1998) 'Latin American feminisms 'Go Global': trends of the 1990s and challenges for the new millennium' in S. Álvarez, E. Dagnino and Arturo Escobar (eds), *Cultures of Politics, Politics of Culture: Revisioning Latin American Social Movements*, Boulder, CO, Westview Press, pp. 293–324.

Batliwala, S. (1996) 'Transforming of political culture – Mahila Samakhya experience', *Economic and Political Weekly*, 31, 1248–51.

Burawoy, M., Blum, J. A., Gille, Z., Gowan, T., Haney, L., Klawiter, M., Lopez, S. H., Ó Rain, S. and Thayer, M. (2000) *Global Ethnography: Forces, Connections and Imaginations in a Postmodern World*, Berkeley, CA, University of California Press.

Clarke, J., Gewirtz, S. and McLaughlin, E. (eds) (2000) *New Managerialism, New Welfare?*, London, Sage Publications with the Open University.

Cooper, C. M. (2006) '"This is our way in": the civil society of environmental NGOs in South-West China', *Government and Opposition*, 41, 109–36.

Desai, V. and Imrie, R. (1998) 'The new managerialism in local government: North-South dimensions', *Third World Quarterly*, 19, 635–50.

De Waal, A. (1997) *Famine Crimes: Politics and the Disaster Relief Industry*, Oxford, James Currey.

Duffield, M. (2001) 'Governing the borderlands: decoding the power of aid', *Disasters*, 25, 308–20.

Hardt, M. and Negri, A. (2000) *Empire*, Cambridge, MA, Harvard University Press.

Hoogvelt, A. (2001) *Globalization and the Postcolonial World: The New Political Economy of Development*, 2nd ed., Basingstoke, Palgrave.

Lönnqvist, L. (2006) 'The Paris Declaration on aid effectiveness: an overview', *ONTRAC*, 33 (3) http://www.intrac.org/pages/previous_ontracs.html or from INTRAC, Oxford.

Mawdsley, E., Townsend, J., Porter, G. and Oakley, P. (2002) *Knowledge, Power and Development Agendas: NGOs North and South*, Oxford, INTRAC.

OECD (2005) Paris Declaration on aid effectiveness, online at http://www.oecd.org/document/18/0,2340,en_2649_3236398_35401554_1_1_1_1,00.html.

———. (2006) Joint Evaluation of General Budget Support, online at http://www.oecd.org/dataoecd/42/38/36685401.pdf.

O'Neill, O. (2002) *A Question of Trust: The BBC Reith Lectures 2002*, Cambridge, Cambridge University Press.

Otto, D. (1996) 'Nongovernmental organizations in the United Nations system: the emerging role of international civil society', *Human Rights Quarterly*, 18, 107–41.

Petras, J. (1997) 'Imperialism and NGOs in Latin America', *Monthly Review*, 49, 10–27.

Porter, G. (2003) 'NGOs and poverty reduction in a globalizing world: perspectives from Ghana', *Progress in Development Studies*, 3, 131–45.

Porter, G. and Lyon, F. (2006) 'Groups as a means or an end? Social capital and the promotion of cooperation in Ghana', *Environment and Planning D*, 24, 249–62.

Pratt, B. (2006) 'Aid harmonisation and challenges for civil society', *ONTRAC*, 33, 1, online at http://www.intrac.org/pages/previous_ontracs.html or from INTRAC, Oxford.

Sharma, A. (2006) 'Crossbreeding institutions, breeding struggle: women's empowerment, neoliberal governmentality, and state (re)formation in India', *Cultural Anthropology*, 21, 60–95.

Townsend, J. G. (1999) 'Are non-governmental organizations working in development a transnational community?', *Journal of International Development*, 11, 613–25.

Townsend, J. G., Zapata, E., Rowlands, J., Alberti, P. and Mercado, M. (1999) *Women and Power: Fighting Patriarchies and Poverty*, London, Zed Books.

Townsend, J. G., Porter, G. and Mawdsley, E. E. (2002) 'The role of the transnational community of non-governmental organisations: governance or poverty reduction?', *Journal of International Development*, 14, 829–39.

———. (2004) 'Creating spaces of resistance: development NGOs and their clients in Ghana, India and Mexico', *Antipode*, 36, 871–99.

Townsend, J. G. and Townsend, A. R. (2004) 'Accountability, motivation and practice: NGOs North and South', *Social and Cultural Geography*, 5, 271–84.

Tvedt, T. (1998) *Angels of Mercy or Development Diplomats? NGOs and Foreign Aid*, Oxford, James Currey.

Zapata, E., Townsend, J. G., Rowlands, J., Alberti, P. and Mercado, M. (2002) *Las mujeres y el poder: la lucha contra el patriarcado y la pobreza*, Mexico City, Plaza and Valdez.

Part 3

Gender, Sexualities and Global Processes

CHAPTER 8

Shifting Ground(s), Remapping Strategies and Triad Analytics

V. Spike Peterson

Even the most frantic drawing of ethnic/community boundaries will encircle social "matter" in rapid states of change. (Jacobs, 2000: 228)

In examining globalization as we proceed into the twenty-first century, we find that differences proliferate, conflicts escalate and the pace of change accelerates, even as global dynamics also have homogenizing effects and a historical long-view exposes continuity. Categorical separations that were commonplace between subject and object, public and private, political and economic, domestic and international, increasingly break down in the face of postmodern challenges, sub- and trans-national political identifications, and local-national-global linkages. In this context of conceptual and empirical transformations, boundaries – and the ground(s) they mark – are shifting, forcing us to re-map what recently was (or seemed to be) familiar terrain.

In this chapter, I begin by considering the politics of epistemology: I review positivist givens and critical responses, describe how feminists map empirical-analytical intersections, and conclude that modernist mapping strategies are inadequate for postmodern conditions. I then introduce an alternative mapping device – 'triad analytics' – that articulates identities, meaning systems, and social practices/institutions as interactive and interdependent (co-constituting). In the next section, I consider the politics of identity by reviewing salient issues and illustrating, through the example of nationalism, the importance of identity for better mapping strategies. The last section considers the politics of states and markets by exposing the foundational dichotomies that underpin conventional framing and by discussing both the neglect of identities and their importance for political practice. A short conclusion summarizes our re-mapping needs and the advantages of a triadic re-framing.

The politics of epistemology

Although challenged from numerous vantage points, positivist epistemologies continue to dominate academic study of social relations, especially in the discipline of international relations (IR). In brief, positivist methods and knowledge claims presuppose categorical separations of subject-object, fact-value and theory-practice.[1] The binary logic of these foundational dichotomies conforms to the objectivist metaphysics that underpins Western philosophy. What renders this logic so *politically* consequential is that it infuses and biases not only our scientific knowledge claims but our conceptual maps – our symbols, categories, identities, paradigms, worldviews – more generally. Of particular significance is how dichotomies differentiate concepts both oppositionally (as mutually exclusive, static and oversimplified categories) and hierarchically (as asymmetrically privileged categories). As a consequence, positivist dichotomies frame 'ways of knowing' that are problematically reductionist, ahistorical and noncritical. They are also masculinist insofar as the privileged terms in foundational dichotomies – reason, culture, public – are associated with masculinity and the devalued terms – affect, nature, private – are associated with femininity (Peterson and Runyan, 1999).

Critics argue that empiricist and mono-disciplinary perspectives, which emerge from and reproduce positivist dichotomies, frame social inquiry too narrowly and leave too much of significance out of the picture. Consider how Realist preoccupation with Cold War power politics obscured the importance of economic, socio-cultural and psychological factors that were decisive in 'bringing down communism.' A neglect of inter-subjective meaning systems and the politics of identification impairs our ability to understand nationalism, fundamentalism and even terrorism. And unless we pay attention to the significance of symbols and the social construction of 'value', we cannot effectively analyze global financial markets and their dependence on various forms of intersubjective 'trust.'[2]

In contrast to feminists and geographers, mainstream IR scholars continue to resist the challenges posed by critical and interpretive perspectives. Moreover, failure to engage critiques of positivism, indeed, a renewal of positivist commitments in the United States, shapes the reception of feminist theory in IR. While references to feminist scholarship are now more frequent, feminist arguments are rarely integrated into mainstream or even critical and interpretive analyses.[3] That is, in spite of a phenomenal growth in publications, the launch of the *International Feminist Journal of Politics* and remarkable conference visibility, feminist IR remains 'foreign' to the mainstream. More specifically, while 'woman' as an empirical referent has gained visibility, gender as an analytical category – with its critical and transformative implications – is hardly acknowledged. This is due, in part, to epistemological blinders. As long as positivist commitments prevail, the discipline may 'add women' (as an empirical category) to existing analytical frameworks, but gender as an analytical category – as a structural feature of analysis that *transforms* frameworks – cannot be taken seriously. Adding 'women' empirically is one thing, integrating gender conceptually is another (e.g., Peterson, 1992, 2003).

Feminists do, of course, seek women's inclusion, and 'adding women' is an important (and hard won!) objective. But what makes feminism systemically transformative is its analytical critique, which insists on rethinking foundational categories that presuppose masculinism.[4] That is, feminists go beyond other critics of positivism to argue that the foundational dualisms of Western philosophy, including constitutive dichotomies of IR and political geography, are not just empirically but conceptually gendered. Taking gender seriously then requires not only moving beyond the binary blinders of positivism but also acknowledging gender as constitutive of binary framing. In Susan Hekman's words, 'The postmoderns see the error of Enlightenment dualisms but the feminists complete this critique by defining those dualisms as gendered' (Hekman, 1990: 8).

What I want to emphasize is that, in contrast to most non-feminist interpretivists, *feminist critiques of dichotomies are inseparable from their critiques of oppression.*[5] Specifically and significantly, feminists take seriously the relational implications of rejecting dichotomies. I identify two complementary dimensions of this relational orientation: the contextual and conceptual. The former emphasizes bringing the abstract critique of dualist thought into relation with its concrete (historical, empirical) effects. Historical-empirical contextualization illuminates the contingent linkages among concepts, practices, agents and institutional arrangements. For example, Merchant's (1980) study of the scientific revolution embedded masculinist concepts (e.g., modernist constructions of rationality, objectivity) in male-dominated historical conditions (e.g., 'conquering of nature,' European state formation and colonialism, and industrial capitalism). And McClintock's (1995) study of British imperialism chronicles the intersection of gender, race and class in the symbols and practices of European nationalism, colonial power and uneven market dynamics.

Feminists thus put flesh on the observation that the model of the rational individual presupposed in scientific ways of knowing is the same (Eurocentric, masculine) individual presupposed in economic contracts and political agency. One consequence, which feminist studies confirm again and again, is that females cannot simply be added to categories that are defined by maleness (which implies the absence of femaleness). To do so exposes the (masculine) gender of the category (for example, the assumption of male experience in constructions of the public, political identity and politics per se). Either females cannot be added (they are marginalized), or they must become 'like men' (they are masculinized), or *they are included, which includes femaleness, and the meaning of the category is transformed.* This brings us to the second, conceptual, dimension of a relational orientation.

If the contextual dimension highlights the empirical and political implications of bringing categories into relation, the conceptual dimension highlights the analytical implications. The binary logic of dichotomies frames our thinking in mutually exclusive categories so that masculinity, reason and objectivity are defined by the absence of femininity, affect and subjectivity. Once we reject the categorical separations presupposed in dichotomies, not only does the boundary between them change but so does the meaning of the polar terms: they are not mutually exclusive but in relation, which permits more than the two possibilities posited in either-or constructions. Moreover, changing the meaning of the terms and bringing them into relation (exposing their interdependence) changes the theoretical frameworks within which they are embedded.

Hence, a critique of masculinity, reason or objectivity does not entail the elevation of femininity, affect or subjectivity (at the expense of masculinity, reason or objectivity) but a recognition of their *relationship* in historically specific contexts. Rather than assuming an unproblematic categorical separation of terms, which promotes static explanations, better mapping requires that we specify how terms are related; this requires situating terms and events in historical context, which promotes contextualized and dynamic understanding. This is a complex task, but the more appropriate one for understanding – not acritically reproducing – social relations. This task also suggests how a relational orientation is simultaneously contextual and conceptual: by bringing terms into relation, feminists not only contextualize the categories politically, economically, socio-culturally, but also re-conceptualize the categories and theoretical frameworks, with implications for political identifications and strategies.

In sum, modernist ways of knowing are masculinist and they are political – embedded in and reproducing particular relations of power – because they naturalize the marginalization, objectification and corollary exploitation, of all which are devalued by association with the feminine: not only 'women' but also nature, effeminate men and colonized 'Others.' In other words, the ostensible 'naturalness' of sex difference and masculine dominance is generalized to other forms of domination, which has the effect of legitimating them as equally 'natural' hierarchies. In this crucial sense, feminist critiques are not simply about male-female relations but about *all social hierarchies that are naturalized (depoliticized, legitimated) by devalorization of the feminine*. The argument here is that 'adding women' (as an empirical category) may be an effective strategy for improving the lives of 'women,' but it falls far short of taking gender (as an analytical category) seriously. The latter entails deconstructing the naturalization of structural hierarchies in their multiple (and interconnected) forms. Hence, it involves improving the lives of *all* – not just women – whose oppression is naturalized by devalorization of the feminine.[6]

What these points demonstrate is that masculinist ways of knowing marginalize women as agents and gender as an analytical category. A litany of dichotomies privilege (elite) male experience and androcentric accounts at the expense of female experience (in all its diversity) and the experience of all who are denigrated as feminine. One consequence is distorted knowledge claims and inadequate theories, leaving us – sometimes intentionally but always dangerously – ignorant of important social dynamics. Another and inextricable consequence is the reproduction of identities, discourses and conditions that favour diverse but always gendered social hierarchies.

Remapping devices: introducing an alternative analytics

I have argued that conventional maps are inadequate. As a contribution to analytical re-mapping, I introduce an alternative 'framing' of social relations. In *The Science Question in Feminism*, Harding (1986: 17–18) identified three aspects through which gendered social life is structured and (re)produced. Gender identity is 'a form of socially constructed individual identity only imperfectly correlated with either the "reality" or the perception of sex differences.' Gender symbolism is 'the result of assigning dualistic gender metaphors to various perceived dichotomies that rarely have anything to do with sex differences.' Gender structure is 'the consequence of appealing to these gender dualisms to organize social activity.' Although the particular referents for these aspects of gender vary cross-culturally, they are interrelated within any particular culture. By reference to these three aspects, not only our identity as subjects but also our meaning systems and social institutions are gendered. Thus, Harding's interrelated aspects reveal the pervasiveness and potency of gender in structuring our world(s) and confirm the importance of 'taking gender seriously' in our study of 'reality.'

I have recast Harding's discussion as a mapping device that encourages us to reframe how we think about theorizing (and practicing) social life. Cast as 'triad analytics'[7] the framing simply posits identities, meaning systems and social practices/institutions as co-constituting dimensions or processes of social reality. It moves away from dichotomized constructions (e.g., material-symbolic, structural-discursive, empirical-analytical) that encumber conventional theorizing (and divide academic disciplines). It draws attention to identity/subjectivity and to the social hierarchies and 'micro-power' that structure subject formation.[8] And it insists that these aspects be understood as mutually constituted, hence interactive, dynamic and historical.

In short, and as I habitually cast it, the triad framing reminds us that gender shapes 'who we are' (identities, subjectivities, sexualities, allegiances), 'how we think' (symbols, concepts, discourses, collective meaning systems), and 'what we do' (actions, practices, institutions, social structures). Stated differently, the triad integrates ways of 'being,' 'knowing' and 'doing.' It thus affords an interactive, multi-level, multi-variable and transdisciplinary orientation. It can also facilitate (which is my intention) conversations among diverse theoretical perspectives. On the one hand, the triad makes reference to, or can be linked with, features of social life that are familiar in modernist, positivist and critical accounts (e.g., agents, ideology, institutions). On the other hand, the triad takes subject formation seriously, privileges relational rather than dichotomized analytics and 'opens new spaces' for theory/practice; these are 'moves' more familiar in postmodernist accounts.

To clarify the need for conceptual remapping, in an earlier section I considered the politics of epistemology. Issues raised in that discussion confirm our need for maps that take 'how we think', including foundational categories and ontological starting points, seriously. A triad analytics permits us to do so, even as it insists that abstractions and discourse be understood in relation to practices/structures and identities. In the next section, I consider the politics of identity, both as a substantive topic in its own right, and to suggest why identity and subjectivity warrant the attention that a triad analytics affords but traditional accounts preclude.

The politics of identity

Whereas feminists have long been interested in the politics of identity and identification, scholars in political science and geography have conventionally neglected these areas of inquiry. Until recently, the latter disciplines tended to take for granted both a Eurocentric model of the modern subject (as unitary, autonomous, interest-maximizing and rational) and a (Eurocentric) spatial model of public sphere agency and territorial states. In these accounts, the dichotomy of public-private locates political action in one but not the other sphere; the dichotomy of internal-external distinguishes citizens and order within from 'Others' and anarchy without; and the dichotomy of culture-nature (civilized-primitive, advanced-backward, developed-undeveloped) 'naturalizes' uneven geopolitical power.

Empirical and epistemological transformations challenge the adequacy of these conventional accounts. In terms of the former, state-centric political identity no longer monopolizes but shares the stage with a growing number of non-territorial claimants. Sub- and trans-national social movements transgress territorial boundaries in favour of identities 'grounded' on ecological, anti-nuclear, ethnic, feminist, religious and other non-state-based commitments. Uneven flows of information, culture, people, technology and capital involve human migrations and diasporic identities that complicate territorial frames of reference. The globalization of production and finance undercuts national economic planning, eroding state sovereignty and the political identities it presupposes, even as supra-national forces alter state power and sub-national conflicts expose the illusion of homogeneity promoted in nationalist narratives. In short, identities conventionally 'grounded' in state territoriality are losing ground to a politics of new-or even 'non'-space(s).

In terms of epistemological transformations, critiques of positivist-empiricism have altered our understanding of agents and subjectivity. In contrast to the modernist conception of a unitary rational actor, contemporary social theory illuminates the multiplicity of subject locations (implying multiple identifications) and their dynamic interaction 'within' the self *and* in relation to the self's environment. In short, identities are socially constructed as ongoing processes: they are embedded in and interact with historically specific social contexts composed of inter-subjective meaning systems, practices, institutional structures and material conditions. Hence, the study of identities must be historical, contextual and dynamic: asking not only how identities are located in time and space but also how they are reproduced, resisted and reconfigured.

Identities are politically important because they inform self-other representations, embed subjects in meaning systems and collective agency, and mobilize purposive, politically significant actions. They are important windows on 'reality' because 'internal subjective selfchange and external objective social change' are inextricable (Bologh, 1987: 147). When we neglect identities, and cultural dynamics more generally, we cannot account for significant social practices. For instance, we lose sight of how racism and the identities it cultivates shape uneven development and political conflicts. In related but even starker terms, we lack adequate understanding of how people are willing to kill and be killed so that a particular group can thrive.

Feminists have a number of reasons for attending to political identity and the politics of identification. First, constructions of femininity and masculinity that inform our identifications as women and men have unbounded implications for the lives we lead and the world(s) we live in. Inextricable from constructions of sexuality and desire, these implications extend to the most intimate activities as well as the most global social dynamics (Zalewski and Parpart, 1998; Hooper, 2001).

Second, to the extent that personal gender identities constitute a 'core' sense of 'self,' they fundamentally condition our self-esteem and psycho-sociological security. This means that challenges to gender ordering may appear to threaten a personal identity in which we are deeply invested. A fear of loss or destabilization may then fuel resistance to deconstruction of gender ideologies, with many – mostly negative – implications for feminist movement.

Third, feminists have criticized biological explanations that essentialize maleness and femaleness. Consistent with their critiques of positivist science, they argue that masculine and feminine are historically contingent social constructions.

Fourth, feminist studies have established that the identity of the modern subject – in models of human nature, citizenship, the rational actor, the knowing subject, economic man and political agency – is not gender-neutral but masculine (and typically European and heterosexual). There is now a vast literature exploring the many ways that androcentric identities, theory and practice marginalize women and all feminized 'Others.'

Fifth, if a universal category of 'woman' is a necessary condition of feminist movement, then the many differences among women contravene that condition. Hence, contemporary feminisms are both challenged and enriched by struggles to address diversity without abandoning solidarities enabled by shared experience and necessary for emancipatory politics (Grewal and Kaplan, 1994; Alexander and Mohanty, 1997; Mohanty, 2003).

Finally, identity groups (whether based on ethnicity, race, religion or nationality) that have been most closely associated with political power have also been historically based on gender inequality (Yuval-Davis and Anthias, 1989; Yuval-Davis, 1997; Peterson, 1999). As members of these groups, women have an interest in their 'success,' including the group's acquisition of political power vis-à-vis competitors. But, insofar as these groups reproduce masculine dominance, identification with and support for them is problematic for feminists.

For all of these reasons, and more, feminists have taken the lead in cross-disciplinary and wide-ranging studies of identity, identification processes and their relationships to power at local, national and global 'levels.' Nationalism, of course, is a particular focus of identity studies and has been particularly well-mapped by feminists. Indeed, today's scholarship on gendering nationalism is vast, reflecting both the development of analytical approaches and the proliferation of ethnic and nationalist conflicts in recent decades. Gender is a structural feature of nationalist projects in co-determining senses: the identities mobilized in nationalist activities are gender-differentiated (resolute leaders, supportive caretakers); the practices of nationalism are gender-differentiated (men at the war-front, women at the home-front), and the symbols and discourse of nationalism are deeply gendered (masculine protectors of the motherland, feminine signifiers of the nation and cultural identity). We see these relationships horrifically at work in the example of rape as a weapon of war. 'Men' are expected to defend their motherland and protect their women. Rape is not only a metaphor of national humiliation, suggesting the failure of men to defend their territory and the loss of manhood in defeat, but also an embodied practice whereby the 'Other' threatens group reproduction by impregnating the group's women with 'alien' seed. Recent ethno-nationalist conflicts have demonstrated all too well how rape is a weapon of war, how performing gender identities involves violence, and how the female body is not only figuratively but literally a battleground. In short, the gendering of nationalisms is not a coincidence but integral to how we identify with, think about, and go about making war.[9]

This discussion of identity has begun to illustrate the advantages of a triad analytics. In the next section, I briefly consider the politics of states and markets and how these are specified and analyzed (or not) in IR. The discussion suggests how positivist legacies not only impoverish our understanding of states and markets, but also deny the politics of identity in relation to state practices. By implication, triad analytics offers a more productive framing.

The politics of states and markets

Replicating disciplinary divisions and consistent with positivist dichotomies, conventional accounts in IR separate political activities associated with states from economic activities associated with markets. In IR, politics is spatially located within the territorial boundaries of the state, to be distinguished from anarchy (the absence of 'authentic politics') outside of the state and/or from market activities (myriad individual decisions) that are not territorially 'grounded.' More frequently, reference to public and private spheres invokes mutually exclusive 'spaces' for political and economic behavior respectively. (Note that in this framing, the private sphere of 'the family' – including its reproductive activities and identity cultivating practices – drops out of sight, and hence, out of our analyzing maps).

As spatial 'spheres', we tend to locate public and private within states, but the dichotomy is foundational to IR as well (Youngs, 1999; Peterson, 2000). Consider that it is exclusively political, diplomatic and military actors – masculinized subjects and identities associated with the public sphere – that are accorded agency and visibility in theories of the state and international politics. In this conventional framing economics, culture, ideology, identities and social reproduction disappear, as do workers, migrants and all dependents. Given this binary framing (familiar in modernist accounts), power can be apprehended (mapped?) only as direct, top-down, coercive, juridical, power-over; not as indirect, productive, normative, disciplinary and power-to (familiar in feminist and interpretive accounts).

As a conceptual map that continues to shape IR inquiry, realist preoccupation with power politics has had the predictable effect of marginalizing economics and the paradoxical effect of neglecting theories of the state (Ferguson and Mansbach, 1996). As foci of inquiry, the history and reproduction of states are largely set aside in favour of a discipline-defining focus on the meaning of sovereignty and security in an inter-state system already in place and assumed to be structurally unchanging. Sovereignty, the distinctive feature of the modern system, is the right of states to exercise complete jurisdiction within mutually exclusive territorial domains. In these accounts, the dichotomy of public-private locates legitimate use of force in the public realm of the state and the dichotomy of internal-external projects this legitimacy outward, expressed as the state's right to make war (Ruggie, 1993: 151).

The neglect of history and presumption of territoriality have impoverished IR theory, rendering it particularly inadequate in the context of global restructuring. On the one hand, ignorance of history has exacerbated the tendency toward static and reductionist understanding: as many critics have observed, prevailing theories deal poorly with change and simply deny fundamental transformations (Buzan and Little, 2000). On the other hand, elevation of politics (understood territorially) over economics has precluded sophisticated and critical analyses of market dynamics. In the absence of such analyses, the globalization of capital stymies our understanding: we rely too much on liberal-capitalist orthodoxies, we know too little about unregulated financial markets and non-territorial power, and we lack any credible alternatives to a model of unbridled accumulation that is ultimately (ecologically, if not morally) self-destructive.[10]

Globalization, understood here as structural shifts in transnational capital relations, has prompted a revival of interest in states and questions of sovereignty. In the face of what most regard as profound changes in the capacity of state agents to 'manage' national economies, IR scholars are compelled to turn their attention to the relationship between states and markets, politics and economics. This is a rapidly growing literature, itself marked by divergent analytical and political commitments but crucial for new understandings – and conceptual re-mappings – of global *political economy*.[11]

But political economy must also acknowledge the politics of identity. As nationalist struggles demonstrate, identities are key to mobilizing actions taken on behalf of, in allegiance to and resistance against the state (and other polities). And today, global migrations and non-territorial diasporas generate new identity processes with important political effects. These identities transgress, physically and electronically, territorial boundaries and state-centric accounts of community. At the same time, identities are increasingly salient for analyzing market activities. On the one hand, consumption has always been gendered (Firat, 1994; de Grazia and Furlough, 1996). On the other hand, contemporary niche marketing both targets and creates particular consumer identities (Friedman, 1994). For some sectors, especially in the rich North, identity as consumers is displacing identity as citizens (Williams, 1996; Hennessey, 2000).

Yet IR has only recently turned its attention to the politics of identity.[12] Earlier accounts for the most part took state-centric identities for granted, so much so that little effort was made to theorize even nationalist sentiments. As one consequence, IR was ill-prepared to comprehend the momentous developments that culminated in the 'fall' of communism, or to contribute much to the analysis of ethnic conflicts as these increasingly shape world politics. Similarly, religion and its enduring effects on identity and activity, including state and intra-state conflicts, are rarely a focus of conventional IR studies; nor are the pervasive effects of culture, broadly conceived. These important omissions are due in part to disciplinary assumptions that relegate the study of mental states, emotional commitments, and socio-cultural phenomena to psychology, sociology and the humanities. It also reflects positivist/empiricist acceptance of dichotomies that privilege science, reason, structures and the public as appropriate subjects of study, at the expense of religion, emotion, culture and the private as unsuitable subjects for study in IR. This of course exacerbates the divide between structural and cultural, material and textual, modernist and postmodernist that distinguishes the dominant epistemologies in social science and humanities and hence prevents more holistic and productive knowledge of social phenomena. It also prevents IR from developing richer, more adequate and more politically astute analyses within its own field of expertise.

Conclusion

This chapter has argued that we need new mapping strategies to situate ourselves and effectively negotiate the unfamiliar terrain of globalized 'new times' and a new world order. Empirical and epistemological challenges interact to problematize conventional accounts of epistemology, identity, states and markets. In the latter, foundational dichotomies set the boundaries of epistemological assumptions (fact-value, empirical-analytical, structural-textual), disciplinary fields (politics-economics, political science-IR, sciences-humanities), politically salient identifications (citizen-alien, scholar-activist, men-women), and the meaning of politics and power (public-private, domestic-international, coercive-discursive). Yet precisely these dichotomies and the 'grounds' they establish are brought into question by today's empirical and epistemological turbulence.

To address these challenges and as a contribution to new mapping strategies, I introduced an alternative 'triad analytics.' This framing juxtaposes the familiar categories of concrete practices (actions, institutions, social structures, etc.) construed as 'what we do,' and abstract categories (concepts, language, ideology, etc.) construed as 'how we think'. But it insists on complicating this familiar juxtaposition in two crucial, even transformative, ways. First, it rejects oppositional framing in favour of understanding the material and symbolic relationally, that is, as *interactive* and *interdependent* (mutually constituting) features of social reality. They may be analytically distinguished for heuristic purposes, but they are inextricable in reality. Second, this framing insists that 'what we do' and 'how we think' are also inextricable from 'who we are.' This draws our attention to issues of identity, personhood and subjectivity that have been too long neglected, even excluded, from socio-political theories, and especially, accounts of power and politics.

In sum, triad analytics rejects oppositional dichotomies in favour of *relational* thinking and mapping; it alerts us to the power of identity dynamics in political practice and theory; and it permits more holistic, dynamic and critical (because reflexive) understandings of social reality. It offers not a definitive map (a contradiction in terms) but a definitive shift in mapping strategies, and a more productive orientation to unstable terrain.

Notes

1. As further clarification, I understand positivism/empiricism as a commitment to epistemic realism ('whereby the world comprises objects the existence of which is independent of ideas or beliefs about them' [Campbell, 1992: 4]) and its corollary metaphysics of binary oppositions (assuming a correspondence theory of truth and categorically separating subject and object, fact and value). These commitments are distinguished from interpretive positions that understand language, knowledge and power as co-constitutive. I take the latter to be the common insight that distinguishes poststructuralism and postmodernism (and what Campbell [1992: 247] casts as the logic of interpretation) definitively from positivism/empiricism (which rejects this co-constitution) and arguably from constructivism (insofar as it theorizes power differently) and critical theories (insofar as they theorize language differently). While I applaud the recent expansion of constructivist approaches in IR (see especially Locher and Prügl [2001]; but also Kinsella [2003]), I understand constructivism as more positivist than interpretive: it acknowledges that concepts and ideas can have material consequences, and insists on the interaction of agent and structure, thus importantly "softening" the rigid separations of positivism and complicating reductionist analyses. But it remains tied to positivist claims of objectivity (understood as requiring access to some ahistorical fixity of meaning, some version of unmediated, pre-discursive reality) and a referential model of language. Over-simply, constructivists acknowledge that language shapes power but not that it *constitutes* power, that it produces power. Lack of agreement on how to characterize ontological and epistemological starting points renders this both an oversimplified and contestable description of complex distinctions and relationships. I caution the reader against assuming too much from this brief description and offer it simply to help situate my argument.
2. For important recent work on finance and risk, see Deuchars (2004); Best (2005); De Goede (2005); Sinclair (2005).
3. Youngs (1999: 4) refers to the 'superficial paradigmatism' of IR, which 'emphasizes distinctions rather than connections across different theoretical approaches.' On feminist studies in IR, international political economy (IPE) and global political economy (GPE), see Zalewski (2002); Chowdhry and Nair (2002); Peterson (2002, 2005); Agathangelou and Ling (2004); Tickner (2005); Waylen (2006); Steans (2006).
4. My comments here presuppose an interpretive feminism (see note 1) that rejects positivist essentializing binaries. Feminists vary significantly in terms of ontological and epistemological commitments, and not all share my critique of binary oppositions.
5. I make this point especially because resistance to interpretive/poststructuralist positions is often justified by casting them (mistakenly, I believe) as anti-political. See Hewitson

(1999: 21–29) for a succinct and especially clear rebuttal of the most frequently voiced criticisms against interpretive/poststructuralist approaches.

6. I elaborate these points and their implications for bridging feminist and queer theories in Peterson (1999) and in much greater depth in Peterson (2003).

7. I use 'analytics' rather than 'theory' or 'analytical framework' to convey in one word a sense of the positive connotation of pattern or order (as in the structure of a theory, how its parts fit together) without the negative connotation of being static (which attends the alternative reference to 'analytical framework').

8. In terms of individual identities, we are all 'subjected' to gender-specific socialization. As a consequence, we do not think about or act in the world as abstract 'humans' but as embodied, acculturated, therefore gendered (and raced, classed, etc.) beings. Whatever other identities we simultaneously embrace, and deem in particular situations to be most salient, gender is never wholly absent. The argument is that gender shapes (though it does not determine and need not dominate) all of our identities, or subjectivities. Consider how race, age, class, sexuality, ethnicity, ability and nationality have differently patterned meanings and therefore constitute differently patterned experiences for women and men. Moreover, the dichotomy of gender identities is inextricable from the history and practice of heterosexism, so that 'who we are' can appear both obvious (insofar as the male-female dichotomy is assumed and reproduced through categorical distinctions in appearance and performance of sexed identities) and deeply complicated (insofar as the sex binary itself is a social construction, and gender and sexuality are complex and fluid).

9. Important recent work on war and empire includes Harvey (2003); Eisenstein (2004); Waylen and Rai (2004); Youngs (2006).

10. Some recent analyses include Peterson (2003); Mittelman (2004); Steger (2004); Eschle and Maiguashca (2005); Rupert and Solomon (2006); Hawkesworth (2006).

11. Examples from diverse perspectives include Camilleri et al. (1995); Strange (1996); Shaw (1997); Youngs (1999, 2007); Palan (2000); Tetreault et al. (2003); De Goede (2006); Payne (2006). For specifically feminist treatments of IPE see, e.g., Marchand and Runyan (2000); Rai (2002); Bakker and Gill (2003); Peterson (2003, 2005); Waylen (2006).

12. See, for example, Lapid and Kratochwil (1996); Peterson (1999); Doty (1996); Keyman (1997); Zalewski and Parpart (1998); Ling (2001); Hooper (2001); Persaud and Walker (2001); Smith and Owens (2005).

References

Agathangelou, A. M. and Ling, L. H. M. (2004) 'The house of IR: from family power politics to the *Poisies* of worldism', *International Studies Review*, 6 (21), 21–49.

Alexander, M. J. and Mohanty, C. T. (eds) (1997) *Feminist Genealogies, Colonial Legacies, Democratic Futures*, New York, Routledge.

Bakker, I. and Gill, S. (eds) (2003) *Power, Production and Social Reproduction: Human In/security in the Global Political Economy*, Houndsmill, Hampshire, Palgrave Macmillan.

Best, J. (2005) *The Limits of Transparency: Ambiguity and the History of International Finance*, Ithaca and London, Cornell University Press.

Bologh, R. (1987) 'Marx, Weber, and masculine theorizing' in N. Wiley (ed.), *The Marx-Weber Debate*, Beverly Hills, CA, Sage.

Buzan, B. and Little, R. (2000) 'Why international relations has failed as an intellectual project, and what to do about it', paper presented at the 41st Annual Convention of the International Studies Association, Los Angeles, CA.

Camilleri, J., Jarvis, A. P. and Paolini, A. J. (eds) (1995) 'Preface' in *The State in Transition*, Boulder, CO, Lynne Rienner Publishers.

Campbell, D. (1992) *Writing Security: United States Foreign Policy and the Politics of Identity*, Manchester, Manchester University Press.

Chowdhry, G. and Nair, S. (eds) (2002) *Power, Postcolonialism and International Relations: Reading Race, Gender and Class*, New York, Routledge.

De Goede, M. (2005) *Virtue, Fortune and Faith: A Genealogy of Finance*, Minneapolis, University of Minnesota Press.

———. (ed.) (2006) *International Political Economy and Poststructural Politics*, London, Palgrave.

De Grazia, V. and Furlough, E. (eds) (1996) *The Sex of Things: Gender and Consumption in Historical Perspective*, Berkeley, University of California Press.

Deuchars, R. (2004). *The International Political Economy of Risk: Rationalism, Calculation and Power*, Hampshire, Ashgate.

Doty, R. (1996) *Imperial Encounters: The Politics of Representation in North-South Relations*, Minneapolis, University of Minnesota Press.

Eisenstein, Z. R. (2004) *Against Empire: Feminisms, Racisms, and the West*, London, Zed Books.

Eschle, C. and Maiguashca, B. (eds) (2005) *Critical Theories, International Relations and 'the Anti-Globalization Movement': The Politics of Global Resistance*, London and New York, Routledge.

Ferguson, Y. H. and Mansbach. R. W. (1996) *Polities: Authority, Identities and Change*, Columbia, SC, University of South Carolina Press.

Firat, A. Fuat. (1994) 'Gender and Consumption: Transcending the Feminine?' in J. A. Costa (ed.), *Gender Issues and Consumer Behavior*, Provo, UT, Association for Consumer Research, pp. 205–28.

Friedman, J. (1994) *Consumption and Identity*, London, Harwood Academic Press.

Grewal, I. and Kaplan, C. (eds) (1994) *Scattered Hegemonies: Postmodernity and Transnational Feminist Practices*, Minneapolis, University of Minnesota Press.

Harding, S. (1986) *The Science Question in Feminism*, Ithaca, NY, Cornell University Press.

———. (1991) *Whose Science? Whose Knowledge?*, Ithaca, NY, Cornell University Press.

Harvey, D. (2003) *The New Imperialism*, Oxford, Oxford University Press.

Hawkesworth, M. E. (2006) *Globalization and Feminist Activism*, Lanham, Rowman and Littlefield.

Hekman, S. J. (1990) *Gender and Knowledge: Elements of a Postmodern Feminism*, Cambridge, Polity Press.

Hennessey, R. (2000) *Profit and Pleasure: Sexual Identities in Late Capitalism*, New York and London, Routledge.

Hewitson, G. J. (1999) 'Conclusion,' in *States of Conflict: Gender, Violence and Resistance*, London, Zed Books, pp. 217–37.

Keyman, E. Fuat. (1997) *Globalization, State, Identity/Difference*, Atlantic Highlands, NJ, Humanities Press.

Kinsella, H. (2003) 'For a careful reading: the conservativism of gender constructivism', *International Studies Review*, 5, 294–97.

Lapid, Y. and Kratochwil, F. (eds) (1996) *The Return of Culture and Identity in International Relations Theory*, Boulder, CO, Lynne Rienner.

Ling, L. (2001) *Postcolonial Learning: Conquest and Desire between Asia and the West*, London, Palgrave.

Locher, B. and Prügl, E. (2001) 'Feminism and constructivism: worlds apart or sharing the middle ground?' *International Studies Quarterly*, 45 (1), 111–29.

Marchard, M. H. and Runyan, A. S. (2000) 'Introduction' in M. H. Marchand and A. S. Runyan (eds), *Gender and Global Restructuring: Sightings, Sites and Resistances*, London, Routledge, pp. 1–22.

McClintock, A. (1995) *Imperial Leather: Race, Gender and Sexuality in the Colonial Contest,* New York, Routledge.

Merchant, C. (1980) *The Death of Nature: Women, Ecology and the Scientific Revolution,* New York, Harper and Row.

Mittelman, J. H. (2004) *Whither Globalization? The Vortex of Knowledge and Ideology,* London and New York, Routledge.

Mohanty, C. H. (2003) *Feminism Without Borders: Decolonizing Theory, Practicing Solidarity,* Durham, NC, Duke University Press.

Palan, R. (ed.) (2000) *Global Political Economy: Contemporary Theories,* London and New York, Routledge.

Payne, A. (ed.) (2006) *Key Debates in New Political Economy,* London and New York, Routledge.

Persaud, R. B. and Walker, R. B. J. (2001) '*Apertura*: Race in International Relations', *Alternatives,* 26 (4), 373–76.

Peterson, V. S. (1992) 'Transgressing boundaries: theories of knowledge, gender, and international relations', *Millennium,* 21 (2), 183–206.

———. (1999) 'Sexing political identity/nationalism as heterosexism', *International Feminist Journal of Politics,* 1 (1), 21–52.

———. (2000) 'Rereading public and private: the dichotomy that is not one', *SAIS Review* XX, 2, Summer–Fall, 11–29.

———. (2002) 'On the Cut(ting) Edge' in M. Brecher and F. Harvey (eds), *Critical Paradigms in International Studies,* Ann Arbor, University of Michigan Press, pp.148–63.

———. (2003) *A Critical Rewriting of Global Political Economy: Integrating Reproductive, Productive, and Virtual Economies,* London and New York, Routledge.

———. (2005) 'How (the meaning of) gender matters in political economy', *New Political Economy,* 10 (4), 499–521.

Peterson, V. S. and Runyan, A. S. (1999) *Global Gender Issues,* 2nd ed., Boulder, CO, Westview Press.

Rai, S. M. (2002) *Gender and the Political Economy of Development,* Cambridge, Polity.

Ruggie, J. G (1993) 'Territoriality and beyond: problematizing modernity in international Relations, *International Organization,* 47 (1), 139–74.

Rupert, M. and Solomon, M. S. (2006) *Globalization and International Political Economy: The Politics of Alternative Futures,* Lanham, MD, Rowman & Littlefield.

Shaw, M. (1997) 'The state of globalization: towards a theory of state transformation', *Review of International Political Economy,* 4 (3), 497–513.

Sinclair, T. J. (2005) *The New Masters of Capital: American Bond Rating Agencies and the Politics of Credit-worthiness,* Ithaca, NY, Cornell University Press.

Smith, S. and Owens, P. (2005) 'Alternative approaches to international theory' in J. Baylis and S. Smith (eds), *The Globalization of World Politics: An Introduction to International Relations,* 3rd ed., Oxford, Oxford University Press, pp. 271–93.

Steans, J. (2006) *Gender and International Relations,* 2nd ed., New Brunswick, NJ, Rutgers University Press.

Steger, M. B. (ed.) (2004) *Rethinking Globalism,* Lanham, MD, Rowman & Littlefield.

Strange, S. (1996) *Retreat of the State: The Diffusion of Power in the World Economy,* Cambridge, Cambridge University Press.

Tetreault, M. A., Denemark, R. A., Thomas, K. P. and Burch, K. (eds) (2003) *Rethinking Global Political Economy: Emerging Issues, Unfolding Odysseys,* London and New York, Routledge.

Tickner, J. A. (2005) 'What is your research program? Some feminist answers to international relations methodological questions', *International Studies Quarterly,* 49, 1–21.

Waylen, G. (2006) 'You still don't understand: why troubled engagements continue between feminists and (critical) IPE', *Review of International Studies,* 32, 145–64.

Waylen, G. and Shirin, M. R. (eds) (2004) 'Special issue: gender, governance and globalization, *International Feminist Journal of Politics,* 6 (4).

Williams, S. (1996) 'Globalization, privatization, and a feminist public', *Indiana Journal of Global Legal Studies*, 4, 97–105.

Youngs, G. (1999) *International Relations in a Global Age*, Cambridge, Polity.

———. (ed) (2006) 'Theme issue: feminist international relations in the age of the war on terror: ideologies, religions and conflict', *International Feminist Journal of Politics*, 8 (1).

———. (2007) *Global Political Economy in the Information Age: Power and Inequality*, London, Routledge.

Yuval-Davis, N. (1997) *Gender and Nation*, London, Sage.

Yuval-Davis, N. and Anthias, F. (eds) (1989) *Woman-Nation-State*, London, Macmillan Press.

Zalewski, M. (2002) 'Feminism and/in international relations' in M. Brecher and F. Harvey (eds), *Millennial Reflections on International Studies*, Ann Arbor, University of Michigan Press, pp. 330–41.

Zalewski, M. and Parpart, J. (eds) (1998) *The "Man" Question in International Relations*, Boulder, CO, Westview.

CHAPTER 9

Gender Inequalities and Feminist Politics in a Global Perspective

Jill Steans

Introduction

In the past decade, feminist scholars have cut into the globalization debate in distinctive ways. While there is no one uniform approach, collectively, this body of work has shown how gender is central to our understanding of the material, ideological and discursive dimensions of globalization (Marchand and Runyan, 2000; Basu et al., 2001; Guzman, 2002; Rai, 2002; Beneria, 2003; Peterson, 2003; Sarker and Niyogi De, 2003; Chow, 2003; Davids, 2005). In recent years, our understanding of the world gender order has also been greatly enhanced by work that focuses on men and masculinities in relation to patterns of investment, trade and communication in the world economy and in global financial institutions (Connell, 1998). While there is no one approach to globalization, feminists concur that attempts to understand globalization, or indeed any other phenomenon with profound social, economic and political consequences are inevitably driven by normative concerns. As with much critical analyses, feminist approaches take seriously issues of power and exclusion in dominant – that is, neoliberal – discourses of globalization (Carr and Chen, 2004). For example, feminist approaches to globalization point to the ideological nature of so-called 'value free' economic theories. By concentrating on the impersonal structures of states and markets, it is not possible to see how women's activities have been demoted to the 'private' sphere, nor is it possible to see that women and men enter into the formal economy as the bearer of a gender identity (Tickner, 1992; Sylvester, 1994).

Feminist work on globalization addresses a number of core concerns: the impacts of global restructuring, notably changing working practices and new forms and conditions of employment; the changing role of the state and the relationship between the state, the market and the household, particularly in regard to health and social-welfare provision; new and enduring forms of inequality, including inequalities in the distribution of resources both locally and globally; the domain of national, regional and international governance; and how ideas are themselves significant in producing and reproducing certain kinds of social relations of inequality (Dominelli, 1991; Afshar and Berrientos, 1999; Wichterich, 2000; Breman et al., 2000; Marchand and Runyan, 2000; Dickenson and Scaeffer, 2001; Black and Brainerd, 2002; Pyle and Ward, 2003; Oostendorp, 2004; Hausman et al., 2006).

Feminist analyses go beyond the gender-specific 'impacts' of globalization, to explore the ways in which gender is relevant to our understanding of emerging sites of resistance (Moghadam, 1999; Marchand and Runyan, 2000; Amoore, 2000; Brawley, 2003). In the usage employed in this paper, 'feminist politics' refers to the strategies adopted by a large, and in many ways diverse, group of non-governmental organizations (NGOs) to influence decision-making and policy-making processes at national, regional and international levels (Pietila and Vickers, 1994; Meyer and Prugl, 1999). Women are not always passive victims of globalizing forces beyond their control. A 'transnational women's movement', forged around a normative identification with women's rights and/or other key gender issues, has gradually emerged since the United Nations (UN) Decade for Women (1976–85). In contesting specific forms of gender inequality in national, regional and global contexts, women's NGOs are also 'challenging and thereby refashioning globalization' (Harcourt, 1999: 403).

The first section of this chapter views globalization through 'gender lenses' (Runyan and Peterson, 1993). It traces out the global dimensions of gender inequalities and identifies a number of key global gender issues. The second section sketches some of the ways in which feminist groups and women's NGOs have attempted to bring these issues to global attention, play a role in shaping debates in policy-making forums at national, regional and international levels and, in some cases, push for alternative strategies and policies to improve the status and position of women in different societies throughout the world.

Gender inequality in global perspective

This chapter starts from the position that gender inequalities must be viewed in global perspective. In part, this is because when adopting a global perspective, it quickly becomes evident that gender remains a significant indicator of social inequality in all societies across the world. While the lives of women in different societies across the world are in many respects different, the position of women globally reveals many similarities. Women operate in a disadvantaged position in all societies, although the nature of that disadvantage may vary. Gender inequalities that derived from cultural beliefs or practices often perpetuate the lower status accorded women in the family, the workplace, community and society and continue to be a pervasive factor in women's experience of poverty (Nussbaum, 2000)[1]. The effects of globalization have been gender-differentiated because of the differences between men and women in terms of access to and control over assets and economic resources (Cagatay and Erturk, 2004). Although Bhagwati (2004) has defended globalization as a powerful force for social good in the world, recent work casts doubt on this contention:

> The world economy has neither produced sustained growth rates, nor significant poverty reduction over the past two decades. Just as growth does not automatically trickle down to the poor households, nor do incomes increases in poor households automatically trickle down to women and girls. (Cagalay and Erturk, 2004: v)

While a 2006 report by the World Economic Forum revealed that:

> Gender-based inequality is a phenomenon that transcends the majority of the world's cultures, religions, nations and income groups in most societies, the

differences and inequalities between men and women are manifest in responsibilities each assign, in activities they undertake, in their access to and control over resources and in decision-making opportunities. (Hausman et al., 2006: 3)

Moreover, though the specific and cultural contexts cannot be ignored, it is evident that globalization has generated new forms of inequality between nations, regions and social groups, marked by class, gender and ethnicity (World Bank, 2006). Thus globalization is leading to more complex forms of social relations and social inequalities that are, in part, explained by the outcomes of trade agreements[2], investment strategies, the changing international division of labour, the uneven nature of economic growth and differential distribution of debt, resources and incomes across countries and social groups and, in part, by political responses at national, regional and international levels (Carr and Chen, 2004; Oostendorp, 2004; Cagatay and Erturk, 2004).

Gender inequalities are not easily disentangled from inequalities rooted in class, or that arise from racial or ethnic discrimination and one must be sensitive to the specificity of gender relations within particular cultures and societies.[3] A key concern of feminist scholarship has been the need to develop a richer, more nuanced conception of globalization that addresses social relations of inequality, marked by gender, ethnicity and class. Feminist scholarship has also been particularly attuned to issues of specificity and difference. Feminists have guarded against the privileging of the global at the expense of the local (Runyan, 1996; Basu et al., 2001). Gender relations have to be understood in terms of specific societies and cultures, but also in relation to dynamic interactions between global and local sites (Steans, 1999).

Global restructuring: opportunities and inequalities

To some degree, globalization has opened up new possibilities for women to enter the workplace which in turn has played a role in shaping and reshaping women's (and men's) identities and expectations (True, 2003). The changing nature of production and labour relations has framed many of the key questions and issues within the social sciences, but until relatively recently, it has been the changing face of labour in the public realm – men's labour – that has been the main focus of attention. It has been assumed that relations between the state, the market and the domestic or private realm are mediated through male heads of households.

However, in the past two decades, women have entered the paid workforce in all OECD countries in increasing numbers, partly as a consequence of de-industrialization and moves to a service economy (Birdsall and Graham, 2000). The degree to which women have entered paid employment in countries across the world has varied to some degree according to cultural context and according to the age and marital status of women in specific societies. Nevertheless, there has been an overall increase in the number of women working in the formal economy as a result of a combination of factors that range from financial necessity, particularly in heavily indebted countries and/or where men have been forced to migrate as a consequence of declining employment opportunities in local and national economies, to the desire for an independent income that then widens the realm of choice and autonomy that individual women might enjoy. The employment of women has also been encouraged by national and international development agencies because this has been seen as a way of improving the status of women in specific societies.[4]

However, the increase in women's employment cannot in itself be taken as evidence of a trend towards greater gender equality. The benefits or costs to women of 'opportunities' opened up by globalization have varied according to a range of factors. Women who are highly trained, well-educated and have marketable skills have often benefited from expanding employment opportunities in OECD countries and in the transitional economies of the former Eastern bloc (Harris and Seid, 2000; True, 2003). To some degree, globalization has challenged conventional ideas about gender roles. For example, the EU claims that the shift in the European economy increasingly towards the service sector and greater flexibility in working times and locations, has brought about changes in family roles and challenged conventional gender relations built around the male breadwinner, female homemaker model of gender relations. (Commission of the European Communities, 1995). It is certainly the case that in many OECD countries, the decline of the male 'breadwinner' and female 'homemaker' roles and the gendered division of responsibilities embedded in such constructions, have been undermined to some degree by the decline of heavy industry and manufacturing and consequent increases in male unemployment.

However, the demise of Fordism has coincided with a decline and weakening of organised labour. New employment opportunities for women tend to be in the expanding service sectors of economies or as a result of growth in flexible and part-time employment (Birdsall and Graham, 2000; Dickenson and Schaeffer, 2001). Women still continue to bear the major burden of responsibilities for the family and the home in societies across the world. In the developing world particularly, women are especially vulnerable to economic recessions or shock:

> Such events worsen women's already inadequate access to healthcare, schooling and job training. Women's burden of unpaid work increases as families try to save on paying for health care and other services. With less of a say in decision making, women have less protection for the rights and are left more exposed to threats associated with economic crisis. (Fukuda-Parr, 2004: 39)

Thus, while globalization might work to challenge to some degree the meaning and implications of gender constructions in specific societies, gender-determined lifestyles continue to push women towards certain types of employment that are relatively low paid and insecure (Birdsall and Graham, 2000). It is widely acknowledged that in the past two decades the position of such marginal workers has deteriorated as a consequence of 'transformations in the global economy that have affected all industrial democracies' (Pierson, 1994: 182). Many countries and governments in the South particularly lack the resources and mechanisms to protect those who have lost livelihoods in the context of globalization (Cagatay and Erturk, 2004, 43).

Of course, capitalism by its very nature generates inequalities in outcomes, in terms of the distribution of property, incomes and resources more generally. One might argue that social inequalities are not necessarily a problem or concern if the overall effect of globalization is to facilitate economic activity, generate growth and help to bring about the conditions in which a reduction in overall levels of poverty and higher levels of human welfare becomes possible. However, globalization is seemingly characterised by a dichotomy between economic and technological changes and social progress. Even in areas of the world where economic growth has been rapid, this growth has not been matched by social progress in general terms and by improvements in relative position of women in particular (UNDP, 2000). In the developing world, there is some evidence that the occupational gender wage gap falls with increasing economic development and trade, but this is not always the case:

> The lack of evidence of a narrowing impact and evidence of a widening impact of FDI net inflows on the high skill occupational gender gap in poorer countries shows that globalization may not lower and in some instances increases the gender gap. This finding complements earlier studies documenting an increase in wage inequality after trade liberalization in a number of developing countries. (Oostendorp, 2004: 31)

As the least unionised and most poorly paid of all workers, women have been particularly vulnerable to market policies that have characterised global economic restructuring in the 1990s. While some women have gained in terms of employment, others, who are less skilled or who have little control over assets, have lost their livelihoods as a result of import competition (Catagay and Erturk, 2004). Where women have taken up paid work, they tend to earn less than men for comparable tasks, work longer hours and make up a disproportionate number of people working in the informal sector. Such new opportunities for paid work are reversible as a result of the entry of newcomers into the international arena, technological upgrading in exports or the relocation of capital to other countries (Catagay and Erturk: 2004: 43).

Attempts to translate paid employment into financial independence for women are often thwarted by lack of access to capital, inadequate education and training and by unequal burden of family responsibilities. In many areas of the world, the burden of debt and of economic policies, which are themselves conditioned by international processes, contribute to further gender divisions within societies (Hooper, 1994a). In many developing countries, the employment of women rather than men in Export Production Zones has occurred because women have been seen as a relatively cheap and passive workforce, although, there is growing evidence that women are now joining trade unions in increasing numbers (Marchand, 1995; Moghadam, 1999; Carr and Chen, 2004).

The changing relationship between states, markets and households

Feminist analysis of globalization extends not only to transformations between economy and state, but also between the state, the economy and the household. Gender relations are not locked into the realm of the cultural or private, but are rather socially produced and reproduced in relation to division between the 'public' and 'private'. Gender is a key factor in the social division of labour between the public world of work and the so-called 'informal economy' of the home and domestic servicing and reproduction.

The state does not simply reflect social or cultural values in relation to gender roles and the distribution of social resources, but rather reproduces gender relations by legislating in the area of marriage, divorce and family law, in the domain of policy-making on family planning and sexual health, as well as welfare and unemployment entitlements, labour legislation, taxation and rights of citizenship more generally. For example, in the post–Second

World War period, the male breadwinner/female homemaker as the 'norm' of gender relations underpinned welfare provision and social policy in many OECD countries (Mishra, 1996: 25; Dickenson and Schaeffer, 2001). Some feminists were critical of the welfare state because of its perceived patriarchal nature (Dominelli, 1991). And yet, some benefits did accrue to women through welfare provision or child-care benefits, for example, and so the question of how far and in what areas states now choose to re-negotiate the boundaries of the public and the private are of great significance.

A major theme to emerge from the early globalization literature was that a shift in decision-making power from the state to the market place was occurring. The capacity of governments to control events within nation-states and national economies was also reduced by the flow of decision-making power away from national institutions to supranational entities like the IMF and regional bodies like the OECD and the European Union (EU). In developing countries, the autonomy of the state was circumscribed to a much greater degree perhaps, as United Nations development agencies and especially multilateral economic institutions like the World Bank and IMF played a greater role in devising development strategies, grounded in neoliberal economic principles, that promoted marketization and moves to export led growth strategies around the world. Contemporary approaches to globalization are more likely to recognise that globalization is mediated through the political economy of the nation-state (Weiss, 1999). However, the state operates in the context of global economic trends that over time engender shifts in its own roles and functions (Mishra, 1996). Over the past decade, an increasing number of commentators have called for the state to assume a bigger role in ameliorating inequalities (Stiglitz, 2003). However:

> The neoliberal policies of the past two decades have further constrained the capacity of the state to address the needs of women and girls. Gender bias in macro-economic policies, which have always existed, have been further accentuated. (Catagay and Erturk, 2004: 43)

To some degree these 'global trends' have encouraged a shift away from the 'social democratic' model of citizenship in many Western countries since the late 1970s, as states have placed greater emphasis on the efficacy of the market over the state in the provision of many welfare 'goods' and services. Again, one must be careful not to overstate the degree to which the state has cut back welfare provision, or withdrawn from areas like health-care provision and social policy. It is evident that the degree to which responsibility for such areas of life continues to fall on states or is shifted to the private sector or to the family depends on a number of factors including the ideological disposition of governments and their core constituencies of support (Newman, 2001). Nevertheless, globalization and 'the structural dependence of the welfare state on a relatively closed economy' have been put forward as significant factors in explaining welfare state retrenchment in many OECD countries (Mishra, 1996: 5). The impact on women of shifts in policy and especially public provision varies according to class. The impact on upper- and middle-class women has been cushioned somewhat by their ability to obtain services from the market, while the position of lower-class women has significantly worsened. However, overall welfare reform, or cutbacks more generally, have a disproportionate impact on women, particularly where they work to transfer the burden of care from the public to the private sphere.

It has long been recognised that women are primarily responsible for the general health and welfare of whole societies. Indeed, recognition of the crucial role that women play here has underpinned development strategies promoted by UN agencies, that have simultane-ously sought to promote the status of women, for example in health, education, control of reproductive function, access to independent income and credit, or in some cases, to support women in their 'traditional' roles. Today, in many developing countries, the need to earn hard currency to service debt is prioritised over government expenditure on welfare, re-sulting in a deterioration of health and welfare for poorer people especially and increasing the burden of unpaid work on women particularly. In parts of the world, girls are still less likely to get food and health care than boys. Sustainable development cannot be achieved unless measures are taken to slow down the growth of the world's population, yet some 300 million women world wide still have no access to effective family planning and contra-ceptive services. Underlying issues of population growth and sustainable development are more fundamental problems of poverty and inequality that affect decisions on the number and spacing of pregnancies (Hartmann, 1995).

The degree to which women are disproportionately affected by economic restructuring is by no means confined to the 'developing' world. In Central and Eastern Europe, there is evidence that women are losing jobs as the region adjusts to the rigours of the global market-place and are also taking up the burden of care which results from cuts in the social sector. Some women have benefited from the transition to the market, but the decline in state provision of health care, housing and certain welfare benefits has had an adverse impact on poorer women. Others have suffered significant losses.

Feminist politics

Understanding feminist politics

There still exists a widespread 'common-sense' assumption that gender inequality can only be properly understood in the context of particular cultural values and practices. Our con-ceptual maps have tended to reinforce ideas or images of the world as neatly divided into territorially bounded nation-states and national cultures. Thus, strategies devised to im-prove the status of women are sometimes resisted on the grounds that they 'interfere with culture' or infringed upon sovereignty. Similarly, feminism is often presented as a Western ideology of no relevance to women in developing world. The 'second wave' globalization literature, to which the first edition of this book made a valuable contribution, called into question conventional methods of conducting social inquiry which utilised a nation-state framework. In challenging the nation-state (national culture) framework, the characterisa-tion of gender as a private or cultural matter, or feminism as a Western ideology, is called into question. Feminist analysis also highlights the ways in which identities are formed and mapped into symbolic and political identifications which are both narrower and wider than the nation-state and nationalist constructions of identity (Steans, 2006). This is evidenced in the growth of a transnational women's movement that is held together by a normative commitment to greater gender equality and an improvement in the status of women across the world.

Adopting a strong cultural relativist position on gender and gender inequality is prob-lematic for many reasons, not least of which is the problem of the appropriation of discourses of 'culture' and 'tradition' to serve the interests of certain social groups and/or elites. The notion of a distinctive national culture, for example, disguises internal differences within nations marked by gender and class, and minority cultural groups. Positing some imagined homogenous community belies the degree of contestation that can and often does exist on issues of 'culture' and on what 'tradition' requires (Nussbaum, 2002). Culture and values are not static but change over time. At certain moments agents can have considerable influence in reshaping expectation and identities and in facilitating the emergence of new frameworks of social organization. Feminism is no more foreign than socialism or nationalism. The growth of a feminist movement within certain societies has been linked to the rise of secular, nationalist movements in parts of the third world in reaction to imperialism (Jayawardena, 1986).

Feminist analysis of globalization challenges the 'common sense' view that gender discrimination is only a matter for particular cultures, or a 'domestic' issue, of concern to sovereign states only, if at all. Today Western ideologies, values, technologies and commercialism impact an increasing number of societies and people. Processes of globalization networks, including migration and the growth and spread of transnational communication, break down cultural boundaries to some degree. Powerful gendered images disseminated by telecommunications and global media bring alternative representations of gender roles and values, while the introduction of fertility-control techniques also poses fundamental challenges to indigenous cultural values and traditional practices. To interpret the spread of Western values as a form of imperialist domination is also something of an oversimplification. For example, the discourse of human rights has been embraced by a wide variety of groups in their efforts to achieve democratic reform, or to otherwise challenge authoritarian political regimes (Lawson, 1998). Moreover, people and communities have always been open to ideas from other societies and cultures. The social and cultural meaning and knowledge available to people is not confined to the boundaries of nations and/or states. To some degree, today human rights, democracy and, indeed, feminism are all ideas that are known 'inside' most societies (Nussbaum, 2000).

Resisting neoliberal globalization

Economic restructuring, debt, even the negotiation of trade agreements can and do create the conditions for transnational alliances which in turn press for social and economic change (Brawley, 2003; Amoore, 2000). Women's resistance to global processes might take the form of agitation for more transnational union representation in both factory and home-based work (Moghadam, 1999). Moghadam argues that: "massive entry into the work force whether as professionals or proletariat has coincided with the political mobilisation of women and the expansion of women organising" (1999: 379).

However, women have mobilised also as critics of neoliberal globalization in transnational feminist networks (Moghadam, 1999: 379). Jan Pettman identifies organizations like GABRIELA in the Philippines, the Third World Movement Against the Exploitation of Women and EMPOWER, the campaign to end child prostitution in Asia, as examples of women using their own experiences as a point from which to assess and construct knowledge and theory of global political economy and develop strategies for change. In this process international alliances are forged. While Pettman recognises that there is no homogeneous identity among women, she also notes many common experiences which open up oppor-tunities for alliances around key issues (Pettman, 1998).

Gender relations are open to bargaining like other forms of social relations and amenable to change. Gender issues – previously considered private or cultural – have been brought into the realm of politics. For example, violence against women which has previously been regarded as a private matter, or something that might be condoned in certain cultures under specific circumstances, is now commonly accepted as a violation of human rights (Chinkin, 1999). Recognition of violence against women as a human rights issue necessarily challenges the sanctity of the patriarchal family structure and the role of men in mediating relations between women and the state.

In foregrounding issues of gender, feminist approaches to globalization are careful not to neglect the continuing relevance of the local, the specific and the cultural in understanding how globalization impacts specific societies and gender relations particularly. It is not the status of feminism and feminist analysis as such that is problematic, therefore, but rather a lack of sensitivity on the part of the theorist towards questions of difference. Chandra Mo-hanty has argued that feminist solidarity can only be achieved if activists and feminist theorists are attentive to the experiences and voices of marginalized communities of women and make efforts to construct an inclusive paradigm for thinking about social justice. This 'particularised viewing allows for a more concrete and expansive vision of universal justice' (Mohanty, 2002: 511).

Human dignity can be realized and protected in various ways. In certain cultural con-texts, the meanings attached to femininity and masculinity can serve to give women social power that translates into particular claims to resources. Moreover, some aspects of culture and national identity are clearly embraced and enjoyed by women. It cannot be simply assumed that all women share a singular collective identity and common interests by virtue of their gender alone.

The 'transnational women's movement' is not a monolithic entity, but reflects differ-ences and diversity among women (Grewal and Kaplan, 1994; Ferree and Martin, 1995). Indeed, as Tohidi argues, one fundamental challenge for any global feminist movement is that the conception, objectives and strategy of feminism in different nations and regions have become intertwined with very different economic, socio-cultural and political condi-tions (1994: 111). Clearly, one needs to view feminist politics in regional, national and local contexts too.

Strategies and objectives adopted by specific NGOs differ somewhat according to the specific issue area or interests of groups and how priorities are identified in different social, cultural and political contexts. In the run up to the Fourth United Nations Conference on Women held in Beijing in 1995, regional forums were set up to decide on priority issues for women in particular regions, which were then incorporated into NGO lobbying documents. Regional Expert Reports prepared for the Fourth UN Conference on Women in Beijing recognised explicitly, and indeed placed a great deal of emphasis upon, broad disparities between North and South, rural and urban and rich and poor women (Hooper, 1994a, 1994b, 1994c). In so doing, these reports demonstrated an awareness of how gender in-equalities were tied up with forms of inequality based on class or race or ethnicity. The implementation of a growing body of human rights laws often involves achieving a balance between respecting cultural diversity and promotion of women's human rights.

However, diversity and difference does not preclude solidarity on specific issues. As NGOs worked to modify the text of the Draft Platform of Action in the run up to the Beijing conference, they were concerned to make visible the massive economic inequalities that existed between women and that greatly add to the burden of not only women in the 'third world' but also working-class women and women from ethnic minorities in the West. Women's NGOs in Europe, Latin America and the Asia-Pacific were united in rejecting the dominant neoliberal economic paradigm that underpinned structural adjustment programmes and policy making at organizations like the World Bank because it was seen to be detrimental to rights of women. Throughout all stages of the preparatory process, NGOs worked to highlight the gender-specific effects of globalization and global restructuring and draw attention to the 'negative' and 'damaging' impact of structural adjustment policies forced on indebted states by the International Monetary Fund. Feminists have increasingly recognised the need to look at issues of low pay and poverty in a global context.

Furthermore, that issues of population growth, sustainable development, environmental degradation and reproductive rights are now being recognised as gender issues and finding their way on to the agenda of international politics, is in no small part due to pressure from NGOs. Feminist groups have stressed the urgency of overcoming poverty and addressing the needs of rural women, female-headed households and women who work in the informal sector. The problem of the 'double burden' has been raised as a concern not just for particular women but whole communities. Women's NGOs around the world have called for alternative development models that emphasise sustainability, equitable and humane development (DAWN, 1991). Access to food and water, appropriate technologies, recognition of both waged and unwaged work as essential to the social and economic well-being of countries have also been raised as key gender issues. NGOs have pressed for inclusion of unpaid work in national accounts and in social and economic indicators.[5] Thus, in this context, feminist politics has both reflected diversity and drawn upon some common problems and perceived interests among women, who are in other ways divided by class, ethnicity, nationality and other differences.

Feminist politics in global governance

Feminist politics needs to be understood in global perspective, because it is concerned with NGO activity in not only local and national sites but in regional and international settings. Moreover, the UN has played a key role in facilitating networking, providing the web that links non-governmental organizations across national borders. One of the ways in which NGOs have worked to promote awareness of gender issues and promote the status of women has been by utilising the platform offered by the UN conferences on women which have taken place since 1975 and which have attracted an ever-increasing number of participants, both at the inter-governmental level and in the parallel NGO forums.

Women's NGOs engage directly in processes and networks of global governance. The United Nations has long accepted that it has responsibilities in improving women's economic status; promoting women's education; improving access to reproductive health care; and in fully integrating women into the development programmes. In accepting these responsibilities, the UN has responded to pressure from NGOs. Since 1975 there have been four major UN conferences on women, which have resulted in concrete action plans to improve the status of women in all areas of life, including employment, reproductive health, family life, politics and human rights, and regular meetings to review progress. In 1985, at the Nairobi conference that drew the UN Decade for Women to close, a *Forward Looking*

Strategies for the Advancement of Women to the Year 2000 (FLSAW) document was produced that set an agenda that was later reviewed at Beijing.

Women's NGOs have been central to efforts to move gender issues from the margin to the centre in the UN's work. Following the UN Decade for Women, efforts began to mainstream – incorporate into policy as a matter of course – gender issues into development policies and projects. Since the beginning of the UN Decade for Women in 1976, most UN agencies have included sections that are specifically charged to advance the interests of women. As debates about gender and development have shifted from an emphasis on 'bringing women in', to an analysis of gender relations, to an understanding of the gender dimension of environmental concerns, and to human rights issues, 'mainstreaming' in common usage has also come to mean making gender a central concern in other areas within the remit of the UN's work. Thus the International Conference on Population and Development held in Cairo in 1994 saw the affirmation of women's empowerment as the key to successful population and development strategies, while the World Summit on Social Development, held in Copenhagen in 1995, afforded opportunities for NGOs to push for recognition of the relationship between female poverty, unemployment and attendant social disintegration.

In the current literature, much greater emphasis has been placed on the ideational or discursive dimensions of globalization (Hay and Marsh, 2000). This has led to more sustained attempts to understand the relationship between material forces – the complex set of structural transformations and changes in social relations across the world, generated by the competitive pressures of an increasingly global capitalist economy – and ideas, specifically the neoliberal rhetoric of globalization widely embraced by elites within business and commerce and among many national and international policy-makers. The rhetoric of globalization has involved dominant interpretations and claims about the nature, extent and implications of globalization that, in turn, set the boundaries of what is deemed to be 'appropriate' and 'feasible' in relation to policy-making.

During the 1980s and for much of the 1990s, the rules and 'norms' that have underpinned economic policy-making in organizations like the IMF and World Bank reflected an underlying set of neoliberal norms among elites, although there is evidence that today the World Bank at least recognises that the state must play a role in ameliorating inequalities, including gender inequalities. These same norms have been contested by oppositional groups. Women's groups have tried to shape the global rules and influence the decision-making process and in so doing have often raised explicit opposition to neoliberalism (Meyer and Prugl, 1999). During the 1980s and 1990s, feminist groups were among the most vocal critics of structural adjustment policies foisted on indebted countries across the South and former Eastern bloc by the IMF and World Bank. Many developing countries complain that goals agreed at UN conferences on poverty eradication, social progress and equality were being undermined by economic liberalization, structural adjustment policies, the continuing debt crisis, the decline in aid flows to developing countries and the attendant marginalization of countries and poor people (United Nations, 1995).

NGOs have become more influential since the UN conferred official status on them through the Economic and Social Council (ECOSOC). The Fourth UN Conference on Women was the largest UN conference up until that time. More NGOs than ever before were affiliated to the inter-governmental conference, while some 30,000 people participated in the NGO forum. The NGO Forum Final Report (1996) remarked that the Fourth UN

Conference on Women was not only the largest international gathering of women ever, but also a global strategic planning meeting where women came together to define an action agenda for the twenty-first century. NGOs also campaigned to be closely involved in the implementation and follow-up process, a move that, if successful, could go some way to strengthening the gender and development agenda in governments and sensitising it to the needs of female citizenship. Moreover, globalization has created the conditions for transnational alliances among women's NGOs. The rapid growth and expansion of telecommunications allow the exchange of information and facilitates networking more generally (Harcourt, 1999). The network established at Huairou, the home of the Beijing NGO forum, was at the time by far the most active computer network at any UN and/or NGO Forum (NGO Forum on Women, 1996).

Conclusion

Over the past decade, approaches to globalization have emerged that more fully capture the nuances of globalization, expand the scope of analysis to include gender, ethnicity and class, and highlight the complex connections and interactions between global, national and local spaces and sites. Key issues that have emerged in what has been characterised as the 'third wave' of the globalization literature are the continuing relevance of politics and the scope for agency and change. The emphasis on the ideational or discursive dimensions of globalization draws attention to the dangers in accepting a 'hyper-globalist' thesis – capitalism has its own logic and dynamic and is largely 'out of control' – since this generates a sense of political defeatism and quietism. The accent on 'the discursive or ideational processes in the mediation of globalizing tendencies' also opens up a greater role for states in shaping globalization (Hay, 2001: 8). However, the understanding of politics must also embrace a range of civil-society groups that operate in local, national, regional and global settings Critical approaches point to the need to identify and analyse both 'globalising forces and counter-hegemonic tendencies' (Hay, 2001: 8). Counter-hegemonic tendencies might loosely embrace active resistance to neoliberal globalization as seen in recent anti-globalization protests, and in efforts that are more reformist in nature, but that might nevertheless involve demands for fairly comprehensive and wide-ranging changes in policies and how they are implemented.

The politics of the anti-globalization movement are not fully understood, but it is clear that alliances are forging around issues of inequality, marginalization and exclusion. 'Counter-hegemonic projects' necessitate creative thinking about possible alternatives models of citizenship, democracy and human rights. Of course, politics takes place in a world of great inequalities, indeed growing inequalities, in respect to resources and incomes, that determine to a great extent the ability of NGOs and other civil society organizations and movements to organize and participate in meaningful ways. Moreover, despite growing pressure from civil society organizations, decision-making bodies and institutions and processes of governance are still largely dominated by states. Arguably, the UN is being eclipsed by the IMF and the World Bank in areas relevant to development and social welfare and these institutions are, in turn, dominated by highly developed industrial countries.

Serious concerns are being raised that conditions of economic austerity, the cutting of development aid, growing levels of poverty and other factors like the current re-organization of relationships between UN agencies and bodies and NGOs all mitigate against the full participation of women in the political process (Meyer and Prugl, 1999; Global Policy Forum, 2000; Steans, 2002). Moreover, where women have participated, it is undoubtedly the case that Western NGOs have played a larger role in shaping debates within UN than women's groups and organizations from the South. The number of NGOs from the South attending international conferences, or otherwise participating in national and international policy debates, formulation and implementation has grown over the past two decades, but are still seriously underrepresented in all of these forums. Overall, women's NGOs have had some success at the local, national and international level, in claiming resources for women, generating support for women's education and on health issues and access to micro-credit, but these efforts have been undermined to a large degree by neo-liberal prescriptions of market-led economic growth that have adverse social consequences.

The greatest challenge in understanding globalization in the future perhaps involves developing a greater understanding of the politics and various sites of resistance to globalization and where possibilities for change emerge. It is also necessary to continually focus on material inequalities and power relations, because these work to constrain and foreclose possibilities for more inclusive visions of citizenship and humane governance. Feminist voices remain central to such critical endeavours.

Notes

1. S. S. McLanahan, L. M. Casper and A. Sorensen, 'undated'. 'Women's roles and women's poverty in eight industrialized countries,' Institute for Research on Poverty Discussion Papers, pp. 978–92, University of Wisconsin Institute for Research on Poverty.
2. See http://www.globalissues.org/TradeRelated/Facts.asp, accessed 14 January 2007.
3. See http://www.osce.org/publications/odihr/2006/09/20640_672_en.pdf, accessed 14 January 2007.
4. Full reference for Global Employment Trends for Women 2004: http://kilm.ilo.org/GET2004/DOWNLOAD/trendsw.pdf, accessed 14 January 2007.
5. See Making Women Count: http://www.makingwomencount.org.

References

Afshar, H. and Berrientos, S. (eds) (1999) *Women, Globalization and Fragmentation in the Developing World,* Basingstoke, Palgrave.

Amoore, L. (ed.) (2000) 'Part three: exploring resistances: the global in the local', in *The Global Resistance Reader,* London, Routledge.

Basu, A., Grewal, I., Kaplan, C. and Milkki, L. (eds) (2001) 'Special issue gender and globalization', *Signs,* 26 (1), 943–1314.

Beneria, L. (2003) *Gender, Development and Globalization: Economics as if all People Mattered,* London, Routledge.

Birdsall, N. and Graham, C. (eds) (2000) *New Markets, New Opportunities? Economic and Social Mobility in a Changing World,* Washington, DC, Brookings Institute.

Black, S. E. and Brainerd, E. (2002) *Importing Inequality? The Impact of Globalization on Gender Discrimination,* Working Paper 9110, Cambridge, MA, National Bureau of Economic Research.

Brawley, M. R. (2003) *The Politics of Globalization: Gaining Perspectives, Assessing Consequences,* Broadview Press.

Breman, J., Das, A. and Agarwal, R. (2000) *Labouring Under Global Capitalism,* Oxford, Oxford University Press.

Cagatay, N. and Erturk, K. (2004) *Gender and Globalization: A Macroeconomic Perspective,* Working Paper 19, Policy Integration Department, World Commission on the Social Dimension of Globalization, ILO, Geneva, May.

Carr, M. and Chen, M. (2004), 'Globalization, social exclusion and gender', *International Labour Review,* 143 (1–2), 129–60.

Chinkin, C. (1999) 'Gender, inequality and international human rights law' in A. Hurrell and N. Woods (eds), *Inequality, Globalization and World Politics,* Oxford, Oxford University Press.

Chow, Ester Ngan-ling (2003) 'Gender matters: studying globalization and social change in the 21st Century', *International Sociology,* 18 (3), 443–60.

Commission of the European Communities (1995) *A New Partnership Between Women and Men,* COM (95) 221, Luxembourg, Official Publications of the EuropeanCommunities.

Connell, R. W. (1998) 'Masculinities and globalization', *Men and Masculinities,* 1 (1), 3–23.

Davids, T. (2005) *The Gender Question in Globalization: Changing Perspectives and Practices,* London, Ashgate.

DAWN (1991) 'Development Alternatives with Women for a New Era', *Alternatives* 1 and 2, Rio de Janerio.

Dickenson, T. and Schaeffar, R. (2001) *Fast Forward: Work, Gender and Protest in a Changing World,* Boston, Rowman and Littlefield.

Dominelli, L. (1991) *Women Across Continents: Feminist Comparative Social Policy,* Hemel Hampstead, Harvester Wheatsheaf.

Ferree, M. and Martin, P. Y. (eds) (1995) *Feminist Organisations: Harvest of the New Woman's Movement,* Philadelphia, Temple University Press.

Global Policy Forum (2000) Available at http://www.global policy.org/ngos/info/ngoun.htm.

Grewal, I. and Kaplan, C. (eds) (1994) *Scattered Hegemonies: Postmodernity and Transnational Feminist Practices,* Minneapolis, University of Minnesota Press.

Guzman, V. (2002) *Gender Relations in a Global World,* New York, UN Publications.

Harcourt, W. (1999) *Women@Internet: Creating New Cultures in Cyberspace,* London, Zed Books.

Harris, R. and Seid, M. (eds) (2000) *Critical Perspectives on Globalization and Neoliberalism in Developing Countries,* Boston, Brill.

Hartmann, B. (1995) *Reproductive Rights and Wrongs: The Global Politics of Population Control,* Boston, South End Press.

Hausman, R., Tyson, L. D. and Zahidi, S. (2006) *The Global Gender Gap,* Geneva, World Economic Forum Report.

Hay, C. (2001) 'Making a virtue of a perceived necessity: globalization, New Labour and the "Third Way" political economy', Plenary lecture delivered at the annual conference of the British Universities Industrial Relations Association, University of Stirling, 4–6 July 2002.

Hay, C. and Marsh, D. (eds) (2000) *Demystifying Globalization,* London, Palgrave.

Hooper, E. (1994a) *Report on the UN ECE Regional Preparatory Meeting for the Fourth World Conference on Women,* Geneva, UN Publications.

———. (1994b) *Report on the UN LAC Regional Preparatory Meeting for the Fourth World Conference on Women,* Mexico, UN Publications.

———. (1994c) *Report on the UN ESCAP Regional Preparatory Meeting for the Fourth World Conference on Women,* Jakarta, UN Publications.

Jayawardena, K. (ed.) (1986) *Feminism and Nationalism in the Third World,* London, Zed Books.

Lawson, S. (1998) 'The culture of politics' in R. Maidment (ed.), *Culture and Society in Asia-Pacific,* London, Routledge.

Marchand, M. (1995) 'Latin American voices of resistance: women's movements and development debates' in S. Rostow, M. Rupert and A. Samatur (eds), *The Global Economy as Political Space: Essays in Critical Theory and International Political Economy,* Cambridge, Cambridge University Press, pp. 89–109.

Marchand, M. and Runyan, A. (eds) (2000) *Gender and Global Restructuring,* London, Routledge.

Meyer, M. and Prugl, E. (eds) (1999) *Gender Politics in Global Governance,* Oxford, Rowman and Littlefield.

Mishra, R. (1996) *Globalization and the Welfare State,* Cheltenham, Edward Elgar.

Moghadam, V. (1999) *Gender and Globalization: Female Labour and Women's Mobilization Journal of World-Systems Research,* 2, 367–88.

Mohanty, C. (2002) 'Under Western eyes revisited: feminist solidarity through anticapitalist struggles', *Signs: Journal of Women in Culture and Society,* 28 (2), 499–535.

Newman, J. (2001) *Modernising Governance: New Labour, Policy and Society,* London, Sage.

NGO Forum on Women: Final Report (1996) New York, UN Publications.

Nussbaum, M. C. (2000) *Women and Human Development,* Cambridge, Cambridge University Press.

Oostendorp, R. H. (2004) 'Globalization and the gender wage gap', *World Bank Policy Research Working Paper 3256,* April.

Peterson, V. S. (2003) *A Critical ReWriting of Global Political Economy: Integrating Reproductive, Productive and Virtual Economies,* London, Routledge.

Peterson, V. S. and Runyan, A. S. (1993) *Global Gender Issues,* Boulder, CO, Westview.

Pettman, J. (1997) *Worlding Women,* London, Routledge.

Pierson, P. (1994) *Dismantling the Welfare State? Reagan, Thatcher and the Politics of Retrenchment,* Cambridge, Cambridge University Press.

Pietila, H. and Vickers, J. (1994) *Making Women Matter: The Role of the UN,* London, Zed Books.

Pyle, J. and Ward, K. B. (2003) 'Recasting our understanding of gender and work during global restructuring', *International Sociology,* 18 (3), 461–89.

Rai, S. (2002) *Gender and the Political Economy of Development,* Cambridge, Polity Press.

Runyan, A. S. (1996), 'The place of women in trading places: gendered global/regional regimes and inter-nationalized feminist resistance' in E. Kofman and G. Youngs (eds), *Globalization: Theory and Practice,* London, Pinter.

Steans, J. (1999) 'The private is global: global political economy and feminist politics', *New Political Economy,* 4 (1), 113–28.

———. (2002) 'Global governance: A feminist perspective' in A. McGrew and D. Held (eds), *Governing Globalization,* Oxford, Polity.

———. (2006) 'Transnational feminist solidarities', *Gender and International Relations,* Cambridge, Polity Press.

Stiglitz, J. (2003) *Globalization and its Discontents,* New York, W.W. North and Co.

Sylvester, C. (1994) 'The Emperor's theories and transformations: looking at the field through feminist lenses' in C. Sylvester and D. Pirages (eds), *Transformations in Global Political Economy,* Basingstoke, Macmillan.

Tickner, A. (1992) 'On the fringes of the global economy' in R. Tooze and C. Murphy (eds), *The New International Political Economy,* Boulder, CO, Lynne Rienner.

Tohidi, N. (1994) 'Modernisation, islamisation and women in Iran' in V. M. Mohagadam (ed.), *Women and National Identity,* London, Zed Books.

True, J. (2003) *Gender, Globalization and Postsocialism: The Czech Republic After Communism,* New York, Columbia University Press.

United Nations (1995) 'Look at the world through women's eyes: NGO Forum on Women, Beijing, 1995.' Final report, United Nations Documents, New York, 1995.

Weiss, L. (1999) *The Myth of the Powerless State,* Cambridge, Polity Press.

Wichterich, C. (2000) *The Globalised Woman,* London, Zed Books.

World Bank (2006) *World Development Report 2006: Equity and Development,* Washington, DC, The World Bank.

CHAPTER 10

Trading Places under Neoliberal Empire

Rethinking Inter-nationalized Feminist Resistance and Solidarities in the Context of 'North America'

Anne Sisson Runyan

In the first two editions of this volume, I examined the gendered impact of and women's resistance to the integration projects of the European Union (EU) and the North American Free Trade Agreement (NAFTA) as primary examples of regional conveyor belts for neoliberal globalization that privileged global capital at the expense of social welfare, equity and justice. I further posited that combinations of grass-roots and cross-border organizing by women in resistance to the Europe of Maastricht and the Americas of NAFTA (and the proposed Free Trade Area of the Americas or the FTAA) offer nascent examples for how to 'link diverse local practices to formulate a transnational set of solidarities' (Grewal and Kaplan, 1994: 19), a process differentiated from 'the old sisterhood model of missionary work, of intervention and salvation' that 'is clearly tied to older models of center-periphery relations' (Grewal and Kaplan, 1994: 19). Although I argued that this process is a product of the forces of 'integration' which exert downward pressures in similar ways in diverse localities, I suggested that it is also a creation of multiply 'placed' but also multiply 'linked' subjectivities (Grewal, 1994: 235), thereby opening up spaces for women to analytically 'trade places' in ways that can build solidarities within and across states to resist and restructure the dominant and dominating logics of regional and global 'integration.' As transnational feminist theorist Inderpal Grewal describes it:

> There can be syncretic, 'immigrant,' cross-cultural, and plural subjectivities, which can enable a politics through positions that are coalitions, intransigent, in process, and contradictory. Such identities are enabling because they provide a mobility in solidarity that leads to a transnational participation in understanding and opposing multiple and global oppressions operating upon them; that is, these subject positions enable oppositions in multiple locations. Multiple locations also enable valuable interventions precisely because the agendas of one group are brought along to interrogate and empower those of another group. (Grewal, 1994: 234)

These contextualized understandings and strategies arising from the development of a more 'heterogeneous consciousness' (Grewal, 1994: 251) can produce and be produced by what I called 'inter-nationalized' feminist solidarities, particularly in the context of contesting regional integration regimes. I used the hyphenation as well as the prefix 'inter' as opposed to 'trans' to stress the politics of difference on at least four levels. First, such solidarities cannot be based on a homogenized notion of 'woman', but rather draw their strength from the 'inter-play' of women's multiple identities, experiences and locations which can reveal differing, yet connected, patterns of domination. Second, 'intersectional' analysis and practices that are attentive to power relations among women are crucial for the development of such solidarities, regardless of their duration, to resist exclusions and silencings. Third, such solidarities are built 'in between' or at the 'interstices' of homogenized national identities that tend to evacuate gender politics. Fourth, terms like 'global' or 'transnational' feminism can also tend to evacuate the politics of difference, including national difference, in gender struggles and elide too easily with the language of capital even as they point to the importance of attending to global and transnational forces like capital.

While instances of 'inter-nationalized' feminist resistance continue to proliferate in resistance to the virulences of current phases of globalization and regional integration projects (see, for example, Eschle and Maiguashca, 2005; Moghadam, 2005; Bandy and Smith, 2005), the purpose of this piece is to more closely examine new sets of divergences and convergences in the context of the imaginary of 'North America' under what is variously referred to as 'neoliberal empire' (Pietierse, 2004), 'unilateral globalization' (Mittelman, 2004), or the 'neo-imperial moment' (Rupert, 2005) particularly in the post-9/11 period, that have implications for thinking about solidarity projects at this historical juncture. This re-focus stems first from the shifting political landscapes in and relations among these states in the face of the ever-tightening US security regime and its economic, political and cultural dimensions. Secondly, it emerges from the analysis, perspectives and experiences arising from gender-based student and faculty exchange projects funded by the North American Mobility Program of the Canadian, Mexican and US governments since the passage of NAFTA, including one in which I am a participant. These shifts and the critiques of them open up new terrains for contestations over and bases of feminist cross-border solidarity projects in the North American context. In particular, I will argue that, on the one hand, there is significant evidence that 'borders matter' in feminist movements, but also have new salience in resistance to neoliberal empire. At the same time, the 'rebordering' efforts by empire are requiring specifically feminist cross-border solidarities that go beyond economic-based critiques of free trade agreements. Finally, I will make the case that regional feminist learning precipitated by 'negative integration' but also aided by feminist border-crossing pedagogies can contribute to that solidarity building.

Re-borderings of and against neoliberal empire

During the heyday of neoliberal globalization prognostications in the 1990s, it was a common imagining that a borderless world would emerge in the face of unprecedented capital, communication and transportation flows. Such economistic arguments have always been particularly strong amongst proponents of free trade who see this as the key to not only economic prosperity but also ending international conflict and increasing democratization.

Thus from a utopian pro-free trade perspective, NAFTA has the capacity for ushering in the following:

> [T]he continuing economic integration of Mexico, Canada, and the United States would foster political steps to merge into a regional union similar to the European Union. Borders would open to allow the free movement of workers, as well as the free movement of goods and capital. The governments of all three countries would work collectively to harmonize their laws and policies and to mitigate the disruption and social dislocation caused by globalization, extending expanded social benefits. Equipped with equal rights and equal benefits, Mexicans, Canadians, and U.S. citizens would forge a common identity as 'North Americans' that would supercede their national identities. A common currency could be established for all three countries. Spanish, English, and French would co-exist as official languages and citizens would develop bilingual and trilingual capacities. New transnational political institutions, comparable to the European Parliament and the European Commission, would be created. . . . The three countries would become truly integrated economically, socially, and politically into the North American Community (NAC) or the North American Union (NAU). (Hawkesworth et al., 2006: 174)

This set of assumptions, however, has long been countered by critics of first the Canadian-US Free Trade Agreement (CUSFTA) of the 1980s and then the North American Free Trade Agreement (NAFTA) of the 1990s who have argued that the neoliberal agenda which underlies these agreements privileges the globalization of capital and corporate power and thus exacerbates, rather than lessens, inequalities among and within these countries economically, politically and socially. Coupled with widening divisions on these levels has been the aftermath of 11 September, in which the governments of Canada and Mexico refused to support the Bush administration's war on Iraq. Meanwhile, the US Homeland Security regime has steadily tightened US borders, further restricting the flow of people, labour and goods with new identification requirements and enforcement procedures for crossing the US-Canadian border (and, indeed, all Western hemisphere borders) and even an impending wall across the entire length of the US-Mexican border. Thus, a far more dystopian picture of North American relations has been unfolding.

According to Canadian feminist anti-free trade/globalization activist and analyst Maude Barlow, the new US security regime has not ended 'integration,' but rather accelerated a number of dark sides of it. In her chronicle of US-Canadian relations post-9/11, *Too Close for Comfort: Canada's Future within Fortress North America* (2005), she notes that with '[E]ighty-seven percent of all Canadian exports going to the United States and some 40 per cent of Canada's GNP...tied to Canada-US trade' after years of NAFTA, Canadian businessmen learned quickly that in the new US security environment, if they 'wanted the border to stay open, they would have to help build a security perimeter around North America and support America's military, energy, and economic interests abroad' (Barlow, 2005: 1–2). These conditions for a continued North American 'partnership' were laid out in the 2005 final report of the Independent Task Force on the Future of North America made up of largely conservative former finance ministers from the three countries that were brought together by the US Council on Foreign Relations.

Undergirding it, according to minutes from closed door sessions, were:

> breathtaking plans the business community has for a North American Union, . . .
> in which Canada would supply resources and political acquiescence, Mexico would
> provide cheap migrant labour for the continent, and the peoples of all three countries
> would see their environmental and social security standards weakened in order to
> promote the interests of an increasingly integrated and powerful business sector.
> (Barlow, 2005: 9)

Its plans for a high-tech security shield, a 'Schenghenization' of immigration including joint visa requirements and common exclusion lists, a common currency union, and the opening up of intra-North American investment, energy production and non-renewable resource exploitation were also codified in the Security and Prosperity Partnership of North America which was signed, also in 2005, by then Prime Minister Paul Martin, then President Vincente Fox, and President Bush in Waco, Texas (Barlow, 2005: 9–11). Since then, Martin and his Liberal party lost to the Conservative party and its leader Stephen Harper in the face of a Liberal party corruption scandal, while Fox's National Action Party (PAN) stayed in power under now President Felipe Calderon who barely (and questionably) defeated leftist Mexico City mayor Manuel Lopez Obrador. Thus, with all three heads of state lined up on the right, Barlow's worst fears of Fortress North America may be more easily realized. The recent wresting of control of the US House and Senate by the Democratic Party, largely as a result of Republican Party corruption scandals, the costs of the war on Iraq, and rising economic insecurity, as well as a possibly short-lived tenure of the Harper minority government and continued contestations over the Calderon presidency may provide some brake on it, but the structural momentum in that direction will be difficult to reverse.

Although the re-rise of the security state is often seen as incompatible with the borderless world imagined by neoliberal globalization adherents, Jan Nederveen Pieterse (2004) argues that the particular 'imperial turn' that the US has taken under 'Bush II' has not supplanted but rather co-mingled with neoliberal globalization, which accounts for the accelerated 'integration' that Barlow observes. As Pieterse puts it:

> The rapid succession from a neoliberal to an imperial project yields a combine of
> American economic and political-military unilateralism and a novel form of ne-
> oliberal empire. The core of empire is the national security state and the military-
> industrial complex; neoliberalism is about business, financial operations, and
> marketing (including marketing neoliberalism itself). The IMF and the World Bank
> continue business as usual, though with less salience and legitimacy than during the
> Clinton years; so imperial policies come in addition to and not instead of the frame-
> work of neoliberal globalization. Neoliberal empire is a marriage of convenience
> with neoliberalism, indicated by inconsistent use of neoliberal policies, and an at-
> tempt to merge the America whose business is business with the America whose
> business is war, at a time when business is not doing so great. (Pieterse, 2004: 45)

Pieterse, however, notes that this is not a completely new hybrid in world history, and this particular formation has been long in the making. He argues that the 'real neoliberalism' gestated in the American South. 'Southern economics has its roots in plantation economics with rural oligarchies and a low-cost workforce that performs manual labour – slaves, seg-regated blacks, rightless migrant workers from Mexico under the Bracero program, and, after 1964, many illegal immigrants' (Pieterse, 2004: 3). The Southern model, 'modernized' but little changed since Reconstruction, of low wages and taxes, few regulations and social services, hostility to organized labour and the maintenance of a racist economic, political and legal order was given the patina of legitimacy by the Chicago School's 'free market' theories and the Reagan administration's policies, enabling the 'export' of it to the rest of nation and the world by the 1980s (Pieterse, 2004: 2–3).

But it is not just the economic order of the American South that has been exported, but also its reactionary culture of religion-based neo-conservativism. As Barlow points out, Southern- and Western-based Christian evangelical groups in the US have become so pow-erful that they have expanded into Canada, opening up Canadian branches, contributing heavily to Conservative campaigns, and flooding legislative offices with right-wing mail against, for example, the Civil Marriage Act allowing same-sex marriage that was instituted in 2005 prior to the installation of the Harper government (Barlow, 2005: 25). Harper shares the views of these groups on 'gays and lesbians, and abortion, but also on small government, privatized health care, environmental regulation, and an aggressive foreign policy backed up by force' (Barlow, 2005: 25), thereby potentially undermining progressive Canadian gains while furthering the nexus between neoliberal globalization and militarized empire on the North American continent that is not just coincidentally bound together by racist, sexist and homophobic ideologies.

In this climate of US-centered 'negative integration', Daniel Drache argues that 'citizens in Canada and Mexico are looking inwards, rather than south or north, for more public and collective goods and to meet new challenges. They are searching for ways to strengthen their national space, not to extend its borders' (Drache, 2004: 84). This is not a new response as critics of CUSFTA and then NAFTA in Canada and Mexico early on pointed to the hege-monic economic relations such pacts would deepen due to the asymmetries in power between the US and its immediate neighbors. For Mexico, the NAFTA years, in which trade among the three countries doubled (Drache, 2004: 70), have been particularly devastating, with poverty levels reaching 50 per cent by 2002, up from 28 per cent in 1984 (Barlow, 2005: 264), while real wages mostly declined post-NAFTA for 90 per cent of the population (Drache, 2004: 71; Gonzales, 2006: 115). Canada has also experienced increasing poverty, particularly among the most vulnerable (children, the elderly, First Nations, and so on) and seen declines in full-time, unionized jobs, while its social spending declined by 15 per cent since 1995 (Barlow, 2005: 128–29). But while the US is most advantaged in this trading relationship, which however constitutes only a fraction of its trade overall, it currently 'ranks dead last in fighting poverty, is at the bottom in terms of functional illiteracy, has one of the lowest levels of life expectancy, has the greatest income inequality, and the highest number of citizens without access to health care' among industrialized states, and its child poverty-rate is second only to Mexico. (Barlow, 2005: 149)

As predicted by critics of CUSFTA and NAFTA, the real winners of these trade agree-ments and the general neoliberal policies of which they are only a part have been especially transnational Corporate America, followed more distantly by Corporate Canada and Cor-porate Mexico. The majority of increased trade since NAFTA is attributable to 'intrafirm trade', while trade increases in general have been largely between the US and Canada and between the US and Mexico, with increasing but still relatively little trade going on between Canada and Mexico (MacDonald, 2006: 134). US corporations account for 60.4 per cent of all Mexican foreign direct investment (FDI) (Gonzalez, 2006: 110), while US FDI in Canada has increased 121 per cent (MacDonald, 2006: 134). Meanwhile, US and Canadian transnational energy and defense contractors have made unprecedented profits, particularly since 9/11 (see Barlow, 2005) and Mexican local and national industries have contracted in the face of transnational capitalist enterprises (Gonzalez, 2005: 115). At the same time, Chapter 11 of NAFTA, which enables corporations to sue the three governments in the pact for trade barriers that result in business losses, has led to the extraction of millions from public coffers in all three countries by transnational corporations (Drache, 2004: 80). The combination of trade liberalization, deregulation, tax cuts and reduced social spending has enriched the top 10 per cent in Mexico and Canada, and especially the top 1 per cent in the US (see, for example, Konigsberg, 2006).

It is little wonder then that many citizens in all three countries would be looking to restore national control over transnational corporate power and (re)invigorate domestic economic security and social safety nets that have been weakened or eroded. But it is also the case that as the 'Homeland Security Act is nationalizing the US side of the border and explicitly extended into Canadian domestic space as part of its stated need to "to protect our nation's critical infrastructure"' (Drache, 2004: 109), the stakes have been heightened for (non-business class) Canadians seeking to distance themselves not only from the neoliberal economic and ideological model of the American South that has been increasingly exported northward during the NAFTA years, but also from the US re-bordering efforts to construct Fortress North America. Such resistance to neoliberal empire entails a different kind of re-bordering suggested by James Mittelman's concept of 'autonomy from below', which is not about the rightest, nativist project of 'fencing-off and attempting to be a fortress' (Mittelman, 2004: 95) either at the behest of the US or simply as a reaction to it, but rather, in Barlow's view, to assert progressive Canadian civil society priorities of and alternative paths to global, social, human and ecological security in combination with 'other moderate countries and people around the world to form a counterweight' (Barlow, 2005: 288).

Faced with a literal US fencing project across its northern border at the same time that remittances from Mexican immigrants in the US, including the majority of the estimated 11 to 12 million indocumented workers in the US, now 'have surpassed oil as the number one source of transborder revenue' (Gonzalez, 2006: 118), the vast majority of Mexicans have a stake in this alternative approach to re-bordering as well. Long identifying more with Latin America than North America, Mexico recently almost joined the spate of Latin American countries whose governments have shifted to the left. After 'twenty years of liberalization,' poverty has increased almost two-fold in Latin America, where the income gap is 'one of the widest in the world' following the US (Barlow, 2005: 264). Thus, along with the leftist political shift at governmental levels, there has been considerable push back on further hemispheric trade agreements, such as the Free Trade of the Americas (FTAA) initiative that has lost considerable traction.

Resisting neoliberal empire within the US, however, requires a somewhat different re-bordering project. As Pieterse argues, as long as the 'self-caricature' and 'self-colonization' of 'American exceptionalism', which is forcing 'the rest of the world [to] subsidize American indulgence and conservativism', especially under the conditions of its 'permanent war project', holds sway, then it is unlikely that progressive forces within the US, who are not immune from such exceptionalism, can meaningfully turn the tide (Pieterse, 2004: 140–41).

In one response to this, feminist political theorist Zillah Eisenstein advocates 'radical plu-ralism', which 'requires a displacement of the US as the privileged site of modernity, democracy, feminism, and so on, and demands an accounting from places "elsewhere" to counter "US empire building" that "Americanizes the globe in its particularly racialized and masculinist forms"' (Eisenstein, 2004: 1). As I argue below, this requires cross-border learn-ing that, in Eisenstein's words, is 'best done by borrowing, dialoguing, mirroring, exchang-ing, arguing' (Eisenstein, 2004: 7) in order to cordon off exceptionalist and imperial impulses and practices.

Regional feminist learning

Although North American trade has proven illusory and problematic as a basis for 'positive integration', it has increasingly brought not only activist and but also scholarly attention to the regional construct of 'North America', generating more critical and specifically feminist comparative analyses of these three states that can contribute to cross-border learning in resistance to neoliberal empire. The neoliberal project of NAFTA has also inspired a ne-oliberal higher education project known as the North American Mobility Program very modestly and jointly funded by the US Department of Education's Fund for the Improve-ment of Post-Secondary Education (FIPSE), Mexico's Secretaria de Educacion Publica (SEP), and Human Resources and Skills Development Canada (HRSDC). Designed to in-crease primarily student and secondarily faculty exchanges among Mexican, US and Canadian universities to increase largely professional cross-border mobility to build 'human capital', most of the funded projects are among business, science and language-learning programs. However, some Canadian, Mexican and US feminist scholars, who have been engaged in gender and trade, border, and globalization studies within North America and beyond, have used this opportunity more subversively to generate exchanges and dialogues to further feminist readings, comparisons and critiques of the region. One such cross-border faculty consortium of feminist political scientists has produced *Women, Democracy, and Globalization in North America: A Comparative Study* (2006), which presents a more com-prehensive, complicated and baseline picture of feminist histories and women's status in relation to the evolving political economies of these countries and the region as a whole than previous work on simply gender and trade in the North American context over the past two decades. What emerges in particular from this study are contributions to the project of de-centering the US in terms of its monopolistic claims on feminism and democracy and even modernity. For example, as the authors point out, 'Mexico and Canada have far more gender democracy than does the United States' (Hawkesworth et al., 2006: 183). Not only is the US the outlier as the only one of the three that has not ratified the UN Convention on the Elimination of Discrimination Against Women (CEDAW), but also lags considerably behind the other two in terms of women's political representation.

Mexico boasts the highest percentage of female federal legislators in the region because of its adoption of gender quotas, allying it more closely with Latin America, which is the 'leading continent when it comes to the introduction of gender quotas in politics', with 11 of the 19 countries adopting them in the 1990s (Araujo and Garcia, 2006: 83). This has arisen out of the combination of Latin American women's grassroots struggles for democ-ratization in the 1970s and 1980s throughout the continent, the development of women's political rights organizations out of this and the influence of UN women's conferences and transnational organizing, and the interests of many Latin American states to adopt 'modern' practices to distance themselves from 'traditional' dictatorial pasts (see Aruajo and Garcia, 2006; Begne, 2006). Although gender quotas in Latin America have also been motivated by international financial institution pressures to model 'good governance in the global market' (Araujo and Garcia, 2006: 88) and such quotas are not 'necessarily an indicator of democracy or even deeper changes in women's general status' (Araujo and Garcia, 2006: 106), they have catapulted Mexico to twenty-seventh in the world in terms of women's office-holding compared to the US at fifty-seventh. The US is a particular outlier throughout much of the developed and, increasingly, parts of the developing world when it comes to the modern trappings of 'legal and party' quotas and proportional representation for women and ethnic minorities, having 'simply rejected them out of hand' (Krook et al., 2006: 216), particularly as the racist, anti-feminist and anti-democratic ideology and political economy of the 'real neoliberalism' of the American South has taken hold nationally. Although it is doubtful that US empire is willing to learn from its Southern neighbors in this regard, it constitutes an object lesson for US claims on modernity as does the recent recognition and legalization of same-sex civil unions in Mexico City.

Canada ranks thirty-first in women's political representation worldwide in the absence of 'hard' quotas but in the presence of a Charter of Rights and Freedoms with significant gender justice components. As a result, it is ranked at the top in terms of 'feminist public policies, such as reproductive freedom, paid maternity leave, paid family leave, protection from violence against women, equitable employment policies, guarantees against pregnancy discrimination, access to health care, social-welfare benefits' (Hawkesworth et al., 2006: 183), and most recently same-sex marriage rights. To try to protect these considerable gains, Canadian feminists, through their national coalition, the National Action Committee on the Status of Women (NAC), became the leading feminist actors in the hemisphere against CUFTA and NAFTA. According to Laura MacDonald's numerous comparative accounts of women's organizing in resistance North American and hemispheric trade agreements (see, for example, MacDonald, 2002, 2005, 2006), NAC's shift in the 1980s from a liberal, white middle-class interest group to one more inclusive of women of colour and working-class women in which economic issues took center stage at a time when power was shifting to the Conservatives and budgets were being slashed enabled it to 'frame' trade as a women's issue and take a national and regional lead on this. In contrast, the US National Organization for Women (NOW) remained a largely liberal public interest group that was almost exclusively absorbed in fighting attacks by the New Right in the US, particularly on abortion, and there was almost no feminist organizational presence in US-based anti-NAFTA coalitions. In Mexico, although national women's movements had existed over time, none had been consolidated into an ongoing national organization, in part because of class divides and class-based social movements, and only a few small, under-resourced women's organizations had a trade focus, despite Mexican women having the greatest familiarity with the poverty-producing impacts of structural adjustment and trade liberalization and the celebrity of indigenous women in the anti-NAFTA Zapatista movement. These major differences and the considerable unevenness in women's movement formations and trajectories underline the significance of national contexts and the reality that borders matter; however, the picture has been changing somewhat.

According to MacDonald (2005), by the late 1990s in the wake of anti–World Trade Organization (WTO) protests in Seattle and other large scale anti-globalization demonstrations at which women began to organize special gender- and trade-focused sessions where US women in particular learned that they were outside of the conversation in an organized way, a dent had been made in the US silence on gender and trade with the formation of the Coalition for Women's Economic Development and Global Equality (Women's EDGE). Although not attracting NOW, Women's EDGE is a part of the Women's Committee connected to the Hemispheric Social Alliance (HSA) that formed in resistance to the FTAA and the International Gender and Trade Network (IGTN), which formed in 1999 to engage in 'research, advocacy, and economic literacy around issues of trade and development' through seven regional networks of women (MacDonald, 2005: 35). These infrastructures, while still marginalized within larger anti-globalization organizations which they must repeatedly pressure to include a gender analysis (see also Eschle, 2005), are nevertheless creating a 'greater opening toward the gender and trade linkage in the United States' and providing 'greater coordination' in Latin America for gender and trade initiatives (MacDonald, 2005: 32).

Although 'US feminists have had trouble shifting their gaze from the local to the global and with incorporating macro-economic analysis' (MacDonald, 2005: 32), they have been sources of assistance in relation to the northward incursions of US right-wing evangelical groups seeking to undermine reproductive and lesbian and gay rights in Canada, that, as Barlow points out, are inseparable from the designs of negative integration on the basis of neoliberal empire. In her recent comparative study of *Abortion Politics in North America* (2005), Melissa Haussman argues that because the US has the largest anti-choice and pro-choice movements in the world, the particular influences on its neighbors in the NAFTA years makes the regional study of reproductive politics imperative. While Mexico remains the outlier in the region in terms of nationally codified abortion rights due to the internal unholy alliance of the PAN party with the Mexican Catholic Archdiocese and its pro-life organization, Pro-Vida, access to abortion in the US and Canada has eroded significantly in the face of health-care budget cuts and state and provincial efforts to reduce who can exercise abortion rights under what circumstances and what procedures are available to do so. Although pro-choice struggles are particularly focused on national and sub-national electoral politics and courts, as reproductive politics has transnationalized through UN women's and women's issues conferences that made gains in the international recognition of reproductive rights and the backlash on the part of transnational fundamentalist actors seeking to reverse those gains, it has also increasingly regionalized. For example, Haussman points out the US-based National Abortion Federation (NAF) has attracted Canadian pro-choice organizations to its network as US-based anti-choice groups like Operation Rescue and the Army of God pressed across the border to recruit members and engage in violent tactics against Canadian abortion providers.

> In essence, as the opposition has heated up its attacks and been shown to be increasingly willing to cross borders for annual protests on both Parliament Hill and Capitol Hill, attempts at blockades of clinics, and to attend recent papal visits in Toronto and Mexico City, the pro-choice network has realized that it has a transnationally focused movement with which to contend. Its strategies have been both defensive, in terms of keeping more legislatures and the US Congress from whittling

away existing abortion rights but also a highly sophisticated strategy of information sharing across borders on a consistent basis to describe common tactics of pro-life groups and especially to alert other countries when violent offenders seem to be headed there. (Haussman, 2004: 97)

At the same time, although the 'Catholic Church has the most overt power to organize politically it has ever held in Mexico . . . transnational linkages have appeared between the IPPF [International Planned Parenthood Federation] and its Mexican, Canadian, and US offices – IPAS and the DF Ministry of Health – to provide aspiration equipment' (Haussman, 2004: 136). A cooperative relationship has also formed between the Mexican Group for Information on Reproductive Choice (GIRE) and the US Center for Reproductive Law and Policy 'to research and publicize the uneven access to abortion in Mexico' (Haussman, 2005: 136).

While much of this cross-border learning and organizing could be seen as fitting the pattern of what Sonia Alvarez (2000) refers to as 'transnational IGO-advocacy logic' in which expert feminist non-governmental organizations (NGOs) ally to direct their efforts upward in attempts to change international and national policies, there are nascent elements of what Alvarez calls 'internationalist identity-solidarity logic' that emphasizes 'identity, reciprocity, affinity' and 'complementarity' among and between feminist NGO and local women's struggles (Desai, 2002: 32) in their horizontal relations and organizing on the ground within their issue areas. A more fully articulated case of 'internationalist identity-solidarity logic' at work is in the Coalition Against Violence Toward Women and Families at the US-Mexico Border, which was formed in response to the murders and mutilations of mostly Mexican women maquiladora workers in Mexican border cities that began in the 1990s and continue. Comprised of community activists, labour unions and feminist academics and NGOs from Mexico, the US, Canada, and the Caribbean, participants

> can act autonomously and pursue different priorities. Some focus on work with the victims and their families, particularly in terms of fundraising for anti-violence services. . . . Others emphasize systemic policy change and the need to challenge authorities. . . . The shared goal of all participants is to draw public attention to the murders, demand judicial responses and to broaden the range of voices being heard. (Coronado and Staudt, 2005: 144)

What participants also share is the view that analysis of and actions to stem violence against women in and beyond the region 'must be acknowledged as central to resistance to globalization' and are best carried out in the spirit of *'comprimiso,'* which requires that research and activism be guided by a caring relationship with and deep obligation to those it is intended to assist (Coronado and Staudt, 2005: 144–45). Such an orientation can help, in Bice Maiguasha's view, to move beyond a 'politics of identity' to 'forge a shared political identity' formed through 'negotiating differences' and engaging in 'dialogical practices' in order to advance the 'struggle against particular relations of oppression that are reproduced simultaneously in the economic and socio-cultural realm and that are reinforced by the state' (Maiguasha, 2005: 135–36).

Despite such developments in feminist cross-border learning and cooperation, the authors of *Women, Democracy, and Globalization in North America* are not sanguine about the prospects for the spread of gender quotas from Mexico northward, the adoption of the panoply of Canadian gender rights southward, or the leavening of imperial designs and anti-feminist assaults in and beyond the US under a potential NAU. They foresee instead continuing and deepening asymmetries and inequalities within and among these nations as long as cross-cutting neoliberal and 'securitization' policies hold sway. To the degree that feminist cross-border learning remains confined to 'single issue' politics among small, under-resourced, but still rarefied in the sense of non-grass-roots, NGOs that do not inter-connect their struggles to resistance to neoliberal empire, it is unlikely that further negative integration will be stemmed, much less positive integration be developed. At the same time, to the degree that feminist struggles for gender democracy in multiple forms and contexts are seen by anti-'free' trade and anti-globalization activists as outside of and immaterial to resistance to neoliberal empire, it is less likely that such interconnected analysis and mobilizations will occur. As Catherine Eschle argues, a 'feminist intersectional analysis of globalization opens up space for the recognition of the multiple axes of oppression and identity that structure and motivate but also limit mobilization' (Eschle, 2005: 1,751). It also allows for apprehending neoliberal empire 'in its exploitative, racialized, masculinist, militarist forms' (Eisenstein, 2004: 21). Thus, as I argue below, nascent cross-border feminist learning can be aided by developing border-crossing feminist pedagogies that make these interconnections in the North American context.

Border-crossing feminist pedagogies

In an attempt to heal the wounds and rifts particularly among women of colour created over the *longue duree* of conquest, slavery, colonialism, neocolonialism, neoliberalism and the contemporary rise of empire in all their gendered, racist, heteronormative and militarized manifestations, Caribbean feminist Jacqui Alexander articulates and recommends *Pedago-gies of Crossing* (2005). Although it is the crossing of the Middle Passage and the particular experiences of domination and resistance it represents which informs her thinking, she uses it metaphorically 'to apprehend how it might instruct us in the urgent task of reconfiguring new ways of being and knowing and to plot the different metaphysics that are needed to move away from living alterity premised in difference to living intersubjectively in relation-ality and solidarity' (Alexander, 2005: 7–8). Pedagogies, for her, are about bringing forth 'subjugated knowledges that are produced in the context of the practices of marginalization in order that we might destabilize existing practices of knowing and thus cross fictive boundaries of exclusion and marginalization' and developing 'the reciprocal investments we must make to cross over to a metaphysics of interdependence' (Alexander, 2005: 6–7). She particularly tasks women's, ethnic and postcolonial studies, which share to varying de-grees 'a nationalist representational intellectual impulse', to better migrate across disciplines and 'state-constructed borders' to develop new frameworks for resisting state practices of control and surveillance in a time of empire (Alexander, 2005: 252–53). Susan Friedman refers to this as developing feminist 'geopolitical literacy' that is most centrally about the de-colonizing approach of 'avoiding the reinscription of self/other centrisms' that structure material and cultural formations and identities (Friedman, 1998: 130) and must accompany the development of relational economic literacies advocated by feminist critics of global-ization and 'free' trade.

In a very modest response to such calls, another group of women's and gender studies specialists in Mexico, Canada and the US, of which I am a part, are in the midst of another subversive use of the neoliberal North American Mobility Program to link subjugated knowledges on women's human rights, citizenships and, most importantly, identities in a North American context. In our collective reflections on this project thus far and the practices it demands to 'move' students and faculty across not only state, institutional and programmatic, but also linguistic, cultural, ideological and identity boundaries, we have critically acknowledged how deeply the academy is enmeshed in what Alexander calls the 'policing functions of the state' as we confront the various bureaucratic barriers and Homeland Security–inspired apparatus involved particularly with student exchanges that, as Alexander points out, are now surveilled in the US under the Patriot Act (Alexander, 2005: 252). Our own mostly state institutions are also set up almost as fortresses with wildly different calendars and crediting systems, even within the same country, and our own curricular requirements also serve in varying degrees as barriers to border-crossing feminist pedagogies.

At the same time, we have critiqued the neoliberal conceptualization of 'mobility' that underlies the funding program, which assumes and privileges those who are most typically 'mobile subjects' – middle to upper class, white(ned) males with no family responsibilities or need to maintain jobs to pay for their education and, thus, can most easily spend a semester or more away. Compounding the gender and class bias in mobility is the differential funding available from each federal entity, with the least available to the Mexicans and the most to the US participants. This structural inequity that reproduces North-South or center-periphery relations between and among these countries also obscures the relative class privilege of private university students in the South versus public university students in the North and the gender, race and sexuality discriminations that operate across the three states that produce center-periphery relations within them. Also obscured by the statist assumptions of the funding program is that students 'contained' within these states are unitary 'national subjects' who have not already migrated from outside of North America or are representative of cultures other than hegemonic ones in each country. At the base of this program as well is the neoliberal approach to education that reduces cross-border knowledge production to a matter of language acquisition and the transfer of technique to homogenize skills and practices, not to reveal and critique power relations.

Such feminist reflections are informing our thinking and praxis that is very much in progress, particularly in relation to summer institutes in Canada and Mexico we worked into our project to better enable more of our feminist students – who constitute atypical mobile subjects as largely women from working-class backgrounds representing a range of race, ethnic, national and sexual identities (albeit still privileged as university students) – to participate by spending a shorter time away than a semester as well as a more intense, collective space for students and faculty for 'borrowing, dialoguing, mirroring, exchanging', and 'arguing' to nurture mobile subjectivities. Beyond bringing the emergent comparative historical, political and economic data on women in North America to the fore, we are concerned with such questions as what bodies and whose identities are stopped at the literal and metaphorical borders between and within these states for what hegemonic purposes and what feminist perspectives, issues and practices migrate or fail to translate or be (literally) translated at what cost to feminist resistances across the region? In the process, we are challenging ourselves and our students to rethink our own feminist identities, knowledge and perspectives, not in service to some imagined NAU, but rather in a conscious attempt to develop border-crossing feminist pedagogies that have capacities to contribute not only to inter-nationalized feminist resistance to neoliberal empire but also solidarities for de-colonizing feminist ways of knowing and doing.

References

Alexander, J. (2005) *Pedagogies of Crossing: Meditations on Feminism, Sexual Politics, Memory, and the Sacred*, Durham and London, Duke University Press.

Alvarez, S. (2000) 'Translating the Global: Effects of Transnational Organizing on Local Feminist Discourses and Practices in Latin America', Meridians 1, 29–67.

Araujo, C. and Garcia, A. I. (2006) 'Latin America: the experience and impact of quotas in Latin America' in D. Dahlerup (ed.), *Women, Quotas and Politics*, London and New York, Routledge, pp. 83–111.

Bandy, J. and Smith, J. (eds) (2005) *Coalitions across Borders: Transnational Protest and the Neoliberal Order*, Lanham, MD, Rowman & Littlefield Publishers.

Barlow, M. (2005) *Too Close for Comfort: Canada's Future within Fortress North America*, Toronto, McClelland & Stewart.

Bayes, J., Begne, P., Gonzalez, L., Harder, M., Hawkesworth, M. and MacDonald, L. (2006) *Women, Democracy, and Globalization in North America: A Comparative Study*, New York, Palgrave Macmillan.

Begne, P. (2006) 'Women and the struggle for democracy in Mexico' in J. Bayes et al. (eds), *Women, Democracy, and Globalization in North America: A Comparative Study*, New York, Palgrave Macmillan, pp. 29–50.

Coronado, I. and Staudt, K. (2005) 'Resistance and *compromiso* at the global frontlines: gender wars at US-Mexico border' in C. Eschle and B. Maiguashca (eds), *Critical Theories, International Relations and the 'Anti-Globalisation Movement': The Politics of Global Resistance*, London and New York, Routledge, pp. 139–53.

Desai, M. (2002) 'Transnational solidarity: women's agency, structural adjustment, and globalization' in N. Naples and M. Desai (eds), *Women's Activism and Globalization: Linking Local Struggles and Transnational Politics*, New York, Routledge, pp. 15–33.

Drache, D. (2004) *Borders Matter: Homeland Security and the Search for North America*, Halifax, Fernwood Publishing.

Eisenstein, Z. (2004) *Against Empire*, London, Zed Books.

Eschle, C. (2005) '"Skeleton women": feminism and the anitglobalization movement'", *Signs*, 30, 1741–70.

Eschle, C. and Maiguashca, B. (eds) (2005) *Critical Theories, International Relations and 'the Anti-Globalisation Movement': The Politics of Global Resistance*, London and New York, Routledge.

Friedman, S. S. (1998) *Mappings: Feminism and the Cultural Geographies of Encounter*, Princeton, NJ, Princeton University Press.

Grewal, I. (1994) 'Autobiographic subjects and diasporic locations: 'Meatless Days' and 'Borderlands'' in I. Grewal and C. Kaplan (eds), *Scattered Hegemonies: Postmodernity and Transnational Feminist Practices*, Minneapolis, University of Minnesota Press, pp. 231–54.

Grewal, I. and Kaplan, C. (1994) 'Introduction: transnational feminist practices and questions of post-modernity' in I. Grewal and C. Kaplan (eds), *Scattered Hegemonies: Postmodernity and Transnational Feminist Practices*, Minneapolis, University of Minnesota Press, pp. 1–36.

Haussman, M. (2005) *Abortion Politics in North America*, Boulder and London, Lynne Rienner Publishers.

Hawkesworth, M., Harder, L. and Bayes, J. (2006) 'Future prospects for women, globalization, democracy in North America' in J. Bayes et al. (eds), *Women, Democracy, and Globalization in North America: A Comparative Study*, New York, Palgrave Macmillan, pp. 173–88.

Konigsberg, E. (2006) 'The new class war: the haves vs. the have mores', *New York Times*, 19, November, Section 4, pp. 1, 3.

Krook, M. L., Lovenduski, J. and Squires, J. (2006) 'Western Europe, North America, Australia and New Zealand: gender quotas in the context of citizenship models' in D. Dahlerup (ed.), *Women, Quotas and Politics*, London and New York, Routledge, pp. 194–221.

MacDonald, L. (2002) 'Globalization and social movements: comparing women's movements' responses to NAFTA in Mexico, the U.S., and Canada', *International Feminist Journal of Politics*, 4, 151–72.

———. (2005) 'Gendering transnational social movement analysis: women's groups contest free trade in the Americas' in J. Bandy and J. Smith (eds), *Coalitions Across Borders: Transnational Protest and the Neoliberal Order*, Lanham, MD, Rowman & Littlefield Publishers, pp. 21–42.

———. (2006) 'Globalization and gender in Canada' in J. Bayes et al. (eds), *Women, Democracy, and Globalization in North America: A Comparative Study*, New York, Palgrave, pp. 145–72.

Maiguashca, B. (2005) 'Globalisation and the "politics of identity": IR theory through the looking glass of women's reproductive rights and activism' in C. Eschle and B. Maiguashca (eds), *Critical Theories, International Relations and the 'Anti-Globalisation Movement': The Politics of Global Resistance*, London and New York, Routledge, pp. 117–36.

Mittelman, J. H. (2004) *Whither Globalization? The Vortex of Knowledge and Ideology*, London and New York, Routledge.

Moghadam, V. H. (2005) *Globalizing Women: Transnational Feminist Networks*, Baltimore and London, Johns Hopkins University Press.

Pieterse, J. N. (2004) *Globalization or Empire?* New York and London, Routledge.

Rupert, M. (2005) 'In the belly of the beast: resisting globalisation and war in a neo-imperial moment', in C. Eschle and B. Maiguashca (eds), *Critical Theories, International Relations and the 'Anti-Globalisation Movement': The Politics of Global Resistance*, London and New York, Routledge, pp. 36–52.

CHAPTER 11

International Sex and Service

Jan Jindy Pettman

This chapter will revisit the notion of an international political economy (IPE) of sex[1] through a focus on international domestic work and transnational sex, especially involving women from poorer Southeast Asian states. It will do so in light of intensifying globalization processes, and the recent profusion of writings on these global flows. There are now a number of specific site studies of sex tourism and of women as labour migrants, in particular as domestic workers. Also, there are new configurations in feminist theoretical and political debates about international sex and sexualised service industries. This chapter will review these writings as a way of considering the continued relevance of positing an IPE of sex.

An international political economy of sex?

The notion of an IPE of sex is a way to make visible, and make sense of, forms of unequal international exchanges which are both gendered and sexualised (Pettman, 1996). It pays particular attention to women who are 'out of place', and 'on the move', beyond the bounds of protection, of either their men/families, or their state.[2] These moves are impelled by the changing global division of labour, the particular hierarchies of state and region, and gender dynamics in the context of globalization.

In the IPE of sex I traced different kinds of border crossings and transnational work that are identified as women's work, including international domestic work, sex tourism, military-base sex, and mail-order brides. Women's bodies are commodified and circulated along transnational circuits which bring together power and wealth, structure and agency, identity and culture, within a global frame. They are marked by unequal relations between rich and poor (states and classes), between men and women, and between different women.

In my chapter on the IPE of sex, I made several moves which I wish to revisit here. It sought to identify and track bodies and borders, bodies crossing borders – between states, between the inside and the outside, between local/national and the international, and between the public and the private. It considered these body/border crossings within the context of globalization processes and global power relations structuring and segmenting labour markets. In so doing, it recognised asymmetrical power relations, while refusing to reduce these crossings and consequent transnational work experiences to structural imperatives or generative compulsions alone. It recognised the complex personal, family and community politics which underlie individual decisions to migrate and noted the role of states in mediating and controlling both migration and restructuring.

The IPE of sex applied a gender lens to these crossings, for it makes a difference when these are women's bodies. In the process, it aimed to contribute feminist knowledge to globalization studies, and to contribute a focus on the impact of globalization on women's bodies and gender relations to feminism as well.[3] Tracing bodies disrupts the usual disembodied accounts and refusals of IR/IPE. It makes visible something of the mess, pain, pleasure and pressure of everyday life and of moving. It should make visible sexual difference, too – for in seeing bodies, we can see different bodies, and differences marked on and read from 'the body'. However, we need to take care about how we speak of bodies and sexualities, lest we become complicit in the kinds of representation which figure 'third world' and minoritised women's bodies as erotic, and/or victimised, and so replicate voyeuristic and predatory uses of other women's bodies, as bodies for others. The challenge then is to write gendered, feminist, embodied and fleshy accounts of women's lives[4], work, and journeying, within the context of contemporary globalization processes.

This chapter revisits the notion of an IPE of sex with a particular focus on visible and lucrative forms of international trade in women's bodies: 'out' migration of women for transnational domestic service work and for sex work; and border crossings of men (mostly) for exotic/tourist sex.

Globalization

Globalization is a shorthand term for global processes and practices, and for understanding about the changes that have become especially manifest since the ECW. Globalization reconfigures relations between capital and labour, and between states and markets, summarised in the assumption that 'the market rules'. It does so in part because of the current dominance of neo-liberal and globalization ideologies which privilege 'the market' as inevitable, so that it comes to dominate. This naturalising of market and globalization processes has the effect of disguising the history and politics, including the repeated practices of power which set up market rights and discredit other ways of imagining society, economy and international relations.

Globalization is propelled by a revolution in technology and communications which underlies the 'third industrial revolution' (Scholte, 2000; Peterson, 2002). It both produces and is produced by the push to deregulation, free trade and especially the remarkable rise of finance capital. Production is transformed and frequently transnationalised. States act more like firms, competing for and facilitating international capital (Cerny). Production for export is privileged. Restructuring or structural adjustment downgrades social provision and reduces state responsibilities for direction of state economies and for the welfare of citizens. Social costs are increasingly privatised, adding to the burden of responsibility for physical and social reproduction in families, which usually means women. It increases the personal costs of everyday life for those women who must extend more time, effort and energy on survival and family maintenance work. As well, it reduces state employment in those sectors – for example, education, health and community welfare – where women predominate.

These pressures are compounded by unemployment or underemployment more generally. More and more people are 'on the move' for work or just to survive. Increasingly those who move are women (Pettman, 1998). This relates in part to gender relations in the family. Women are more likely than men to maintain contact with home, send remittances and return. In some families and areas, women are also more expendable, as they would on marriage leave home to contribute to husbands' family and/or be costly to marry. As well, the gender effects of globalization have rapidly increased the demand for women's labour, constructed through ideologies of femininity – as temporary, supplementary, pliant and patient – as cheap labour (Enloe, 1992). This applies to factory work on the global assembly line, and to the kinds of sex and service work which are amongst the fastest growing sectors of the global economy.

Globalization is an uneven process. It aggravates existing inequalities and creates new ones. Some states and classes have done well from the changes, though the triad of North America, Western Europe and Japan still rule. But the Asian miracle saw substantial growth in East Asia including Singapore from the 1970s, and in some Southeast Asian states from the 1980s. There is much anticipation and anxiety regarding China, as it marketises while maintaining authoritarian communist rule. The Asian crisis of 1997 undermined talk of 'Asia rising', but a number of the states so affected are now in recovery (with the obvious exception of Indonesia). In the 1990s, the fall of European state socialism and dismantling of the Soviet Union universalised the market and subjected many people to the rigours of restructuring and growth in unemployment and social insecurities. At the same time, significant parts of the world appear to have been abandoned or bypassed, left only as reservoirs of labour, combatants or natural resources.

This uneven impact of globalization and its unequal patterns of wealth and power underlie the restructuring of labour on a global scale. Within and across states, labour is increasingly polarised between professional and skilled workers associated especially with market management and the new techno-economies, and unskilled or deskilled service and manufacturing workers. Labour is increasingly flexiblised, casualised and feminised; channelled into piecemeal, outwork, sweatshops, informal or shadow work. These changing conditions reflect and affect reduced worker protection, in the name of competition and productiveness. Women, especially young women[5], make ideal employees where cheap labour is at a premium, making up most of those employed in export-processing zones for example. But even where men are still employed, they experience forms and conditions of work formerly more associated with women (Peterson, 2003).

It is important to recognise that these forms of labour are not residual or premodern. They are an integral part of the current global market and its restructuring. They are not an unfortunate side effect of globalization but intrinsic to it, for they service the global elites and global capital. This work challenges us to theorise the relationship between formal and informal economy, and between public and private, including paid labour in private or domestic places, and to take the reproductive economy seriously (Gibson et al., 2001; Gibson-Graham, 1996; Peterson, 2003).

Chang and Ling (2000) pursue this connection through their identification of two rather different globalization processes. The first is the popular view, of global finance, production, trade and communications, where the difference between 'core regions' and 'deadlands' is masked by privileging aggressive market competition, which they call 'technomuscular capitalism' (28). The second process is 'more explicitly sexualised, racialised, and class-based . . . low-wage, low-skilled menial service provided mostly by female migrant workers' (27). This they identify as a regime of labour intimacy, the intimate Other to techno-muscular capitalism. They argue that 'techno-masculinst' capitalism's 'structural adjustment' policies of the 1970s–1980s account for today's 'global feminisation of labour intimacy in a globalised service economy' (34).

Sassen (2000) also stresses that such service work is a crucial component of contemporary globalization. She notes 'a growing presence of women in a variety of cross-border circuits that have become a source for livelihood, profit-making and the accrual of foreign currency' (2000: 503), which she names 'counter-geographies of globalization'. They overlap with some of the major dynamics that compose globalization: the formation of global markets, the intensification of transnational and trans-local networks and development of communications technologies' (503–4). These dynamics generate a shadow economy that operates in part through institutional structures of the formal economy. Women are crucial in these counter-geographies, including through the 'feminization of survival, because it is increasingly on the backs of women' that family survival, business profits and government revenue are secured (506). Global cities are 'strategic sites for the specialized servicing, financing and management of global economic processes . . . [and] the incorporation of large numbers of women and immigrants in activities that service strategic sectors in both shadow and formal economic activities', as 'serving classes', sustaining new global economies (510).

Labour migration

Globalization restructures national economies and inserts workers into global circuits of production and exchange. It also restructures labour so as to maintain a global reserve of labour, and to direct cheapened workers into a segmented labour market through the extensive use of labour migrants.

Labour migration has always been a feature of capitalism and of development. It waxes and wanes, and follows particular tracks across state borders and into global flows, depending on both the global political economy in general, and on particular hierarchies of power and wealth within that frame. Goss and Lindquist (1998) note continuities of global labour migration over time. Patterns of uneven development are crucial, but so too are migration regimes, dual labour markets, social networks and individual negotiations. They distinguish between three phases of labour migration: 1830–1940, 1940–70 and the contemporary phase from the 1970s, marked especially by growth in contract labour and temporary work migration. Nowadays, most expect to and are expected to return home. Large numbers of illegal workers dramatically demonstrate the significance of national borders and the tension between deregulated capital flows and restrictions on migration by state governments. Again, this tension is not an unresolved or residual factor. Rather, 'the border remains a vital part of the construction and reproduction of an international labour reserve, and it is used to systematically segment national labour markets' (Goss and Lindquist, 1998: 16).[6]

These markets and systems are structured by the global division of labour and by labour and migration regimes, including border patrols and migration policies, and both sender and receiving states' policies and practices regarding contract workers. Crossing the border conditionally as contract labour or illegally, or becoming illegal through overstaying or breaking conditions, compounds both the vulnerability and the exploitability of migrant workers. It separates them from host state workers, frequently setting these workers against each other, or at least reducing the likelihood of solidarity.[7] It leaves labour migrants in a strange in-between, where often they cannot claim either citizen or worker rights.

However, references to 'globalization' can disguise particular flows and localized features. 'The question . . . is how within the generalised production of a global labour reserve, regional and bilateral systems develop and remain distinctive' (Goss and Linquist, 1998: 18). Here, 'global' is the context and the overall set of structuring relations. Within that frame, historical, colonial, regional and neighbour migrations set particular tracks; return migration, transnational family connections and social networks, and recruiting businesses sustain already existing links and flows.

For this reason, we need to attend to migration systems: networks of states or regions linked together through sustained migration. Examples include contract workers from South/Southeast Asian states to the Middle East and both contract workers and undocumented workers from poorer South and Southeast Asian states into richer Asian states. These and other systems and flows reveal an IPE of migration, clearly mapped in flows from poorer to richer, from employment surplus to labour demand states, feeding the 'absorptive patches of global capitalism' (Aquilar, 1998: 4). Some states become providers of migrant labour, others become destinations and siren calls. For example, the Philippines has 6.97 million people residing and working overseas, 2.9 million as overseas contract workers (OCWs), and 1.8 million as undocumented workers – though estimating the latter is particularly complicated (Asis, 1999). In 1997 for the first time Philippines workers going to other Asian countries outnumbered those going to the Middle East, as international sex and service flows come to predominate. Saudi Arabia remains the largest single destination, followed (in order) by Hong Kong, Taiwan, Japan, United Arab Emirates, Singapore and Malaysia (Battistella, 1998). This list indicates changes in migration status over time, with Taiwan emerging as a newer, significant state. The inclusion of Japan is a reminder that 'migration denying' states like Japan and South Korea do have increasing numbers of foreign workers, too (Moon, 2000).

Migrant workers fill particular niches in the labour market in receiving states. Here again we find labour market segmentation, with professional, managerial and other skilled workers often highly mobile, sought-after and rewarded and other workers classified as unskilled or deskilled service workers.[8] Increased feminisation of migrant labour flows marks the growing importance of international service work, and the gendered division of labour within it (Willis and Yeoh, 2000). I have asked questions concerning women's work that are relevant here (Pettman, 1996). Why is it women who are overwhelmingly responsible for reproductive work almost everywhere? Why is womens' work so often regarded as a labour of love, as not really work at all? And why is it routinely unpaid or underpaid? Clearly gender roles, constructions of femininity and masculinity, and the association of domestic work with the private sphere all play a role, even where family form and cultural differences also figure. Clearly too these constructions not only give women who also work outside the home (be it in subsistence, informal or formal sector) double loads, but 'catch' them in negotiating the contradictions and competing demands of these loads.

International domestic work

Women occupy difficult border zones between the public and private, and between productive and reproductive work. These difficulties are compounded when we add yet another border, the international or state-to-state border. Many women are on the move in attempts to fulfil family or household obligations, though some may also be in flight from families or communities, and others make their own way. Furthermore, many women move across state borders to do 'women's work', including domestic work. They enter and live in other homes and families (in the intimate economy) as servants or paid workers – and as foreigners (Wong, 1996). Their work sites and kinds mean that they are often outside public view, as non-citizens and as house-workers. They are often not subject to industrial legislation and worker protections (where they exist).

Focusing on international domestic workers facilitates a double move familiar to feminist international relations observers. Globalization affects women differently from men, because, among other reasons, women are already located differently within labour markets at home and in destination countries. Globalization feeds demands for particular kinds of servicing work which are largely identified with women. On the other hand, women's experiences, choices, mobility and work are now significantly affected by globalization, which many development and in-state studies overlook.

International domestic work reflects the transformation of economies and households, for example as more women go 'out' to work, or to provide care for children, older and ill people as states reduce or withdraw support.[9] Rich state labour shortages mean that the search for domestic labour moves beyond state borders, rather than negotiating changes in gender relations and the sexual division of labour within households.

The international 'trade in maids' is now increasingly visible, and requires analysis of class and gender relations, within a global frame. Thanh-Dam Truong traces the extension of the sexual division of labour in households and national economies into the global labour market, in what amounts to a massive 'transfer of reproductive labour from one class, ethnic group, nation or region to another' (1996: 33).[10] This formation depends on the continuing assumption that reproduction is women's responsibility.

While the scale and visibility of the international domestic worker (IDW) trade is new, migration for domestic work is not. There are now many single-state studies. For example, Wong (1996) traces the history of domestic service in Singapore.[11] In the early twentieth century this included the *mui tsai* system of unpaid domestic servitude where very young girls, including those bought in China, were given into the employer's family. Restrictions on this trade in the 1930s initiated largescale migration of women into domestic service, for many of the 190,000 Chinese women who migrated to Malaya and Singapore between 1934 and 1938. In the 1960s and 70s, domestic workers were increasingly drawn from amongst poorer local women, but the transformation of the economy and the growth of the manufacturing sector led to a shortage of local recruits. At the same time, increasing numbers of women participating in the paid labour force increased the demand for paid domestic labour. From the early 1980s, the demand was increasingly met through recruiting 'foreign' domestic workers. By 1984, one household in every 10 employed a foreign domestic worker.

Singapore now has the highest proportion of foreign workers of any Asian state, some 30 per cent of its work force. The bulk of these workers are (men) in the construction industry and (women) in domestic work. They are regarded as a labour reserve, to accommodate local labour shortages. Now there are some 100,000 IDWs in Singapore, three-quarters from the Philippines, one-fifth from Indonesia, the rest mainly from Sri Lanka (Yeoh and Huang, 2000). These workers face stringent controls to ensure that their stay is short-term, including a rigorous allocation system, with government holding an employer security bond, and a two-year work permit on condition they do not marry a Singaporean or become pregnant. Despite government regulation and surveillance, they are excluded from the operations and possible protection of the Employment Act because their employment is treated as a private contract between the domestic worker and her employer (Yeoh and Huang, 2000).

There is a racialisation and nationalisation hierarchy of IDW that is reflected in local agencies' newspaper advertisements and in popular associations of particular characteristics and skills with particular nationalities. Those from the Philippines are most in demand and more expensive. They are characterised as good English speakers, quick learners and more competent, but also as bold and streetwise, and potential trouble. Indonesians are ranked next, as hardworking and obedient, while Sri Lankans are least regarded, stereotyped as lazy, and backward (Willis and Yeoh, 2000). The trade in IDWs thus reflects and reproduces a racialised hierarchy of women and of states (Pettman, 1998). These differences are reflected spatially and through social networks too, as women from different states meet in different city locations on their day off, for example (Wong, 1996).

Globalization feeds on the bodies of women. The international trade in women in sex and service now attracts considerable publicity which also feeds on stories of abuses to and pain of women's bodies (Tadiar, 1997). At the same time, these stories of suffering are used to deploy women's bodies to stand in for the national body, also suffering under globalization.

Particular states become labour producers and exporters; particular kinds of labour are both sexualised and nationalised. So the Philippines becomes identified internationally as a 'nation of servants', generating a kind of transnational shame (Aguilar, 1999). International domestic workers (along with sex work; see below) become emblematic of this shame (Tadiar, 1997; Rafael, 1997; Hilsdon, 2000). Women's bodies on transnational circuits are utilised as evidence of the Philippines government's failure to provide for its people, and of its servicing global capital and the US military through selling off its citizens' bodies (Pettman, 1998). Here, too, transnational mobilities and the changing global division of labour reflects, and reproduces, a racialised hierarchy of women and of states.

Yet how do we account for the fact that many labour migrants, including IDWs, opt for return migration, renew contracts or help recruit other family members or neighbours? Why do so many tell stories of adventure accomplishment, excitement or liberation, even if at personal cost? Aquilar asks how we can 'understand international labour migration from the perspective of the migrant actors, whose generally positive assessment of their employment in other countries baffles and contradicts the sentiments of academics, rights advocates and other observers' (Aguilar, 1999: 2–3). He proposes understanding labour migration as ritual, as a secular journey which involves struggle, quest and transformation. In this context, he complicates the currently popular view of women migrating as part of family income strategy, arguing that 'family' can function as a reason for going or for not going; and that family rhetoric might legitimise women's desire to escape, or for adventure, learning or income.

Anne-Marie Hilsdon refers to Filipinos working overseas as engaging in a rite of passage. She listens to migrant workers, whose recountings are not all of exploitation, danger, loneliness or loss (1998). IDWs reconstruct their identities and experiences to make sense of their own lives and worth. They frequently mobilise identities as self-sacrificing and dutiful wives, mothers and citizens – in part to distance themselves from the sexualising and victim imagery they so frequently face (Chang and Ling, 2000; Tadiar, 1997). They are clearly active in making sense of their own experiences of work and travel, as they are in forging new identities and networks in the new places. Among the most famous is the colourful, noisy and lively meeting of Filipinas in the middle of the CBD in Hong Kong on Sundays, their day off. They move from private constriction to public display, causing considerable local agitation in the process.

These stories and sites call attention to identity formation and performance through mobility, work and return; and to networks that sustain or propel these mobilities. Public knowledge about IDWs is produced through moral panics, NGO activism, transnational alliances, media portrayals, political/policy formulations and academic texts, as well as through forms of cultural production and testimony of the women themselves. It is a challenge to negotiate the tension between structure and agency, power relations of domination and resistance, and collective identities and individual identifications. Which ways of writing can give import both to the dynamism and power of globalization processes and an international political economy of sex, and those who make their own way – though not in circumstances of their own making?

International sex

If it is difficult to write of international domestic service, it is even more difficult to write of international sex, and of the global sexual economies in which such sex takes place. These economies demonstrate the usefulness of gender analysis and the significance of sexuality in IR/IPE. They also demonstrate the dangers of reproducing the sexualisation and always/already victim of 'Third World Woman'.[11]

International sex refers to migration across state borders for sex work and the sex that results from such migration; and to sex tourism, where the buyer goes travelling for sex. Sex worker migration is often associated with trafficking in women for forced prostitution. In fact, trafficking is not only of women, nor only for prostitution, but is an aspect of labour migration more generally (Kempadoo, 2005). Trafficking is a symptom of the border, and of border patrols: many who wish to migrate for work must seek out recruiters, agents and traffickers to get across (Skrobanek et al., 1997; Skedlon, 2000; Ucarer, 1999). Representations of trafficking as always and only coercive and deceptive are not necessarily true. However, the illegal border crossing places many in debt or in danger from the traffickers or those with whom the traffickers trade.

There is also considerable evidence of violent and vicious trafficking, and of children and women forced into sex work in situations where both the illegality of the work and their illegal status as migrants compound the dangers. Many stories are dreadful, telling of violence and greed, betrayal and deceit, at the intersections of sexism and racism, business and poverty, maldevelopment and debt (personal and national) and protection rackets that frequently include border and police personnel (Asia Watch, 1993; Matsui, 1996; Brown, 2000). These stories provide evidence and motivation for campaigns against trafficking, and for those who oppose sex work more generally as intrinsically demeaning to and dangerous for women. For example, the Coalition against Trafficking in Women (CATW) argues that as long as there is prostitution there will be trafficking (this point seems hard to resist). It therefore adopts an abolition position against prostitution (Barry, 1995). International sex in this telling is a moral issue, an abuse of women's and human rights. This abolitionist strand is in the tradition of international organising that goes back one hundred years or more, and was until recently dominant in global organising.

But not all the women engaged in sex tourism, nor all trafficked into prostitution, are hapless victims. Many who are trafficked for prostitution are recruited by someone they know, some with the agreement or complicity of family members; a number engage in return migration. Many of those engaged in sex tourism in Thailand, for example, construct themselves as dutiful daughters, asserting the contribution they make to their families (Skrobanek et al., 1997; Cook, 1998; Pettman, 1999). Like the IDWs, these may be personal testimonies and performances to salvage honour and justify costs. They can also be read in a search for agency, and within the understanding that many other forms of work available to poorer women are dangerous and damaging, too.

These stories confirm poverty as a form of coercion which makes prostitution a viable option. But only in some cases is desperate poverty or displacement a key (the proportion itself fiercely contested). Again, the women's own accounts complicate our explanations, as for example family income strategies for survival jostle with a desire for consumer goods or improved lifestyle. Rather than blame, Sanitsuda Ekacai suggests it might be more useful to ask why, in Thailand for example, are options for improved goods or even living so restricted that sending a daughter into sex work may seem the only choice? (quoted in Bishop and Robinson, 1998: 213).

Listening carefully is also essential for constructing effective strategies. The Thai Foundation for Women's (FOW) *The Traffic in Women* (Skrobanek et al., 1997) reports on Thai women and trafficking for sex research action. Its authors locate trafficking as an aspect of transnational migration, and as a global issue related to 'the international division of labour, the migration policies of sending and receiving countries, and the impact of all these on female labour migration, both nationally and internationally' (9). They identify traffic in women as a grave violation of human rights. They explore strategies against trafficking in partnership with women affected by trafficking, and in so doing, they reveal the complexities of this task. Those who have been trafficked may return to sex work, or may recruit others to it, after their return home. Project workers were attacked by some mothers who were receiving money from their daughters and did not wish to know, or did not wish others to know, how the money was earned. Those who did provide testimony concerning their own bitter experiences could be made more vulnerable. Project workers soon became aware that 'the promotion of understanding had to be structured in such a way that it did not offend families whose daughters were abroad, and so that it did not add to the discrimation against sex workers' (91). But others were grateful for more information, and wished to organise to prevent their daughters from entering the international sex trade.

The FOW project is an example of many NGOs and commentators who do attempt to accommodate the nuances, and to attend to the voices and needs of those caught up in international sex. One current strategy distinguishes between trafficking and forced prostitution on the one hand and sex work on the other. The Global Alliance Against Trafficking in Women (GAATW), and the FOW Project are examples of this strategy. It has become influential in international organising for women's rights and against violence. For example, the 1993 Vienna Declaration on the Elimination of Violence Against Women included trafficking and forced prostitution as violence against women, but did not include prostitution per se; and the 1995 Beijing Platform for Action of the fourth UN Conference on Women reiterated this distinction These distinctions were contested through the politics around the adoption of the 2000 UN Trafficking Protocol (Sullivan, 2003; Kempadoo, 2005).

The voluntary/coerced distinction is, however, difficult to maintain, as the element of choice is suspect in conditions of economic need, lack of options, and asymmetrical power relations, including gender relations within the family. The distinction might also have the unintended effect of undermining the rights and safety of 'voluntary' sex workers by privileging the innocence of 'forced' workers (Pickup, 1998). This critique is taken further by organised sex workers, who argue that the distinction reproduces the dichotomy between free-choice first-world sex workers, and coerced third-world sex workers, perpetuating the victim image of the latter (Murray, 1998)[13]. It also facilitates ongoing state and police surveillance of the sex scene, encouraging forms of 'protection' and intervention that deny the human rights and worker rights of sex workers.

Recently the views of non-Western sex workers have become increasingly visible, revealing that organization and rights talk are not the monopoly of the West. Kempadoo and Doezema (1998) have brought together a range of 'third world' sex worker organizations and voices, and traced their growing participation in global organizing. Their emphasis is mainly on working conditions, rejecting the victim approach, and urging 'the respectful recognition of subjectivity and personal agency'. They continue:

> Explorations of agency encountered in *Global Sex Workers* identify sites of transformative practices within the context of both structural constraints and dominant relations of power in the global sex industry. By underlining agency, resistances to and contestations of, oppressive and exploitative structures are uncovered, and the visions and ideologies inscribed in women's practices made visible. Such analyses position sex workers as actors in the global arena, as persons capable of making choices and decisions that lead to transformations of consciousness and changes in everyday life. (8–9)[12]

These different positions regarding prostitution reflect sex wars among women's and feminist organizations campaigning for action on the global stage, which replay differences over sex, sexuality and work (Pettman, 1997; Sullivan, 2003). They are deeply felt and have profound consequences for strategy and action: for example, over whether organizing principles should be women's rights, workers' rights or migration rights; and around issues of victim and agency.

There is a global sex industry, and an IPE of sex among sex workers too. For example, in Amsterdam in the 1970s and 80s, migrant sex workers were predominantly from Southeast Asia and Latin America. After the fall of European state socialism, increasing numbers came from Central and East Europe (Marchand et al., 1998). These shifts replicate the racialised, nationalised hierarchy of states and women amongst sex workers in first world locations. They support the 'poverty/dislocation' model, and suggest that marketization and integration into the global economy mean integration into the global sexual economy, too.

'In this libidinal new world order in which gendered sexualities are signifiers of the organizing principles of national economies and their political status in the international community, the Philippines functions as a hostess nation' (Tadiar, 1998: 927). Tadiar traces the move, similar to the IDW context (above), from the actual woman's body to the symbolic use of woman's body to stand in for the body politic, or the national body. In the Philippines, 'the prostitute' becomes a metaphor for the nation within international relations and the global political economy, and for the nation's losses in globalization processes. This felt threat is a direct response to the feminisation of Philippines' labour, restructured under global capitalist compulsions, including workers' insertion into forms of labour to do with international sex and service. 'Prostitution thus pertains not only to the metaphorical construction of the Philippines as both female and feminine – signifying its lack of political and economic power and its status as possessed territory with permeable boundaries – but also to the actual conscription of female workers and their sexualised labour' (Tadiar, 1998: 932).

This metaphorical use of women's bodies to indicate the anxiety around globalization is familiar in international relations, using the nation's women to symbolise penetration, rape, danger and boundary transgressions more generally. These uses can elide the bodies and experiences of actual Philippines women, including those engaged in a complex international political economy of sex, first providing US military-base sex, and now sex tourism.[13]

In Thailand, very different politics and rhetoric surround its sexual economy (though it is often put together with the Philippines with regard to sex tourism). Within Thailand, the public uses of 'the prostitute' and discourse around international sex are heavily constrained by what Bishop and Robinson (1998) call the 'unspeakability' of something about which many people know, but most do not wish to acknowledge (see also Cook, 1998). They note that it has become easier to speak of international sex and local sex since another global phenomenon, HIV/AIDS, enabled and funded talking about paid sex as a public health issue. Behind such support is concern at the potential threat to tourist dollars and hard currency for the government. Bishop and Robinson provide a close reading of ways in which sex tourism has been represented in popular, media, political and academic commentaries from outside Thailand, as well. They note the continuing absence of sex tourism in most tourism literature,[14] and the paucity of reports which do flesh out what I am calling an IPE of sex. They trace both to 'a very political economy' and a cluster of cultural representations that are infused with colonial, national, racialised and gendered associations and identities. The politics of representation to which they draw attention return us to the difficulties of writing sex tourism without reproducing the Thai or Filipina or Asian woman as both always/already victim, and/or as sexualised (Law, 2000). They are also a reminder of, and caution against, the uses of the prostituted body for different kinds of politics, including feminist politics.

International sex and service

Globalization has restructured women's lives and gender relations across state boundaries, as surely as it has reconstituted inter-state relations and international political economy. Globalization has propelled many women's moving across state borders, including into forms of international sex and service which are the focus of this chapter. It has also prompted women's and feminist organizing against the abuses and inequalities which are inherent in these forms of work – though not inevitable for every woman in that work.

There is a global political economy of sex, which links maldevelopment, poverty and unemployment into transnational flows and a global division of labour, which are gendered. Intimate economies of sex and service are increasingly internationalised. Women's experiences as international sex and service workers generate NGO activism and transnational campaigns. These in turn contribute to public knowledge and ways of understanding both the work and the transnational circuits along which the women move (Mohanty, 2003; Pettman, 2004).

Stivens (2000: 22) notes that 'the acute issues of who may speak for and about whom have consumed feminisms in the last decades'. However, '[g]lobalisation would appear to make any simple opposition between "Western" and "third world" women problematic'. Many who bewail or celebrate globalization remark that political and economic effects can no longer be contained within national boundaries; nor might individual states be appropriate or effective targets for action. The gendered effects of globalization require global forms of solidarity and action in response.

Globalization propels forms of restructuring and demands on women's choices, time, work and bodies that necessitate global responses. Indeed, as noted above, it is often the very bodily effects and assaults of globalization that have generated women's and feminist activism and organization. Languages and strategies differ, depending on different understandings of both women/gender relations and globalization. These connections are shaped by transnational travelling and global effects, and by forged transnational and global connections. They utilise new global technologies like e-mail and the Internet. They are also an aspect of globalization and nourishing transnational solidarities and communities, generating what Stivens (2000: 26) calls a global feminist public.

Notes

1. Developed in my 1996 chapter, and in *Worlding Women*, 1996.
2. Though note that 'protection' can be dangerous for women, who cannot necessarily control the conditions of protection.
3. In the last decade, feminist attention to globalization has flourished. See for example Marchand and Runyan, 2000; Mohanty, 2003; Pettman, 2004).
4. See Beasley and Bacchi (2000) for a pursuit of social flesh, in this case regarding women's citizenship.
5. In this chapter I usually use the catch-all term 'women', though closer examination in many of these cases reveals many young women and girl children.
6. Border control and surveillance of border crossers and national minorities have intensified in the wake of 9/11 and the subsequent 'war on terror'; security impacts directly on economic migrants as well as refugees and others on the move.

7. For a fascinating exception, see transnational affiliations and organizing for migrant-worker rights in South Korea (Moon, 2000).
8. Deskilling is particularly obvious in the case of Filipina nurses, teachers and other qualified women who move across state borders as IDWs.
   There are also questions here regarding the relations between both older and more recent migrants, and between recent migrants of different class and identity background, for example men from South Asia into Singapore and Malaysia, some as construction workers and others as professionals.
9. My 1996 chapter notes that a home-state woman is usually responsible for the hire and supervision of IDWs, raising difficult issues for feminists regarding complex racialised and nationalised politics and unequal power relations among women, too.
10. Rather differently, Yeats (2004) identifies 'global care chains' situated at the nexus of globalization, migration and care labour. See also the *Globalizations* (2006) symposium on transnational gendered care work.
11. Pearson and Theobald (1998) caution that a focus on sex work rather than factory work can become complicit with popular sexualisation of Thai women, for example, and make it difficult for activists to organize and campaign for women's rights as workers. This confirms the difficulties of writing sex across racialised and national lines (Pettman 1999). See also Laura Hyun Yi Kang 'Si(gh)ting Asian/American Women As Transnational Labor', Positions 5 (2) 1997, 403-38.
12. See the Inter-Asian Cultural Studies Forum (2006) on the introduction of the language of 'sex worker' and increased visibility and voice of sex workers in several Asian states.
13. Though feminist organizations like GABRIELA, both deploy the 'prostitution' motif to critique US and sexploitation, and work closely with sex workers in support of the latter's strategies and choices (Pettman, 1996).
14. I have written elsewhere about both IR and tourist studies 'missing the body' (Pettman, 1997: 1999).

References

Aguilar, F. (1999) 'Ritual passage and the reconstruction of self-hoodin international labour migration', *Sojourn*, 4 (1), 98–139.

Asian and Pacific Migration Journal (1996) Special issue on Migration in Asia, 5 (1).

Asia Watch Women's Rights Project (1993) *A Modern Form of Slavery: Trafficking of Burmese Women and Girls into Brothels in Thailand*, New York, Human Rights Watch.

Assis, M. (1999) 'Introduction', *Asian and Pacific Migration Journal*, 8 (1/2), 1–14.

Bakker, I. (ed.) (1994) *The Strategic Silence: Gender and Economic Policy*, London, Zed Books.

Barry, K. (1995) *The Prostitution of Sexuality: The Global Exploitation of Women*, New York, New York University Press.

Battistella, G. (1998) 'Migration in the context of globalization: issues and implications', *Asian Migrant*, 11 (1), 10-16.

Beasley, C. and Bacchi, C. (2000) 'Citizen bodies: embodying citizens – a feminist analysis', *International Feminist Journal of Politics*, 2 (3), 337–58.

Bishop, R. and Robinson, L. (1998) *Night Market: Sexual Cultures and the Thai Economic Miracle*, New York, Routledge.

Brown, L. (2000) *Sex Slaves: The Trafficking of Women in Asia*, London, Virago.

Chang, K. and Ling, L. H. L. (2000) 'Globalization and its intimate other: Filipina domestic workers in Hong Kong' in M. Marchand and A. Sisson Runyan (eds), *Gender and Global Restructuring*, London, Routledge, pp. 27–43.

Cook, N. (1998) '"Dutiful daughters" estranged sisters: women in Thailand' in K. Sen and M. Stivens (eds), *Gender and Power in Affluent Asia*, London, Routledge, pp. 250–90.

Enloe, C. (1992) 'Silicon tricks and the two dollar woman', *New Internationalist*, January, 12–14.

Gibson, K., Law, L. and McKay, D. (2001) 'Beyond heroes and victims: Filipina contract migrants, economic activism and class transformations', *International Feminist Journal of Politics*, 3 (3), 365–86.

Gibson-Graham, K. (1996) *The End of Capitalism (As We Knew It): A Feminist Critique of Political Economy*, Oxford, Blackwell.

Goss, J. and Lindquist, B. (1998) 'Placing movers: conceptualizing international migration in Asia and the Pacific', paper to 'Moving Cultures: Remaking Asia-Pacific Studies' conference, Honolulu.

Hilsdon, A-M. (1998) 'The good life: cultures of migration and transformation of overseas workers in the Philippines', *Pilipinas* 28, 49–62.

———. (2000) 'The Contemplacion fiasco: the hanging of a Filipino domestic worker in Singapore' in A. Hilsdon et al. (eds), *Gender Politics and Human Rights in Asia and the Pacific*, London, Routledge.

Huang, S. and Yeoh, B. (1998) 'Discourse on foreign maids in Singapore: constructions of the national self and the Other', Workshop on Migrations in Contemporary Southeast Asia, Singapore.

Kempadoo, K. (1999) 'Slavery or work? Reconceptualising Third World prostitution', *Positions*, 7 (1), 225–38.

———. Kempadoo, K. (ed.) (2005) Trafficking and Prostitution Reconsidered: New Perspectives on Migration, Sex Work and Human Rights, Boulder, CO: Paradigm Publishers.

Kempadoo, K. and Doezema, J. (eds) (1998) *Global Sex Workers: Rights, Resistance, and Redefinition*, New York, Routledge.

Law, L. (2000) *Global Sex Work: Desire in a Time of AIDS*, New York, Routledge.

Lim, L. L. (ed.) (1998) *The Sex Sector: The Economic and Social Bases of Prostitution in Southeast Asia*, Geneva, International Labor Organization.

Matsui, Y. (1996) *Women of the New Asia; from Pain to Power*, Bangkok, White Lotus.

Millennium (1998) Special issue, 'Gendering "the international"', 27 (4).

Moon, K. (2000) '"Migrant workers" movements in Japan and South Korea' in C. Murphy (ed.), *Egalitarian Politics in the Age of Globalization*, New York, MacMillan/St. Martin's.

Mohanty, C. (1988) '"Under Western Eyes" revisited: feminist solidarity through anti-capitalist struggles', *Signs*, 28 (2), 499-537.

Murray, A. (1998) 'Debt-bondage and trafficking: don't believe the hype' in K. Kempardoo and J. Diezema (eds), *Global Sex Workers: Rights, Resistance, and Redefinition*, New York, Routledge, pp. 51–64.

Pearson, R. and Theobald, S. (1998) 'From export processing to erogenous zones: international discourses on women's work in Thailand', *Millennium*, 27 (4), 983–94.

Peterson, VS (2003) *A Critical Rewriting of Global Political Economy*, London and New York, Routledge.

Pettman, J. (1996a) 'International sex and service' in E. Kofman and G. Youngs (eds), *Globalization: Theory and Practice*, London, Pinter, pp. 191–208.

———. (1996b) *Worlding Women: A Feminist International Politics*, London, Routledge.

———. (1997) 'Body politics: international sex tourism', *Third World Quarterly*, 18 (1), 1022.

———. Pettman , J (2004) 'Global politics and transnational feminisms', in L. Ricciutelli, A. Miles, and M. McFadden (eds) *Feminist Politics, Activism and Vision: Local and Global Challenges*, London and New York, Zed Books.

———. (1998) 'Women on the move: globalization and labour migration from South and Southeast Asian States', *Global Society*, 12 (3), 389–403.

———. (1999) 'Sex tourism: the complexities of power' in T. Skelton and T. Allen (eds), *Culture and Global Change*, London, Routledge and Open University Press.

Pickup, F. (1998) 'Deconstructing trafficking in women: the example of Russia', *Millennium*, 27 (4), 995–1022.

Rafael, V. (1997) 'Your grief is our gossip. Overseas Filipinos and other spectral presences', *Public Culture*, 9 (1), 267–91.

Sassen, S. (2000) 'Women's burden: counter-geographies of globalization and the feminization of survival', *Journal of International Affairs*, 53 (2), 503–24.

Scholte, JA (2000) *Globalization: A Critical Introduction*, London, Macmillan.

Skeldon, R. (2000) 'Trafficking: a perspective from Asia', *International Migration*, 38 (3), 7–30.

Skrobanek, S., Boonpakdi, N. and Janthakeero, C. (1997) *The Traffic in Women: Human Realities of the International Sex Trade*, London, Zed Books.

Stivens, M. (2000) 'Introduction: gender politics and the reimagining of human rights in the Asia Pacific' in Hildsdon et al. (eds), *Gender Politics and Human Rights in Asia and the Pacific*, London, Routledge, pp. 49–62.

Sullivan, B. (2003) 'Trafficking in women: alternate migration or modern slave trade?' *International Feminist Journal of Politics*, 5 (2), 67–91.

Tadiar, N. X. (1997) 'Domestic bodies of the Philippines', *Sojourn*, 12 (2), 153–91.

———. (1998) 'Prostituted Filipinas and the crisis of Philippine culture', *Millennium*, 27 (4), 927–54.

Truong, T-D (1996) 'Gender, international migration and social reproduction', *Asian and Pacific Migration Journal*, 5 (1), 27–52.

Ucarer, E. M. (1999) 'Trafficking in women: alternate migration or modern slave trade?' in M. Meyer and E. Prugl (eds), *Gender Politics in Global Governance*, Lanham, MD: Rowan & Littlefield, pp. 230–44.

Willis, K. and Yeoh, B. (eds) (2000) *Gender and Migration*, Cheltenham, Edward Elgar.

Wong, D. (1996) 'Foreign domestic workers in Singapore', *Asia and Pacific Migration Journal*, 5 (1), 117–37.

Yeats, N. (2004) 'Global care chains: critical reflections and lines of enquiry', *International Feminist Journal of Politics*, 6 (3), pp. 369–91.

Yeoh, B. and Huang, S. (2000) 'Home and away: foreign domestic workers and negotiations of diasporic identity in Singapore', *Women's Studies International Forum*, 23 (4), 29–43.

CHAPTER 12

The Global Politics of Sexual Dissidence

Migration and Diaspora

Jon Binnie and Tracy Simmons

Introduction

The impact of feminist interventions within political geography and IR has created the space to examine the global politics of sexual dissidence. This chapter sets out to theorise the global politics of sexual dissidence as a supplement but also challenge to feminist perspectives on global politics that have sometimes tended to reproduce a heteronormative perspective in overlooking same-sex sexualities and transgender politics. Sexual dissident sexualities have generally been neglected in theories of globalization (though, for an exception, see Scholte, 2000). However, recent years have witnessed a dramatic growth of work examining the global and transnational politics at the intersection of law, geography, cultural studies, postcolonial studies and lesbian and gay/queer studies. This body of work has much to contribute to understandings of globalization more generally.

Queer politics and theory have both sought to challenge the stability of categories such as gay and lesbian and to provide a deconstructive analysis and examine the exclusions associated with mainstream gay identity politics. The focus within queer politics was on alliances across boundaries of sexual and other categories. However in his discussion of queer, Bell (1994) suggested that queer politics has reproduced exclusions rather than eliminated them. Other writers have been critical of queer theory's marginalization of transgender politics (Namaste, 1996). Moreover, Eng et al. (2005: 12) argue that: 'much of queer theory nowadays sounds like a metanarrative about the domestic affairs of white homosexuals'. See also Puar's (2006: 86) acknowledgement of the limitations of labels and terms to denote sexual dissident identities and practices, as she 'note[s] the inadequacy of these terms, because they are overdetermined and vague, too specific yet too broad'. It is this very inadequacy and unsustainability of terms and labels to categorise identities and practices that has been a significant issue for activists engaged in research on global sexual politics.

This chapter does not offer an exhaustive overview of material on the globalization of sexual dissidence which we use as an umbrella term to cover non-normative sexual practices and identities. However, it seeks to provide a discussion of how the politics of sexual dissidence have been approached within theories of globalization and how insights from research on non-normative sexualities can inform both understandings of transnational political practices and theories of globalization. The first half of the chapter concerns more general debates concerning same-sex and transgender sexualities in relation to both theories and practices of globalization. The second half focuses on questions of migration and diaspora. The conclusion offers some ideas and suggestions for future research.

Beyond the globalization of gay identity: contested formations of transnational sexual politics, practices and identities

The adoption of the rainbow flag of gay liberation by movements across the globe reinforces the notion that lesbians and gay men may constitute a non-national ethnic group based on a common experience of homophobic expression. The emergence and proliferation of Pride events across the globe in cities as diverse as Sao Paulo, Taipei, Istanbul and Zagreb to complement the longer standing, more documented and studied events, such as in Sydney's Mardi Gras (Markwell, 2002), would appear to lend empirical weight to the emergence of gay identities and communities across the globe based on public statement – a declaration of 'coming out'. The high media profile of global gay sporting events such as the Gay Games – which seek to proclaim solidarity among those oppressed because of their sexuality across the globe – is a means of institutionalising a global gay identity (Waitt, 2005). This solidarity is based on a universal notion of a common gay identity across the globe based on resistance to homophobic oppression.

The idea of a universal gay identity that transcends time and space is one that has considerable resonance to many gay men. See for instance Allen (1996) cited in Binnie (2004: 37): 'Gay men the world over live similar lives and dream similar dreams. . . . I know I often feel closer to a gay foreigner I've known for five minutes than to heterosexual relations I've known all my life'. The notion of a common gay identity across national borders is also asserted in academic commentary – for instance, Ralph Bolton is quoted in Sonia Katyal (2002: 120):

> And over the years I discovered that, despite differences of dialect, the language of gay men in places I have been is the same; we are one tribe in diaspora, whether living in Trondheim or Zagreb, San Juan or Oaxaca, San Francisco or Atlanta, Las Vegas or Chicago. We are indeed everywhere and in all walks of life.

Of course it would be tempting to interpret statements such as Allen's and Bolton's as naïve and ethnocentric – reproducing an essentialising Western gaze on diverse sexual cultures. Oswin argues (2006: 787): 'It is by now widely recognized that Western bias within queer scholarship and activism is a violence directed against queer cultures around the globe'. A concern with difference and the desire to demonstrate solidarity with sexual dissidents across the globe needs to be balanced with recognition of the dangers of generalisation from the particular. To what extent are same-sex identities fractured by differences along the lines of race, class and gender? How does a global gay identity relate to transgender rights? It is how to interpret the politics of globalized struggles for sexual rights that is now the subject of a considerable body of work.

Dennis Altman's influential essays on 'The globalization of gay identity' sought to understand the emergence of lesbian and gay rights movements in the global South with a particular focus on Asia (Altman, 1996, 1997). He suggested that there was a strong American influence on the development of these movements. Other writers have highlighted the role of new media in the development of gay and lesbian identities and communities in Asia (Berry et al., 2003). Altman's work has spawned considerable debate on how to theorise the development of lesbian and gay movements in the global South. The contested notion of a universalized gay identity across the globe and the extent to which it forges and promotes solidarity across national boundaries, or whether it reproduces colonising tendencies and causes harm to sexual dissidents in the global South, has been a key focus of work in this area. Questions of how sexual acts and practices map on to identities is a central facet of debates about the global politics of sexual dissidence. For instance, in taking Dennis Altman to task for his universalizing tendencies in his writing on the global gay, Lisa Rofel (1999: 455) argues: 'For Altman, invocations of universalism, whether by Westerners or by Asians, appear to be self-evident and self-referential rather than rhetorical strategy, double-voiced dialogism, the locational politics of representation, or strategic essentialism'.

One of the main issues associated with the notion of the emergence of a global gay identity is the use of evolutionary narratives that frame the West as ahead of the rest on the escalator towards ever greater rights of self-determination and autonomy. Some writers have sought to challenge evolutionary narratives that chart a path of development from folk, indigenous or 'traditional' configurations of same-sex practices to a modern, politicised gay marked by visibility and greater publicity (Hoad, 2000). Spatial rhetorical strategies configure and fix the West as 'progressive' and 'liberated' contrasted with the 'backward' non-West. Indeed the focus on fixity is problematic – is the West monolithic, stable, knowable? (Binnie, 2004; Oswin, 2006). This critique of evolutionary narratives of development of a gay identity has brought to the fore perspectives on sexual dissidence informed by postcolonial theory (see for instance, Hawley, 2001). But also present are the colonializing tendencies of contemporary activism and theory, as Oswin (2006: 787) argues: 'the desire to know and coexist equitably with the "other" too often contains its own colonizing moves'. Any consideration of sexual dissidence in a global context needs to understand the imprint of colonialism on sexual subjectivities which has consequences for contemporary formations of same-sex sexualities (see for instance, Aldrich, 2003; Hawley, 2001; Hayes, 2000; Phillips, 2006). We also need to acknowledge the multiple contexts of colonial tendencies – for instance as postcolonial theoretical perspectives are adopted by writers on post-socialism. Carl Stychin (2003: 137) asks in the conclusion to his essay on Romanian sexual politics and EU accession: 'to what extent can European actors avoid the colonial impulse? COC Netherlands is now working actively on a lesbian and gay empowerment project in the Republic of Moldova. Will this be a force for "liberation," or should it be seen as an example of the colonization by the West?'

This section has examined the contested nature of theories around the global politics of same-sex sexualities. At the start of this section, we set out some of the main areas that have been the focus of work on globalization and same-sex sexualities. The tensions reflected in transnational activism around sexual politics is one area of contention in these debates. The next section focuses on these tensions and the distinction between theory and practice in the discussion of transnational activism and sexual politics.

From theory to practice: transnational activism and sexual dissidence

The distinction between theoretical work and activist practice is not always clear-cut. The queer transgender activist academic Nico Beger (2004) has written an exemplary study of the tensions between activist practice and deconstructive tendencies of queer theory. He worked for ILGA-Europe lobbying to secure reforms in the EU based on legally recognised categories of dissident sexualities, while simultaneously applying a deconstructive analysis of the very categories that activists were deploying in these struggles. Deconstruction of categories of identity may be desirable to safeguard against the essentialising of identity, but at the same time it can be disempowering when trying to effect practical legal change. As Jennifer Hyndman (2003: 4) notes: 'While critical geopolitics is useful for a feminist geopolitical analysis, its deconstructive impulses are to my mind insufficient to generate change for building alternative futures'. In addition to the relevance of deconstructive analysis for practical activist struggles, we also need to recognise that well-intentioned 'progressive' interventions may have damaging or harmful consequences. For instance, outside activist interventions can play into conservative nationalist politicians' claims that homosexuality is a foreign import. On the other hand, we can point towards the unintended queer effects of reactionary legislation. Section 28 in the UK was a homophobic piece of legislation which galvanised lesbian and gay activism and increased media visibility rather than marginalization.

The earlier discussion of a universal gay identity and whether this may have harmful effects has an immediate consequence for the most appropriate forms of political organization and intervention. In her wide-ranging discussion of global sexual rights, with particular focus on Thailand and India, Sonia Katyal argues that the focus in rights struggles on gay rights based on a Western model of gay identity as opposed to indigenous labels and categories may play into conservative nationalist politicians who argue that homosexuality and therefore gay rights are a foreign import. Katyal notes that campaigns in India for the rights of MSM (men who have sex with men) draw upon the colonial origins of Section 377 of the Penal Code that is used to punish same-sex sexual activity: 'it is perhaps most ironic that the laws that have been used towards prosecution are the very emblem of colonial exports and have long been abandoned by the country from which it originated' (2002: 162). Katyal argues how campaigns by gay and lesbian activists in India use Section 377's colonial origins as a way of powerfully critiquing nationalist arguments that a gay identity is a Western imposition (2002: 167).

The distinction between focussing on securing rights that protect an *identity* versus rights that safeguard self-determination in sexual practices is one that Katyal argues needs to be better foregrounded in both activism and scholarly work on transnational sexual politics. She argues that 'many Western activists and scholars often fail to recognize that arguments for legal protection on the basis of sexual orientation can collide with, rather than incorporate, these preexisting social meanings of same-sex sexual activity' (2002: 100). She highlights the danger that these preexisting formations of same-sex sexual activity – such as *kathoey* in Thailand – are interpreted as 'backward' and will be inevitably superseded by a Western model gay identity. It is ironic that modern Western gay identity is often taken for granted as if it is uniform, easily understood, knowable, intelligible and recognisable. However, there is also a danger that the Western model of gay identity, based on a distinctive gay lifestyle, may itself be less stable, fixed. Thus Katyal (2002: 154) argues: 'The proliferation of competing identities demonstrates the difference between the concept of a fixed and stable perceptions of gay identity and the more fluid sexuality of many men and women throughout the world'. In some respects, the turn towards focussing on constructions of sexual dissidence in transnational contexts may be seen in the context of the emergence of a post-gay identity in some Western societies. In many Western societies the successes of law reform and changing societal attitudes towards sexual dissidence have dissolved the glue that fixed the bonds of solidarity between sexual dissidents. These bonds were forged in the context of a common threat from a homophobic state, but in era of law reform, with policing policies and practices that seek to protect sexual dissidents from violent attack, there is no strong external threat to unite the community as in the past. For instance, Henning Bech (1997) has suggested that in late modern societies such as Denmark, we are witnessing the end of the modern homosexual identity.

Reading some accounts of global sexual politics, specifically those that focus on the international tourist practices of gay white men, one could be forgiven for thinking that white gay men are uniformly affluent and privileged transnational actors. However, it is important not to forget that the global platform for LGBT rights is still highly problematic, as Doris Buss and Didi Herman recognise in their analysis of the growing transnational dimension of Christian Right activism: 'the international realm is in itself inhospitable to lesbian and gay activism. Many countries strongly resist any recognition of the rights of sexual minorities, and human rights violations against lesbians and gay men continue with little apparent international condemnation' (2003: 122). Thus we must treat with caution representations that over-emphasise the power that lesbian and gay activist groups are able to wield at the global level. ILGA (The International Lesbian and Gay Association) is the highest profile NGO working at the global level to improve the legal status of lesbians, gay men, bisexuals and transgendered people. ILGA was founded in Coventry in England in 1978 and now has over four hundred groups affiliated to it in over ninety countries. This spectacular growth in the scale and organization of transnational activism around same-sex sexualities is both reflective of globalization but also constitutive of it. ILGA's lack of consultative status at the UN has been a persistent problem for activists pressing for LGBT rights to be recognised at a global political level. Until very recently, only two LGBT NGOs have enjoyed consultative status at the UN – the Australian group Coalition of Activist Lesbians and International Wages Due Lesbians. The granting of consultative status to ILGA-Europe (the European region of ILGA), the German lesbian and gay rights organization LSVD and Danish lesbian and gay rights organization LBL, by the United Nations Economic and Social Council (ECOSOC) in December 2006 heralded a major breakthrough in the recognition of LGBT groups at the UN. Reflecting the growing focus on transgender politics within transnational sexual-dissident activism, ILGA organised an event at the UN Human Rights Council to highlight transgender rights and have stated their intention to press for a UN resolution to protect the rights of transgender people (ILGA, 2007). However, progress in getting LGBT groups consultative status at the UN has been painfully slow and recent successes have been followed by failure – for instance in early 2007 ECOSOC denied consultative status to the Quebecois NGO Coalition *gaie et lesbienne du Québec* while at the same time granting the status to the Ethics and Religious Liberty Commission of the Southern Baptist Convention and the American Conservative Union.

The growing visibility of lesbian and gay rights as an issue at the UN has also helped to crystallise the work of the Christian Right. According to Buss and Herman (2003: xxiv), 'an invigorated international civil society has placed issues like women's rights and sexual equality on the international agenda, which alarms the CR'. While there has been considerable work on how transnational activism is taking place to secure human rights for LGBTQ people, and around reproductive rights, there is also research examining the ways in which the Christian Right is organising at the global, supranational scale to promote its own agenda to fight against these attempts to claim rights (Buss and Herman, 2003; Herman, 2001; Kobayashi and Ray, 2006).

In this section we have noted the focus on identity categories within global rights activism, as opposed to sexual acts and practices risking further marginalizing of indigenous and other configurations of sexual dissident identities and practices that do not conform to a Western model of gay identity. The recent history of sexual citizenship politics demonstrates that rights won for some are normally at the expense of those whose marginality is further reproduced through law reform.

Migration and sexual dissidents

Migration and diaspora are two areas that clearly highlight the importance of recognising different constructions of sexual identity across space. Indeed, rural-to-urban migration is seen as a central experience in the narratives of sexual dissidents (Castells, 1983; Weston, 1995; Chauncey, 1994). In respect of this, a common trope in the literature is concerned with migration as a necessary part of building a lesbian, gay and bisexual identity and tied to narratives of coming out and escaping from the restrictive 'home' of origin (Cant, 1997; Sinfield, 2000; Phelan, 2001). Though this work generates important theoretical and ethnographic insights, it has a tendency to be, as Stychin observes, limited to an 'American focus' and concerned with movement within nation-states (2003: 95). However, further work concerned with transnational migration and diaspora foregrounds how movement across borders impacts the types of sexual identity formations and categories that operate at different spatial scales. Moreover, the ability of sexual dissidents to migrate depends on the specific citizenship frameworks at the national and regional levels. Therefore, migration and diaspora highlights the uneven impact of political, social and legal developments in the arena of queer activism across the globe.

The contestation of sexual identity within different locations is articulated in work on queer diaspora. This framework is influenced by postmodern perspectives that problematize 'essentialist' notions of belonging and identity which makes it an attractive way to explore questions of identity in the context of queer transnational networks. One way this is illustrated is by Manalansan's (2000) ethnographic research on Filipino gay men in New York City, where the performance of the 'Santacruzan' Catholic ritual serves to symbolically represent a queer diasporic Filipino experience, which playfully negotiates a connection between a country of origin and the marginalizing space of the settled community in New York City. In this sense, it is a reminder of how queer diasporic communities may be involved in negotiating and re-creating connections with the 'homeland' often seen as the country of origin through symbolic use of space in the country of entry. This is reflected in Petzen's (2004) examination of how queer Turkish migrants or Türkiyelis in Berlin deploy a range of strategies in the disruption of public space. In Petzen's account, such 'management of space' involves a negotiation and contestation of dominant racism and prejudices within the wider German queer community and that within Türkiyelis community. In other words, the presence of queer Türkiyelis in a range of public spaces such as multicultural festivals and queer events offers the opportunity for Türkiyelis to challenge and parody racial and sexual stereotypes. These two accounts explore the way in which diasporic communities may contest or rearticulate sexual and ethnic identities, not only significant for the migrant community but for the wider 'host' queer community.

The above accounts do not seek to provide a comprehensive picture of the literature that situates sexual dissidents within a diasporic frame. For example, Fortier (2002) provides an excellent overview of such scholarly work (see also Patton and Sánchez-Eppler, 2000; Gopinath, 1996; Eng, 1997; Puar, 1998; Schimel, 1997). However, the above section indicates how queer diasporic perspectives highlight questions of place, identity and belonging in the narratives of sexual dissidents. Furthermore, such insights return us to persistent questions relating to globalized sexuality that is to what extent it is possible to make universal claims about the experiences of gay migration. What types of and forms of sexual identity are being constructed and how might they consolidate or challenge other identity categories across different spaces? Though 'diaspora' allows a degree of purchase over these debates by fore-grounding the multiplicity and fluidity of identity and its contestation in different national settings, it can only give a partial portrait of the 'gay' migration experience. What is often absent in these accounts is the role of policy and legislation in the regulation of sexual dissidents' movement across borders. A predominance of scholarly work by socio-legal scholars working in the area of sexual citizenship (though not limited to) has been partic-ularly effective in examining how legal frameworks constitute and regulate sexual identities. Moreover, such insights highlight the importance of the spatial dimension of citizenship frameworks that is a recognition of the diverse levels of rights accorded to sexual dissidents within and across different national and regional scales. It is to the legislative and policy developments in the area of same-sex migrant couples, in particular the ability for sexual dissidents to achieve family or spousal reunion, that we turn to in the following section.

Relationship rights and same-sex migrant couples

Over the past decade or so, a major area of lesbian and gay activism has been centred on what can be broadly described as the legal recognition of same-sex relationships. Much of this activism has been centred on arguments for the recognition of same-sex relationships at the national level. The debates concerning rights around marriage and civil partnership have been gaining momentum in both the Northern and Southern hemispheres. At the European level, there are a number of countries now offering registered or civil partnerships, including UK, Finland, Sweden, Norway, Denmark, Germany and Iceland and in the case of the Netherlands, Belgium and Spain, same-sex marriage. Beyond Europe, Australia, Brazil, Israel and New Zealand provide legal recognition of same-sex relationships, with Canada and South Africa offering marriage. However, the development of rights for same-sex couples has been patchy and uneven at the national level particularly within regional and federal political contexts. For example, Spain had initially made available reg-istered partnerships in certain provinces such as Aragon, Catalonia, Navarra and Valencia. Similarly, in Italy as debates continue at a national level for same-sex couples to be recognised in law, civil unions are available in regions such as Tuscany, Umbria, Emilia Ramagna,

Campania, Marche, Puglia, Lazio, Liguria and Abruzzo. Outside the European scale, in the US a number of states are challenging federal and constitutional definitions of marriage as opposite sex (as exemplified by the 1996 Defense of Marriage Act) by offering in the case of Massachusetts same-sex marriage and in Connecticut, Vermont, New Jersey and California, Hawaii and Maine equivalent or limited rights through civil unions (Demian, 2006).

The significance of different citizenship frameworks at the national and regional scale is illustrated by the unfolding pattern of registered partnerships, civil unions and in some case marriage that has been widely discussed, particularly in academic work on sexual citizenship, and has raised questions about the political and cultural implications of the 'relationship' rights agenda (see for example Bell and Binnie, 2000; Cooper, 2001; Richardson, 2004; Stychin 2006). What kinds of rights are being secured, and do they reinforce heteronormative discourses that privilege the monogamous dual-income couple? To what extent is marriage or partnership in itself an assimilative or transgressive move? Though the two poles concerned with assimilative effects of the relationship agenda versus the potential for inclusion and radicalising of traditional institutions such as marriage do not entirely capture the full range of debates on this topic, they do underpin some key arguments advanced by academics and activists. They are also fundamental to the discussion on sexual dissidents and migration, in terms of what definitions and models of the family and relationships are being legitimised in migration policies. Furthermore, to what extent are relationship rights available to indigenous citizens within national spaces comparatively accessible to same-sex migrant couples?

Though indigenous sexual citizens in some spaces are reaping the benefits of legal protection, at the level of immigration such rights are not automatically afforded to same-sex migrant couples. In many cases immigration policies require one partner to be a citizen or have residency before admitting the accompanying partner (Holt, 2004). This makes it particularly difficult for binational couples to gain entry based on their same-sex relationship. In respect of this, same-sex couples cannot always take advantage of hard-won rights for indigenous citizens and are subject to particularly conservative and normative discourse when they seek to migrate from one county to another. The process of migration may involve losing legal recognition of their relationship if similar protections are not available. In some cases the lack of recognition of same-sex relationships for immigration purposes may have a bearing on where sexual dissidents can migrate. For example, consider the case of the United States which despite continued activist campaigns still has no regulations that allow entry based on a same-sex relationship.

The European Union has been a key site for legal and political challenges that illuminate the issue of free movement for sexual dissidents. As mentioned in the previous sections, the EU has been the focus for many activists and NGOs such as ILGA Europe who have been attempting to use the European legal arena to secure rights and in some cases challenge discriminatory practices within nation-states (Beger, 2000; Bell, 2002; Wintemute and Andanaes, 2001). There have been some notable legal successes at the European level, such as the lifting of the ban in 2000 on lesbians and gays serving in the armed forces in the UK (*Lustig-Prean and Beckett v United Kingdom* [1999, 29 EHRR 548]; *Smith and Grady v UK* [1999, 29 EHRR 493]), decriminalisation of homosexuality in *Northern Ireland Dudgeon v. UK* (1981, 7525/76; 4 EHRR 149) and arguments for the equal age of consent for gay men, *Sutherland v United Kingdom* (1998, 24 EHRLR 117). However, there has been less success in cases involving same-sex migrant couples challenging decisions by nation-states that prevent or impede their ability to achieve family reunion.

A key area of policy where there have been a number of changes is in relation to what constitutes a family for the purposes of family reunion, though such changes have been somewhat uneven. In respect of this, one of the major obstacles for same-sex migrant couples is that European Community law defines a 'spouse' for the purposes of family reunion as a married, opposite-sex couple. As previous cases highlight, there has been a tendency on the part of European judiciary to not intervene especially on matters of immigration, and also 'sensitive' issues concerning the 'family' (Bell, 2002). This is fully illustrated by the widely discussed case (Elman, 2000; Toner, 2004; Wintemute, 1995) of *X and Y v. UK* (No. 9369/81, 1983, 32 D 220). This case involved a British-Malaysian male couple, who made a claim of interference to their 'family' life based on Article 8 of the European Convention on Human Rights, as they were unable to achieve family reunion in the UK which at that time had no immigration provision for same-sex couples. The Commission on Human Rights denied the couple's claim on the grounds it did not fall within the ambit of a family but rather private life. In addition, they also argued the couple were 'professionally mobile' and 'it has not been shown that the applicants could not live elsewhere other than the United Kingdom or that their link with the United Kingdom is an essential element of their relationship' (Wintemute, 1995: 104). The 'elsewhere' argument is, as Toner (2004: 102) argues, particularly problematic in view of the fear of ill treatment the couple may receive in Malaysia, where homosexual acts are an offence. More recently, the Family Reunification Directive (Council Directive, 2003/86/EC) which applies to third-country nationals, aims to 'protect' and 'preserve family' life but explicitly proposes a narrow nuclear family model.

The above case highlights a reluctance to recognise claims made by sexual dissidents in terms of the family and also illustrates how European Community law is unable to secure rights for free movement for same-sex couples (see Guild, 2001 for a full discussion). The inclusion of same-sex couples in definitions of the family continues with the EU Freedom of Movement Directive that came into force in May 2006 (UKLGIG, 2006). The Directive 'on the right to citizens of the Union and their family members to move and reside freely within the territory of the Member States' contains provisions that are applicable to same-sex couples (UKLGIG, 2006). A key provision is that countries that do not recognise same-sex relationships should 'facilitate' entry to lesbian and gay couples in a 'durable' relationship (Bell, 2005). However, as the UK Lesbian and Gay Immigration Group (UKLGIG) reports, the directive is a 'partial victory' as the 'right is not given' therefore there is no clear obligation on behalf of the state and once again it relies on national conditions regarding partnership rights (UKLGIG, 2006). The effectiveness of the Directive remains to be seen, but at present the shifts towards strengthening the inclusion of same-sex couples in definitions of the family and spousal rights more generally appear to be in the hands of individual European states. Moreover, the historical development of the EU as an economic marketplace means that migration policies are skewed towards the 'primary' migration of labour workers, which means family reunion rights remain of secondary concern in policy debates (Kofman, 2004).

Clearly, economic imperatives and discourses concerned with increasing global competitiveness shape migration policies and regulations, especially those that seek to identify skilled migrants that can fulfil labour shortages (Raghuram, 2004). As Stychin (2000) succinctly states, '. . . mobility is constrained from the outset by its central relationship to consumption and class, which are all too frequently closely connected to race and gender' (606). Therefore, in examining the policies that do recognise same-sex couples for the purposes of immigration, it is evident how they construct an idealized migrant on lines of sexuality, gender, race and class. First, as in the case of UK and Australia (Stychin, 2003; Holt, 2004), the family reunion provision for same-sex couples is founded on a 'marriage like' model that places emphasis on financial responsibility and 'long-standing' relationships. Conditions, as exemplified by the 1997 unmarried partners' rule in the UK, require proof and evidence of two years of cohabitation, which can be difficult criteria to fulfil for couples who are unable to live together in one country. In this sense, they reproduce a normative model of coupledom that reinstalls 'marriage' as the primary way to define relationships. In addition, by placing emphasis on financial responsibility, white gays and lesbians with 'marketable skills' have more chance of realising their transnational citizenship than others (Bell and Binnie, 2000: 120). Such a model also reproduces traditional gendered assumptions that are based on a male 'bread winner' model (Ackers, 1998) with the 'sponsored' partner positioned as 'dependent' (and often prevented from working full-time and seeking public funds) to the 'lead' migrant. Couples who utilise 'spousal' reunion regulations as outlined above find themselves subject to surveillance and intrusion into the validity of their relationship and solvency. Such surveillance is particularly trained on non-white sexual citizens, reflecting a preoccupation with identifying migrants who might use such provision falsely, which resonates with recurring immigration discourses concerned with 'marriages of convenience' (Bhabba and Shutter, 1994; Wray, 2006).

As the above section highlights, though recognition of same-sex couples for the purposes of immigration perhaps reflects an emerging pattern of liberalisation and inclusion in social policies for sexual dissidents, questions still remain about what costs come with gaining citizenship (Stychin, 2003; Bell and Binnie, 2000). In this sense there is a danger that the granting of rights continues to be founded on a narrow heteronormative 'marriage'-like model that constrains the ability for sexual citizens to organise their intimate life in more diverse ways. Aside from these concerns, migration still remains an important site for lesbian and gay activists. This can be illustrated by a recent case involving a UK-based female same-sex couple who lost their case in the High Court; they sought to have their marriage, which was obtained in Canada, recognised in the UK (Minto, 2006). Current campaigns mobilized by queer activist groups such UKLGIG and ILGA have been concerned with the situation relating to lesbian and gay men seeking asylum and refugee status based on the grounds of sexuality. Once again this invites questions about how these campaigns are framed, particularly how utilising international 'human rights' discourses may produce heteronormative, Westernised conceptions of sexuality based on 'victimhood'. This seems to echo a general critical discussion about how a lesbian and gay human rights agenda might be advanced and what model of sexuality emerges from these debates (Sanders, 1996; Stychin, 2004). Migration and diaspora has been and continues to be central to debates about the contestation of sexual identity, bringing to the fore the importance of space and boundaries both figuratively and literally in the lives of sexual dissidents.

Conclusion

In this chapter a common theme running through the varied theoretical debates concerned with global politics and sexual dissidents is the importance of recognising the spatial context.

For these debates, the location and setting have a bearing on what models and categories of 'gay' identity are being articulated and how they might be contested. As the first section clearly shows, they bring into play postcolonial perspectives that critically challenge the advancement of what can be seen as a distinctly Western and therefore one-dimensional assertion of what constitutes a gay identity. Such critical interventions provide a useful way to examine the colonial legacies on the cultural and legislative frameworks concerning same-sex activity. What has also been shown is that it is deeply problematic to view a monolithic, Western gay imaginary. As the section on migration and diaspora illustrates, the impact of legal and political processes in the EU has been by no means linear and uniform. Moreover, the different levels of rights available for sexual dissidents remain vitally important in the context of migration. A key example is in the US, where discriminatory immigration practices towards same-sex couples are very much in evidence today. However, transnational activism remains a powerful way to organise and keep LGBT rights on the agenda of international politics, especially in view of the slow response by the UN and EU to recognise queer NGOs and lobby groups in an official capacity. What this chapter has also illustrated is how sexuality should not be viewed as a 'niche' topic against broader macro theories of the 'global' but rather a rich vantage point to explore from a range of disciplinary perspectives the sexualised spaces and discourses of globalization. In turn, lesbian and gay/queer scholars also need to critically consider in what way the 'global' figures, or is being articulated, in their examinations of sexual identities and culture – all the more prescient as transnational practices and polices continue to shape the lives of sexual dissidents.

References

Aldrich, R. (2003) *Colonialism and Homosexuality*, London, Routledge.

Allen, J. (1996) *Growing Up Gay: New Zealand Men Tell Their Stories*, Auckland, Godwit Publishing.

Altman, D. (1996) 'Rupture or continuity: the internationalization of gay identities', *Social Text*, 14 (3) 77–94.

———. (1997) 'Global gaze/global gays', *GLQ: A Journal of Lesbian and Gay Studies*, 3, 417–36.

———. (2001) *Global Sex*, Chicago and London, University of Chicago Press.

Beger, N. (2000) 'Queer readings of Europe: gender identity sexual orientation and the (im)potency of rights politics at the European Court of Justice', *Social and Legal Studies*, 9 (2), 249–70.

———. (2004) *Tensions in the Struggle for Sexual Minority Rights in Europe: Que(e)rying Political Practices*, Manchester, Manchester University Press.

Bell, D. (1994) 'In bed with the state: political geography and sexual politics', *Geoforum* 25, 445–52 .

Bell, D. and Binnie, J. (2000) *The Sexual Citizen, Queer Politics and Beyond*, Cambridge, Polity.

Bell, M. (2002) *Anti-Discrimination Law and the European Union*, Oxford, Oxford University Press.

———. (2005) *EU Directive On Free Movement and Same-Sex Families*, Brussels, ILGA Europe. Available at http://www.ilga-europe.org/europe/campaigns_projects/freedom_of_movement. accessed 19 June 2004.

Berry, C., Martin, F. and Yue, A. (eds) (2003) *Mobile Cultures: New Media in Queer Asia*, Durham, NC, and London, Duke University Press.

Binnie, J. (2004) *The Globalization of Sexuality*, London, Sage.

Buss, D. and Herman, D. (2003) *Globalizing Family Values: The Christian Right in International Politics*, Minneapolis, University of Minnesota Press.

Cant, B. (1997) *Invented Identities? Lesbians and Gay Men Talk about Migration*, London, Cassell.

Castells, M. (1983) *The City and the Grassroots*, Berkeley, University of California Press.

Chauncey, G. (1994) *Gay New York*, New York, Basic Books.

Cooper, D. (2001) 'Like counting stars? Re-structuring equality and the socio-legal space of same-sex marriage' in R. Wintemute and M. Andanaes (eds), *Legal Recognition of Same-sex Partnerships, a Study of National European andInternational Law,* Oxford, Hart, pp. 75–96.

Council Directive (2003/86/EC) On the Right to Family Reunification, 22 September 2003, *Official Journal of the European Union.* Available at: http://eur-lex.europa.eu/LexUriServ/site/en/oj/2003/l_251/l_25120031003en00120018.pdf, accessed 30 July 2007.

Demian. (2006) 'Immigration roundup, a survey of welcoming countries', Partners Task Force for Gay & Lesbian Couples. Available at: http://www.buddybuddy.com/immigr.html, accessed 5 March 2007.

Elman, R. A. (2000) 'The limits of citizenship, migration, sex discrimination and same-sex partners in EU law', *Journal of Common Market Studies,* 3 (8), 729–49.

Eng, D. (1997) 'Out here and over there: queerness and diaspora in Asian American studies', *Social Text,* 15 (3–4), 31–52.

Eng, D. with Halberstam, J. and Munoz, J. E. (2005) 'Introduction: what's queer about queer studies now?' *Social Text,* 84–85, 23(3–4), 1–17.

Fortier, A. M. (2002) 'Queer diaspora' in D. Richardson and S. Siedman (eds), *The Handbook of Lesbian and Gay Studies,* London, Sage, pp. 183–97.

Gopinath, G. (1996) 'Funny boys and girls: notes on a queer South Asian planet', in R. Leang (ed) *Asian American Sexualities: Dimensions of the Gay and Lesbian Experience,* London and New York, Routledge, pp. 119–27.

Guild, E. (2001) 'Free movement and same-sex relationships, existing EC Law Article 13 EC', in R. Wintemute and M. Andanaes (eds), *Legal Recognition of Same-Sex Partnerships: A Study of National European and International Law,* Oxford, Hart, pp. 677–89.

Hawley, J. (ed.) (2001) *Postcolonial, Queer: Theoretical Interventions,* Albany, NY, State University of New York Press.

Hayes, J. (2000) *Queer Nations: Marginal Sexualities in the Maghreb,* Chicago, University of Chicago Press.

Herman, D. (2001) 'Globalism's siren song: the United Nations in Christian Right thought and prophecy', *Sociological Review,* 49, 56–77.

Hoad, N. (2000) 'Arrested development or the queerness of savages: resisting evolutionary narratives of difference', *Postcolonial Studies,* 3 (2), 133–58.

Holt, M. (2004) 'Marriage-like or married? Lesbian and gay marriage, partnership and migration', *Feminism and Psychology,* 14 (1), 30–35.

Hyndman, J. (2003) 'Beyond either/or: a feminist analysis of September 11th', *ACME: An International E-Journal for Critical Geographies,* 2, 1–13.

Katyal, S. (2002) 'Exporting identity', *Yale Journal of Law and Feminism,* 14, 97–176.

Kobayashi, A. and Ray, B. (2006) 'Moral crusades, transnational activism and human rights', paper presented at the session on The Politics of Transnational Activist Networks: Translation, Theory, Practice, Association of American Geographers, Chicago, March.

Kofman, E. (2004) 'Family-related migration: a critical review of European studies', *Journal of Ethnic and Migration Studies,* 30 (2), 243–62.

Manalansan IV, M. F. (2000) 'Diasporic deviants/divas: how Filipino gay transmigrants "play with the world"', in C.Patton and B. Sanchez-Eppler (eds), *Queer Disaporas,* Durham, NC, Duke University Press, pp. 183–203.

Markwell, K. (2002) 'Mardi Gras tourism and the construction of Sydney as an international gay and lesbian city', *GLQ: A Journal of Lesbian and Gay Studies,* 8 (1–2), 81–99.

Minto, D. (2006) 'Marriage ruling an insult', *Pink Paper,* 9 August, 10.

Morgan, W. (2000) 'Queering international human rights law', in C. Stychin and D. Herman (eds), *Sexuality in the Legal Arena,* London, The Athlone Press, pp. 208–25.

Namaste, K. (1996) 'Tragic misreadings: queer theory's erasure of transgender subjectivity', in B. Beemyn and M. Eliason (eds), *Queer Studies: A Lesbian, Gay, Bisexual, and Transgender Anthology*, New York, New York University Press, pp. 9–23.

Oswin, N. (2006) 'Decentering queer globalization; diffusion and the 'global gay'', *Environment and Planning D: Society and Space*, 24 (5), 777–90.

Patton, C. and Sanchez-Eppler, B. (eds) (2000) *Queer Diasporas*, Durham, NC, Duke University Press.

Petzen, J. (2004) 'Home or homelike', *Space and Culture*, 7 (1), 20–32.

Phelan, S. (2001) *Sexual Strangers, Gays, Lesbians and Dilemmas of Citizenship*, Philadelphia, Temple University Press.

Phillips, R. (2006) *Sex, Politics and Empire: A Postcolonial Geography*, Manchester, Manchester University Press.

Puar, J. (1998) 'Transnational sexualities: South Asian (trans)nation(alism)s and queer diasporas' in D. Eng and A. Hom (eds), *Q and A: Queer in Asian America*, Philadelphia, Temple University Press, pp. 405–22.

———. (2006) 'Mapping US homonormativities', *Gender, Place and Culture*, 13, 67–88.

Raghuram, P. (2004) 'The difference that skills make, gender, family migration strategies and regulated labour markets', *Journal of Ethnic and Migration Studies*, 30 (2), 303–21.

Richardson, D. (2004) 'Locating sexualities, from here to normality', *Sexualties*, 7 (4), 391–411.

Rofel, L. (1999) 'Qualities of desire: imagining gay identities in China', *GLQ: A Journal of Lesbian and Gay Studies*, 5 (4), 451–74.

Sanders, D. (1996) 'Getting lesbian and gay issues on the international human rights agenda', *Human Rights Quarterly*, 18, 67–108.

Schimel, L. (1997) 'Diaspora, sweet diaspora: queer culture to post-Zionist Jewish identity' in C. Queen and L. Schimel (eds), *PoMoSexuals: Challenging Assumptions about Gender and Sexuality*, San Francisco, CA, Cleiss Press, pp. 163–73.

Scholte, J. (2000) *Globalization: A Critical Introduction*, London, Macmillan.

Sinfield, A. (2000) 'Diaspora and hybridity: queer identity and the ethnicity model' in N. Mirzoeff (ed.), *Diaspora and Visual Culture: Representing African and Jews*, London, Routledge, pp. 95–114.

Stychin, C. (2000) 'A stranger to its laws, sovereign bodies, global sexualities, and transnational citizens', *Journal of Law and Society*, 27 (4), 601–25.

———. (2003) *Governing Sexuality: The Changing Politics of Citizenship and Law Reform*, Oxford, Hart.

———. (2004) 'Same-sex sexualities and the globalization of human rights discourse', *McGill Law Journal*, 49, 951–68.

———. (2006) '"Las Vegas is not where we are": queer readings of the civil partnership', *Political Geography*, 25 (8), 899–920.

Toner, H. (2004) *Partnership Rights, Free Movement and EU Law*, Oxford, Hart.

UKLGIG (2006) 'Freedom of Movement in Europe', available at http//www.uklgig.org.uk/Europe.htm, accessed 15 June 2006.

Waitt, G. (2005) 'The Sydney 2002 gay games and querying Australian national space', *Environment and Planning D: Society and Space*, 23 (3), 435–52.

Weston, K. (1995) 'Get thee to a big city, sexual imaginary and the great gay migration', *GLQ: A Journal of Lesbian and Gay Studies*, 2 (3), 253–77.

Wintemute, R. (1995) *Sexual Orientation and Human Rights*, Oxford, Clarendon Press.

Wintemute, R. and Andanaes, M. (eds) (2001) *Legal Recognition of Same-Sex Partnerships: A Study of National European and International Law*, Oxford, Hart.

Wray, H. (2006) 'An ideal husband? Marriages of convenience, moral gate-keeping and immigration in the UK', *European Journal of Migration and Law*, 8, 303–20.

Part 4

Politics and Economics of Movements and Space

CHAPTER 13

The Politics of Migration Regulation in the Era of Globalization

Hélène Pellerin

The buzzword 'globalization', like a tidal wave, has carried with it many social and economic dynamics that are now defined in terms of globalizing tendencies. International migration is no exception to this. But what exactly globalization has done to migration is a legitimate and important question. To some extent, international migration has become global, insofar as globalization means greater circulation of goods, people and capital and also greater velocity in world politics (OECD, 1992). Yet the mobility of people is still much more limited than that of capital or of goods (Richmond, 1994). Another change is qualitative, with a greater diversity of regions involved in migration, as well as a diversity of patterns of migration. Finally, there is also a transformation in the way migration is being managed. Migration has become regional and even global in its management.

This is perhaps the most unexpected development to date, stimulating new scholarship on this aspect of the migration question (Hollifield, 2000; Ghosh, 2000a; Pellerin, 2004). Insofar as migration policies have been historically, at least for most of the twentieth century, a prerogative of state power, the process through which it became a global issue deserves some scrutiny. I argue in this chapter that this was not fortuitous or a rational reaction to the global nature of the problem. Many scholars have described globalization as a process of power reconfiguration (Wood, 1997), of production restructuring (Cox, 1992), and of different spatializations of economic and political practices (Agnew and Corbridge, 1995). In this context, the idea of a necessity to manage migration at the global level can be interpreted as a moment in the redefinition of power relations in this domain. The idea and initial efforts in this direction were provoked by a sense of urgency, a sense of crisis. The relationship between globalization and migration policies can be seen in this context as a crisis of migration regulation, as much as it is a crisis of financial regulation and production regulation.

In the following sections, an examination of the critical moment leading up to the idea of a global regulation of migration will be offered. This examination will allow us to see that a sense of crisis produced a momentum on the part of politicians and experts to do something about the situation. The chapter will then turn to examine the propitious conditions this created for a new world arrangement for managing international migration. This is where the interesting dynamic lies. The study of the pressures to act, to coordinate and control policies of migration allows one to observe the various interests involved, and the projected vision of economic and social space concomitant with these interests.

The 'crisis' of migration dynamics in the 1990s

In the early 1990s, many analysts and international organizations contributed to creating a feeling that the world had entered a critical moment of significant quantitative and qualitative change in the dynamic of international migration. The corollary was the increasing difficulty states encountered in responding to, let alone controlling, this dynamic. Several bodies referred to the acute situation in migration dynamics, involving increased movements, diversification of regions and migration patterns involved, and finally, changes in the relationships between migrants and receiving communities. References were made to an unusual, urgent and often negative migration situation, requiring a response that would curb elements of it, or change it into something else.

The term 'crisis', or 'potential crisis', refers here to some dynamics that have been unleashed by the end of the Cold War, by the continued gap between rich and poor regions of the world and by globalization. The term appeared in the early 1990s to refer to changes or potential changes in migratory flows. There was particular insistence on three dimensions: the increasing volume of migration flows; the greater diversity – geographic, ethnic and at the level of skills of migrants; and finally the challenge posed to states and to the management of migration more generally. The looming crisis can be illustrated by this comment made by an American official at a conference organized under the auspices of the OECD in 1991:

> Two important dynamic phenomena are creating conditions increasingly perceived by both high level policymakers and the mass public in many advanced industrial democracies as having the potential for generating an explosive immigration *crisis*. The first is recent in origin and surrounds the changing East/West relationship following the political and economic reforms in Eastern Europe and the Soviet Union (the 'East'). The second has had a gestation period measured in decades, rather than months. It notes the vast and increasing population 'surpluses' in most of the developing world (the 'South'), points to these surpluses' accompanying implications for economic survival and internal and regional political stability, and highlights the urgency of the search for solutions to the challenge posed by rapidly growing populations. (Papademetriou, 1991: 1; emphasis is mine)

In 1993, the Department of Economic and Social Development of the United Nations published its *Report on the World Social Situation*, in which it also stated the terms of the crisis:

> In recent years, there have been several significant changes in mass migration between countries. After having stabilized – even declined as in the case of Germany – during the first half of the 1980s, immigration flows to some developed countries increased during the last three years of the 1980s. The most dramatic flows were into the United States of America and Germany. There were new destinations, such as Japan and Taiwan Province of China, to which migrants from other parts of Asia were attracted. Countries in southern Europe, such as Greece, Italy and

Spain, which had been countries of net emigration, became countries of net immigration. (UN Department of Economic and Social Development, 1993: 14)

In the early 1990s, the notion of potential or existing crisis came to be part of the official analysis by many organizations, from the International Organization for Migration (IOM), the United Nations High Commissioner for Refugees (UNHCR) to the United Nations (UN), the Organization for Economic Cooperation and Development (OECD), the Council of Europe and the Organization for Security and Cooperation in Europe (OSCE).

Existing facts and trends

In order to assess the extent to which a crisis really occurred, or was about to occur, a closer look at available statistics is warranted. Such examination partly supports that perception, but only if the crisis is given a very specific meaning. Perhaps the first point to mention is that the notion of crisis is based on trends as opposed to absolute and real figures. Globally, migrants represented, in the early 1990s, 2.9 per cent of the world population, compared with 2.2 per cent in the 1970s and 1980s (UNCTAD and IOM, 1996: 6; UN, 2006). This growth has had differentiated impacts throughout the world. The Population Division of the UN produced a report indicating that, from the mid-1970s, the number of international migrants increased steadily, if not significantly, passing from 85 millions in 1975 to 106 millions ten years later, indicating a growth rate from 1.1 to 2.2 per cent for that period (UN Département de l'information, 1995: 35). From 1965 to 1990, the estimated total number of migrants increased, from a world total of 75 millions to 119 millions 35 years later. In the developed world, the number of migrants went from 30 million to 54 million; and in the developing world, from 44 million to 65 million, with the largest increase in Africa, in North America and in Europe (UN Secretariat, 1998). These trends have continued throughout the 1990s, but it should be noted that a large part of this increase is the result of a reclassification of internal migrants into international migrants following the break-up of the Soviet Union in 1991; and the division of the former Yugoslavia and Czechoslovakia in 1992 and 1993, respectively. Moreover, the proportion of migrants in relation to the global demographic growth did not grow significantly between 1990 and 2006. In 1990, the number of international migrants represented 2.9 per cent of the world population, and in 2006, with a population of international migrants near 191 millions, it was representing 3 per cent of the world population. In 2006, it is still Europe that hosted the largest proportion, 34 per cent of migrants, followed by North America (23 per cent) and Asia (28 per cent). Africa hosted 9 per cent of migrants, and Oceania 3 per cent (UN, 2006).

During the 1990s, some significant increases occurred, particularly with regard to refugees and asylum claimants. The large increase in the number of refugees and asylum seekers was particularly acute in some industrialized countries (OECD, 1998; 1996). As a UN report indicates, in 1990, there were 17 million refugees, compared to 9.6 million in 1980 (UN Department of Economic and Social Development, 1993: 20). These numbers have gone down considerably since then, with, in 2005, a total of 8.4 million refugees, the lowest in more than twenty years. This downward trend is also notable in the number of asylum claimants in the world (HCR, 2006).

The steady increase, at least until the end of the 1990s, was a cause for alarm, especially considering the varied levels of intensity around the world. Some specialists argue that the industrialized world and Asia have seen more migrants coming to their regions, proportionately speaking. In absolute numbers less developed countries remain the largest basin of migrants, with 52 per cent of the 125 million migrants in the world in 1994 (UNCTAD and IOM, 1996: 6–7), but the industrialized world focused on the drastic change occurring within its boundaries. Thus in its 1999 edition, the SOPEMI (Système d'observation permanente des migrations internationales) report stated that:

> Over the course of the 1980s and above all at the beginning of the 1990s, migration movements accelerated in many OECD countries. This trend reached its peak in 1993, notably in major immigration countries such as Germany, the United States and Canada. (OECD, 1999: 13)

International organizations and fora have thus insisted on the serious impact of growing and diversified migration flows on industrialized countries. The main argument developed to justify this focus was demographic, based on the comparison of ratios, between the entry of migrants and the birthrate in industrialized countries. Despite an absolute number of migrants far less than in other regions of the world, the industrialized countries, the argument goes, were more affected demographically speaking by the presence of migrants. Developed regions thus saw their population increase thanks to international migration, which provided almost 45 per cent of their net population growth (UN Secretariat, 1998: 12). The demographic impact of migration in the industrialized world is also highlighted by the Population Division of the United Nations, which insists that due to the low birthrate in North America and Europe, the presence of migration represents a significantly more important contribution to population growth:

> Despite the rapid increase in the number of international migrants in developing countries, the latter represented in 1985 only 55% of migrants on a world scale, while the population of the receiving countries represented 76% of the world population. The proportion of international migrants in relations to total population of developing countries thus remained small (1.6% of the total). On the contrary, international migrants represented 4.1% of the population of developed countries. Thus, international migrations continued to be relatively more important in developed countries. (UN, Département de l'Information, 1995: 36)

Regarding the category of asylum claimants and refugees, analysts have claimed that because they were uninvited, their presence made more acute the lack of preparedness of industrialized countries. These flows of migrants were the result of important changes in the global order. Push factors generated a greater number of migrants going to the industrialized world, without a reciprocal pull or demand for them in the receiving countries. Many of these migrants became the undocumented migrants and bogus asylum claimants that industrialized countries witnessed in the early 1990s.

As the figures shown earlier indicate, these trends tended to be reduced with the end of the 1990s, although the incentive for globally managing migration continued. This was made possible because *migration pressures* were considered along with indications of future trends. The term 'migration pressures' refers to latent flows, to potential as opposed to existing flows of people, in relation to the absorptive capacity of receiving regions. The term came to be widely used, starting in the early 1990s, to refer to the potentiality of the crisis rather than its existing manifestations. This came after the unrealized mass exodus that was expected following both the fall of the Berlin Wall, and economic and political degradation in main countries of origin of migration. Under the subtitle 'New migratory movements: a looming crisis?' the UNCTAD and IOM document underlined the fear behind this term:

> The growing concern over international migration in industrial countries not only stems from the rising scale and changing characteristics of contemporary migratory movements, but also from demographic, economic and political forces that could unleash far greater migration movements in future years. (UNCTAD and IOM, 1996: 15)

After the second half of the 1990s, most international bodies referred to potential migration, rather than to real and existing migratory flows, when making their analysis or calling for action. Migration pressures were assessed through changes that could potentially trigger more migration flows to the industrialized world, such as economic globalization, improved telecommunications and transport systems, increasing economic and social gaps between countries and regions, and conflicts. From the beginning of the twenty-first century, migration pressures have been replaced by the focus on illegal migration and risks to security posed by clandestine and uncontrolled migration flows.

The call for a new global migration order

The discourse on international migration as expressed by various international organizations contributed to the sense of imminent crisis and the urgency of a response. Even when statistics and figures did not corroborate such an impression, the discourse remained focused on the need for a response, reliant on the efforts of the international community as a whole. More precisely, a particular migration order was going to be created, or rather reconstituted, following the changes from the post–World War II period. The discourse on the crisis of international migration provided the incentive for states to work together. But why did this happen? Did not states manage migration on their own? Yes, they did, to a certain extent. Thus, in response to this new face of migration, most countries have modified their immigration policies, particularly by increasing restrictions. Data compiled by the UN Department for Economic and Social Information and Policy Analysis confirmed this increase in the number of countries reducing immigration between 1986 and 1994, in both developed and developing countries (UN Département de l'information, 1995).

But these reductions were not considered enough, as migration flows could then move to other, less restrictive places. Moreover, with the growing transitory nature of migration flows, there was a sense that a multilateral framework, covering an ensemble of regions of origin, of transit and of destination, was necessary. Trends in the 1990s unveiled the ineffectiveness of existing measures and mechanisms, thus encouraging a different kind of response. This special response did not change fundamentally the modalities of migration management in that states were still going to be the main locus of controls, yet the objectives and areas involved were to be different. The global management took the form of a stronger co-ordination in migration policies and controls, with the participation of countries of origins and of transit. The call for a global approach also referred to the adoption of collective objectives and priorities. The migration order to unfold was about agenda setting[1].

Globalization has affected the management of international migration in the same way that it affected the expansion of financial capital, namely through a deregulation and re-regulation of spaces of circulation. In the case of international migration, this dynamic translated into new sets of objectives where the freedom to move had to be respected, but in the framework of a more selective model of migration. Orderly migration became the organizing principle (Ghosh, 2000a). New categories of migratory flows came to be defined, with an emphasis on the useful and good migration flows, that of highly skilled migrants increasingly in need in a knowledge economy, and the illegal migration associated with human trafficking, criminal activities and terrorism. As for the categories of the post-War order, refugees and labour migration, they became progressively marginalized. The space of migration management also expanded with greater cooperation and even harmonization of policies and controls between regions of origin and of destination.

Most of the international fora dealing with migration directly or indirectly participated in this new agenda setting, with the aim of better co-ordinating states' objectives and strategies. One significant moment was the 1994 UN-sponsored International Conference on Population and Development (ICPD). Third in a series of population conferences occurring every ten years since 1974, the ICPD highlighted the need for bringing together sending and receiving countries in order to address the causes of emigration and in order to 'alleviate the massive and uncontrolled international migration flows' (Singh, 1998: 97). The ICPD also marked the beginning of a more steady cooperation between various organizations on the matter: the IOM and the UN; the Council of Europe and the UN Economic Commission for Europe; the European Union, the G7 and the OECD, to name a few initiatives (UN ECE et al., 1994a: 394–404). The OECD, which had been addressing questions of migration flows and policies in its member countries since 1975, also started to recognize the need for a more co-ordinated approach in the 1990s and worked accordingly through its Development Assistance Committee (DAC) and its SOPEMI reports. Hence, in its 1995 report, it emphasized the importance of international co-operation, particularly on two issues: co-ordinating policies relating to asylum, and the involvement of Central and East European countries in efforts to control migration flows (OECD, 1995; 1998).

The Inter-governmental Consultations on Asylum, Refugee and Migration policies in Europe, North America and Australia (IGC), created in 1985 as an informal consultation group, also became more focused on developing common solutions to asylum and migration issues 'among like-minded states for implementation in other fora' (Shenstone, 1992: 75). The Council of Europe too worked first on identifying common trends among its member countries, then called for more collaboration between the European Union, the United Nations and the United Nations Population Fund. Finally, added to this already large list of initiatives, regional processes were created in the mid-1990s to promote more co-operation on migration matters. Two of them can be mentioned here: the International Centre for Migration Policy Development (ICMPD) created in 1993, a joint initiative of Switzerland and Austria, receiving diplomatic status in 1997, and co-operating with other inter-governmental organizations and states. It should be noted that the ICMPD constituted an important influence in the elaboration of the Schengen system among European countries, prior to its inclusion into the European Union; and the Regional Conference on Migration or Puebla Process, involving sustained co-operation between North and Central

American states on migration matters, particularly on issue of combating migrant trafficking (Pellerin and Overbeek, 2001).

Of all these initiatives, the role of the IOM should be underlined, for its logistical and agenda-setting efforts. In the 1990s, the IOM was involved in administrative and other support in organizing several meetings at both regional and international levels to discuss issues of migration regulations. It also acted as executive agency for a think tank on the question, a project called the New International Regime for Orderly Movements of People (NIROMP) (Ghosh, 2000a). Recognizing that international migration is no longer the exclusive national concern of sovereign states, that it had become a more global and interdependent phenomenon (IOM, 1996: 9), the organization called for a global and comprehensive approach to the problem.

This call was answered by the UN in recent years, with the creation of a Global Commission on International Migration (GCIM) in December 2003. Its report, published at the end of 2005, recognized the central and continuing importance of migration globally, and proposed a series of recommendations serving to make it beneficial for all parties, namely sending and receiving countries, and migrants themselves (GCIM, 2005). As it was rightly observed, the report was a significant achievement for the consensus it showed among the different experts, on the need for bringing migration to the centre of the world agenda (Hansen, 2006). And equally noteworthy was the insistence on the need for a multilateral and comprehensive approach, with greater coordination among states, and with the involvement of international financial institutions and the private sector (Escobar Latapi, 2006). The UN wanted to keep the momentum and acted upon some of the GCIM recommendations, with the organization of a first in a series of annual High-Level Dialogues on Migration in September 2006.

Towards a new global migration order

The new migration order is made up of a set of rules, priorities and a configuration of power destined to embrace the contours of the global political economy. It is also a locus of struggles between different visions and principles. The ambitious call for a global regulation of migration can be understood in this sense as an attempt by dominant forces to impose a particular view of mobility onto others[2]. It involves at least three areas of action, debate and struggle: migration patterns suiting a new economic space and logic; migration policies reflecting new power configuration between states and markets; and integration questions contributing to new models of state-society relations.

A new economic and spatial logic

The post-war migration order, as Zolberg aptly summarized it, served specific interests and priorities:

> [T]he resumption of international movement in the post-World-War-II period and its expansion to an unprecedented level . . . [r]esulted from an interaction between new immigration or immigration-relevant policies adopted by the industrial democracies in the service of their own economic and political objectives as well as the vast

enlargement of the pool of potential migrants in the world at large . . . . [T]his development took place within the framework of an international political economy reconstructed under the leadership of internationalist-minded American capitalists, who sought to prevent the reenactment of interwar catastrophes by liberalizing the international movement of capital and goods, while allowing individual countries some possibility of protecting their internal labour markets from major oscillations . . . . [I]n short, the importation of foreign workers on a temporary basis was a convenient device for achieving this objective. (Zolberg, 1996: 46–47)

The current phase is more attuned to the globalization phase of capitalist expansion, with a different spatialization of economic activities. This requires international migration and the mobility of people, but a very selective one. Capital holders and skilled migrants are priorities, while states need to keep their migration policies flexible to respond to the needs of a flexible labour market. Unskilled migrant labour, which was the main migration category in the post-war period, becomes secondary, with industrialized states consenting to temporary schemes only for sectors where production could not be delocalized, such as construction, agriculture, food processing and unskilled services. The discussions at the World Trade Organization for creating a GATS visa for some service suppliers, the growing interests of industrialized receiving countries in attracting, often on a temporary basis, highly skilled labour capable of contributing directly and significantly to economic growth, and the recent interest by the World Bank, the International Monetary Fund and the IOM for greater mobility of human and social capital, sometimes referred to as a diaspora resource model (Bhagwati, 2003), are all indications of this emerging paradigm. Two characteristics of this new paradigm therefore are the subordination of labour migration not solely to labour markets' needs in host societies, but also to the projections of global competitiveness of key economic sectors, and less reliance on states involvement in regulating and supporting labour migration.

Regions that are not part of centres of growth, like the largest part of the African continent, tend to receive a different treatment in the global regulation of migration, notably by being excluded from the privileges of mobility. The Trilateral Commission had called, in 1993, for a right of people to stay where they are (Meissner et al., 1993). The European Population Conference adopted a similar posture when it recommended that 'governments should encourage persons in need of international protection to stay, to the extent possible, in the safe areas nearest to their countries of origin.' (UN ECE et al., 1994b: 23). This trend has been confirmed by the growing emphasis placed by industrialized countries on migration controls beyond their borders, through interregional partnerships, and through the externalization of some of their procedures (OXFAM, 2005). Even the development-migration nexus of the interwar period is being reformulated. Rather than sending money to poor regions through official public aid, donors and international financial institutions focus on liberalizing trade and capital markets, and on reforming the state, in order to create endogenous conditions of developments that will eventually limit the push factors (Escobar Latapi, 2006).

Part of the new spatialization of economic activity is reflected in the regionalization of migration regulation. The regionalization of migration controls is evident in the form and the content of cooperation that is involved. Most international co-operation takes place between regionally close partners, with less developed countries. Regional cooperation often includes two aspects: technical cooperation in matters of migration controls and restrictions, and the promotion of mechanisms facilitating the mobility of specific categories of migrants. The first aspect is well known: it takes the form of official agreements, like the Schengen Agreement which creates a common space for security, liberty and justice within which there is mobility of factors of production including people, provided that they are legally within the territory. Other arrangements provide also for cooperation on border controls, such as the Euro-Mediterranean Agreements, between the EU and North African and Middle Eastern countries (Pastore, 2002). The second dimension of regionalization of migration policies is less documented and publicized: it relates to the adaptations of domestic laws and/or of immigration laws to facilitate the harmonization of control mechanisms on the one hand, and also to facilitate the circulation of certain categories of migrants on a short-term basis, often through private recruiting agencies, on the other. This latter set of changes concerns new policies such as types of visas, new requirements for residency and access to employment for spouses. Hence, within the North American Free-Trade Agreement (NAFTA), and subsequent free-trade agreements between Canada and Chile and Costa-Rica, clauses exist on the migration of some categories of professionals. The actual process of labour market integration is governed in large part by the private sector, notably with the work of recruiting agencies and employers' designing demands for foreign labour (Kuptsch, 2006). Another example would be the Regional Conference on Migration or Puebla Process that brings together North and Central American countries. This regional forum seeks to harmonize migration policies through the process of legislative and policy reforms in send-ing regions (Pellerin, 1999).

Through these various schemes, policy-makers from the advanced industrialized coun-tries seek to foster greater co-operation and coordination for the freer mobility of skilled people, intellectuals and students. At the same time, compatible and complementary mea-sures to curb the flows of unwanted migrants are discussed, designed and progressively implemented, helping in this way to share the costs of migration controls among all regions involved. The global management of migration thus serves to regulate competition for highly skilled workers among industrialized countries, and to bring sending states into the sharing of the costs of controlling migration.

A new power configuration in migration practices

The new world migration order is based on a series of compromises that took place between the various interests involved. Of these, which range from communities in sending and receiving regions, to NGOs dealing with human rights, to economic sectors and state, only a few managed to get their objectives and priorities met. The new migration order is one that promotes first and foremost the interests of regionally and globally oriented industries, receiving states and minimally, the interests of Northern NGOs.

Perhaps the most obvious losers in this new migration order are sending states. Although the post-war period was not designed with equal benefits to sending and receiving states, in practice many sending countries managed to negotiate relatively good terms for exchanging migrants and capital, particularly in the context of a great demand for unskilled labour in many industrialized countries. This period could be referred to as a competitive bilateral model, where sending states were competing for larger quotas and receiving countries competed for attracting migrants (Pastore, 2002). The Cold War rhetoric in the Western world also served sending states insofar as the freedom of movement principle was almost sacrosanct. In the current period, however, the benefits occur mostly to receiving regions. Before they can receive assistance, sending states have to demonstrate that they do everything possible to keep their people in.[3] Moreover, with the focus on the root causes of migration, the industrialized world has put the magnifying glass on sending states and societies and is scrutinising their practices very critically, notably those related to population growth and distribution. Finally, the experience of migration export strategies adopted by some states is increasingly presented as a best practice that other less-developed countries should seek to emulate. The Philippines, with a large volume of expatriates, is said to benefit from remittances, and also, from protections and guarantees for its workers abroad (Battistella, 1995).

Host states of the industrialized world see their interests well promoted in this new migration order. Not only are their sovereign prerogatives over who comes in and out not fundamentally questioned, they also deploy new efforts to deal with the consequences of the entry of migrants, and have a new legitimacy to convince sending regions to adopt compatible policies. And the aftermath of the attacks on the World Trade Center increased the legitimacy of industrialized countries in their search for migration control, in the name of security. In this new context, even asylum claimants are now subordinated to a security logic. Countries in the industrialized world increasingly externalize their controls, in order to avoid having to grant rights and entitlements to people they do not want on their territory (OXFAM, 2005).

Within receiving states it is particular economic interests that are well protected. Neo-liberal economic reforms implemented in all of the industrialized countries in the 1990s reflected the interests of particular economic sectors, those focused on the new economy of knowledge, and on globally oriented economic activities, financial and otherwise. In this context some of the key priorities of the new migration order are related to flexibility, competitiveness and liberalization. In one of its recommendations, the European Population Conference insisted on the promotion of temporary forms of migration for regional developments (UN ECE et al., 1994b: 22). The OECD has echoed this approach by presenting, in its annual reports since the late 1990s, the use of temporary migration as a convenient measure to respond to flexible labour markets. Many European countries have resumed guest-worker programs in recent years, notably Germany, the Netherlands, Norway, the United Kingdom, Ireland, Belgium, Sweden, Greece, Italy and Spain (Castles, 2006; Ruhs, 2005). It is also important to note that even the fight against terrorism and irregular migration has received the support of private employers, notably in North America. In order to ensure that borders remain open for the circulation of goods and capital, the Coalition for Secure and Trade-Efficient Borders was actively involved in demanding from Canadian authorities closer cooperation with the United States administration (Coalition, 2001). The more recent Security and Prosperity Partnership of North America (SPP), signed in 2005 between Canada, Mexico and the United States, even has a feature for incorporating fully the private sector in the establishment of closer cooperation between the three countries on issues of border security, emergency management and other cross-border questions (SPP, 2006).

A clear illustration of the interests being promoted by this global migration order lies in the concept and practice behind the notion of *orderly migration*. As the IOM defines it, orderly migration is one that 'follows agreed procedures and allows for the safety and protection of the rights of everyone involved' (IOM, 1995). Another term also used, *regulated openness*, perhaps conveys better the intent of the concept. Far from a complete liberal view of free and unfettered movements across countries, international migration should 'follow a pragmatic approach focusing on what is politically achievable and operationally viable' (Ghosh, 2000c: 25). The right to move thus becomes subsumed under the need for an orderly, that is predictable, and manageable environment for state policy. The freedom to move becomes a logic for efficient economic growth. As one specialist put it: 'Increased temporary mobility related to trade in services and investment should make it easier for countries in different stages of development to better exploit their comparative advantages' (Ghosh, 2000b: 228).

In this context, the interests promoted by NGOs are not very well served by the new migration order. Questions of human rights are addressed only minimally in international or regional gatherings. The UN Convention on the Rights of Migrants promoted by many human rights groups took thirteen years to come into force due to the slow ratification rate by member states. It came into force in 2003. In early 2007, the Convention counts 36 ratifications and 15 signatures. It is noteworth that it has not been signed by any industrialized countries, except Mexico and Turkey. The NGOs involved, mostly from the industrialized countries, tend to play a marginal role in negotiations at the regional level, and even more minimally at the international level[4]. When issues of human rights of migrants are taken into consideration, they are limited to minimal procedural rights, such as in conditions of detainment of irregular migrants, or they are framed in the combat against human trafficking, thus reducing the variety of migrant abuses to the criminal offence of clandestine crossing (Satterthwaite, 2005). The *UN Convention against Transnational Organized Crime* (2002) and its two protocols, the *Protocol Against the Smuggling of Migrants by Land, Sea and Air* (2003), and the *Protocol to Prevent, Suppress and Punish Trafficking in Persons, Especially Women and Children* (2004), constitute an important legal framework in which minimal human rights are considered.

The promotion of a new state-society model

The comprehensive approach to global governance of migration involves a large number of questions, from population growth to population distribution and international migration. In such a broad framework, even issues of integration of migrants have become the object of attention for global regulation. Integration measures were not part of the post–World War II migration order, as the issue remained a national prerogative. In the current period, however, the question has become the object of close examination and discussion among industrialized countries and within some international organizations. It has become one key element of the new migration order partly to face past failures, but also to better manage their consequences. The issue of managing diversity is becoming a central concern. As one specialist wrote:

> If states, especially advanced industrial democracies, cannot control who enters, they should turn instead to the question of how best to deal with the consequences of such entries. (Weiner, 1996: 181–82)

In the context of globalization and neoliberal reforms, integration measures become important for at least two reasons. First, they constitute an important permissive or propitious factor conditioning the mobility of people. If people cannot integrate well, the social order and its legitimacy are at stake, and there is a disruption in the free flow and self-regulated distribution of people according to economic criteria of profitability and productivity. In a context of growing tensions, xenophobic feelings and the rise of extreme-right forces, particularly in Europe, the question of integration becomes a sensitive political one that confronts entrenched interests.

One model of integration that came to be particularly popular in global circles in the 1990s is multiculturalism, which was promoted by many states and private organizations. The model serves to fight xenophobia, promote tolerance, and the harnessing of diversity. In Canada, it is seen as an efficient mechanism to maintain social order and even to gain a competitive edge on global markets. It is in these terms that the multicultural models of Canada and the United States were praised at the international and regional levels, notably at the OECD and in Europe. But despite the support business provided to multiculturalism, especially for the purpose of encouraging the development of a diverse workforce to tap global markets and maintain competition (Council of Europe, 1998: 9), its features started to be called into question in Europe in the late 1990s (Joppke, 2004).

The second reason why integration measures became important was that they address directly the role of the state in regulating society. With neoliberal reforms there has been a shift in costs and responsibilities for integration away from the state, into the hands of private agencies, or in the hands of migrants themselves. In other words, ethnic communities, NGOs and charity organizations bear the brunt of integration operations, while states become responsible largely for the policing dimension of migration. The delegation of functions to private organizations comes in the form of promoting self-reliance of ethnic and migrant communities. Moreover, the more recent focus on the migration of highly skilled labour also fit into this approach. Highly skilled migrants are presumed to be more fit for host societies, with less need for specific integration measures. The onus of their integration has fallen increasingly on the migrants themselves. And recent immigration reforms in the Netherlands, in the United Kingdom and in France, with the necessity for migrants to show their ability to civic integration, is confirming this trend (Joppke, 2004; Mony, 2006).

With these various efforts, the discussion of integration measures at the global level imprints a particular model of functions and responsibilities on states, individuals and various communities. This tends to promote a state-society model more in line with neoliberal principles of the state's withdrawal from social responsibilities and support.

Conclusion

Justifying the current global effort at regulating migration, one observer noted that there are many reasons, political, economic and humanitarian, for doing so at the turn of the twenty-first century:

> A unique convergence of three types of factors is now challenging states to strengthen their mutual cooperation. First, on a domestic level, state policies and behaviour are now largely shaped by the dominant power groups that have strong links with the

global market and thus have a strong interest in stable inter-state relations. Second, states are also under pressure to increase cooperation among themselves in order to operate in the transnational space to: maintain peace and order; enhance economic prosperity through expansion of trade and investment; ensure an efficient global system of transport and communication; fight extra territorial terrorism; protect the environment; manage the 'global commons'; and so on. A third set of transnational factors that are also having a gradual but perceptible impact on state behaviour concerns an evolving sense of common human values and a growing concern for humanity, such as the respect for basic human rights and protection of people in extreme danger or distress. (Ghosh, 2000b: 244)

Beyond more effectiveness and responsiveness, however, it is a new migration order that is in the making at the world level, with a set of priorities that reflects objectives, interests and priorities more in line with the globalized political economy. Concretely, the changes brought about by this new migration order have so far taken essentially two forms. First has been the transformation of state policies and priorities through a harmonization of legislation, statistics and control policies. The second mechanism is the elaboration of legal instruments for anchoring the newly defined principles into binding obligations for the international community. The latter, that takes the form of agreements, treaties, conventions, but also administrative reforms in countries of origin and of transit, is much less developed and less known. With these measures the global agenda on migration priorities is generating a new consensus among industrialized states and social forces about migration dynamics, the spatial organization of the economy, and the ideological programme of neoliberalism and state reduction.

Such order in the making obviously has consequences that go much beyond the control of borders. The challenge is for a progressive agenda to be set forth, particularly in a context where very different interests are mobilized around migration issues: rising xenophobic politicians and public opinion in many industrialized countries, the ongoing fight against terrorism across borders, and the search for a more globalized labour market for skilled people. In the early 1990s, a crisis of numbers triggered the initial efforts of states to global regulation. A security crisis that started in 2001 provided a continued incentive for constructing a global regulation framework for migration. These crises led to a focus on states' concerns for the security of their borders, with very little room for development and human rights concerns. In this context, of the two most popular progressive scenarios – the development of a transnational form of citizenship and the protection of migrant rights – only the latter still receives some attention by states, and only in a minimalist version.

Notes

1. The post-war period also witnessed international efforts to promote a co-ordinated set of rules and principles around migration. It was at that time that the High Commissioner for Refugees was established as a permanent and more internationally focused organization replacing the International Refugee Organization. It was also in 1951 that the International Organization for Migration, then called the PICMME (Provisional Intergovernmental Committee for the Movement of Migrants from

Europe), was established to oversee the transport of migrants. Finally, it was also in 1949 that the first convention on migrant labour came into force, through the ILO. These various efforts and organizations produced a set of principles that were to define the post–World War II migration order, notably around industrial growth in the Euro-Atlantic area.

2. The new global migration order is ambitious in that it aims to be comprehensive and embraces many facets of the migration process, from short-term policies like controls on the circulation of people, the duration of stay, the labour market, and social integration, to longer-term objectives such as demographic growth, development orientations, concerns for the regions of origin, such as employment and investment opportunities, voluntary return of migrants, and rights of individual migrants.

3. It is illustrative of this trend that the Inter-governmental Consultations on Asylum, Refugee and Migration Policies in Europe, North America and Australia focuses its efforts on burden-sharing measures and on re-admission agreements rather than on assisting sending states and migrants to stay where they came from (IGC, 1994; 1997).

4. Just to give an example, at the World Population Plan of Action during the period 1988–1989, more than half of the NGOs participating in financial or technical assistance to population cooperation were located in the United States and most of the rest were in continental Europe (UN ECE et al., 1994b: 402).

References

Agnew, J. and Corbridge, S. (1995) *Mastering Space: Hegemony, Territory and International Political Economy*, London, Routledge.

Appleyard, R. T. (1992) *International Migration: Challenge for the Nineties*, Geneva, IOM.

Battistella, G. (1995) "Philippine overseas labor: from export to management", *ASEAN Economic Bulletin*, 12 (2), 257–74.

Bhagwati, J. (2003) "Borders beyond control", *Foreign Affairs*, 82 (1), 98–104.

Castles, S. (2006) 'Guestworkers in Europe: a resurrection?', *International Migration Review*, 40 (4), 741–66.

Coalition for Secure and Trade Efficient Borders (2001) *Rethinking our Borders: A Place for Action*, Ottawa, December.

Council of Europe (1995) *Recent Demographic Developments in Europe*, Strasbourg, Council of Europe.

———. (1998) *Initiatives by Employers to Promote Employment and Integration of Immigrants*, Strasbourg, Community Relations Series.

———. (1999) *Current Trends in International Migration in Europe*, Social Cohesion and Quality of Life, online at www.coe.fr/dase/en/cohesion/action/publi/migrants/managing.htm.

Cox, R. W. (1992) 'Global Perestroika' in R. Miliband and L. Panitch (eds), *New World Order? The Socialist Register*, London, Merlin Press.

Escobar Latapi, A. (2006) 'The Economy, Development, and Work in the Final Report of the GCIM', *International Migration*, 44 (4), 15–24.

GCIM (2005) *Migration in an Interconnected World: New Directions for Actions: Report of the Global Commission on International Migration*, Geneva, Global Commission on International Migration.

Ghosh, B. (ed) (2000a) *Managing Migration: Time for a New International Regime*, Oxford, Oxford University Press.

———. (2000b) 'New international regime for orderly movements of people: What will it look like?' in B. Ghosh (ed.), *Managing Migration*, Oxford, Oxford University Press, pp. 220–47.

———. (2000c) 'Towards a new international regime for orderly movements of people' in B. Ghosh (ed.), *Managing Migration*, Oxford, Oxford University Press, pp. 6–26.

Hansen, R. (2006) 'Winners and losers, democrats and demagogues, welfare and work: commentary on the GCIM', *International Migration*, 44 (4), 25–36.

High Commission for Refugees (2006) *Refugees. World Trends in 2005*, online at www.unhcr.org.

Hollifield, J. (2000) 'Migration and the "New" international order: the missing regime' in B. Ghosh (ed.), *Managing Migration*, Oxford, Oxford University Press.

IGC (Intergovernmental Consultations on Asylum, Refugee and Migration Policies in Europe, North America and Australia) (1994) *On Readmission Agreements*, working paper, August.

———. (1997) *Report on the Concept of Burden-Sharing*, October.

IOM (International Organization for Migration) (1996) *IOM News*, Nov/Dec.

———. (1995) *Overview of International Migration: Migration Management Training Programme*, online at http:www/iom.int/iom/publication/entry.htm, accessed July 2000.

———. (1999) *Technical Cooperation on Migration (TCM)*. IOM's contribution towards migration policy-making and strengthened migration governance, October, online at http:www.iom.int/tcm/entry.htm.

Joppke, C. (2004) 'The retreat of multiculturalism in the liberal state: theory and policy', *The British Journal of Sociology*, 55 (2), 237–57.

Kuptsch, C. (ed.) (2006) *Merchants of Labour*, Geneva, International Labour Organization, International Institute for Labour Studies.

Lithman, Y. G. (2000) *Spatial Concentration and Mobility*, Metropolis International, online at www.international.metropolis.net/frameset_e.html.

Lohrmann, R. (1998) 'Migrant, refugees and insecurity', IOM statement at the international seminar on 'Globalization: A challenge for Peace – Solidarity or exclusion?', Milan, October, online at http://www.iom.int/IOM/Statements/Lohrmann_milano_1998_10_29.htm, accessed 3 July 2000.

Meissner, D. M., Hormats, R. D., Garrigues Walker, A. and Ogata, S. (1993) *International Migration: Challenges in a New Era*, report to the Trilateral Commission 44, NYMony, P. (2006) 'Country report: France', *The Rights of Migrant Workers in the European Union*, Shadow Reports for Estonia, France, Ireland and the United Kingdom, Bonheiden, Europe Platform for Migrant Workers' Rights, 59–80.

Muus, P. J. and van Dam, E. W. (1996) 'Comparative research on international migration and international migration policy', Document for the European Commission, Luxembourg, June.

OECD (1991) *Trends in International Migration*, SOPEMI Annual Report 1991, Paris, OECD.

———. (1992) *Trends in International Migration*, SOPEMI Annual Report 1992, Paris, OECD.

———. (1993) *Trends in International Migration*, SOPEMI Annual Report 1993, Paris, OECD.

———. (1995) *Trends in International Migration*, SOPEMI Annual Report 1994, Paris, OECD.

———. (1996) *Trends in International Migration*, SOPEMI Annual Report 1996, Paris, OECD.

———. (1998) *Trends in International Migration*, SOPEMI Annual Report 1998, Paris, OECD.

OECD (1999) *Trends in International Migration*, SOPEMI Annual Report 1999, Paris, OECD.

OXFAM (2005) *Foreign Territory: The Internationalisation of EU Asylum Policy*, Oxford, Oxfam.

Papademetriou, D. (1991) 'Confronting the challenge of transnational migration: domestic and international responses', paper presented at the International Conference on Migration, OECD, Rome, March.

Pastore, F. (2002) 'Aeneas's route: Euro-Mediterranean relations and international migration' in D. Lavenex, E. M. Uçarer (eds), *Migration and the Externalities of European Integration*, Lanham, Lexington Books, pp. 105–24.

Pellerin, H. (1999) 'The cart before the horses? The coordination of migration policies in the Americas and the neoliberal economic project of integration', *Review of International Political Economy*, 6 (4), winter, 468–93.

———. (2004) 'Economic integration and security. New key factors in managing international migration', *Choices*, 10 (6), July 1–26.

Pellerin, H., and Overbeek, H. (2001) 'Neo-liberal regionalism and the management of people's mobility', in A. Bieler and A. Morten (eds), *Social Forces in the Making of the New Europe*, London, Palgrave.

Richmond, A. (1994) *Global Apartheid*, Oxford, Oxford University Press.

Ruhs, M. (2005) 'The potential of temporary migration programmes in future international migration policy', paper prepared for the Policy Analysis and Research Programme of the Global Commission on International Migration, online at http://www.gci.org/attachments/TP3.pdf.

Salt, J. (1993) *Migration and Population Change in Europe*, United Nations Institute for Disarmament Research, Research Paper no. 19, New York, United Nations.

Security and Prosperity Partnership of North America (2007) *A North American Partnership*, online at http://www.spp.gov, accessed in April.

Shenstone, M. (1992) *World Population Growth and Population Movements: Policy Implications for Canada*, Policy Planning Staff Paper no. 92/7, Ottawa.

Singh, J. S. (1998) *Creating a New Consensus on Population*, London, Earthscan.

Statterthwaite, M. (2005) 'Crossing borders, claiming rights: using human rights law to empower women migrant workers', *Yale Human Rights and Development Law Journal*, 8, 1–66.

UN ECE, Council of Europe, UNPF (1994a) *European Population Conference.* Proceedings vol. 1, New York and Geneva, United Nations.

———. (1994b) *European Population Conference.* Proceedings vol. 2, New York and Geneva, United Nations.

UNHCR (1993) *Les Réfugiés dans le Monde 1993. L'enjeu de la Protection*, Paris, La Découverte.

UN Department of Economic and Social Affairs, Population Division (1998) *International Migration Policies*, New York.

UN Department of Economic and Social Development (1993) *Report on the World Social Situation*, New York, Population Division.

UN Département de l'information économique et sociale et de l'analyse des politiques (1995) *Aperçu de la Situation démographique dans le Monde en 1995*, New York.

UN Department of Economic and Social Affairs (2005) *Trends in Total Migrant Stock*, New York.

UN Secretariat (1998) *Migrations internationales et Développement*, New York, Rapport concis.

UNCTAD and IOM (1996) *Foreign Direct Investment, Trade, Aid and Migration*, Current Studies Series A no. 29, Geneva, United Nations.

Waever, O., Buzan, B., Kelstrup, M. and Lemaitre, P. (1993) *Identity, Migration and the New Security Agenda in Europe*, New York, St. Martin's Press.

Weiner, M. (1996) 'Ethics, national sovereignty and the control of immigration', *International Migration Review*, 30 (1), 171–97.

Wood, E. M. (1997) 'Modernity, postmodernity or capitalism?' *Review of International Political Economy*, 4 (3), 539–60.

Zolberg, A. R. (1996) 'Immigration and multiculturalism in the industrial democracies' in R. Bauböck, A. Heller and A. R. Zolberg (eds), *The Challenge of Diversity: Integration and Pluralism in Societies of Immigration*, Aldershot, Avebury, pp. 43–66.

CHAPTER 14

Citizenship, Migration and Globalization

An Issue of Social Cohesion

Ahmet Icduygu and Banu Senay

Introduction

This chapter offers some thoughts about investigating the migratory context of citizenship which is changing dramatically in our globalizing world. It also presents some discussions about citizenship as an institution that provides social cohesion. It addresses two distinct but interrelated issues; first, the role of globalization in producing a new genre of citizenship, and second, the association between international migration, the emergence of ethnically diverse societies and social cohesion. Contemporary globalization has caused a number of changes in the institution of citizenship, as it implies 'a move away from territorialism in geography . . . together with a move away from statism in governance' (Scholte, 2004: 2). Contemporary globalization and the rise of transnational spaces have loosened crucial affective underpinnings of citizenship. While the globalization-citizenship linkage has received considerable attention in the last two decades, the debate has primarily focused on three main aspects (Castles and Davidson, 2000: 6): the destabilization effect of globalization over the 'national-state'; the question of how globalization undermines the homogenization ideology of the nationalist project; and the growing mobility of people across national borders. All these processes generated by globalization, together with increasing international migratory flows, challenge, in turn, the notion of social cohesion which is defined as the interdependence between members of a society, shared loyalties and solidarity (Jenson, 1998). Social cohesion is deeply connected to the institution of citizenship since it is about feelings of a common identity and sense of belonging to a community. Many material conditions in the current international mobility associated with global trends have made the sustainability of social cohesion unviable in numerous societies of our modern times. This process has had important implications for re-thinking the notion of citizenship in a global world.

Over the past few years, issues of immigration, integration, ethnic and religious diversity and social cohesion have become intense sites of concern through the world. Whereas some decades ago these issues would be confined within the realm of 'low-politics', they have recently been at the heart of many debates related to nationhood, national identity, national security, national cohesion and so forth. This tendency to place an overwhelming emphasis on the term 'national' is accompanied by a parallel discourse which portrays immigrants as a 'threat to the nation' and 'obstacles to social cohesion'. Even such changes at the discourse level demonstrate how issues of immigration have become highly politicized (Vasta, 2006: 2). However, this politicization goes beyond the discourse level and has its repercussions in state policies and practices towards immigrants today. In many countries, the introduction of compulsory programmes for new immigrants such as language tests and citizenship courses has become common. These legal amendments, which are promulgated in the name of easing the way for migrants to integrate into the life of the host country, signal a general shift towards more restrictive approaches to immigration or what Joppke (2004: 237) defines as the 'retreat of multiculturalism in the liberal state'. The process of the downscaling of multiculturalism is not only a Europe-wide phenomenon, but can even be observed in traditional immigrant-receiving countries such as Australia and Canada. In September 2006, for instance, the Department of Immigration and Multicultural Affairs in Australia released a discussion paper titled 'Australian citizenship: Much more than a ceremony' which suggests a citizenship test be introduced in order to assist social cohesion and successful integration into the community (2006: 11). According to the discussion paper:

> A formal citizenship test could be an important part of the process of assisting people to fully participate in the Australian community as it would provide a real incentive to learn English and to understand the Australian way of life. (2006: 11)

A return to an assimilationist perspective and civic-integrationist policies is even more pronounced in Europe (Cheong et al., 2007; Kofman, 2005; Schuster and Solomos, 2004; Back et al., 2002). This can be explained with regard to the foundations of multicultural policies in Europe. Whereas in countries like Australia and Canada multiculturalism is entrenched as an identity option for society as a whole, European multiculturalisms have always been for immigrants only (Joppke, 2004: 247). The move away from liberal migration policies in Europe has become more severe in the aftermath of the terrorist bombings in the London metro in July 2005 and the November 2005 riots in Paris banlieues. Propagated by the governments of most states, populist politicians and parties, and the media, immigrants were portrayed as perils to the unity and cohesion of most European states. 'Immigration has been framed as a security risk, igniting xenophobia and the fear of the Other' (Cheong et al., 2007: 42). Even in countries like the Netherlands and Britain, which had applied more inclusive policy frameworks for immigrants, not only has multiculturalism been strongly criticized, but national identities and obligations have been re-asserted. Since 1998, various civic and language requirements wer ? introduced by the Dutch government in an attempt to ensure that new immigrants integrate into Dutch society and culture to a much greater degree than in the past and coercive measures have been taken up to withhold citizenship for those who do not achieve the expected civic and language grades (Vasta, 2006: 1). Likewise, in Britain, nationhood practices, such as citizenship courses and ceremonies, have been institutionalized to incorporate non-British Others (Home Office, 2002, cited in Cheong et al., 2007: 26). With some similar concerns, Kofman (2005: 464) argues that 'this new social contact seeks to circumscribe transnational and diasporic identities and to reassert attachment to the core values of the nation-state of potentially disruptive citizens'. Such growing emphasis on the commitment and obligations of immigrants focuses attention away from the responsibilities of the receiving countries and obscures the positive side of immigration flows.

This chapter highlights the context in which the contemporary large-scale globalization and international immigration have modified the conventional understanding of citizenship and social cohesion and proposes a framework for re-thinking citizenship. The crucial question here is how the projects and policies still being produced at the national level are responding to the pressure engendered by globalization and whether they encourage the emergence of new forms of membership to the larger political community. Do state policies and practices leave some space for a progressive form of citizenship so as to empower the position of immigrants, or are they cautiously attempting to preserve and activate the already existing forms of state membership?

In today's modern states, citizenship indicates a symbolic reality of the equality of its members (Heater, 1999: 1). It signifies a bundle of rights and duties, connotes a sense of identity, and implies a variety of civic virtues, so that those members are assumed to live in an environment of social cohesion (Kymlicka and Norman, 2000: 30). At the same time, by drawing a lucid line for criteria of inclusion and exclusion, citizenship stands as the most important determining element of the membership in a political community. Meanwhile, as often noted, various elements of uncertainties that modern states face today make it much more difficult for the institution of citizenship to deal with the paradoxes of inclusion and exclusion. Indeed, arrivals and residence of foreigners as migrants in a nation-state pose a question of this kind. As mentioned by Sassen (2002: 5), 'these signal a deterritorializing of citizenship practices and identities, and of discourses about loyalty and allegiance'. Without having certain rights and duties, without feeling a sense of identity, and without exercising various civic virtues, can these immigrants easily become a part of the societies they live in? This is a widely debated, but, as yet, unresolved question (Icduygu, 2005). Considering the challenges of international migration in the age of globalization, some scholars, for instance, emphasize a fundamental shift away from national citizenship, as a nation-based inclusion, to post-national citizenship (Soysal, 1994), which is a more individual-based universal conception of inclusion. However, the concept of post-national citizenship has been questioned by other scholars who have contended that individual-based universal conception of inclusion cannot be implemented and enforced without the consent of nation-states.

Having addressed the key problematic issues in the debate on 'what to do with the citizenship position of immigrants in receiving countries', the main points of departure of the arguments of this chapter are three-fold: (a) in general, citizenship constitutes a dynamic sociological and political ground on which we can analyze the dynamic nature of the integration questions of immigrants which have given rise to the recent impasse of the state-centric approaches in integration policies and practices; (b) more specifically, there are four elements defining the *modis operandi* of citizenship, namely legal status, identity, civic virtues and social cohesion. In the context of globalization and international migration, we have witnessed the increasing legitimacy crisis of such an operation of citizenship, whose manifestations can be observed within each element of citizenship as they are de-articulated and re-articulated in various migratory contexts; (c) the pressures on the modern notion of citizenship reveal that it is necessary for us to see that an empowerment of immigrants cannot be fully achieved without the implementation and dissemination of a more individual-based universal conception of inclusion that is a post-national understanding of citizenship.

Given the salience of intensified international migration flows, the issue of access to citizenship rights is of increasing global importance. Arguments in favour of facilitating access to citizenship by alien residents have been challenged on both ideological and structural grounds. The former has brought into focus the relationship between the formal and informal implications of citizenship and its practical consequences, including viewing citizenship as either a cause of or an effect of immigrants' integration into the receiving societies. The latter implies an extension of the debate to, and a fresh emphasis on new forms of citizenship, such as dual citizenship, multiple citizenship, transnational citizenship or postnational citizenship. Consequently if citizenship is considered important both symbolically and practically, what remains crucial in these debates is the need for a critical re-thinking of citizenship.

Migration, citizenship and integration: a question of challenge and opportunity

Contemporary globalization has encouraged increased complexity with respect to the functions and practices of citizenship in migrant receiving countries. After several decades of experiences of immigration in many countries around the world, the potential effects of naturalization on the integration of immigrants in receiving countries continue to be hotly debated. At the centre of this debate is the question of whether naturalization is a cause of or an effect of the integration of immigrants. The cause side of the debate views as positive the effects of liberal naturalization policies and practices on the likelihood of immigrants' increasing incorporation into the social, political and economic spheres of the receiving countries that would have otherwise not occurred. Implicit in this position is the assumption that the desire to integrate into the receiving country and the demand for acquiring citizenship can be manipulated by liberalizing the naturalization policies and practices. The optimistic assessment of the linkages between migration, citizenship and integration is exemplified by the relatively relaxed naturalization procedures of traditional immigration countries such as Australia and Canada.

Advocates of the effect side of the debate argue that more rigid naturalization policies and practices may produce a clearer desire for immigrants to incorporate into the social, political and economic spheres of the receiving countries, and then, try to take out the citizenship of these countries. In the absence of liberal naturalization procedures, it is assumed that immigrants who desire to take out citizenship more than anything else will first seek and adopt methods of incorporation to the societies where they live. The effect side of the argument notes the desires of immigrants to integrate and incorporate themselves into various spheres of receiving countries as a necessary precondition for naturalization. This relatively conservative position, indeed, tends to determine the naturalization policies and practices in many European countries.

While these debates are voiced in many locations, the intensification of migratory flows continues to pose both challenges and opportunities for many nation-states and citizens involved in such flows. Today many nation-states host thousands of foreigners who are citizens of other countries. Thousands of people hold multiple citizenships and live in more than one country. Thousands are disenfranchised since they cannot become citizens in their countries of residence. Consequently, international mobility can end up with situations of crisis for many people regarding their citizenship. The anomalous status of citizens reveals that new approaches to citizenship, which take account of a new understanding of citizenship, are needed. For instance, as Ong (2006: 501) noted, transnational practices enhance the capacity of immigrants to negotiate national spaces and to claim citizenship-like entitlements 'as free individuals to confront globalized insecurities by making calculations and investments in their lives'. The crucial question here is whether the current policies and practices encourage the formulation and practice of a progressive form of citizenship, and what parameters one can think of in relation to this possible form which has the potential to empower immigrants.

Migration as a space of assemblage for citizenship: processes of disarticulation and re-articulation

In their seminal work on citizenship in diverse societies, Kymlicka and Norman (2000: 30) contend that citizenship at an individual level can be addressed from three different dimensions. Citizenship, first, implies a *legal status* held by citizens which determines the range of rights and obligations available to them. A second aspect of citizenship would be *identity*, which implies membership in one or more political communities and, at the same time, comprises various particular identities, such as class, race, ethnicity, gender, profession, and sexual preference, etc. Third, citizenship is about a person's *civic virtue* which can be defined as an asset for acting virtuously and participating in the life of one's political community. In addition to these three individual-level aspects of citizenship, Kymlicka and Norman add a fourth element, which differs from the former three by operating at the community level: *social cohesion*. It includes concerns about social stability, political unity and civil peace. These four aspects are deeply interrelated with each other and, through a dialogical relationship, they re-enforce one another. The combination of these aspects and the continuously changing nature of interrelatedness between them give citizenship its dynamic characteristic as a 'status', a 'sense of belonging', an 'activity', and as a 'social and political institution'.

At the individual level, the interrelatedness between the aspects of legal status, identity and civic virtue also has some very significant implications for the articulation of citizens' perceptions and experiences over their citizenship (Icduygu, 2005: 204). For instance, the legal status defines the content and extent of citizenship rights and obligations available to citizens, but, at the same time, the range of these rights and obligations provide a plethora of sentiments and moral dispositions concerning their identities. All these sets of rights and duties shape the way identity is constructed and the way citizens perceive their identities. Similarly, the presence/absence of legal rights not only shapes the feelings of citizens over their identities, but also determines the range of political activities available to them. In a similar vein, citizens' involvement in civic activities cannot be viewed separately from the way they define their identities. Identity might operate as a motivating source for their civic activism. The panoply of these aspects is deeply interconnected with social cohesion as well. The main ingredients of social cohesion from a Durkheimean's angle can be identified as 'shared loyalty and solidarity', which come into play as an outcome of some social-political elements such as rights, duties, identities and civic virtues.

In an ideal type of non-migration setting, the articulation of these aspects of citizenship appears to be relatively more stable. The four elements of citizenship are somehow compounded and practiced somewhat moderately in the daily lives of individual citizens. For instance, citizens are more likely to have a deeper knowledge about the scope of rights they are to enjoy and the duties they are responsible for, and there is less likelihood for an ambiguity about the way they feel about their identities. They may behave as active and responsible citizens in their particular communities. However, in a migratory setting which transcends national boundaries, the migrants' perceptions and experiences over their citizenship and various aspects of citizenship become relatively ambiguous since their citizenship status, once determined by membership in a nation-state, become unattached from its national basis. Whereas the political context, which formerly served as the basis for the formation of their citizenship status, was the nation-state that they were a member of in the pre-migratory stage, this context is replaced by a totally new setting following their migration to the receiving country. Thus, international migration operates as 'a space of assemblage' whereby the four dimensions of citizenship become disarticulated from each other. Indeed, besides international migration, the destabilizing impact of globalization contributes to accentuating the distinctiveness of each of these dimensions (Sassen, 2002: 5). During this process of 'disarticulation', there occur 'mutations', as Ong (2006) puts it, within each aspect of citizenship, and more broadly, within the whole notion of citizenship. Here we should not consider the process of 'disarticulation' as occurring only within each different aspect of citizenship, but should also recall the deep interconnectedness of these aspects, and, as a result, the question of how these links among the components of citizenship are affected, too.

The process of disarticulation involves the immigrants' assessment and questioning of their citizenship status in the new setting of the receiving country. This is most visible regarding immigrants' perceptions of the legal status aspect of citizenship. In the new sociopolitical environment of the receiving country, the content and the extent of legal rights and duties held by migrants alter. Immigrants in their new social space can no longer claim rights simply through the institutional arrangements of their countries of origin. The nature of the legal status, which indicates what one can do, what capabilities one has (Barbalet, 1988: 16), becomes subject to transformation. A new form of legal status is produced which is not necessarily determined according to the national arrangements of the destination country or according to the idea of membership in a nation-state. Immigrant groups can also claim rights and benefits associated with citizenship within the framework of international human rights which are vested in individuals rather than national governments and have the potential to empower them against the receiving state. So, 'while in theory political rights depend on membership in a nation-state, in practice, new entitlements are being realized through situated mobilizations and claims in milieus of globalized contingency' (Ong, 2006: 499). To put it more amply, full membership in a political community no longer operates as the sole criteria to be endowed with legal rights and duties. According to Urry (1999: 313),

> Citizenship has been conceived of within the west in terms of national risks that may face anyone living within a given territory, national rights that those possessing full membership should receive, and national duties that are appropriate for all such citizens of a society.

He adds that the global flows have changed the ability of the states to mobilise nations in pursuit of societal goals. Today, he says, they have acquired more of a regulative function rather than holding an absolute power to set the rules.

> The hybridisation of cultures, the global refugee problem, the importance of trav-
> elling cultures, some growth of a global dwellingness, diasporas, and other notions
> of the 'unhomely' . . . these configurations weaken the power of the society to draw
> together its citizens as one, to govern in its unique name, to endow all with national
> identity and to speak with a single voice. (Urry, 1999: 314)

Although the scrutiny of international human rights has increased rapidly in the age of globalization, there are still problems with respect to the enforcement and implementation of these rights since it is still national states that are authorized to enforce and implement those rights. In her study of guest-workers-turned-immigrants in Western Europe, Soysal (1994) found that these immigrants had been incorporated into their host societies not as citizens but through 'universal personhood', which supplants nationhood as the defining focus of citizenship. Soysal calls this new type of citizenship as *postnational* citizenship, one in which state sovereignty is contested but not yet replaced. The transition from citizenship rights to human rights, Soysal (1994) argues, is partial: nation-states are declining but not disappearing, yet no new structure has emerged to replace the nation-state.

In the migratory setting, it is not only rights and obligations that become disarticulated, but also identity. Although traditionally, identity came to be termed almost exclusively with 'national identity', given the impact of international migration this analogy is no longer easily applicable. International migration appears as a site whereby individuals begin to reassess their sense of belonging and attachment to their nation, state and nation-state. At this stage, it is not only their membership in a nation-state that shapes their perceptions of their identities, but various other sources of identity might also provide them with a sense of membership. These sources of identity may include race, class, ethnicity, religion, gender, profession, and so on. For instance, a female migrant coming from a rural society may not be allowed to work in the traditional setting of the sending country, but the same person can cling to her gender identity after finding employment in the receiving country. Or, a Muslim migrant may become a more practicing Muslim, such as experiencing a closer adherence to Islam after his or her arrival in the receiving country. After arriving in Germany, for instance, a Turkish citizen of Kurdish origin may begin to feel more Kurdish than Turkish; or after migrating to France a Moroccan citizen with Berber origin may define himself or herself with the identity of being a Berber rather than being a Moroccan. They may give over-emphasis to their existing identities, or suppress them. Hall (1990: 225) de-fines identity as 'the names we give to the different ways we are positioned by, and position ourselves within, the narratives of the past. In this sense, identities are both imposed and self-made. Migration plays a de-constructive role by positioning the migrant in a totally new socio-political environment and blurring the distinction between private and public realms. Various identities that were previously held in the private realm can find acceptance in the public realm within the migratory setting. Indeed, the opposite is also possible.

Migration also problematizes the disarticulation and re-articulation of the activity side of citizenship, that is, civic virtue. In most cases there are fundamental differences between the civic traditions of the sending and receiving countries. When we consider that the majority of migrant groups worldwide are moving from the Southern and Eastern parts of the world to the Northern and Western parts, it is possible to argue that the civic (civil society) traditions of these origin countries are not compatible with the civic traditions of the Western (and Northern) countries where the bulk of the migrants go. Practically, this incompatibility becomes visible as we observe them mostly in the homeland-centered civic activities of migrant communities in the receiving countries. It is very common for immigrant communities to set up migrant associations or clubs in the destination countries. These associations are most commonly known as hometown associations and are formed by migrants from a particular community with common origins. There are ongoing debates as to whether migrant associations foster or hinder the integration of migrant communities in the receiving countries. Although the main aims of hometown associations are to promote support for the benefit of their communities and to assist in the adaptation of newcomers, the scope of their activities has extensively broadened. Often they are very much involved in homeland-centric political activities. Some of the projects carried out by these associations serve for the domestic development of the country of origin. In addition to their functions of sending remittances to the families of migrants in the sending countries, they may also organize and promote humanitarian projects, such as rotating credit, building schools and hospitals, providing informal insurance, organizing sportive and cultural facilities and so forth. Thus, it is possible to argue that the scope of the activities of hometown associations has extended as to encompass the growth and well-being of the destination areas. Through these sorts of activities, the associations also enhance the migrants' attachment to the community of origin – in a way making their integration into the receiving country more difficult.

On the other hand, one must note that, as Kaya and Kentel (2005: 12) implicitly refer to it, the broad networks of communication and transportation between the countries of origin and countries of destination play a significant role in the formation of a migratory citizenship site among transnational communities which connect citizens both to their homeland and to the rest of the world. Consequently, it becomes much easier for immigrants to live on both banks of the river in terms of their legal status, identities and civic virtues. This situation refers to the challenges and opportunities posed to social cohesion by the institution of citizenship in the receiving societies. Under the influence of contemporary globalization, the nature of social cohesion in those societies has become increasingly global as well.

This whole process of disarticulation – throughout which the content and extent of the legal status, identity and civic virtue aspects of citizenship are transformed – is continued by a new process of re-articulation. The legal rights and obligations of migrants, their sense of identity and their civic participation are re-formed in the new setting of the destination country. At this stage, citizenship has the potential to empower the migrant groups, though it may not solve all kinds of problems they encounter. We will next discuss how a citizenship model could become an empowerment tool for immigrants in receiving countries.

Acquisition of citizenship in the migrant-receiving countries: empowering migrants

The re-articulation of the various aspects of one's citizenship is very much linked to the nature of the post-migratory setting in the destination country. It is possible to think of two different settings: (a) a setting in which immigrants have relatively straightforward procedures for the acquisition of citizenship in the receiving country, and (b) a setting in which immigrants are subject to demanding or very tough measures to acquire the citizenship of the receiving country. It is obvious from the discussion above that the former setting has the power of re-articulating the elements of legal status, identity and civic virtues which are essential for the enhancement of social cohesion and incorporation of migrants in the receiving societies. In short, the process of the acquisition of citizenship itself is explicitly empowering for immigrants, as it provides more than a legal status, involving various dimensions of identity-constructing and civic virtue-building.

In most migrant-receiving countries, the integration of migrants into mainstream society is seen as a prerequisite for granting citizenship to them. The main expectation of the governments or societies of these countries is that migrants should first integrate into the society, fulfil their obligations by participating towards the common good of the society, have a deep insight about the historical and cultural background of the country so that they deserve the right to demand a status of citizenship. In short, citizenship, from this perspective, is seen as an outcome of integration rather than a tool for empowering migrant groups in this integration process. This type of thinking treats citizenship mostly in terms of its legal status. Even if it considers the importance of the three elements of citizenship, namely legal status, identity and civic virtues, it does so by reducing them to the uniform notion of citizenship and by ignoring their dynamic interconnectedness. It inherits the assumption that the integration of migrants in the receiving society will provide them with a set of rights and endow them with various entitlements so that they will feel like a full member of the society. However, although acquiring the citizenship status of the receiving country is of crucial importance to an immigrant, gaining formal access to citizenship is only one aspect of this. As Castles and Davidson (2000: 84) put it, 'equally important is the extent to which people belonging to distinct groups of the population actually achieve *substantial citizenship*, that is, equal chances of participation in various areas of society, such as politics, work, welfare systems and cultural relations'. Similarly, Higgins (1999: 290) highlights the essential distinction between the formal and substantive dimensions of citizenship. This distinction signifies that citizenship is not simply a status that endows citizens with a set of rights and entitlements, but at the same time, it is a status that enables persons with the opportunity to realize those rights and entitlements. 'All citizens formally possess civil, political and social rights, but not all possess the means of realizing, and hence, enjoying the substantive benefits of citizenship' (Higgins, 1999: 290). Hence, one can argue that an attempt to formulize a model of citizenship that is capable of empowering migrants in the setting of the receiving country must take the complex and multi-faceted nature of citizenship into consideration in which its various aspects re-enforce one another.

Similar to citizenship, the notion of empowerment is also a complex, multi-level construct that can be viewed as both a process and an outcome (Higgins, 1999: 303). At the individual level, empowerment involves a sense of efficacy, belief in personal abilities, and feelings of greater control over one's own life. But, apart from these, it also implies a sense of connectedness to and togetherness with others, which give it the quality of a society-level

phenomenon (Shields, 1995; Lord, 1994; Wallerstein, 1992). Empowerment, from this angle, is thus directly linked to the four aspects of citizenship. Having access to formal rights
plays an empowering role by providing migrants a sense of membership and identity in the
receiving society, but it is also through the practices and experiences of participation that
migrants feel like having a deeper control over their lives. This is partly related to the civic
virtue aspect of citizenship. Participation helps to foster a sense of community which in
return makes immigrants feel more empowered, as they begin to feel like a part of the social
cohesion in the country they live in.

In short, arguments in this chapter support the views that citizenship should first not
be seen as an outcome, but rather as a means for the empowerment of migrants in the
receiving societies, and second, empowerment can be achieved by taking the whole interrelated aspects of citizenship into consideration, rather than dealing with the notion of
citizenship as a monolithic entity. However, the question of what kind of a citizenship model
is necessary to incorporate migrants into the societal structure of the receiving country is
not a simple one. The answer to this question reveals the necessity of addressing this question
from various dimensions, in particular by taking the *universality, duality (multiplicity), flexibility* and *functionality* aspects of a new model of citizenship into account.

Universality aspect: an inclusive model of citizenship that is capable of empowering
migrants must inherit the principle idea that everyone is a citizen by virtue of membership
in a given territorial space, but before that, by virtue of being a person. Traditionally, nationhood has provided the moral resource for the conceptualization of modern citizenship
given the fact that the roots of modern citizenship are traced back to the French Revolution
(Turner, 1994: 159; Crowley, 1998: 167; Janoski, 1998: 12; Barbalet, 2000: 101). However,
the conception of nation-based citizenship is insufficient to cope with the complexities related with globalization. There is a need for an individual-based citizenship that will be
formulized with reference to the universality of human rights.

Duality (multiplicity) aspect: the ambiguous position of migrants in terms of their status
of citizenship poses an immense problem not only to migrants themselves, but also to the
sending and receiving countries. Therefore, the issue of dual (multiple) citizenship is significant both in terms of the naturalization policies adopted in the migrant-receiving states and
also for the empowerment of citizens (Hammar, 1989). As Icduygu and Keyman (1999: 53)
argue, dual or multiple citizenship, which is based on the premise of membership in a state
as a legal entity rather than as a nation-based identity, inherits the assumption that individuals with different ethnic and national origins can co-exist in a single state under the
meta-identity of citizenship. Therefore, the right to hold dual/multiple citizenship can help
to secure the position of immigrants in both sending and receiving countries without necessarily obliging them to be withdrawn from their former rights and freedoms. It also has
the potential to lessen the degree of moral disturbance that migrants might feel concerning
their identities and their sense of belonging.

Flexibility aspect: various socio-political demands of immigrants can concretely be
translated into a set of 'flexible forms of citizenship' that would allow them to be incorporated into the immigrant-receiving societies (Ong, 1993: 501). The naturalization policies
of the migrant-receiving states must have a degree of flexibility in order to meet the needs
of different types and different generations of immigrants. For instance, those policies may
distinguish between immigrants who are intending to be permanent settlers and migrants
who intend staying temporarily. Similarly, those policies should take into account that the

transnational links of the first generation of migrants tend to be stronger than those of other generations: the first-generation-migrants' practices of civic virtue may be overwhelmingly home country-based, and those migrants might tend to preserve and revitalize their previously held identity characteristics, but these can change in time in line with their further adaptation and integration into the receiving country. Therefore, for instance, in the case of first-generation migrants, receiving countries may ease their requirements and expectations of being knowledgeable about the social and cultural heritage of the country. Similarly, an empowering model of citizenship must understand that the identities of migrants can be multiple, and not necessarily nation-based. In short, the government of the receiving states should accept the principle that different practices of citizenship can be applicable to different types and different generations of immigrants (such as the debates on German citizenship in the early 2000s).

Functionality aspect: if citizenship amounts to the four functional elements – legal status, identity, civic virtues, and social cohesion – if it is the foundation of a democratic society, and if an active and cautious citizenry is essential to the practical functioning democracy, we can conclude that there is a crucial need for more relaxed citizenship policies and practices which offer more liberal naturalization procedures (Icduygu, 1996: 158). In achieving this liberalization, it is important to grasp that acquisition of citizenship is mostly a matter of pragmatic or functional choice rather than a normative, moral and psychological commitment process.

Conclusion

The debate over issues of immigration, citizenship and integration is both longstanding and deeply rooted. This chapter implicitly highlights the fact that the debate regarding the linkage between the acquisition of citizenship and the integration of immigrants in receiving countries presents a dilemma: integration through citizenship versus integration for citizenship. In other words, should integration be based on the acquisition of citizenship or should citizenship be based on the result of integration? The view of integration through citizenship takes on the assumption that those immigrants who acquired citizenship of the receiving country are mature enough to take an active role in their process of integration. However, the view of integration for citizenship presumes that the immigrants should pass certain measures of being incorporated into the social, political and economic spheres of the receiving countries that test their maturity to become citizens of those countries.

Under the influence of increased globalization, the linkage between immigration and citizenship is also hotly debated and intensely questioned. The key aspect of globalization which makes a post-national citizenship more likely in the future is the non-functionality of conventional notion of citizenship. For instance, Heater (1999: 160) wrote the following:

> Has citizenship as a state-defined status outlived its usefulness? Students of International Relations refer to the emergence of the post-Westphalian state, a style of polity that, they suggest, is superseding the sovereign territorial state recognized by those mid-seventeenth-century treaties. Can this new, less autonomous state, moulded by migratory, sub-national and trans-national forces, still support a form of citizenship designed in and for different conditions? The influences of two trans-national forces in particular cast doubt on the sustainability of citizenship in its

traditional form. One is the increasingly accepted validity of universal human rights; the other is the globalization of trade, communications and, most importantly, financial transactions.

As we have argued that the individual-level elements of citizenship – legal status, identity and civic virtues – have become disarticulated from each other in the global assemblages of international migratory settings, and then re-articulated with universalizing criteria of global assemblages of transnational settings, it is possible to conclude that these three elements of citizenship have the potential to make the incorporation of immigrants more straightforward and comfortable. Attention should then be paid to their contribution to the whole issue of social cohesion, which is the societal-level element of citizenship.

In closing, evidence from the existing literature indicates that the citizenship position of immigrants is important as it largely determines the social, political, economic and cultural engagements in the receiving society. In other words, citizenship is something empowering for individuals. It is within this context that what seems to be needed for a better incorporation of immigrant populations is a new formulation of citizenship with the elements of universality, duality (multiplicity), flexibility and functionality, rather than an exclusive and restrictive formulation of citizenship that puts emphasis on the commitment and duties of immigrants. The post-national conception of citizenship more readily allows immigrants to re-articulate the dynamic elements of legal status, identity and civic virtues and social cohesion which, in turn, contribute to better integration of immigrants into the receiving society. As the granting and withholding national citizenship is today exclusively in the hands of the nation-state, it seems that there are consequences and responsibilities for the states of both migrant sending and receiving countries which are the main players in determining the rules and regulations of a new form of citizenship such as a post-national one. It is widely recognized that recent processes of socio-political changes, associated primarily with globalization, appear to be creating the opportunities for the development of a new formulation of citizenship.

References

Back, L., Keith, M., Khan, A., Shukra, K. and Solomos, J. (2002) 'New Labour's white heart: politics, multiculturalism and the return of assimilation', *Political Quarterly*, 73 (4), 445–54.

Barbalet, J. M. (2000) 'Vagaries of social capital: citizenship, trust and loyalty' in E. Vasta (ed.), *Citizenship, Community and Democracy*, Basingstoke, MacMillan, pp. 91–106.

Castles, S. and Davidson, A. (2000) *Citizenship and Migration: Globalization and the Politics of Belonging*, London, MacMillan.

Cheong, P. H., Edwards, R., Goulbourne, H. and Solomos, J. (2007) 'Immigration, social cohesion and social capital: a critical review', *Critical Social Policy*, 27 (1), 24–49.

Council of Europe (2005) *Concerted Development of Social Cohesion Indicators: Methodological Guide*, Strasbourg, Council of Europe Publishing.

Crowley, J. (1998) 'The national dimension of citizenship in T.H. Marshall', *Citizenship Studies*, 2 (2), 165–78.

Department of Immigration and Multicultural Affairs (2006) 'Australian Citizenship: much more than a ceremony', discussion paper, Commonwealth of Australia, Canberra.

Gorham, E. (1995) 'Social citizenship and its fetters', *Polity*, 28 (1), 25–47.

Hall, S. (1990) 'Cultural identity and diaspora' in J. Rutherford (ed.), *Identity: Community, Culture and Difference*, London, Lawrence and Wishart, pp. 195–310.

Hammar, T. (1989) 'State, nation and dual citizenship' in R. W. Brubaker (ed.), *Immigration and Politics of Citizenship in Europe and North America*, Lanham, MD, German Marshall Fund of the United States.

Heater, D. (1999) *What is Citizenship?*, Cambridge, Polity Press.

Higgins, J. W. (1999) 'Citizenship and empowerment: a remedy for citizen participation in health reform', *Community Development Journal*, 34 (4), 287–307.

Home Office (2002) *Secure Borders, Safe Haven: Integration with Diversity in Modern Britain*, London, Home Office.

Icduygu, A. (1996) 'Citizenship at the crossroads: immigration and the nation-state' in E. Kofman and G. Youngs (eds), *Globalization: Theory and Practice*, London, Pinter, pp. 150–62.

———. (2005) 'The international migration and citizenship debate in Turkey: the individual level of analysis' in E. F. Keyman and A. Icduygu (eds), *Citizenship in a Global World: European Questions and Turkish Experiences*, London, Routledge, pp. 196–216.

Icduygu, A. and Keyman, E. F. (1999) 'Globalleşme, Anayasallık ve Türkiye'de Vatandaşlık Tartışması' ('Globalization, Constitutionalism, and Citizenship Debate in Turkey'), *Doğu Batı*, 2 (5), 143–56.

Janoski, T. (1998) *Citizenship and Civil Society*, Cambridge, Cambridge University Press.

Jenson, J. (1998) *Mapping Social Cohesion*, Canadian Policy Research Networks, CPRN Study No. 03, Ottawa.

Joan, W. H. (1999) 'Citizenship and empowerment: a remedy for citizen participation in health reform', *Community Development Journal*, 34 (4), 287–307.

Joppke, C. (2004) 'The retreat of multiculturalism in the liberal state: theory and practice', *The British Journal of Sociology*, 55 (2), 237–57.

Kaya, A. and Kentel, F. (2005) *Euro-Turks: A Bridge or a Breach between Turkey and the European Union?*, Brussels, Centre for European Policy Studies.

Kofman, E. (2005) 'Citizenship, migration, and the reassertion of national identity', *Citizenship Studies*, 9 (5), 453–67.

Kymlicka, W. (2000) 'Citizenship in culturally diverse societies: issues, contexts, concepts' in W. Kymlicka and W. Norman (eds), *Citizenship in Diverse Societies*, Oxford, Oxford University Press, pp. 1–41.

Lord, J. (1994) 'Personal empowerment and active living' in H. A. Quinney, L. Gauvin and A. E. T. Wall (eds), *Toward Active Living*, Windsor, Human Kinetics, pp. 213–18.

Ong, A. (1993) 'On the edge of empires: flexible citizenship among Chinese in diaspora', *Positions*, 1 (3), 745–78.

———. (2006) 'Mutations in citizenship', *Theory, Culture, and Society*, 23 (2–3), 499–531.

Sassen, S. (2002) 'The repositioning of citizenship: emergent subjects and spaces of politics', *Berkeley Journal of Sociology*, 46, 4–25.

Scholte, J. A. (2004) *Globalization and Governance: From Statism to Polycentrism*, Centre for the Study of Globalization and Regionalization Working Paper No. 130/04.

Schuster, L. and Solomos, J. (2004) 'Race, immigration and asylum: New Labour's agenda and its consequences', *Ethnicities*, 4 (2), 267–300.

Shields, L. (1995) 'Women's experiences of the meaning of empowerment', *Qualitative Health Research*, 5 (1), 15–35.

Soysal, Y. N. (1994) *Limits of Citizenship: Migrants and Postnational Membership in Europe*, Chicago, The University of Chicago Press.

Turner, B. (1994) 'Postmodern culture/modern citizens' in B. Van Steenbergen (ed.), *The Condition of Citizenship*, London, Sage, pp. 153–68.

Urry, J. (1999) 'Globalization and citizenship', *Journal of World-Systems Research*, 5 (2), 311–24.

Vasta, E. (2006) 'From Ethnic Minorities to Ethnic Majority Policy: changing identities and the shift to assimilationism in the Netherlands', COMPAS Working Paper No. 26.

Wallerstein, N. (1992) 'Powerlessness, empowerment and health: implications for health promotion programs', *American Journal of Health Promotion,* 6 (3), 197–205.

CHAPTER 15

Advertising and Cities

A Relational Geography of Globalization in the Early Twenty-first Century

Peter J. Taylor

Introduction: cities and services

One of the most important functions of cities has always been to operate as service centres. They are where you go to access facilities for provision of all manner of services – economic, political, social, cultural – that help to sustain the myriad of projects that are our lives. Cities are characterised by the services they offer: they are shopping centres, administrative centres, cultural centres and much else besides. In other words, they are foci of the everyday lives of billions of people. In this chapter, I concentrate upon one type of service, advanced producer services, and within this sector, one service industry, advertising. The reason for this choice is that advanced producer services, and advertising in particular, provide specific insights into the processes that have generated and are sustaining contemporary globalization. Today many cities can be categorised and analysed as global service centres in a world city network (Taylor, 2004).

Advanced producer service firms provide for the needs of other firms, hence they are sometimes called, simply, 'business services'. Corporate law, management consultancy, investment banking and advertising are all service sectors that provide high value-added professional, creative and/or financial services for their company clients. Under conditions of contemporary globalization, many of these service firms have chosen, or felt compelled, to 'go global' in the provision of their services. Always traditionally associated with larger cities, in recent decades they have been implicated in the rise of world or global cities (Sassen, 2001). In studies at GaWC, these services have been treated as the agents of world city network formation, a skeletal structure through which globalization operates (Taylor, 2004).

This chapter is divided into seven sections. First, the importance of advanced producer services for globalization is described and explained. Second, one particular service, advertising, is considered as particularly apt to provide insights into globalization; its American origins make it specifically interesting. Third, the advertising industry is depicted in the early twenty-first century, its specific and unusual organization is outlined and its globality affirmed. Fourth, cities are treated as marketplaces for the industry's products: leading cities are identified. Fifth, cities are treated as network nodes wherein firms' use of cities beyond their local markets is analysed. Sixth, combining city roles as places and network nodes, profits are estimated across cities to indicate the geography of firms' 'revenue-take'. Finally, in a conclusion that focuses on using the results to inform the geography of globalization, both the borderless world concept and the simple core-periphery model are found to be wanting.

Advanced producer services in globalization

Business services are as old as business and therefore many advanced producer services are older than the modern world-system – maritime insurance, commercial (merchant's) law, audit accountancy and some financial instruments for example. But other such services are strictly modern, such as advertising and management consultancy. To provide their particular service, these firms require close relations with their clients. A successful firm builds up a client-base over time and it is this that defines the worth of the company. Traditionally, firms have been quite local, typically single city-based. Firms would normally be identified by their city: a 'New York law firm', a 'Liverpool insurance company', an 'Amsterdam bank', and so on. From the late nineteenth century onwards, through mergers and acquisitions and stimulated by national regulation of professions and companies, many such firms began to operate at a national scale. Varying to some degree with the physical expanse of countries, big city banks became national banks, big city insurance companies became national insurance companies, and so on. With this geographical change, the firms changed, like their public service counterparts expanding at the same time, going beyond a single locality could only be coped with through bureaucratisation. Instead of being customised for a known local client, products had to become relatively standardised in a national market. Many advanced producer services were not that 'advanced' by the mid-twentieth century. All this changed with globalization and the final up-scaling of business services.

In the 1970s, two distinct advanced technologies, computers and communications, combined to create a new enabling infrastructure for global organization. As it became more pervasive and sophisticated, this global infrastructure was able to provide a semblance of the immediacy of the original city business service for transnational service activities: the loss of old relations based upon contiguity replicated by new relations based upon simultaneity (Castells, 1996). Thus up-scaling to the global would not mean simply building bigger bureaucracies than existing national firms, advanced producer services could enhance their being as expert, customised service providers, but now at a global scale. Of course, there was nothing inevitable about this up-scaling – economic circumstances had to be right. The possibilities of this infrastructure were first exploited by large multinational corporations creating the new international division of labour: commodity production in the 'third world', command functions and product development in the 'first world'. However, these corporations were major clients of the leading business service firms, and as the corporations became more global so also did their service needs. Hence service firms were threatened with losing important clients unless they could provide a 'global service'. Many responded in the 1980s by creating new offices where their clients did business, but this highly dependent strategy soon gave way to business-service firms developing their own global locational strategies (Kim, 1995; Leslie, 1995; Tharp and Jeong, 2001). By 1990, the thinking was that if you are going to invest in providing a transnational service it is dangerous to remain dependent on a few old clients; rather, take the opportunity to gain more new clients in new markets. The resulting organization of global service firms is a multiple location office strategy so that a 'seamless service' (i.e., as was once offered in a single locale) is provided across the world.

It was Sassen (1991) who first associated this new global dispersal of services with concentration in key cities, which she termed 'global cities'. She interpreted these cities – the archetypal cases are New York, London and Tokyo – as postindustrial production sites: 'The "things" that a global city makes are services and financial goods' (5). This involves four key functions: corporate headquarters (command centres of the world economy), service provision of advanced producer services, sites of production of innovation in these services (requiring face-to-face interaction), and markets for these products and innovations (via headquarters) (3–4). The literature deriving from this work has been criticised for focussing on just the major metropolitan areas in globalization. In fact, all cities have been affected by ubiquitous globalization processes – there can be no such thing as a 'non-global city' – and this is reflected in studies incorporating a wider range of cities as 'globalizing cities' (Marcus and van Kempen, 2000) or simply 'cities in globalization' (Taylor, et al. 2006). The latter approach has expanded Sassen's concern for advanced services in a few 'global cities' to the office networks of global service firms across many cities worldwide (Taylor, 2004).

These global service firms are located in the ubiquitous office tower blocks that dominate contemporary world cities (Taylor, 2004). These very visible offices constitute the invisible nodes of myriad electronic networks. The 'office work' generates flows of information and knowledge – advice, instruction, planning, design, strategy (supplemented by air travel for face-to-face meetings as necessary) – that are the product they are selling to service global capital in today's intensely integrated world economy. This professional/creative/financial knowledge behind expert services generates such products as multiple inter-jurisdictional law contracts, financial instruments in 24-hour money markets, global advertising campaigns, multiple tax jurisdiction accountancy audits, investment banking advice on multinational acquisitions, and numerous management consultancy activities. Thus have advanced producer services come to be a critical cutting-edge economic sector in globalization since 1990.

Advertising: from Americanization to globalization

Within advanced producer services, advertising has become a key facilitator in contemporary globalization (Bagchi-Sen and Sen, 1997). The industry has been fuelled by ever-increasing consumer expenditure that relies on advertising to develop, sustain and spread markets for the products of capitalism. It is through the success of advertising campaigns that capital is realised globally. This 'global consumer world' is a projection of a consumerism that was largely pioneered in US society in the first half of the last century; many of the features that today we identify as globalization (e.g., 'global brands') were originally experienced trans-nationally as 'Americanization' in the mid-twentieth century. The modern advertising industry was both a creator of, and created by, this original US mass consumerism, and advertising continues to be the archetypal American advanced producer service in contemporary globalization.

As a relatively new producer service, advertising was a central player in the creation of a new framework for capitalism that we call American hegemony. With US advances in manufacturing building upon British industrial hegemony to create new mass production, a need was generated for a complementary mass consumption. The advertising industry developed as a major service sector in the 1920s to meet this need 'to speed the flow of goods through the national market place' (Marchand, 1986: 2). This was the 'American speciality' industry (Mayer, 1991: xv) that created a 'consumer modernity' as the cultural face of American hegemony (Taylor, 1999). Advertisers were the arch agents of this new modernity, the promoters of new fashions and ideas in the 'new American tempo' (Marchand, 1986: 4): 'they brought the good news about progress' (1). Today, no longer so American-dominated but still 'selling modernity', advertising's contemporary role can be seen as speeding the flow of goods through the global world market.

But this is a naïve interpretation of advertising. Although the industry would peddle itself as the consumer's 'ambassador' providing information on goods to buy, in reality advertising practitioners operated as 'consumption engineers' (Marchand, 1986: 29). Their purpose was never simply to expand markets, they operated on behalf of their clients to create partial monopoly rents through the branding of commodities. By developing and maintaining brands, advertisers added value to products allowing their clients either to sell more at the same price or sell about the same at a higher price (Mayer, 1991: xi–xii). Trademarks, like patents and copyrights, provide monopoly powers but in the former case without the time limits. Thus American hegemony has created 'a world of brandscapes', to extend Mayer's (1991: 27) evocative description geographically to contemporary globalization.

Initially, when US producers in the 1920s were concerned about overproduction, advertisers were hailed as 'guardians of uninterrupted growth' (Marchand, 1986: 2), as the solution, no less, to capitalism's propensity for disruptive economic cycles. Obviously this accolade only lasted to the next severe downturn, but the 1930s in no way eclipsed advertising. By now the industry was embedded into the new social matrix that was American consumer capitalism. This is reflected today, ironically given the 1920s beliefs, in advertising's particular sensitivity to cyclical changes. This illustrates the industry's continued centrality to modern capitalism: it is widely used as a key indicator of either signs of rise or decline both in national economies and in the world economy. In more recent times, advertising has kept consumer capitalism going through good times and bad. By creating wants and converting them into needs, it has stimulated a huge growth in personal debt that has sustained a massive growth of the world economy through the 1990s, and which has been credited with the 'soft landing' in the early 2000s. In the contemporary period, the industry appears almost (but only almost) to be living up to its supposed power identified by its promoters in the 1920s (Monle and Johnson, 1999; Coopers and Lybrand, 1992).

The advertising industry in the early twenty-first century

Nachum (2000: 27) points out that advertising firms 'are in a unique position in which there is a separation between those who buy their services and those who "consume" them': their customers are commodity producers who pay for adverts, their 'consumers' are the potential commodity buyers. This 'in-between position' has several important ramifications.

The advertising industry is distinctive in its organizational structure. As it has grown, major transnational corporations have emerged through the usual processes of mergers and acquisitions (Ducoffe and Smith, 1993; Kim, 1995). However, this growth process causes problems for advertising practice because the value of a business being taken over is largely a function of its client list. But acquisitions and mergers will often bring the accounts of rival clients together into one advertising firm. Obviously advertisers cannot service clients that are in competition, but neither does it make commercial sense to choose between clients and lose a lucrative contract. The solution to this conundrum has been to create a dual-level organization structure (Banerjee, 1995; Tharp and Jeong, 2001).

All global advertising firms operate in practice under the umbrella of 'holding companies/groups' (e.g., WPP) that constitute a collection of 'advertising agencies' (e.g., BBDO Worldwide) with 'firewalls' between them so that clients in competition can be serviced within the same group but by different agencies. There is a division of knowledge work: the holding companies do the strategic managerial work, and the advertising agencies provide the creative design producer services. The vast majority of the literature of advertising treats the agencies and their creative work. However, here I am concerned for the economic geography of advertising and therefore the focus is on the consolidated financial results of holding companies.

A typical transaction in this industry involves a minimum of three firms – manufacturing (client) company, advertising company (agency within holding company), and media company (e.g., TV corporation). The basic unit of the transaction is an advert created by the advertising firm about the manufacturing firm's product to be transmitted by the media firm. The sale to the media is recorded as the billings for the advertising company. It is commonly used as a measure of the size of advertising companies: Table 1 lists the 18 holding companies in 2001 that had billings above a billion dollars.[1] These data on advertising firms are reported in the *Advertising Age*'s annual reports, which is the data source used for this study. For some years, billings are reported for leading city markets but this ended in 2002, so the final city data is reported for 2001 (in the 2002 Report). This is the reason for providing a cross-sectional analysis of advertising in 2001, the early twenty-first-century geography of my subtitle. In Table 1 the ranked list companies is fairly typical of corporate concentration processes producing contemporary globalization: there are a few very important companies tailing off to many smaller companies all vulnerable to further acquisition.[2] In this case, there are four dominant companies and a further five important companies; these nine will be one focus in subsequent analysis.

Table 1   Major advertising firms in 2001

World rank	Advertising firm	Headquarters	Billings ($millions)
1	WPP Group	London	75,711
2	Interpublic Group of Companies	New York	66,689
3	Omnicom Group	New York	58,080
4	Publicis Group	Paris	52,892
5	Havas Advertising	Paris	26,269

World rank	Advertising firm	Headquarters	Billings ($millions)
6	Dentsu	Tokyo	20,848
7	Cordiant Communication Group	London	13,388
8	Grey Global Group	New York	12,106
9	Hakohodo	Tokyo	6,862
10	Asatsu-DK	Tokyo	3,501
11	Carlson Marketing Group	Minneapolis	2,611
12	Tokyu Agency	Tokyo	1,783
13	TMP Worldwide	New York	1,706
14	Dako Advertising	Tokyo	1,585
15	Aspen Marketing Group	Los Angeles	1,262
16	Panoramic Communications Doner	New York	1,194
17	Yomko Advertising	Detroit	1,071
18	Yamiko Advertising	Tokyo	1,022

Source: *Advertising Age* Annual Report 2002

The conventional way in which advertising firms are paid is 15 per cent of the billings (*The Economist*, 1990; Natchum, 2000). This is called the commission and constitutes the revenue accruing to the company. This practice can be interpreted as ensuring the integrity of the profession: competition is not reduced to the cheapest, but choice is made on creative product preferences. However, like all such control of professional remuneration, it also provides a gross monopoly position for the service providers, ensuring no undercutting and therefore good profits for all work (Johnson, 1972). Nevertheless, this arrangement is not always strictly adhered to and may be negotiable. In addition, holding companies bring together more than just advertising, incorporating services such as provided by PR agencies where the payment is by negotiated fee. *Advertising Age* reports provide data on the income derived from billings which, as billings minus costs (salaries, estate, etc.), are typically between 10 per cent and 15 per cent of billings. These data will be used to estimate differences in advertisers' 'take' across cities to see whether the globalization processes described in this paper incorporate any core-periphery tendencies.

Place: cities as markets

As noted above, Sassen (1991/2001) has highlighted cities as markets of advanced producer services as key features of her 'global cities'. *Advertising Age* reports have provided data on selected cities for their 'local shop billings' for cities. These are city markets for advertising. In 2001, *Advertising Age* reported its fullest set of cities in two lists, one for the USA and one for the rest of the world. From these data, the top forty city advertising markets in the world can be identified: they are listed in Table 2.

Table 2   Top 40 city advertising markets

City	Billings ($millions)
New York	57,238
Tokyo	38,664
London	23,814
Chicago	15,213
Paris	12,441
Detroit	8,337
Los Angeles	8,226
Milan	6,095
San Francisco	5,855
Frankfurt	5,513
Sao Paulo	5,480
Duesseldorf	4,744
Boston	4,156
Toronto	4,151
Amsterdam	4,121
Madrid	4,116
Sydney	3,960
Minneapolis	3,621
Dallas	2,457
Hong Kong	2,097
Istanbul	1,965
Mexico City	1,944
Brussels	1,883
Buenos Aires	1,670
St. Louis	1,651
Atlanta	1,620
Miami	1,473
Austin	1,434
Athens	1,413
Hamburg	1,386
Vienna	1,380
Kansas City	1,330
Philadelphia	1,319
Mumbai	1,280
Copenhagen	1,275
Zurich	1,272
Taipei	1,203
Columbus	1,201
Singapore	1,155
Seattle	1,044

Source: *Advertising Age* Annual Report 2002

The advertising market is very uneven across cities, but the latter are reasonable worldwide in distribution. Clearly New York dominates, followed by Tokyo and then London. These are Sassen's (2001) three global cities, the leading cities of the three main globalization regions: Northern America, Western Europe and Pacific Asia. Other cities are unevenly distributed among these regions; in all, there are seventeen in Northern America (all but one in the USA), fourteen in Western Europe and five in Pacific Asia (if we include one from Australia). In addition, non-core zones are represented through Sao Paulo, Mexico City, Buenos Aires and Mumbai.

Although US cities dominate the list, they constitute only 40 per cent of the total cities and, overall, cities from 24 different countries are listed. This reflects first, the ascendancy of the US in this industry, and second, beyond the USA, the pattern of concentration of the advertising market in large metropolitan regions dominating individual countries (the only country outside the USA to have more than one city in Table 1 is Germany). In the US, there is a similar pattern: large metropolitan regions are featured as major advertising markets.

In conclusion, the top forty advertising 'local shop' markets consist of large affluent cities in the 'global North' and mega-cities in the global South with relatively large proportions of middle class consumers.

Network: cities as nodes

If, as indicated above, some cities do work beyond their local market for global campaigns, then local marketplace billings do not constitute all the work done in a city. *Advertising Age* reports only provide 'local shop' data for cities; there are no data on extra-local work. However, for 2001, there is a breakdown of the top thirty advertising firms in terms of agencies, which list all their offices. Further, billings are provided for offices, and therefore these can be summed city by city to provide estimates of a city's overall work. For this exercise there is no reason to stick with the cities with the largest forty city markets; in Figure 1 all cities accruing billings above $100 million from top firms are depicted. These ninety-eight cities are displayed by total billings across major world regions. The pattern is highly centralised in a few major advertising centres, but there is also representation across all regions – even Sub-Saharan Africa has Johannesburg (and, in addition, Nairobi, Cape Town and Harare just miss the cut). This is the basic relational geography of advertising in the early twenty-first century.

Figure 1: The Distribution of top advertising companies billings across world regions, 2001

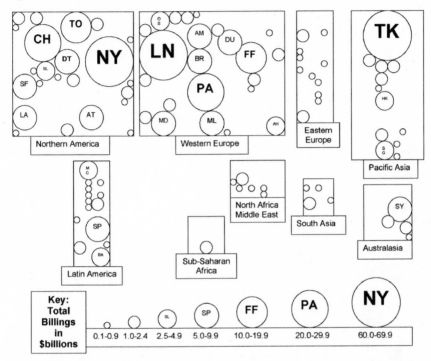

City codes: AH Athens; AM Amsterdam; AT Atlanta; BA Buenos Aires; BR Brussels; CH Chicago; DT Detroit; DU Dusseldorf; FF Frankfurt; HK Hong Kong; LA Los Angeles; LN London; MC Mexico City; MD Madrid; ML Milan; OS Oslo; PA Paris; SF San Francisco; SG Singapore; SL St. Louis; SP Sao Paulo; SY Sydney; TK Tokyo; TO Toronto

To separate out local and non-local work requires return to cities for which there is data on local shop billings: I focus on the twenty-five cities with the largest top thirty billings. In Table 3 these cities are listed in rank order for top thirty firms' billings and top nine firms' billings (the latter nine are leading firms in Table 1 above). Several features clearly emerge. First, Tokyo and London are much nearer to New York in these statistics compared to just local billings (Table 2). Second, this relative reduction of New York's position is complemented by a general reduction in rank for other US cities: they dominate the bottom half of the Table 3's two rankings. This tendency can be directly expressed by computing the ratio of firm billings sums to local shop billings: cities are ranked by this ratio in Table 4. Here we see nine US cities in the bottom twelve ranks for the top thirty ratios (the exception is Atlanta) and all ten cities ranked in the bottom eleven for top nine ratios. This is intriguing ... and complex.

Table 3   Leading firm's city billings, 2001 (millions)

City	Top 30 billings	City	Top 9 billings
New York	68,379	New York	27,381
Tokyo	67,921	Tokyo	25,615
London	63,236	London	21,756
Chicago	24,433	Paris	13,101
Paris	22,603	Chicago	7,389
Toronto	16,208	Frankfurt	7,297
Frankfurt	11,429	Milan	6,035
Detroit	9,032	Los Angeles	5,462
Madrid	8,556	Dusseldorf	4,526
Sao Paulo	8,474	Madrid	4,210
Milan	8,095	Sao Paulo	3,817
Atlanta	6,312	Amsterdam	3,359
Brussels	6,006	Toronto	3,296
Amsterdam	5,951	Detroit	3,128
Dusseldorf	5,487	Mexico City	2,942
San Francisco	5,221	Sydney	2,856
Sydney	5,140	San Francisco	2,172
Los Angeles	5,079	Boston	2,103
Mexico City	3,816	Hong Kong	1,882
Hong Kong	3,222	Brussels	1,824
Dallas	2,423	Dallas	1,464
Seoul	1,603	Seoul	1,036
Minneapolis	1,477	Atlanta	925
Philadelphia	562	Minneapolis	255
Boston	483	Philadelphia	0

Source: Derived from *Advertising Age* Annual Report 2002

Table 4   Leading firm's city billings in relation to city markets, 2001

City	Top 30 billings/city market	City	Top 9 billings/city market
Toronto	4.092	Mexico City	1.343
Brussels	3.104	Paris	0.996
London	2.697	Frankfurt	0.988
Atlanta	2.408	Milan	0.981
Tokyo	1.855	Brussels	0.969
Madrid	1.775	Dusseldorf	0.946
Mexico City	1.742	Hong Kong	0.933
Sao Paulo	1.741	London	0.928
Paris	1.718	Sydney	0.884
Hong Kong	1.597	Madrid	0.873
Sydney	1.591	Amsterdam	0.837

City	Top 30 billings/city market	City	Top 9 billings/city market
Frankfurt	1.547	Toronto	0.832
Amsterdam	1.483	Sao Paulo	0.784
Chicago	1.406	Tokyo	0.700
Milan	1.316	Boston	0.527
Dusseldorf	1.147	Los Angeles	0.518
Detroit	1.137	Dallas	0.453
New York	1.116	New York	0.447
San Francisco	1.023	San Francisco	0.426
Dallas	0.749	Chicago	0.425
Seoul	0.524	Detroit	0.394
Los Angeles	0.482	Atlanta	0.353
Minneapolis	0.243	Seoul	0.339
Philadelphia	0.236	Minneapolis	0.042
Boston	0.121	Philadelphia	0.000

Source: Derived from *Advertising Age* Annual Report 2002

There are two counter tendencies producing the results in Table 4. First, as regards the position of US cities, this relates to its being the origin country of the modern advertising industry. As noted previously, the advertising industry developed in American cities in the first half of the twentieth century and diffused from here to other parts of the world. As a diffusion centre, it generated a complex mixture of local companies, some of which grew and became international and contributed to the growth of advertising in cities in other countries. Although some companies from other countries came to be international as well, the USA remained the country least penetrated from outside. It remained a rich mixture of local and international companies with the local remaining more prominent than cities elsewhere. Thus there are relatively less extra-local billings: local firms are dominant. The limiting case in Table 4 is Philadelphia where none of the top nine global firms even have an office (i.e., they record zero billings). This indicates a market embeddedness of local firms leading to global firms not attempting to enter that particular local city market. Why more 'local' firms in the USA? It is here that city markets are especially well-developed in advertising and local knowledge leads to good profits. In these circumstances there is less incentive for such firms to expand beyond the local: outside New York, there have been relatively fewer global firms originating in the US compared to equivalent cities outside the US. (This feature of a large lucrative US service market not encouraging global expansion is found generally in advanced producer services – see Taylor and Lang, 2005.)

Second, beyond the USA, there are cities that have billings beyond their 'local shop' to encompass larger national or even trans-national markets. In Table 4 the classic case is Toronto's dominance of the Anglo-phone Canadian market that results in top thirty companies billing more than four times the city's local market. The cities in the top half of both lists in Table 4 are the media capitals (TV, main national press, etc.) of relatively large national advertising markets, with Germany having two centres, and including third-world examples. Mexico City actually records higher billings for the top nine firms than for its whole local market, and for seven other major media centres their billings are almost as large as the local shop (i.e., over 90 per cent). There is an interesting exception and that is Atlanta for the top thirty firms whose billings are over twice the local city billings. This indicates the city's media dominance over the US Southeast region attracting global firms but outside the top nine.

In conclusion, the results from this section show a distinctive multiple-centred US advertising market, such that there is a greater distinction between USA/non-USA than the usual global North/global South contrast. The origin of the modern industry as an American invention continues to feature in its geography under conditions of contemporary globalization.

Place and node: cities in globalization

Does this US distinctiveness indicate that the market for advertising products has not really globalized? A very good way to answer this question is to compare profit rates across cities. If the advertising industry constituted separated markets, then profits would presumably vary greatly depending on local circumstances. On the other hand, globalization of markets (resulting from opening up service markets) should smooth out differences through the usual supply-and-demand processes. Unfortunately, there are no data available of overall profit rates in cities, but they can be estimated from information provided in *Advertising Age* reports.

The profit estimation method requires the assumption that profit rates are relatively smooth across the office networks within a company. Obviously it is at this decision-making level that profit differences will be addressed: withdrawing work from low-profit offices, increasing work in high-profit offices. Using this premise, if we have profit rates of firms and the mix of firms in a city, these two pieces of information can be combined to estimate the profit generated in a city. In fact, *Advertising Age* reports provide company data on income as well as billings and their ratio can be interpreted as a gross measure of profit; I will term it a firm's 'estimated revenue rate' (for a more detailed discussion of profit in this industry, see Taylor, 2006). I will focus on just the top nine advertising companies since they are definitively global in their scope. However, this entails omitting Philadelphia and Minneapolis from the twenty-five cities due to their zero and very low presences of top nine companies, respectively (Table 4). 'Estimated global revenue rates' are computed for the remaining twenty-three cities using proportions of billings each company has in each city. These figures are interpreted as the 'revenue-take' across cities and are reported in Table 5.

Table 5   Notional 'takes' from billings, 2001

Cities	Takes %
Tokyo	12.85
Dusseldorf	12.29
San Francisco	11.94
Seoul	11.86
Brussels	11.63
Atlanta	11.62
Chicago	11.54

Cities	Takes %
New York	11.52
Toronto	11.48
Los Angeles	11.38
Amsterdam	11.38
Hong Kong	11.25
Dallas	11.18
Mexico City	11.12
Sao Paulo	11.08
Madrid	11.02
London	10.98
Paris	10.91
Frankfurt	10.88
Boston	10.72
Milan	10.63
Sydney	10.51
Detroit	10.42

Source: Derived from *Advertising Age* Annual Report 2002

The main point that Table 5 illustrates is the low range of revenue-take percentages across the cities and, unlike Table 4, US cities are distributed across the range. This suggests that the major holding companies are operating a reasonably unified world market: clearly the 15 per cent commission rate method of billing is reflected in these takes, resulting in figures a little below the commissions received. However, like all markets, the global advertising market is not a perfect market and this is reflected in the small differences in revenue-takes. These market differences will be the result of both local and non-local influences. The top and bottom of Table 5's ranking illustrate this. The Tokyo market is a seller's market: it is largely serviced by Japanese companies with resulting 'monopolistic tendencies' creating high revenue-takes. In contrast, the Detroit market is a buyer's market: a market where a few (motor company) customers dominate to hold down revenue-takes. This simple supply/demand contrast between two cities on opposite sides of the world suggests that place and network market affects are operating globally. Further, the fact that the two global South cities in the table, Mexico City and Sao Paulo, are at opposite ends of the ranking suggests there is no North-South contrast in revenue-takes in this particular industry.

Conclusion: geography of globalization

I have dealt with one particular industry in some detail, justifying my choice by its importance for consumer modernity as represented by contemporary globalization. In this conclusion, I will draw out specific findings that provide insights into this globalization. Of course, advertising is just one industry, and a peculiar one at that as discussed, and therefore it is necessary to be careful in drawing more general conclusions. Nevertheless, there are some simple notions about the geography of globalization that require comment and for which advertising does provide a glimpse of a more complex geography. These are the notions of a borderless world and elemental application of core-periphery ideas.

The findings in this chapter clearly show the continuing importance of the 'national' in a global industry. Although with its propagation of global brands, advertising appears to be the epitome of contemporary globalization, its practice is anything but 'a world without borders' however well known the brand. Advertising is a cultural pursuit, and as such, has to be mindful of cultural differences: the same product has to be presented in different ways in different national contexts (Kanso, 1991; Leslie, 1995; West, 1996; Natchum, 2000). Furthermore, the main media for advertising, TV, and also press and radio, have remained largely national in organization across the world (Morley and Robins, 1995).

To provide a seamless global service for a client, an advertising firm requires a two-level approach. In selected cities, typically New York, global strategy is devised with the client and much of the creative work is done. But in rolling the campaign out across the world, the product has to be adapted country by country. This requires a nation-state distribution of offices, usually one office per country. There is little need for trans-national regional offices or intra-national regional offices (outside the US) because this is not the way the media is organized. Thus, there are offices in the 'media city' (usually capital city or largest city) of countries across the world (Taylor et al., 2004). Overall, production is through a combined national-global economic geography: borders remain important in advertising.

The findings in this chapter look superficially similar to the 'new international division of labour', but this is emphatically not the case. The latter is about using cheap labour in poor countries for production organized and consumed in richer countries. But in advertising, the labour is professional and creative, in the media cities across the world high value-added work is carried out, and it has been shown that company's revenue-takes vary little. Interpretation of these findings for remuneration is complicated; we have to go back to the fact that the industry is a service provider and that the service being provided is itself quite unusual. As an expert knowledge service, the professionals are not only the labour, they embody the industry's 'raw material' in the knowledge they input into the production of the commodity. Thus labour 'loyalty' is essential and is reflected, not only in high renumeration, but also through 'hand-cuff' contracts to stop labour movement that would lead to client movement. The value of an advertising company is ultimately dependent on its professionals and their client portfolios. Obviously the labour costs in this industry cannot be treated in same way as for industries producing more tangible commodities (Natchum, 1996, 2000).

This can be interpreted as the latest expression of what Wright (1997: 15) refers to as 'the problem of the "middle class" among employees'. Specific powers in the labour market through managerial or professional skills lead to 'loyalty rents' (17), resulting in new privileged class locations. These are what Wallerstein (1984) has called the 'cadres' of the world economy, the middle-class facilitators of capitalist accumulation. But the question now arises whether 'global cadres', reinforcing their power on the back of new enabling technologies to expand their geographical reach, are qualitatively different from their predecessors. Have they moved from a privileged non-capitalist class position to becoming part of the capitalist class itself? This is what the literature on trans-national class formation suggests. This alternative interpretation, or rather 'upgrading', of 'cadres' appears to be a good fit of the global advertising results.

Sklair (2002: 98) premises his identification of a 'trans-national capitalist class' with the assertion that 'direct ownership or control of the means of production is no longer the exclusive criterion for serving the interests of capital, particularly not the global interests of capital'. He goes on to specify 'globalizing professionals' as one of four components of this contemporary capitalist class: they are the 'technical fraction' (99). Of course, this does not mean that ownership is no longer relevant; it has also changed towards what Clark (2002) terms 'pension-fund capitalism'. The upshot is that the 'capitalist interest' in advertising accounts is reflected not in 'profits' alone, the revenue takes, but in their combination with renumeration of globalizing professionals. The key point is that the geography of this trans-national capitalist class, while concentrated in the global North, is distributed across major metropolitan areas throughout the world. There is no longer a simple core-periphery pattern; rather, there is a new complex geography of interweaving core-making and periphery-making processes operating through all major cities across the world. The advertising industry shows a new relational geography of core-making processes straddling the old, seemingly static, North-South divide. Contemporary globalization is not making a more equal world – quite the opposite in fact – but it is reshuffling geographies of inequalities in quite remarkable ways that were hardly imaginable a generation ago.

Acknowledgement

Asli Ceylan Oner (Virginia Tech) collected the *Advertising Age* data.

Notes

1. 'Billion' here means one thousand million.
2. For instance, in 2005 WPP kept its number 1 spot by adding Grey's companies to its ownership portfolio.

References

Bagchi-Sen, S.and Sen, J. (1997) 'The current state of knowledge in international business in producer services', *Environment and Planning A*, 29, 1153–74.

Banerjee, A. (1994) 'Transnational advertising development and management: an account planning approach and a process framework', *International Journal of Marketing*, 13, 95–124.

Castells, M. (1996) *The Rise of Network Society*, Oxford, Blackwell.

Clark, G. L. (2000) *Pension Fund Capitalism*, Oxford, Oxford University Press.

Coopers and Lybrand (1992) *The Advertisement Industry: An Examination*, London, Coopers and Lybrand.

Ducoffe, R. H. and Smith, S. J. (1993) 'Mergers and Acquisitions among Advertising Agencies', in A. Alexander, J. Owers and R. Carveth (eds), *Media Economics: Theory and Practice*, Hillsdale, NJ, Lawrence Erlbaum Associates, Inc, pp. 309–30.

Economist, The (1990) 'The advertising industry', *The Economist*, 9 June, pp. 13–14.

Johnson, T. J. (1972) *Professions and Power*, London, Macmillan.

Kanso, A. (1991) 'The use of advertising agencies for foreign markets: decentralized decision and localized approaches?' *International Journal of Advertising*, 10, 129–36.

Kim, K. K. (1995) 'Spreading the net: the consolidation process of large transnational advertising agencies in the 1980s and early 1990s', *International Journal of Advertising*, 14, 195–217.

Leslie, D. A. (1995) 'Global scan: the globalization of advertising agencies, concepts and campaigns', *Economic Geography*, 71, 402–25.

Marchand, R. (1986) *Advertising the American Dream: Making Way for Modernity, 1920–1940*, Berkeley, University of California Press.

Mayer, M. (1991) *Whatever Happened to Madison Avenue?* Boston, Little, Brown.

Monle, L. and Johnson, C. (1999) *Principles of Advertising: A Global Perspective*, New York, Haworth Press.

Morley, D. and Robins, K. (1995) *Spaces of Identity: Global Media, Electronic Landscapes and Cultural Boundaries*, London, Routledge.

Nachum, L. (2000) *The Origins of International Competitiveness of Firms: The Impact of Location and Ownership in Professional Service Industries*, Cheltenham, UK, Edgar Eldar.

Sassen, S. (1991/2001) *The Global City*, Princeton, NJ, Princeton University Press.

Sklair, L. (2002) *Globalization: Capitalism and Its Alternatives*, Oxford, Oxford University Press.

Taylor, P. J. (1999) *Modernities: A Geohistorical Introduction*, Cambridge, Polity.

———. (2004) *World City Network: A Global Urban Analysis*, London, Routledge.

———. (2006) 'The rise of "global" advertising from 1990', *GaWC Research Bulletin*, No. 195.

Taylor, P. J., Catalano, G. and Walker, D. R. F. (2004) 'Multiple globalizations: regional, hierarchical and sectoral articulations of global business services through world cities', *The Services Industries Journal*, 24, 63–81.

Taylor, P. J. and Lang, R. E. (2005) *US Cities in the World City Network*, Washington, DC, The Brookings Institution (Metropolitan Policy Program, Survey Series).

Tharp, M. and Jeong, J. (2001) 'Executive insight: the global network communications agency', *Journal of International Marketing*, 8, 111–31.

West, D. (1996) 'The determinants and consequences of multinational advertising agencies', *International Journal of Advertising*, 15, 128–39.

Wright, E. O. (1997) *Class Counts*, Cambridge, Cambridge University Press.

CHAPTER 16

The Governmentalization of World Politics

Philip G. Cerny

Introduction

In the social theory of Michel Foucault, 'governmentality' is the art of modern liberal (or 'neoliberal') governing. Its core lies in the practices which have grown up over the past three centuries for creatively shaping (and transcending?) the interaction between the supposed antipodes of (a) the 'totalization' of modern bureaucratic institutions and (b) the 'individualization' of people through capitalist commerce and personal consciousness. This essentially modern (but also postmodern) 'governmental rationality', for which 'governmentality' is a shortened form, is, however, not merely an admixture of (a) and (b) in and of themselves, but rather an ongoing process of manipulation of the two into a creative synthesis – the 'art' of governmentality. This chapter argues that globalization is an extension of the same (not merely analogous) practices to world politics. This wider process of governmentalization is instantiated in:

- the development of institutions or regimes of so-called 'global governance', both inter-governmental and supranational
- the crystallisation of uneven pluralist (or 'neopluralist') processes of group politics across and below borders
- the marketization of the state and the spread of more complex processes of pro-market regulation
- the 'privatization of governance' across borders
- the spread of transnational norms such as human rights
- the renewed incorporation of more and more people, cutting across class, into a paradoxically politically promoted and regulated culture of individualistic 'empowerment' that embeds liberal capitalism at new levels.

Thus, world politics involves neither an embryonic 'global state' nor an integrated 'world marketplace' as such, but a complex, multilayered, fungible and increasingly hegemonic set of simultaneously globalizing and governmentalizing political practices – in particular, the management of processes of convergence and divergence through the emergence of new 'varieties of neoliberalism' in politics and public policy. But governmentalization by its very nature is always incomplete. In this context, the traditional power politics of national interests constitutes a predictable but anachronistic backlash.

Governments and government in international relations

The central conundrum of international relations as both academic discipline and political practice concerns the extent to which order, security and public goods can be provided in the international system without the existence of a state-like – sovereign or quasi-sovereign – international government that could exercise authority over the separate states within that system.

- Realists and neorealists posit the prevalence of a number of essentially inter-state practices such as power balancing, hegemony and the like to explain why internally hierarchical, self-interested states effectively cooperate while retaining a strong incentive to defect (Waltz, 1979; Keohane, 1986).
- American 'neoliberals' – a term used quite differently in Europe, as we will see later in this paper – look to the growth of international institutions and regimes that can reduce transactions costs, thereby increasing the absolute benefits of cooperation to a point where the costs of defection are effectively outweighed (Keohane, 1984; 1986).
- English School analysts look to international norms, especially those embedded in practices of diplomacy, as the main path of developing cooperative practices (Buzan, 1993; Little, 1995).
- Economic and sociological globalization theorists see 'bottom up' developments such as the spread of markets, firms, new technologies, civil society, culture and the 'global village,' and so on, across borders as the key variables. These are seen increasingly to outflank and enmesh states, which remain key structures but in partially transformed ways, in a denser web of relations, creating strong incentives not only to cooperate but also to restructure states and regimes themselves as interests and practices converge (Cerny, 1999, 2000a; Held, et al., 1999; Scholte, 2000; Hülsemeyer, 2003).
- Finally, some theorists see the emergence of a 'global state' (Shaw, 2000), albeit structured rather more loosely than traditional domestic states.

In all of this, of course, idealists differ as to the best way to make the international system more stable, peaceful and prosperous. Each of these approaches has its place in an understanding of how the international system is, or may be, changing as we go further into the twenty-first century. Each reflects a significant but partial reality. However, each underplays in different ways the interaction of three key factors in bringing about the kinds of structural change we have been witnessing over the past half century or so. In the first place, they all underestimate the role of agency – the autonomous, political conduct of human individuals and groups, rather than structural change, in the wider processes they describe. Second, they miss the dialectical element in processes of change – the fact that these human agents are continually attempting to actively manage, shape and manipulate change in ways that must reconcile tensions and contradictions inherent in those processes. Finally, they too often misunderstand and caricature analogous processes of change within states themselves over the past three centuries or so, creating too stark a picture of the distinction between government at a domestic level and international relations – the so-called 'inside/outside distinction' (Walker, 1992). In this chapter, an attempt will be made to fill these gaps with reference to the concept of *governmentality* as developed by the French social theorist Michel Foucault (Burchell et al., 1991; Foucault's chapters and the other analyses in *The Foucault Effect*, especially the introduction by Colin Gordon, are the most concise statements of this theory, although they are complemented by recently published lectures [Foucault, 2004a and 2004b; see also Lemke, 2006]). Governmentality, I argue, captures a dynamic and on-going element of the process of governing which, although originally developed primarily at the domestic level, is now at the heart of international political change.[1]

In Foucault's terminology, 'governmentality' is the art of modern liberal (or neoliberal) governing. It has come to characterise the dominant practices of liberal states and economies since the eighteenth century and has been the fundamental reason for their success in pro-viding both security, on the one hand, and market-based prosperity, on the other. It is thus a political practice of modern capitalist states, indeed the prevailing practice. It is govern-mentality – rather than other forms of statehood such as the 'police' state characterized by the supremacy of *raison d'État*, the rule of the capitalist class, the ascendancy of Saint-Simonian bureaucracies in both public and private sectors (the 'administration of things'), the invisible hand of the market, or the political forms of liberal democracy, etc. – that has enabled successful liberal democratic states to survive, adapt and develop (see also Foucault, 2004a and 2004b, for a more extended analysis). Indeed, all these major modern forms of social organization fail when put into practice in isolation or where one is set hierarchically above the others. Rather it is the art of weaving them together – the art of 'governing', in Foucault's sense, although many in the Anglophone world might think of it rather as the art of 'politics' – into a whole which is greater than the sum of the parts that enables and empowers the elements of modern society to work together effectively in the first place.

In today's globalizing world, I argue, governmentality is an ongoing and expanding process – being understood, learned and practiced above, across and beyond the level of the state. It is increasingly being redefined not only in terms of actors' capacity to weave together elements of successful liberal practices at the level of national societies, regions or cultures, but also in the perceived necessity to *link together and actively manage* the various layers of contemporary globalizing liberal capitalist society and the relationships among them. It involves the ability to navigate not just between states, as diplomats have tradi-tionally done, but among those uneven and multiple layers, through negotiation, policy innovation, power brokering, policy transfer and the like. But in all of these processes, the art or practice is basically the same when practiced *across* state borders as it has been throughout the modern period *within* national states. In this sense, globalization and gov-ernmentalization are inextricably intertwined. Globalization itself is being brought about above all through a process of the governmentalization of world politics – of the transfer of practices that are seen and thought to be those, pragmatically arrived at for the most part, that have enabled liberal states to be so successful domestically, to the international and transnational levels. Thus it is not necessary for there to be a world government, in either the realist or the idealist sense, for governmentality to become generalized, first in the de-veloped liberal capitalist world, and increasingly elsewhere. All that is required is an expansion of the hegemony of those practices learned from the domestic sphere, now in-creasingly put into practice in innovative ways globally.

The roots of governmentality

Governmentality is not embodied in institutions as such. Rather the practices of governmentality are what enable institutions to work in the first place. It is not merely norms or ideas that count, but actors with on-the-job experience in managing the contradictions and tensions inherent in governing and their ability to impart those practices to others through social learning. And it is not simply that economic growth and prosperity emerge because of some spontaneous bottom-up, self-generating process. These factors are in turn dependent upon two kinds of practices: (a) the way actors engage in political practices that enable markets to thrive, not merely to avoid 'market failure' but also to make them more efficient, competitive, etc. and also (b) the way the system as a whole empowers individuals to become 'homo economicus' at one level while at the same recognizing that pursuit of their self-interest is also at one and the same time part of a wider social process that is to the general good. This process therefore involves an ongoing effort to reconcile *apparently incompatible* structural tendencies in circumstances where those incompatibilities continually reappear, get refashioned and reshaped in political processes, and are frequently exacerbated by the conflicting interests and values of the wide range of actors in question.

The capacity for such a dynamic synthesis – the balancing act at its heart – has been forged in the historical experience of liberal states. The category of 'liberal' states, of course, includes both those societies which have been liberal (or liberal capitalist) throughout the modern era, on the one hand, and, those that have become liberal capitalist only through a series of historical tests – only having become liberal more recently and/or having gone through periods of bureaucratic authoritarianism of one kind of another – and that have become more liberal for various reasons (the 'demonstration effect' and a desire to emulate prosperous, 'developed' societies, popular demand for liberal democracy, the rise of newer capitalist elites, defeat in war, etc.). The core of this balancing act lies more specifically in a wide range of practices which have grown up over the past three centuries for creatively shaping – and consciously attempting to transcend – the interaction between the supposed antipodes of (a) the 'totalization' of modern bureaucratic institutions and (b) the 'individualization' of people through capitalist commerce and personal consciousness.

The modern experience involves both. Nevertheless, images of modernity presented by both modernists and postmodernists often emphasize and privilege the former, whether in terms of Le Corbusier's architecture and urbanist giantism; images of fascism and state communism – authoritarianism mixed with mass politics – and even the state Panoptikon presented by Foucault himself (Foucault, 1981); the Second Industrial Revolution factory with its integrated mass production lines and economies of scale, with Henry Ford's 1913 factory at River Rouge and the Model T achieving iconic status in this regard; or Hollywood's domination of world cultural production (Bohas, 2006). Saint-Simon's idea of 'the administration of things' as the wave of the future, also represented in Foucault's work by reference to the Cameralist school and the notion of 'police' in social theory (with the state presented as knowing what is best for people), along with the rise and fall of political totalitarianism, represents this tendency (Foucault, 2004a and 2004b). And indeed, the capacity for governments to collect and use information about people has expanded dramatically with the development of information and communications technology. Human lives today can potentially be 'micro-managed' in ways that were easier to escape even in authoritarian societies of old while systems of economic production and exchange often resemble Weber's notion of capitalist organization rather than the diffuse and decentralizing fluidity of the market's invisible hand.

But merely to raise this point highlights an equal and opposite critical reaction. After all, modernism is also about the spread of notions of individual freedoms and human and civil rights; about markets where the efficient allocation of resources in theory depends upon millions of micro-choices; about liberal democratic political systems where citizens and voters do actually have some say in the choice of their governors; and about pluralist political processes in which a range of groups contest and engage in bargaining within the public policy process. Of course, some actors are more endowed with resources and power than others. However, in what Charles Lindblom called 'neo-pluralism' (Lindblom, 1977), those social, economic and political actors with the greatest access to material and social resources generally marshal those resources in uneven and complex ways in order to pursue their own interests in what is still a relatively open political process. They predominate, but they do not necessarily control. Even powerful actors are unlikely to agree with each other on a range of matters across the board, although they may have common priorities such as the promotion of some version of capitalism. And other groups also have resources to mobilize and rules to appeal to. They can frequently exert leverage and punch above their weight in crucial situations. Thus even in a neo-pluralist political process, outcomes are determined not by simple coercion and/or structural power but, even more significantly, by how coalitions and networks are built in real-time conditions among a plurality of actors. This sort of modernism is more like modernism in literature, especially poetry, characterised by a stylised anarchy that is directed against precisely the kind of giantism implied by the totalising modernism discussed above.

Governmentality, for Foucault, then, involves both the continuous – and uneven – confrontation and management of the multiple incompatabilities of totalization and individualization at a variety of levels and nodal points. But it is much more than just that. Governmentality as an 'art' does not merely juxtapose: it attempts to take advantage of a creative, dynamic tension between the two contrasting and conflicting, but inextricably intertwined, forms of action and structuration. Thus it requires at one and the same time the development, mainly by political actors, of the art of not merely reconciling the two, but also ensuring that the creative disequilibria that result can be channelled into a dynamic process of social and economic growth and development. There is an analogy here with Austrian economics, which dispenses with the notion of equilibrium but sees economic development as the management of continually transmuting and dynamic disequilibria in innovative directions (Thompson et al., 1991). Even more, Foucault's approach to modernity in general, as well as to governmentality in particular, is set explicitly in the philosophical context of the Scottish Enlightenment – in the tradition of Adam Ferguson, Adam Smith and David Hume, with their practical, humanist and consequentialist emphasis – as well as in the later utilitarian tradition of Jeremy Bentham (Burchell et al., 1991; Foucault, 2004b: 295–317; for a recent intellectual and political history of the Scottish Enlightenment and its global repercussions, see Herman, 2003).

Without such navigational skills, disequilibria are likely to be set in stone. After all, it was the increasing dominance of one form of disequilibrium – that between workers who possessed only their own labour power and the bourgeoisie who owned capital – that Marx saw as leading to the collapse of capitalist society and that Lenin saw as becoming even more entrenched through liberal democracy, 'the best shell for capitalism.' Karl Polanyi described these developments as involving distinct (if overlapping) time periods – a 'double movement' between periods when the abstract notion of self-regulating markets would hold sway and loosen social bonds, thereby creating a backlash that would lead to anomie, social unrest and resistance, on the one hand, and periods when governments would try to re-establish those bonds and re-embed markets in social values, on the other. The 'Great Transformation' (Polanyi, 1944) was seen as emblematic of lessons having been learned from Fascism and the Great Depression, thereby leading to more socially solidaristic public policy through the industrial welfare state. Of course, globalization is often seen as the double movement revived, as destabilizing forms of market liberalization return (Murphy, 1994).

But in Foucault's account, history is both messier and more coherent at the same time. Not only does the double movement occur throughout at micro and meso levels, as well as the macro level, but its *creative management* is the crowning achievement of the modern liberal state. In this sense, Foucault's supposed radicalism, born in his postmodernist critiques of prisons and asylums with their emphasis on discipline, punishment and control, merges into an almost triumphalist liberal pluralism. Foucault himself makes quite clear (2004a and 2004b) that he sees governmentality not as a method of exercising authority or top-down control but as a creative and constructive art of developing the positive human potential of modern liberal society. Indeed, his notion of governmentality is about the *self-limitation* of government in the interests of achieving practical results. Governmentality is all about the ongoing process of dynamic, innovative, expansionary and, on the whole – despite its unevenness and the smaller-scale tyranny of micro-'circuits of power' – successfully learned practice of reconciliation and management of such supposedly contradictory tendencies. This essentially modern (but also postmodern) 'governmental rationality' – of which 'governmentality' is a shortened form – is therefore not merely an admixture of totalization and individualization, or of security and prosperity, in and of themselves, but rather an ongoing process of manipulation of the two into a creative synthesis. In this sense, governmentality is always a work in progress, never complete.

So what does governmentality involve in more concrete terms? Although Foucault is rather vague on this, focusing as he does on the longer-term history and general principles, it seems to me that there are several lines of development in a range of issue-areas that go beyond Foucault's specific comments but which can be seen in relationship to each other as giving rise to more generalisable 'practices' of governmentality. These practices include, in particular:

- the capacity for the *state administration* to be both an efficient bureaucratic structure in the Weberian sense, rationally organised offices with clear functions and rules, and yet flexible enough to conciliate opposing interests, adapt to new economic and social developments, reflect and act upon 'bottom-up' as well as 'top-down' inputs, allow bureaucrats to innovate, and the like
- the capacity for liberal democratic institutions to be both 'expressive', representing public opinion and pressure groups, yet also 'effective', i.e., capable of providing leadership where necessary and working through adminstratively and managerially coherent processes of public policy formulation, adoption and implementation

- the capacity for *state intervention in the economy* to promote economic and industrial development through central direction and support while at the same time promoting efficient market behaviour, entrepreneurialism, innovation, investment and genuine competition on the part of the private sector in both industry and finance, counteracting 'market failure' but not featherbedding firms
- the capacity of a system of legal and quasi-legal *regulation* not to constrain positive, growth-oriented market behaviour but actually to anchor those markets in an institutional framework that stabilises them, prevents fraud, sanctions contracts but involves clear, legitimate and agreed procedures for *ex ante* litigation, protects property rights and basically enforces market rules of the game
- the capacity of the state in international affairs to promote the wider *competitiveness* of the national economy through trade, finance and production while avoiding the beggar-thy-neighbour temptations of old and new mercantilism and promoting various forms of 'embedded liberalism' (Ruggie, 1982) or, today, perhaps, 'embedded neoliberalism' (Cerny, 2005a)
- the capacity of governments to ensure the economic as well as the physical security of citizens, especially through the *welfare state* and liberal neocorporatist arrangements (Schmitter, 1974), while attempting at the same time to *prevent* the welfare state from undermining the market economy (for example, by costing too much in terms of government spending, especially through 'creeping socialism' or what Sir Keith Joseph called the 'ratchet effect', rewarding dependency, entrenching rigid working practices or otherwise raising costs to business)
- managing *macroeconomic* – fiscal and monetary – *policy* in ways that can flexibly react to quite subtle indicators of overheating and cooling, inflation and deflation, boom and slump.

Each of these balancing acts is partially open-ended, without clear prescriptions as to how to act in particular historical circumstances. Each of them depends on actors gaining on-the-job experience in handling the delicate and challenging issues that are faced on a day-to-day basis. It is in this setting that we need to evaluate Harold Wilson's famous (or notorious) saying: 'A week is a long time in politics'. There are issues of managing tensions between short-term problems, especially if there is a crisis or potential crisis in the offing, and often unpredictable but equally necessary medium- and long-term considerations. There are issues of linking together various horizontal and vertical layers and divisions of government and society, from executive power to the separation of powers to complex ministries (and the relations between them) to layers of regional and local governance to social groups, 'interests' in Arthur Bentley's sense (Bentley, 1908), classes, organised groups like trade unions, 'cause groups' and many others. Indeed, Foucault extensively cites Adam Ferguson's conception of civil society as the key to understanding the process of governmentality (see Ferguson, 1767/1995; Foucault, 2004b). And there are questions of linking and weaving the different processes and policy issue-areas listed earlier into some sort of coherent overall social process of 'governing' in Foucault's sense of the word. Clearly these practices or aspects of the art of governing provide the key to the success of liberal capitalist states (or neoliberal states, as Foucault sometimes would say, further confusing the meaning of that word[2]).

Finally, the overall key to understanding governmentality along all the dimensions listed above – and the intrinsic complex interaction among them – is found in the necessity for *self-limitation* on the part of the state and political actors (Foucault, 2004a and 2004b). The limitations on government, as Foucault argues at length in several places, derive not so much from moral or ethical principles such as rights or liberties. Rather, they are rooted in a kind of systemic pragmatism. Governmental actors do not intervene (or choose not to intervene) in economic and social affairs out of moral principles *per se*, but instead are constantly careful not to overstep their own practical boundaries, because in a complex world – especially a world of *homo economicus*, where the everyday life of the population and the success of market society depend on the spontaneous action and interaction of individuals – the state is forever in danger not only of overreaching itself in terms of efficiency and effectiveness but also of stifling progress and human activity more broadly. States and state actors have to look at the practical and potentially counterproductive effects of trying to control people too closely, for fear of choking off individual initiative, disrupting group solidarity and undermining the very enlightened self-interest upon which society and the state depend for their existence and stability in the modern world. Today, it is often said that policy-makers should pursue policy options according to the criterion of 'what works'. This is also true for Foucault. But the discovery of 'what works' is rooted precisely in the balancing act between Saint-Simonianism and individual or group initiative and continuous activity – Fergusonian civil society – described above.

Governmentality in an age of globalization

Going further – extending the notion of governmentalization as an ongoing process to international relations and international political economy – this chapter argues that governmentalization constitutes the key independent variable in contemporary world politics that the standard approaches to international relations listed at the beginning of this chapter do not quite succeed in capturing. Foucault's own presentation of governmentality is confined to the governance of the domestic political systems of nation-states or of particular policy issue-area and agencies (as is evident from most of the still embryonic literature on this subject). However, at this point – and especially in Foucault's rather broad-brush treatment of the topic – the concept does not yet take us much farther along in specifying how it applies to our original quest to bridge the government or governance gap in international relations theory. But I will try to demonstrate through some illustrative examples analogous to the institutional and policy issue-areas listed above that it is central to that quest. In particular, I see governmentality as the key to understanding what is generally but loosely referred to as the process of globalization. Globalization, I argue here, is primarily and fundamentally an extension of the same – not merely analogous, but fundamentally isomorphic – practices to world politics. The similarity of the balancing acts and governing practices that a wide range of actors engage in – but especially those actors whom I have stylised elsewhere as 'political' and 'social' actors (Cerny, 2000b and 2006a) – suggests that rather than simply adapting their behavior to the structural imperatives of traditional anarchic international relations as distinct from hierarchical domestic state politics, these actors are increasingly learning to adapt and *apply domestic practices* in ways that are *transforming international relations themselves*. In this process, in other words, they are not merely adapting domestic practices of governmentality to the dictates of traditional international relations; rather, they are transferring those practices and using them to manage and shape the process of globalization, in turn changing international relations in quite fundamental ways.

What is perhaps most intriguing about this analysis is the suggestion that governmentality is not only an art or practice in Foucault's sense but also an art or practice that can be exercised and applied in diverse political and institutional settings. In domestic politics, of course, we normally associate these practices with the main developed liberal capitalist states. However, at the domestic level they can not only be represented and embedded in a range of alternative developed 'national models' (Crouch and Streeck, 1997) or 'varieties of capitalism' (Hall and Soskice, 2001), but also found in mixed, quasi-capitalist authoritarian societies. For example, some influential members of the ruling dynastic family in Saudi Arabia some time ago began debating the possibilities for transforming that country into a more participatory model while shunning the idea of actual democratization. Their domestic situation (and location in the Middle Eastern geopolitical cauldron), their economic interdependence with Western oil-consuming countries, the assertive US role in Iraq and elsewhere, their Western education, increasing strains on the alliance between the Saud dynasty and the fundamentalist Wahabi sect, and so on, taken together, seem to be setting the ruling family on the road to attempting to develop some kind of governmentalization without moving towards formal liberal democracy. Other Middle Eastern states are attempting to chart analogous courses, without much success so far, it has to be said. Of course, such attempts in the past have often proved merely transitional in the longer term, empowering as they do the participation of competing and conflicting social, economic and political forces and leading them to demand further democratization. Similar comments could be made about China, Iran and a number of other countries. But that is part of the process of the social learning of the practices of governmentality too.

In the international sphere, an increasing number of actors are involved in a wide range of processes, their successful navigation of which, I suggest, requires approaching and managing those processes according to the domestically learned liberal practices of governmentality. The days of Ruggie's original conception of 'embedded liberalism', when there could be a functional complementarity through the differentiation of function between liberal international economics – especially freer trade and liberalized capital movements – and the Keynesian, welfarist politics of relatively autonomous domestic national economies, has progressively been incorporated into, undermined and transformed by globalization. But in partial contrast to the development of governmentality at the domestic state level, these lessons and practices must of course be applied in a far more structurally *heterogeneous* institutional and processual context. When I say in 'partial' contrast, of course, I am referring to the fact that political scientists and other social scientists in recent years have been discovering (or rediscovering!) the structural and processual heterogeneity of domestic states and societies too (e.g. Rhodes, 1997). The word which is increasingly applied in this context is not governmentality but *governance*, seen as a process. R. A. W. Rhodes has himself stated that in the development of his own usage of the concept of 'governance', at the domestic level he adapted elements drawn from international relations theory, in particular the complex interdependence theory of Keohane and Nye (Keohane and Nye, 1977; Rhodes, personal conversation, 1993). So there is to some extent a two-way process here.

Nevertheless, the key to the quest for bridging the 'government gap' in international relations demands that we recognize that governmentality, being essentially a pluralistic conception, does not require the construction a hierarchical domestic-type state order at international level in order to be practiced effectively. In some ways, indeed, the very heterogeneity of the globalizing international order makes governmentality particularly appropriate to managing and shaping the complex processes of transnational liberal capitalism without being in danger from a reawakening at an international level of totalizing alternatives, whether called fascism, bureaucratic authoritarianism, state communism or whatever. The very fact that there is no international government removes the temptations of totalization. Even empire, in the guise of the current Bush adminstration's attempt to reassert American hegemony and national interests in the world, is based on a form of what William Appleman Williams (1959) called 'informal empire' rather than formal colonial empire, and can be constrained to some extent by various forms of opposition and even resistance as well as, more directly, by the need for coalition-building and international institutional legitimacy. Therefore, the fact that the international system does still involve structural elements that, relatively speaking, can be seen as 'anarchic' paradoxically opens up a range of heterogeneous spaces for the development of governmentalizing practices.

This wider process of international and/or global governmentalization can thus be identified as being instantiated at a number of structurally quite diverse levels and in a range of partly complementary, partly competing arenas or structured fields of action (Crozier and Friedberg, 1977), some of which are listed below. However, it must be added that this process does not merely involve separate forms of governmentalization tailored to each level or arena. Rather it involves a *dialectical process of convergence and divergence*, again both reconciling and creatively managing through what Foucault calls the art or practice of governmentality the dynamic processes of interaction among these levels and arenas, linking them and weaving them together in an evolving – and, of course, incomplete – (neo)liberal capitalist world order. These are some of the key dimensions of this interactive process.

1. The development of institutions or *regimes* of so-called 'global governance', both intergovernmental and supranational, constitute probably the most visible dimension of governmentalization. Actors in these regimes must continually play off the demands of states, economic actors, social interest groups and the like, parlaying them into relatively effective outputs. There are at least two fundamental problematics here. The first is to deal with the issue-area in question in a way that actually does the job. The second is to pursue and promote the continued institutional existence and further development of the regime in question itself. These imperatives can often conflict. For example, actors within or interacting with environmental regimes often see their first order or *a priori* goal to make sure the institution itself is not undermined by states (both developing and developed, in different ways), business interests seeking to avoid the costs of pollution control, and so on; only then can the real issues be tackled (Young, 1994). At the same time, maintaining and expanding those regimes in such conditions will often mean that regulations and substantive policy outputs have to be watered down. The dispute between the United States and other signatories over the future of the Kyoto Protocol is a rather extreme case of this syndrome.

2. Another example was the role of the United Nations with regard to Resolution 1441 and the disarmament inspection regime in Iraq. Which was more likely to undermine UN legitimacy – for the Bush administration's proposals to be accepted by a reluctant Security Council under pressure from the so-called 'hegemon', or for those proposals to be vetoed or otherwise blocked in the Security Council itself, with the US attacking Iraq with only a small 'coalition of the willing'? The challenge, the balancing act, is ongoing, as is seen in the attempt to circumscribe Iran's nuclear ambitions or to deal with the humanitarian crisis in Darfur. In the post–Cold War era, in fact, the United Nations saw its profile and effectiveness increase somewhat overall in the 1990s, but its present role and practices are increasingly seen as problematic.

3. A third example is the World Bank (and to a lesser extent the International Monetary Fund), which effectively shifted in the mid-1990s from imposing more radical market-oriented forms of restructuring represented by the 'structural adjustment' policies of the 1980s and the 'Washington Consensus' of the early 1990s, to a 'post-Washington Consensus', rhetorically, at least, focused on a new overriding goal: poverty reduction. One astute academic observer, Peter Willetts, has said that in his opinion the World Bank has effectively adopted a social democratic approach to globalization (oral intervention at the British International Studies Association annual meeting, London School of Economics and Political Science, December 2002), far from the neoliberalism red in tooth and claw of Thatcher or Reagan (or even George W. Bush).

With regard to such continually expanding and institutionalizing arenas, then, social learning and on-the-job experience of actors – not only within those regimes themselves but also among state actors, economic actors and social actors – are in the process of expanding and adapting forms of governmentality, however unevenly and incompletely, in terms of both the problematics mentioned above of regime durability and policy effectiveness. Of course, the balancing act is a complex and often ambiguous one, as critics of the World Bank's poverty reduction approach are keen to point out. Finally, to the extent that the discourse of 'international institutions' and 'regimes' is increasingly being superseded by that of 'global governance', we can also see a reflection of the extent to which the art and practices of governmentality are altering people's *perceptions* of how the superstructure of the international system is evolving.

1. The crystallisation of uneven pluralist (or 'neopluralist') processes of group politics across and below borders, sometimes called the emergence of 'global civil society', is also a crucial aspect of governmentalization, as Ronnie Lipschutz in particular has pointed out (Lipschutz, 2005; cf. Cerny, 2000b). Actors in both national political systems and international regimes increasingly interact with a wider range of more and more assertive interests, pressure groups, cause groups and the like. Although these categories are still primarily domestic, (a) more and more of those domestic groups have a growing transnational dimension and perceive their interests as embedded in the state of international relations and the international political economy, and (b) certain groups have become effectively multinational and/or transnational (Keck and Sikkink, 1998). Even supposedly 'anti-globalization' protestors have been changing their discourse over the past two to three years in particular, looking towards more social democratic – or 'social neoliberal' – approaches to globalization, opposing key aspects of the *form* of globalization rather than globalization *per se* (Cerny, 2005a).

2. At the same time, however, as in Foucault's original treatment of governmentality, these governmentalising practices involve the acceptance at an international (transnational? global?) level of the opening of markets for trade, finance and production, the liberalization of regulation both at the national level and across borders through what Keohane and Nye (1977) called 'transgovernmental' linkages (cf. Slaughter, 2004), the prioritization of the promotion of international competitiveness as the hallmark of state intervention, and even the marketization of the state itself (Cerny, 2000a). State actors, both politicians and bureaucrats, have over the past three decades been on a steep learning curve about how to adapt government policies themselves to globalization. This has been transforming *domestic* governmental practices in ways which were less viable before the globalization processes of the past three decades or so took shape. Governmentalization in international relations therefore increasingly involves a process which cuts across and links domestic, regional, transnational and intergovernmental levels in a range of creative balancing acts.

3. So far, the institutions and superstructures we have mainly been talking about are public or quasi-public institutions. However, there is also the development of a phenomenon familiar enough with liberal capitalist states, i.e., the emergence of quasi-corporatist transnational private regimes – what David Lake (1999) has called the 'privatization of governance' across borders. Such private organizations in global politics fill crucial parts of the government gap, whether in expanding the effective scope and reach of international diplomacy, the organization of international financial markets (Cerny, 2005b), a range of transnationally organized industrial sectors, the evolving process of administering and managing the Internet, and the like (Ronit and Schneider, 2000). Of course, these developments interact and overlap with the growing role discussed above of interest groups, transnational cause networks and epistemic communities too. Indeed, as Lake argues, the very structure of the traditional international system, blocking as it does the capacity for more state-like world governmental institutions to develop, actually encourages a growing process of experimentation with private and quasi-private institution-building on the part of both private sector actors and public sector actors frustrated by the institutional weaknesses of much of the international governmental superstructure – a form of institutional *bricolage*. Governmentalization proceeds at different levels, as I have argued, and the growth of privatized international governance structures and processes have become a crucial part of filling those gaps.

4. Finally, the governmentalization of world politics, like the governmentalization of the modern state, involves the renewed incorporation and inclusion of more and more people, individuals as well as groups, cutting across class, into a paradoxically politically promoted and regulated culture of individualistic 'empowerment' that embeds liberal capitalism at new levels. This last dimension is actually even more multi-dimensional than the first four dimensions discussed here, becoming an essential element of them all. For just as governmentality in the modern state has entailed the promotion and development of a market-oriented individualization of consciousness, mainly through discourse, so the governmentalization of world politics involves the discursive assertion – and behavioral actualization – of individual empowerment in legitimizing globalization processes. For the World Bank, for example, the adoption of a poverty reduction strategy does not merely involve aid to the poor; it adopts the rhetoric of enabling/empowering the poor to actively participate in capitalist development, incorporating

them into market-friendly practices, and supposedly giving them a stake in the governmentalization process itself (cf. Jessop's use of the concept of Schumpeterian Workfare State: Jessop, 2002).

For the politics of transnational pluralism and civil society, the new international governmentality involves encouraging such groups to develop cross-cutting links with states, global governance institutions, private sector economic organizations and so on, making such 'social actors' (Cerny, 2000b) into active carriers and practitioners of governmentality themselves (Lipschutz, 2005). For the 'competition state' and the reformed, marketized welfare state, rhetoric such as that of the 'Third Way' (Giddens, 1998) is based on a new contractual relationship between welfare recipients (and ordinary citizens) and the state, seeing government support as conditional on the willingness of welfare clients to learn how to involve themselves proactively in work (workfare, etc.) and market exchange. Indeed, globalization rests on a new consumptionism that encourages workers, migrants, and so on, to perceive themselves as *homo economicus* rather than as merely sellers of labour power (Cerny, 2006b; Jessop, 2002). And finally, for the growing sector of private organizations in global politics, there is a new social partnership between business and global governance, a new self-regulatory field of action, which actively integrates international business into wider globalizing norms, including the social neoliberal 'Global Compact' pursued by Kofi Annan when he was Secretary General of the United Nations (Cerny, 2005a).

Conclusions

Closing the government gap in world politics and international relations theory involves neither an embryonic post-Weberian 'global state' nor a fully integrated, bottom-up 'world marketplace', but a complex, multilayered, fungible and increasingly hegemonic set of simultaneously globalizing and governmentalizing political practices. Linking these practices together are not merely a new global elite but rather an increasing pluralization of actors, all learning the art of balancing and managing an expanding process of transnational governmentalization, using still-heterogeneous superstructures to experiment and innovate in policy and discourse – leading in turn to a further, if uneven, pluralization of transnational society, economy and politics. In particular, such actors must creatively manage complex processes of convergence and divergence, mainly rationalized through the emergence of new 'varieties of neoliberalism' in politics and public policy (Cerny, 2005a). In this context, the traditional power politics of national interests constitutes a predictable but anachronistic backlash, especially when linked with the concepts of empire and hegemony in the United States. However, I would suggest that the backlash is likely to be viewed in historical perspective as temporary – as 'one step back' in a longer historical process of combined globalization and governmentalization, which in turn constitute 'two steps forward'. The actors involved in the latter increasingly have a critical stake in the development and expansion of the governmentalization of world politics. The result is a real, if uneven, process of undermining and transcending the 'inside/outside distinction' that has held back international relations theory in the contemporary world. Such a process is a logical – and historical – extension of the 'art' of governmentality as theorized by Michel Foucault.

Notes

1. In partial contrast to Stephen Gill's concept of 'disciplinary neoliberalism' (see Gill, 2002: 130–31), I would argue that the concept of governmentality is more fluid and pluralistic. Although the theme of neoliberalism being entrenched through individual internalization is similar, Foucault's version of neoliberalism is also intended to be liberating and self-empowering rather than simply self-disciplining (Lemke, 2006).

2. 'Neoliberalism' has three different if overlapping meanings that are relevant to this chapter. In the first place, it is derived, for most European observers, from the European use of the word 'liberal', which – in contrast to standard everyday American usage (what former US President George H. W. Bush called the 'L-word', implying Keynesian, welfare statist, interventionist, quasi-social democratic politics) – is more like free market, *laissez-faire* economics or what Americans often call 'classical' or 'nineteenth-century' liberalism. In this sense, Thatcherism in the United Kingdom and Reaganism in the United States, which emphasised limiting and/or reducing the social and economic functions of the state, are the embodiment of late twentieth-century *neo*liberalism, or the rediscovery of nineteenth-century liberalism in the global era. In the second place, for American international relations scholars like Robert O. Keohane (1989), neoliberalism means the institutionalization of complex economic interdependence in international regimes and the evolving *de facto* practices of cooperation such regimes represent – i.e., as will be argued later in this chapter, one partial dimension of the governmentalization of world politics. Finally, there is Foucault's own rather loose use of the word, which seems to me to involve the more advanced forms of liberal capitalism characteristic of the late twentieth century – in some ways a mixture of the other two definitions.

References

Bentley, A. F. (1908) *The Process of Government: A Study of Social Pressures*, Chicago, University of Chicago Press.

Bohas, A. (2006) 'The paradox of Anti-Americanism: reflection on the shallow concept of soft power', *Global Society*, 20 (4), 395–414.

Burchell, G., Gordon, C. and Miller, P. (eds) (1991) *The Foucault Effect: Studies in Governmentality*, Chicago, University of Chicago Press.

Buzan, B. (1993). 'From international system to international society: structural realism and regime theory meet the English school', *International Organization*, 47 (3), 327–52.

Cerny, P. G. (1999) 'Reconstructing the political in a globalizing world: states, institutions, actors and governance' in F. Buelens (ed.), *Globalization and the Nation-State*, Cheltenham, UK, Edward Elgar, for the Belgian-Dutch Association for Institutional and Political Economy, pp. 89–137.

———. (2000a) 'Restructuring the political arena: globalization and the paradoxes of the competition state' in R. D. Germain (ed.), *Globalization and Its Critics: Perspectives from Political Economy*, London, Macmillan, pp. 117–38.

———. (2000b). 'Political agency in a globalizing world: toward a structurational approach,' *European Journal of International Relations*, 6 (4), 435–64.

———. (2005a) 'Neoliberalism' in M. Griffiths (ed.), *Routledge Encyclopedia of International Relations and Global Politics*, London, Routledge, pp. 580–90.

———. (2005b) 'Power, markets and accountability: the development of multi-level governance in international finance' in A. Baker, A. Hudson and R. Woodward (eds), *Governing Financial Globalization*, London, Routledge, pp. 24–48.

———. (2006a) 'Plurality, pluralism, and power: elements of pluralist analysis in an age of globalization' in R. Eisfeld (ed.), *Pluralism: Developments in the Theory and Practice of Democracy*, Opladen, Barbara Budrich on behalf of the International Political Science Association, Research Committee No. 16 (Socio-Political Pluralism), pp. 81–111.

———. (2006b) 'Restructuring the state in a globalizing world: capital accumulation, tangled hierarchies and the search for a new spatio-temporal fix', review article, *Review of International Political Economy*, 13 (4), 679–95.

Crouch, C. and Streeck, W. (eds) (1997) *The Political Economy of Modern Capitalism: Mapping Convergence and Diversity*, London, Sage Publications.

Crozier, M. and Friedberg, E. (1977) *L'Acteur et le système: les contraintes de l'action collective*, Paris, Éditions du Seuil.

Ferguson, A. (1797/1995) *An Essay on the History of Civil Society*, Cambridge, Cambridge University Press, 1995; originally published 1797.

Foucault, M. (1981) *Power/Knowledge: Selected Interviews and Other Writings, 1972–1977*, edited by Colin Gordon, New York, Longman.

———. (2004a) *Sécurité, Territoire, Population: Cours au Collège de France, 1977–1978*, Paris, Gallimard/Seuil.

———. (2004b) *Naissance de la Biopolitique: Cours au Collège de France, 1978–1979*, Paris, Gallimard/Seuil.

Giddens, A. (1998) *The Third Way: Renewal of Social Democracy*, Cambridge, Polity Press.

Gill, S. (2002) *Power and Resistance in the New World Order*, London, Palgrave Macmillan.

Hall, P. A. and Soskice, D. (eds) (2001) *Varieties of Capitalism: The Institutional Foundations of Comparative Advantage*, Oxford, Oxford University Press.

Held, D., McGrew, A. G., Goldblatt, D. and Perraton, J. (eds) (1999) *Global Transformations: Politics, Economics and Culture*, Cambridge, Polity Press.

Herman, A. (2003) *The Scottish Enlightenment: The Scots' Invention of the Modern World*, London, Fourth Estate.

Hülsemeyer, A. (ed.) (2003) *Globalization in the 21st Century: Convergence and Divergence*, London, Palgrave Macmillan.

Jessop, B. (2002) *The Future of the Capitalist State*, Cambridge, Polity Press.

Keck, M. E. and Sikkink, K. (1998) *Activists Beyond Borders: Advocacy Networks in International Politics*, Ithaca, NY, Cornell University Press.

Keohane, R. O. (1984) *After Hegemony: Cooperation and Discord in the World Political Economy*, Princeton, NJ, Princeton University Press.

———. (ed.) (1986) *Neorealism and Its Critics*, New York, Columbia University Press.

———. (1989) *International Institutions and State Power: Essays in International Relations Theory*, Boulder, CO, Westview Press.

Keohane, R. O. and Nye, J. S. Jr. (1977) *Power and Interdependence*, Boston, Little, Brown.

Lake, D. A. (1999) 'Global governance: a relational contracting approach' in A. Prakash and J. A. Hart (eds), *Globalization and Governance*, London, Routledge, pp. 31–53.

Lemke, T. (2006) 'Governance and governmentality' in A. Harrington, B. L. Marshall and H-P. Müller (eds), *Encyclopedia of Social Theory*, London, Routledge, pp. 232–34.

Lindblom, C. E. (1978) *Politics and Markets: The World's Political Economic Systems*, New York, Basic Books.

Lipschutz, R. D. (2005) *Globalization, Governmentality and Global Politics: Regulation for the Rest of Us?*, with James K. Rowe, London, Routledge.

Little, R. (1995) 'Neorealism and the English School: A methodological, ontological and theoretical reassessment', *European Journal of International Relations*, 1 (1), 9–34.

Murphy, C. (1994) *International Organization and Industrial Change: Global Governance Since 1850*, Cambridge, Polity Press.

Polanyi, K. (1944) *The Great Transformation: The Political and Economic Origins of Our Time*, New York, Rinehart.

Rhodes, R. A. W. (1997) *Understanding Governance: Policy Networks, Governance, Reflexivity and Accountability*, Milton Keynes, Open University Press.

Ronit, K. and Schneider, V. (eds) (2000) *Private Organisations in Global Politics*, London, Routledge.

Ruggie, J. G. (1982) 'International regimes, transactions, and change: embedded liberalism in the post-war economic order' in S. D. Krasner (ed.), *International Regimes*, Ithaca, NY, Cornell University Press, pp. 195–231.

Schmitter, P. C. (1974) 'Still the century of corporatism?' in F. Pike and T. Stritch (eds), *The New Corporatism*, Notre Dame, Notre Dame University Press, pp. 85–131.

Scholte, J. A. (2000) *Globalization: A Critical Introduction*, London, Macmillan.

Shaw, M. (2000) *Theory of the Global State: Globality as an Unfinished Revolution*, Cambridge, Cambridge University Press.

Slaughter, A-M. (2004) *A New World Order*, Princeton, NJ, Princeton University Press.

Thompson, G., Frances, J., Levaçić, R. and Mitchell, J. (eds) (1991) *Markets, Hierarchies and Networks: The Coordination of Social Life*, London, Sage Publications.

Walker, R. B. J. (1992) *Inside/Outside: International Relations as Political Theory*, Cambridge, Cambridge University Press.

Waltz, K. N. (1979) *Theory of International Politics*, Boston, Addison Wesley Longman.

Williams, W. A. (1959) *The Tragedy of American Diplomacy*, New York, Norton.

Young, Oran R. (1994) *International Governance*, Ithaca, NY, Cornell University Press.

An earlier version of this chapter was presented at the annual convention of the International Studies Association, Portland, Oregon, 24 February–1 March 2003. I am grateful to Paul Cammack, Natalie Bormann, Stuart Elden, Colin Gordon and Stuart Shields for their comments on that version.

Part 5

Knowledge and Technologies

CHAPTER 17

Globalization in the World Trade Organization

Power, Knowledge and the Reproduction of Inequality in Intellectual Property Governance

Chris Farrands

The World Trade Organization (WTO), created in 1994 from the General Agreement on Tariffs and Trade (GATT), has been a powerful instrument of globalization, regardless of how one defines 'globalization'. More recently, it has faced a series of deep divisions over trade in agriculture and services, which have led to the collapse of the so-called 'Doha Development Round' of trade talks in July 2006. The stakes are indeed high, and at the time of writing most commentators are pessimistic about how the talks can be revived, not least because it appears to many on all sides that the negotiating structure is not fit for its intended purpose. Furthermore, the balance of power between the main actors has shifted, to give more leverage to the large developing countries, including Brazil, India and China. It is perhaps premature to ask whether the 'hegemonic moment' of the United States in the WTO has passed, but it has certainly become more difficult for the older dominant trio, the US, European Union and Japan, to use the WTO to achieve some of their main goals. Yet in key areas, the WTO has gone on consolidating specific forms of power, reproducing dominant discourses of negotiating power, and reflecting the major interests of large multinational companies and trade associations as well as powerful states.

This is the case with Trade Related Intellectual Property (TRIPS) issues, among others on the WTO's agenda. Intellectual property was brought into the WTO remit to ensure the protection of major interests of large global players including communications, IT, software and media firms at a time when their interests were under threat from piracy, as well as to promote a global market in which they could flourish, issues that continue to matter (Anonymous, 2006). Liberalization has encouraged new members, including China, which joined the WTO in 2001 (Wang, 2006). It has helped the established firms, as they had intended; but it has also thrown up new competitive challenges and opened the door to new firms (as have technology changes in the key industries involved). And the new procedures of disputes settlement have sometimes not gone as anticipated: developing states have started to learn how to play the rules of the new system both in political negotiation and legal procedures. In this chapter, I shall argue that the WTO TRIPS system retains a strong bias towards powerful core states and their companies, despite some of the rhetoric of liberalization; but I shall also suggest that the powerful do not have it all their own way, and that unintended effects from the creation of the WTO have also had an interesting and potentially important place in the story of the WTO TRIPS system in the twenty-first century.

What are TRIPS about politically? They represent a redefinition of political space, and at the same time constitute a reallocation – mostly in the form of a further concentration – of structural and symbolic power. Not least, they reach across the boundaries of even the most powerful states. They seem to demand obligations of individual governments, thereby undermining their claim to sovereign authority. They also find new political space at local and global levels. It is this simultaneous redefinition and reconstitution of political space through the working of intellectual property rules in the global political economy which is the starting point of this chapter.

Intellectual property issues have assumed a central role in debates about contemporary global political economy. Alongside their academic interest, their practical political importance was graphically demonstrated in anti-globalization demonstrations on the streets of Seattle in November 1999 and in World Social Forum actions in the early 2000s. Principal amongst the perceived threats of globalization, which they criticised, was the impact of changes in the system of intellectual property regulation. In the 1980s and 1990s, Western governments gave up earlier aspirations to manage the economy through macro-economic policy management. But no sooner was the era of neo-liberal de-regulation announced, than new forms of regulation – or re-regulation – emerged. These new regulatory systems are often managed by private or quasi-governmental institutions rather than by states, at a global level. They have taken over governmental functions, including the allocation of authority and the pursuit of economic security. In disputes procedures within the WTO, they have involved an unprecedented degree of 'automaticity'. The impact of this transfer of power to an autonomous and technocratic global institutional structure, which is often seen as increasingly unaccountable and removed from the possibility of democratic control, has surprised even many of its creators.

Intellectual property, globalization and governance

The creation of a new international level of policy management, which is at the same time a form of dominance, of rule making, and of interest articulation, has been called 'governance' in the globalization literature (Agnew and Corbridge, 1995; Taylor, 1996). The term is ambivalent, expressing a consolidation of hegemonic power in neo-Gramscian literature and a system of interdependent policy cooperation to more liberal authors (cf. the essays in Gill, 1993, especially Cox, 1993). Intellectual property management has proved to be a key battleground of global governance. The conflict is between the new re-regulationism carried forward in the name of neo-liberalism, the old corporatism or paternalism, and a more genuine liberalization, amounting to a possible democratisation, of space and territory. The same kind of conflict has also shaped efforts to manage the Internet and World Wide Web (Berners-Lee, 1999). And it has also affected questions of human reproduction through intellectual property rules in the human genome project, and through the control of biotechnology and pharmaceutical research (May, 2000: 100–107). The new re-regulatory agencies in intellectual property are the TRIPS agreements and the WTO disputes procedure, invented to replace a supposedly ineffective General Agreement on Tariffs and Trade (GATT) adjudication process. Although many of the most important issues arise between developed states, the most powerful impact of the new regulatory system is on developing economies and societies. For the most part, these are also the players least able to protect themselves in global disputes, although countries such as India, discussed in an example below, have considerable resources to promote their cause, and should not be seen, as they sometimes rather patronisingly are, as helpless in the face of global power structures.

Intellectual property issues are not new in political economy. In 1767, the Scottish writer Adam Ferguson (1966: 25–31) noted the importance of innovative knowledge as a factor in wealth creation. David Ricardo (1973: 263) was probably the first to recognise that knowledge creates a monopoly for its holder, which is relatively short-lived, so recognising the time-sensitive nature of knowledge transactions of almost all kinds. In the twentieth century, the economic literature on knowledge became increasingly sophisticated. It recognized the importance of knowledge structures and led to an awareness of the role of knowledge production as the basis for the new economy of the 1980s and 1990s (Boyer and Durand, 1997: 81–85; Strange, 1994; May, 2000). As knowledge-based industries have become increasingly important in production, employment, trade and investment, so they have become ever more important for those who claim to *own* knowledge to maintain control over its worldwide distribution and its capacity to generate income (Sennett, 2006).

Here, there is a problem, for what we call knowledge can mean many different kinds of entity, process or activity. Only some of these can properly be called intellectual property, in the sense that only some of them can be either valued precisely or owned and sold. Others, including 'know-how' and what Polyani (1957) called 'tacit knowledge', may be very difficult to identify as ownable, never mind tradable. But despite some real problems of definition, knowledge of different kinds has become commodified (see the excellent discussion in May, 2000). The goal of seeking rents from knowledge has been a key driver of globalization in the world economy in the last twenty years. In the process, knowledge such as know-how, which was always thought to be embedded in social relations or social structures so that it could not be transferred or reproduced, has become detached from its social foundations and incorporated into the world of tradable assets (Farrands, 1996, 1997).

I have previously discussed the relationship between globalization and the transformation of intellectual property regimes (Farrands, 1996). It is useful to summarize that position before moving to a new development of the argument. There are four critical points. First, and contrary to more optimistic liberal authors (e.g., Ohmae, 1990), globalization can best be understood as a reconfiguration of power. Power may be material or symbolic, it may involve resources, capabilities and will, as in traditional ideas of power, and it clearly involves the ability to set agendas, to define and exercise power through structures, and to occupy and defend a position in a structure of dominance. However, it also involves forms of relationship created by discourse and represented in language, especially in the power relationships of communications. An emphasis on the importance of communications power seen in this way unites writers such as Habermas, Foucault and Arendt, even though we should acknowledge disagreements between them too (Ashenden and Owen, 1999). As Hirst (1998) suggests, the development of the study of international relations involves a plurality of forms of power which are productive as well as constitutive and destructive. Globalization is primarily a reconstitution of power, and in the process a reconstitution of our understanding of spatial and temporal relations and hence, in some respects, of consciousness (Lefebvre, 1991; Agnew and Corbridge, 1995; Taylor, 1996).

Second, globalization weakens the 'adjectival state' – the welfare state, the nation state, the sovereign state, the national security state. But it does not follow that the state as such is *weakened* rather than *changed* by these transformations. Instead, the state demonstrates its enduring power through its adaptive capability (Weiss, 1998). Third, the new focus on intellectual property can be understood as a form of enclosure analogous to the descriptions of the enclosure of common land in economies such as England on the eve of the industrial revolution, an argument later developed especially in Christopher May's work (May, 2000). The sense that what was once held in common, knowledge of everyday remedies, cultural practices, agricultural techniques and so on, is under threat of enclosure through manipulation of intellectual property rules by giant global corporations, is one of the main sources of opposition to TRIPS. Disadvantaged people were stripped of traditional rights by those who had the legislative and juridical power, and who used that power to increase their own wealth, in both the land enclosures and in TRIPS. Fourth, and finally, intellectual property relations – along with much that we call globalization – create a series of inter-related, but not contiguous spaces, spaces which may be conceptual or legal but are always also political, even though they may not strictly speaking be located in an actual territory (Lefebvre, 1991). These spaces may overlap, they may move on different axes, or they may nest – like Russian dolls each containing the next. This partial deterritorialization of political space makes sense if we think of the idea of what has been called cyberspace, but also applies to any of those governance regimes, which are not linked to a specific state territory. As Taylor (1996) suggests, the role of the state is transformed, sometimes diminished, but certainly not always so. And non-state agencies take over regulation functions and become key players in negotiations, including trade associations, lobby groups and (given the very technical nature of TRIPS deals) law firms acting as consultants to all parties.

Evaluating the new WTO regime

My earlier argument was written as the WTO regime first emerged. At that stage, no cases had passed right through the new panel system of adjudication, which had just replaced the former GATT procedures. Since then, several hundred cases have been referred to it, some being negotiated before presentation to a disputes panel, and it is completing disputes adjudications at the rate of two a month (WTO, 2000b; WTO, 2006). As with any legal system, its regulatory force has extended beyond those cases actually referred to it. Its decisions communicate a system of rules and so influence practical decisions on investment, as well as shaping national regulatory decisions. For example, national government decisions are framed with reference to anticipated WTO rulings by officials anxious to avoid obvious clashes which they would lose in the disputes procedure.

The WTO regime emerged from the complex negotiations of the Uruguay Round (Dhanjee and de Chazournes, 1993), largely as a result of the interplay of EU and US interests which were brought to a head very late in the negotiation process. This negotiation evolved in a way that allowed other actors, even powerful, well-informed, developed world actors such as Australia and Canada, very little scope to influence the late-night rush of bargaining.

Lawyers have since prospered hugely on the consequential uncertainties. Power and knowledge were brought together in new ways in the hands of those states and business interests which were already the most powerful in the global system. My earlier assessment imagined the particular difficulties this would cause in marginalizing not only developing states, but also social movements and peoples across the international system, while creating circumstances favouring the interests of global corporations. My central argument still stands. Intellectual property law has not only assumed a great importance in international trade; it has also become a mechanism whereby power relations in international relations as a whole are reproduced, contended and enforced. The transition from the GATT to the WTO was said to herald a new agenda of cooperation, where agriculture, clothing, investment and financial services, intellectual property and piracy issues were all added to the GATT agenda of trade, tariffs and non-tariff barriers, which related mainly to manufactured goods. But this so-called cooperation was always unequal at best. The WTO has had at least one unquestionable impact: its membership, now 151 countries, is more than twice that of the GATT (WTO, 2006). But this may imply that it has succeeded in incorporating within its reach many more countries, rather than that they have wholly willingly accepted its jurisdiction. One way to judge the new WTO system is to ask whether, as against this incorporation, it is capable of producing a remedy for the loss of power, knowledge, traditional culture and economic independence which peoples facing it report (Seyoum, 1993).

My previous argument failed to take account of a number of problems, not least the need to conceptualize power more effectively (see below). Equally, although I touched on the question, I neglected the importance of specific practices of intellectual property regulation in the global arena for developing societies and indigenous peoples. Indigenous peoples live in the developed world (e.g., Canada, Australia, New Zealand) as much as in developing societies. The new intellectual property system provides powerful resources for those large companies, which tend to own most globally traded intellectual property assets. But does it provide any redress at all for the weak actors or small players in the system? The examples which we might turn to suggest that the system has a deep inability to provide effective redress for those who most need it. The result in the short term may well be a yet greater concentration of power in the advanced industrial economies. But such a concentration of power is likely to produce new forms of resistance, including different forms of piracy and quasi-violence (such as hacking or the spreading of computer viruses), as well as actual violence against those who would enforce what is seen as a manifestly unjust system. The enforcers are very often the governments of the marginalized or developing countries acting in effect on behalf of the WTO system. In short, my earlier arguments were not sufficiently pessimistic about the disorderly effects which the new WTO regime would have in the longer run, and failed to recognise sufficiently strongly how far excluded groups and societies would be further marginalized by its impact.

Mike Moore, Director General of the WTO, argued that 'although no-one can claim that the WTO's dispute settlement system compensates for unequal power distribution in the world, it . . . gives small countries a fair chance they otherwise would not have to defend their rights' (*Times of India*, 6 June 2000). The quotation is interesting first because it concedes the potency of structural forms of domination against which developing countries and marginalized peoples struggle. But second, it lodges the claim that the WTO disputes procedures are in effect the least worst system those groups and those people could hope to find. The 'fair chance' they receive is, however, of very dubious fairness.

Conceptions of power in globalization processes

To give an account of the impact of the globalization of knowledge, we need a clear conception of power. The idea of power in the study of international relations, always central
but always contended, still tends to emphasise physical resources and material structures,
whether in versions which look to the balance of power for their explanation or those,
Marxist or neo-Marxist, which look to global production and exchange structures (Hirst,
1998). Psychological factors and ideology find a place in some theories, including classical
sources such as Clausewitz's (1976: 149–52) writing on war, liberal institutionalism and neo-
Gramscian theory. But when writers, whether liberal or postmodern, look to ideas, com-
municative power and discourses, they then tend to neglect the materiality of key power
relations (1993). In particular, the conception of power in post-structuralist writing is weak.
Poststructuralists, including Bourdieu, Foucault, Habermas, Giddens and hermeneutic
writers who draw on Wittgenstein or Gadamer in varying degrees, all write about power.
Yet the poststructuralist literature embodies disagreements about power (cf. Foucault,
1982), and fails to draw together an account able to recognise *both* the materiality *and* the
symbolic and discursive character of contemporary power relations.

More than any other poststructuralist writer, Pierre Bourdieu (1982, 1993) has illustrated the importance of forms of symbolic power in constructing the fabric of social power.
Foucault engages with the power of discourse (Rouse, 1994), whereas Habermas, partly in
overlap with Foucault and partly in dispute with him (Ashenden and Owen, 1999), puts
more emphasis on forms of communication and the ways in which these shape processes of
legitimation. The language of any social relations incorporates dimensions of symbolic
power, including the social relations embodied in dress (what is fashionable or not), music
(what is cool or uncool to listen to at a given moment) or the everyday practice of social
exchange. Bourdieu (1982, esp. chapters 1 and 6) sees more fundamental forms of symbolic
power as rooted in the ever-increasing professionalization of social relations. Professionals,
he argues, are primarily manipulators of symbolic power, whatever else their apparent or
explicit roles may seem to be. They exercise this power through their special role as rulers
of the act of distinction: they exercise their taste and judgement on our behalf (Bourdieu,
1984). The people referred to here are often academics defining the social context of symbolic
power through their debates, television appearances and the definition of what is acceptable
or 'common sense', a term Bourdieu uses, drawing on Gramsci, to indicate a powerful but
generally unspoken hegemony of ideas. But policy-makers and academics combine together.
This is essential in the reproduction of what neo-Gramscian writers call hegemony, although
neo-Gramscians in particular pay insufficient attention to the symbolic forms of power that
Bourdieu examines (e.g., Cox, 1993). Bourdieu's argument is more than valuable: he highlights an essential dimension of power internationally as well as nationally. But he may also
overstate his case. For there is at the same time always a material element to the process of
discriminatory arbitration. The act of discrimination itself creates value: if we want to buy
Madonna's underwear, own the bloody clothes of an assassinated rap star, or touch the piano
on which John Lennon wrote 'Imagine', we pay to own them or to see them. Their unique
status gives them a special value in commercial terms. Symbolic power creates unique value,
which may easily be commodifed. Knowledge may embody symbolic power in varied forms,
but it is never far removed from it, and knowledge power is not understandable divorced
from its symbolic face. Symbolic power and material power are conceptually quite distinct,
and Bourdieu gives insight into the former which we have lacked. But at the same time

symbolic power does not necessarily exist in isolation from the material. Each has a significance for the other, and it is important to recognize, following Bourdieu but also pushing his argument into dialogue with others writers on power, that symbolic and material forms of power *in interaction* shape social life at personal, interpersonal, collective and global levels. This is important particularly in the context of intellectual property disputes since the forms of knowledge which intellectual property involves clearly have, as the earlier discussion suggested, both material and symbolic forms of power and value.

Indigenous peoples

In June 1999, the US Association of Concerned African Scholars (ACAS) produced a paper on the new US Africa Growth and Opportunity Act (H.R. 2489). That legislation had been widely welcomed in the US and Africa as signalling a renewed interest by the Clinton administration in Africa after decades of neglect. But the ACAS working paper (Africa Scholars, 1999) suggested that this new interest was unfortunate: it led to an extension of conditionality, which would control governments and limit the potential of peoples to achieve autonomous development. The paper highlighted intellectual property rules as a means to deprive African societies of control over peoples' lives and resources. The new TRIPS agreement would do little to foster development, but would easily become a means of expropriating indigenous peoples' knowledge and communal experience.

The ACAS working paper is only one of many examples of protest against the impact of the TRIPS arrangements on indigenous peoples. Biopiracy, the patenting of genetic information gleaned in the developing world by developed world corporations which then try to enforce their patents and licences on the original peoples who held that knowledge in a popular form, has become one of the key points of protest against the new WTO rules. Examples range from the neam tree in India to Amazonian and Australasian indigenous medicines. But the principles of procedure in the disputes panels mean that allegations of biopiracy simply do not count as relevant evidence against corporate greed. The rules and procedures seem to be designed to ensure that large companies can act unaccountably. A huge variety of websites asserting opposition to this suggest that new forms of exclusion have provoked a new international organization of resistance through electronic networking ('enetworks'). Tom Goldtooth of the Minnesota Indigenous Environmental Network argued that 'the WTO undermines indigenous peoples' power over their own land and natural resources' and that actions by major corporations amounted to 'theft of our genes and our knowledge' (IEN, 1999; Marinova and Raven, 2006). The indigenous peoples' arguments against the WTO capture both the material and the symbolic faces of power engaged in intellectual property disputes in graphic forms. They also demonstrate the importance of evaluating the impact of WTO procedures from the viewpoint of peoples and communities and not only through the lens of state perspectives.

Pharmaceuticals and chemicals

Other disputes illustrate the complexity of TRIPS-related disputes and their capacity to redefine domestic politics and economic space. India has been one of the most active opponents of aspects of the TRIPS agreements. In the course of the WTO negotiations, India, jointly with other states, won a transitional period for developing economies in which they could adjust to the new regime, holding that an immediate shift to the new rules would impair the competitiveness of their emerging high technology sectors to the advantage of established multinational companies. In pharmaceuticals and agricultural chemicals, this is an especially important issue since India has a large market and the intellectual and industrial capacity to become an even more significant producer in its own right. For their part, the EU countries need to be able to exploit those sectors in which they in turn hold a lead, including pharmaceuticals and fine chemicals. To be able to generate income to achieve a strong market position, both India and the EU need sales, and to get sales they need market control. The result was argued in a case before the WTO disputes panel (WTO, 1998). It was claimed for the EU that India's transitional measures, even before the full adoption of WTO standards, nonetheless needed to respect key aspects of WTO principles. India, it was said, had failed to allow this in its domestic legislation. For its part, India claimed that the EU's interpretation of its obligations was over-intrusive in principle and unworkable in detail. India claimed she had met the obligations she believed she had undertaken. EU lawyers demonstrated to the satisfaction of the panel that she had not. In particular, Indian domestic law should recognise the authority of EU patents to create exclusive marketing rights in India for EU producers (WTO, 1998: 67). This case emphasizes the danger of automaticity of WTO procedures for developing countries, and largely prevents a defence of the need for 'transitional arrangements' as countries move to adapt to WTO demands.

In a separate dispute in the early 2000s, developing countries have raised vital issues about the need for cheaper drugs to combat growing problems with diseases including HIV/AIDs and resistant forms of malaria and tuberculosis. Large global multinationals had done the research and held patents for potentially important drugs, but they were unwilling to allow their expensively researched products to be made cheaply under licence in developing countries. Those countries had the capacity and ability to make the drugs. They also had a possible choice of making them illegally, a threat which made the pharmaceutical majors pause. A large coalition of developing country interests backed by NGOs and some developed country governments pressed for a change in the intellectual property rules to allow the production of drugs under licence for the use of poorer people in the developing world (Kremer, 2002; Abbott, 2005). Following pressure from a group of African states led by Nigeria and South Africa, and joined by others including India, a temporary agreement was reached through the WTO by June 2005. This was in turn replaced by a more permanent agreement in December which was ratified in 2006 (*Financial Times*, 6 December 2005 and 20 June 2006). This is a significant step since the agreement represents a major derogation from the 'norm' of TRIPS agreements, although it is not seen as a precedent for other areas, and many NGOs rightly complained that access to medicines would still be restricted. But in the 2005 pharmaceuticals' agreements, the WTO has provided benefits, which will reach at least some of the people suffering from these major diseases, although many others will still not be able to get treatment. This does suggest something less pessimistic than the largely negative view the earlier edition of this chapter suggested, although it does not wholly overturn that argument.

The dimensions of power in TRIPS

This discussion is also a debate about power in global society. But writing on intellectual property generally fails to recognise the importance of the intersection of quite distinct forms of power which TRIPS disputes invoke. There is a conflict between material, ideational, discursive and symbolic forms of power here which runs through post-liberal and post-structural traditions of explanation. If we try to understand the interaction between symbolic and material forms of power, we can develop a sharper sense of what globalization processes mean: not just that they redistribute power to the already powerful, but also how this can occur and what the texture of the relationships involved might be.

The TRIPS case is an important but depressing one. For it illustrates a raft of issues in international political economy with compelling force. It offers a suggestive analysis of the concentration of power in largely unaccountable hands, including international adjudication panels such as the WTO disputes machinery. The aim of the new WTO procedure was to replace uncertain settlements with binding determination. Its procedures handicap many governments. But, much more than governments, it excludes many people, including social movements and indigenous communities. It is hardly surprising that these excluded groups seek to resist unacceptable outcomes, and hardly unnatural that they should collaborate together to do so. But as these struggles continue, it is increasingly hard to talk about a developing country bloc in TRIPS negotiations: different NGOs and different countries take contrasting positions. For example, Brazil has sought to conciliate between the EU and developing countries in 2005–6, while India has vied for leadership of the developing country group by pursuing a rather more radical agenda, and China has adopted a less activist pose, trying to learn how to use the system and to adapt to its procedures before taking many initiatives of its own (Wang, 2006). And different NGO groups, such as War on Want, have taken more radical positions on indigenous knowledge while other groups have been more conservative. At the same time, as in other areas of global governance, authority to make policy has passed between private (i.e., non-state) agencies, and consultancies have become increasingly important. As a recent paper on EU trade policy suggests, trade talks are no longer simply exchanges of market access between different parties: they have become exchanges of market access on the one side for regulatory power on the other (De Bièvre, 2006). Larger developing countries gain access to markets, to regulatory power, or both, as part of complex deals, while smaller developing countries get less and less. Globalization in trade as in other aspects is, as my arguments claimed in the earlier editions of this volume, a sophisticated differentiation of actors and structures, and not merely a homogenization of all differences.

This discussion also provides insights into the changing role of the state and the changing agenda of trade diplomacy. It illuminates the involvement of NGOs in global politics, and it suggests arguments about the role of global networks in challenging established power. In terms of the study of international relations, the case is a valuable one. But in terms of the experience of the people who are the objects of this politics, not only those in developing countries but also indigenous peoples across the world, in Canada or the western isles of Scotland, as much as those in Amazonia or south Asia, the example of increased powerlessness is not much vitiated by a great deal of activity on the Web and in the streets. For that activity, however much it may have exposed the drama of what the new agreements are bringing, so far shows little evidence of actual achievement in the face of the embedded neoliberal principles in the WTO agreements and procedures.

References

Abbott, F. M. (2005) 'The WTO medicines decision: world pharmaceutical trade and the protection of public health', *American Journal of International Law*, 99, 317–58.

Africa Scholars (1999) *US Africa Growth and Opportunity Act (HR 2489): A Briefing Paper by the Association of Concerned Africa Scholars*, 6 June, online at www.globalexchange.org/economy/rulemakers/AfricaScholars.html.

Agnew, J. and Corbridge, S. (1995) *Mastering Space: Hegemony, Territory and International Political Economy*, London, Routledge.

Anonymous (2006) 'Euro-American bid to tackle rise in intellectual property piracy', *Professional Engineering*, 28 June, 8–9.

Ashenden, S. and Owen, D. (eds) (1999) *Foucault contra Habermas: Recasting the Dialogue Between Genealogy and Critical Theory*, London, Sage.

Berners-Lee, T. (1999) *Weaving the Web*, New York, Harper Collins.

Bourdieu, P. (1982) *Ce Que Parler Veut Dire*, Paris, Fayard.

———. (1984) *Homo Academicus*, Paris, Éditions de Minuit.

———. (1993) *The Field of Cultural Production*, ed. and trans. R. Johnson, Cambridge, Polity.

Boyer, R. and Durand, J-P. (1997) *After Fordism*, trans. S. Mair, Basingstoke, Macmillan.

Clausewitz, C. von (1976) *On War*, Harmondsworth, Penguin.

Cox, R. (1993) 'Gramsci, hegemony and international relations: an essay in method' in S. Gill (ed.), *Gramsci, Historical Materialism and International Relations*, Cambridge, Cambridge University Press, pp. 49–67.

De Bièvre, D. (2006) 'The EU regulatory trade agenda and the quest for WTO enforcement', *Journal of European Public Policy*, 13, 851–66.

Dhanjee, R. and de Chazournes, L. B. (1993) 'Trade related aspects of intellectual property rights: objectives, approaches and basic principles of the GATT and of intellectual property conventions', *Journal of World Trade*, 24, 3–15.

Farrands, C. (1996) 'The globalization of knowledge and the politics of intellectual property: power, governance and technology' in E. Kofman and G. Youngs (eds), *Globalization: Theory and Practice*, London, Pinter, pp. 175–90.

———. (1997) 'Interpretation of the diffusion and absorption of technology: change in the global political economy' in M. Talalay, C. Farrands and R. Tooze (eds), *Technology, Culture and Competitiveness: Change the World Political Economy*, London, Routledge, pp. 75–89.

Ferguson, A. (1966) *An Essay on the History of Civil Society*, Edinburgh, Edinburgh University Press, reprint of 1767 edition.

Foucault, M. (1982) 'The subject and power' in H. Dreyfus and P. Rabinow (eds), *Michel Foucault: Beyond Structuralism and Hermeneutics*, Brighton, Harvester Wheatsheaf, pp. 214–32.

Gill, S. (ed.) (1993) *Gramsci, Historical Materialism and International Relations*, Cambridge, Cambridge University Press.

Hirst, P. (1998) 'The eighty years' crisis: power', *Review of International Studies*, 28, 133–48.

IEN (1999) International Environmental Network website at www.alphacdc.com.ien/intellectual_property.html.

Kremer, M. J. (2002) 'Pharmaceuticals and the developing world', *The Journal of Economic Perspectives*, 16, 67–90.

Lefebvre, H. (1991) *The Production of Space*, Oxford, Blackwell.

Marinova, D. and Raven, M. (2006) 'Indigenous knowledge and intellectual property: a sustainable agenda', *Journal of Economic Surveys*, 20, 587–605.

May, C. (2000) *A Global Political Economy of Intellectual Property Rights: The New Enclosures?* London, Routledge.

Ohmae, K. (1990) *The Borderless World*, London, Fontana.

Polyani, K. (1957) *The Great Transformation: The Political and Economic Origins of Our Time*, Boston, Beacon Books.

Ricardo, D. (1973) *The Principles of Political Economy and Taxation*, edited and introduced by Donald Winch, London, Dent.

Rouse, J. (1994) 'Power/Knowledge' in G. Gutting (ed.), *The Cambridge Companion to Foucault*, Cambridge, Cambridge University Press, pp. 92–114.

Sennett, R. (2006) *The Culture of the New Capitalism*, New Haven, CT, Yale University Press.

Seyoum, B. (1993) 'Property rights versus public welfare in the protection of trade secrets in developing countries', *International Trade Journal*, 7, 341–59.

Strange, S. (1994) *States and Markets*, 2nd ed., London, Pinter.

———. (1997) 'The problem or the solution? – Capitalism and the state system' in S. Gill and J. Mittelman (eds), *Innovation and Transformation in International Studies*, Cambridge, Cambridge University Press, pp. 236–47.

Taylor, P. (1996) 'The modern multiplicity of states' in E. Kofman and G. Youngs (eds), *Globalization: Theory and Practice*, London, Pinter, pp. 99–108.

Wang, Y. (2006) 'China in the WTO: a Chinese View', *China Business*, October–September, 42–50.

Weiss, L. (1998) *The Myth of the Powerless State*, Cambridge, Polity.

World Trade Organization (1998) *India-Patent Protection for Pharmaceutical and Agricultural Chemical Products: Complaint by the European Communities and their Member States*, Report of the Panel, WT/DS79/R, August, Geneva, WTO.

———. (2000) *WTO Annual Report*, Geneva, WTO.

———. (2006) *WTO Annual Report*, Geneva, WTO.

CHAPTER 18

The Multimedia Industry

Networks and Regional Development in a Globalized Economy

Gerhard Fuchs

Introduction

At the interface of economic and social sciences, a specific type of research literature has developed emphasizing the embeddedness of economic activities in social contexts (see for example, Granovetter, 1985; Grabher, 1993a; Amin and Thrift, 1995; Staber, 1996b; Uzzi, 1996; Dobbin, 2004). This literature is concerned with identifying the various institutional mechanisms by which economic activity is coordinated. It attempts to understand the circumstances under which the various mechanisms of coordination are chosen, and is interested in comprehending the logic inherent in the different coordinating mechanisms. The importance of networking of economic actors is one of the central topics in these discussions (Hage and Alter, 1997). Embeddedness in social structures may explain why network arrangements may persist in situations where, at first glance, other forms of governance (such as open markets) may appear more efficient. Mutual trust, social expectations and the forces of tradition can be powerful mechanisms for overriding opportunistic motives and preventing the breakdown of cooperative relationships. So far there is little comparative research on the specific effects of certain types of networking of actors (Smith-Doerr and Powell, 2005). Moreover, technological progress and changes in the global economic system cause us to analyze the effects of certain network-like ties over and over again. In other words and following Granovetter (1973), questions about which ties are strongest and their impact have to be constantly readdressed in relation to the specific object of research.

If we analyze, for example, various sectors of industry, the answers will be different. In this chapter, I discuss the importance of network ties for one specific sector of industry: multimedia. Multimedia is generally considered to be a future-oriented and still emerging industry. I look at the development of this sector from the perspective of economic regions. The research question is: what kind of interorganizational ties of multimedia firms within a certain region are most likely to favour the development and growth of a multimedia cluster?[1] I focus on the difference between intraregional and extraregional ties. This question should be seen against the background of a scientific as well as policy-oriented discussion on the significance of globalization and regionalization for the development of economic regions.

There are two main arguments and each one describes certain kinds of ties as crucial. The first is a 'regionalization thesis'. This is often used in research on industrial districts. It emphasizes the importance of quantity and quality of intraregional networking, not least as a means for protecting one region against the effects of globalization. The second is the so-called 'globalization thesis', which has been gaining in popularity. According to this perspective, the embeddedness of economic flows in regional networks can be expected to decrease in importance with a resultant process of disembedding from regional contexts. But at the same time, global kinds of ties become increasingly important within the context of a globalized economy.

The regionalization and the globalization theses are frequently discussed as contradicting one another, or their relationship is treated as a 'paradox' (see Boekholt and van der Weele, 1998; Huggins, 1997). The assessment presented in this chapter is different. It is that the medium- and long-term development of regional economic areas is dependent on a combination of *both* regional and global ties. Without any doubt, there are conflicts between regional and global ties, but assuming a fundamental contradiction is misleading.

I begin by discussing the strengths and weaknesses of regional and global ties. Then I cover the different kinds of regional and global ties, and their meaning for the development of economic areas in general, and for multimedia clusters in particular. Finally, I present my conclusions.

Strengths and weaknesses of regional and global ties

Regional ties

Pointing out the importance of the regional context for economic development is nothing new. The basic argument can be traced back to the work of Marshall on industrial districts from the late 1890s. Yet this regional context was given little attention (Scott, 1995) until the late 1980s when the rise of 'neo-regionalism' began. The neo-regionalist research perspective consists of various approaches. In the beginning, there were studies on industrial districts of the so-called 'Third Italy' with their distinct pattern of flexible specialization among mainly small companies. Later, regions with similar characteristics were found in other areas, i.e., Baden-Wuerttemberg (Piore and Sabel, 1984; Pyke and Sengenberger, 1992). At the same time, the concept of an 'innovative milieu' developed (Aydalot and Keeble, 1988; Camagni, 1991). This depicted a complex network of social relations within a limited area, promoting the capacity of the respective region to learn and innovate (Camagni, 1991: 3). Related arguments for the importance of the regional level in the development of economic systems, especially its capacity to support the generation of innovations, can be found in the literature on innovation systems, particularly in the literature on regional innovation systems (Braczyk, Cooke and Heidenreich, 1998; Asheim and Gertler, 2005). Finally, works of Porter (1990), Krugman (1991), Enright (1996), Fischer (1998) and Preissl and Solimene (2003) analyse the conditions under which spatially concentrated *industrial clusters* with high productivity and competitiveness develop.

These approaches are partly complementary, but they are also contradictory to a certain extent. This cannot be discussed in detail in this context. Nevertheless, there are some basic arguments that can be extracted which are useful for the present discussion. A testable hypothesis could be the following: if there is a close network between companies and institutions in a certain region, the competitiveness and economic development of this region will be promoted. To emphasize the positive effects of networking it can be said – based on the standard literature on this subject – that regional networks

- enable companies to use a common pool of resources (qualified labour, infrastructure, services of supporting institutions, etc.)
- help companies to exchange knowledge and to generate innovations; most important are 'technology spillovers' among the companies in a region and the possibility to pass on 'tacit knowledge' via networks (Bramanti and Maggioni, 1997: 323)
- help them to be in close contact with clients or users and their special requirements
- facilitate a division of labour so that highly specialized firms can combine and pool competences.

The neo-regionalist research perspective thus discusses the strengths of regional networks or intraregional ties. There has been a lot of criticism concerning this work. Some authors have found fault with the research's emphasis on a few outstanding and successful model regions and its neglect of 'normal regions' with less favourable conditions. It has also been argued that the regions were frequently described using a neo-regionalist vocabulary, without an exact empirical verification of whether there were actually important characteristics to be found, like a structure of predominantly small firms and intensive cooperation between companies (Markusen, 1996; Staber, 1996a: 23; Sternberg, 1998).

Without any doubt, this criticism is partly justified and supports the need for a more differentiated treatment of neo-regionalist arguments. Obviously, the strengths of intraregional networking are only effective under certain regional and sectoral conditions. Regional networking seems to be advantageous

- in sectors with a high amount of small- and medium-sized companies (SMEs). In these circumstances, flexible cooperation with other firms may even replace – at least partially – the advantages of organizational size. Larger companies in contrast can hold necessary competences within their own organization (Almeida and Kogut, 1997).
- in sectors with a high rate of technological change and innovation. Works on innovation research (Feldmann, 1994; Almeida and Kogut, 1997; Gehrke and Legler, 1998) prove that especially research- and knowledge-intensive industries show a tendency for spatial concentration.
- in sectors where predominantly customer-specific rather than standardized products are manufactured, and where the close contact between manufacturer and customer is particularly important (Scott, 1988).

As will be shown below, these conditions can – to a very high degree – be found in the multimedia industry. Thus the neo-regionalist approach may principally be applied to this industry and the strengths of regional ties are even characteristic for this industry.

With innovation becoming increasingly important for the success of regions, and considering the assumption that it is highly dependent on information and knowledge, networking seems to be a key facilitator. It is to be admitted that a precise definition of networks or networking is hard to find in the literature (Smith-Doerr and Powell, 2005). The appeal of the concept seems to stem exactly from the fact that it encompasses important relationships, which are difficult to capture in one definition. Networking capacity at a very basic level can be seen as the disposition of actors to collabourate and communicate to achieve mutually beneficial ends. Actors that network can be employees as well as employers, companies, associations, public funding agencies, research institutes and so on. But to what extent does the globalization thesis contradict the assumptions of the regionalist thesis?

Global ties

Many regions or sectors profit only to a limited degree from regional ties as emphasized in the neo-regionalist research. But there is also an even deeper conflict with the globalization thesis. The most crystallized version of this thesis can be found in various popular publications (Forrester, 1999). It appears in more moderate form in numerous publications by social scientists or economists (Thurow, 1997). Briefly summarized, the thesis argues that because of rapidly advancing globalization, economic structures and flows are increasingly disembedded from regional contexts, and regional embeddedness is losing importance. Companies act on a global level and the most globalized companies become key actors whose strategies will increasingly determine the possiblities for development of certain regions. For Ash Amin (1993: 288), the consequence is: 'The meaning of place is becoming defined within the hyperspace of global corporate activity.'

This perspective emphasizes the importance of global ties. Quantity and quality of intraregional networking are no longer crucial, but the integration of economic regions in worldwide networks is. The position of regions in the organizational structures and networks of *global players* determines the possibilities for economic development. Even the often analyzed *model regions* of the industrial district research come under pressure due to globalization (Fuchs and Wassermann, 2005).

The possible strength of global ties may be to counterbalance the lack of flexibility in regional structures. The strengths of a distinct regional network may change into weaknesses if they hinder the adjustment of regional economies to modified technological and economic conditions. This is also acknowledged by the neo-regionalist research perspective (see Grabher, 1993a on the Ruhr region). Regional economies frequently develop along stable trajectories. External influences are required to prompt departures from them. In this context, Camagni (1991: 3ff) sees the special function of innovation networks in the opportunity they provide for one innovative milieu to come into contact with another. Such contact enables the import of new technological possibilities, organizational models and commercial ideas into the system, as well protection from death by entropy.

For multimedia and other young growth industries in particular, this correlation is most significant. If one compares specific regions (Braczyk et al., 1999), it can be demonstrated that those with strong, mature industries do not necessarily have advantages in multimedia production structures. Networks in established industries do not guarantee a rapid growth in innovative future industries. Exogenous regional strategies aim at establishing competence in new sectors by attracting highly competent actors from outside. In other words, global ties have special strengths where regions want to tread new paths for which previous economic and structural development did not offer favourable starting conditions. Global networking provides links for regions to sectoral centres of excellence in research and development and extraregional markets. Examples for such strategies will be presented later in this chapter.

In a large part of the above-mentioned literature on the globalization thesis, the strengths of global ties are less emphasized than the problems and risks for economic regions. These relate to the restricted abilities of regions to be proactive and the fragility of global ties. Regional policies are forced to provide attractive conditions for global players, probably leading to a process of competitive dumping among the regions. Moreover, globalized companies with weak ties to a specific location will probably remove business units from a region at short notice. The more important these business units are for the economic performance and employment of a regional economy, the more problems arise due to decisions to remove operations from a region.

The combination of regional and global ties as a precondition for successful cluster formation

The neo-regionalist research perspective emphasizes the strengths of regional ties, referring to regional success stories, whereas the globalization thesis points to the importance of global ties in an increasingly internationalized economy. From the viewpoint of economic regions, however, regional and global ties must not be treated as alternatives. The most successful regions in one economic sector are embedded in well-functioning regional as well as global networks. There are four theoretically possible combinations for the intensity of regional and global networking (see table 1). The doubtlessly simplified and stylized[2] distinction is derived from the perspective of certain regions. From now on, I will only refer to specific sectors within regions, however. Based on this assumption, the following four-field table (see table 1) is constructed. Table 2 summarizes examples for the respective combinations from the literature.

Fragmented isolated regions

The situation of an economic area is particularly precarious if there is only little networking among regional companies and no significant integration in global networks. The situation of combined fragmentation (no intra-regional networking) and isolation (no integration in global networks) is generally accompanied by serious weaknesses in the regional economic productivity, particularly with regard to the generation and adaption of innovations. This combination may primarily be observed in connection with fundamental and radical changes, such as the situation of far-reaching social change in the transformation from a socialist to a capitalist economic system. Grabher's study (1995) on East German industry after reunification gives an example of a disembedded transformation economy. Informal networks of extreme importance in the (former) German Democratic Republic broke down and economic relations with other Eastern European countries were under pressure because of monetary union. The integration of this region in West German and global networks gradually developed, but the region's position within these networks has remained weak.

Table 1: Combinations of regional and global ties

Integration in global networks...	Regional networks....	
	... weak	... strong
... weak	I Fragmented isolated regions	II Isolated industrial districts
... strong	III Cathedrals in the desert	IV Global regions

Table 2: Examples from research

Integration in global networks...	Regional Networks	
	.... weak	..... strong
.... weak	I Different industries, former German Democratic Republic (Grabher, 1995) and other transformation economies	III Watch industry, Swiss Jura (Glasmeier, 1995); coal and steel industry, the Ruhr area (Grabher, 1993b)
.... strong	II Information technology, Boston/Route 128 (Saxenian, 1994); electronics industry, Scotland (Molina/Kinder, 1999)	IV Information technology and software, Silicon Valley (Saxenian, 1994); information technology, Taiwan (Kim/von Tunzelmann, 1998)

Isolated industrial districts

Regions that deserve the rank of an industrial district because of a distinct degree of intraregional cooperation, but whose integration in global networks is weak, are called isolated industrial districts. Technological discontinuities are one cause for the development of isolated industrial districts. The study of Glasmeier (1995) on the watch industry in the Swiss Jura may serve as an example. For a long time, this industry was a very efficient, productive and integrated complex of highly specialized companies deliberately cutting itself off through protectionist politics. In the 1970s, this complex did not adapt itself to the emerging quartz technology as quickly as possible and therefore soon lost its leading technological position. There are many more examples of declining industries, such as the coal and steel industry in the Ruhr area where formerly strong intraregional ties later turned into weaknesses (see Grabher, 1993b). The shipbuilding or textiles industry in a variety of European regions could serve as additional examples.

Industrial districts can presumably develop positively during longer periods of time without strong integration in global networks. Yet, without well-functioning global ties the risk increases for industrial districts to be surprised or put under pressure by technological and organizational innovations developed by other regions. The risk is high because isolated industrial districts frequently have a high degree of specialization leading to high productivity in a very limited field, which makes the adaptation to modified conditions difficult. In addition, there are limits to the growth of the domestic market for industrial districts that are difficult to overcome without ties to global players.

Cathedrals in the desert

The somewhat ironical label of *cathedrals in the desert*[3] is given to those regions that are closely integrated in global networks by prominent global players, but do not show the distinct intraregional integration and networking of companies, typical for industrial districts. Integration in global networks generally results from one or several large companies being represented in the region by the head office or other major company units. These globalized companies are not competing with an integrated endogenous economic sector in the region.

As described by Saxenian (1994), one example is the information technology industry in the Route 128–area near Boston. This region accommodates globalized companies, such as DEC, but does not show any distinct regional networking structures. According to Saxenian, this is the reason why the region some years ago had much more trouble than Silicon Valley in adapting to changing conditions on the world market. The electronics industry of Scotland is another example. According to Molina and Kinder (1999), a remarkable electronics industry cluster developed in Scotland based primarily on foreign direct investments. But the externally dominated companies are integrated into endogenous companies only to a very limited extent[4]. Particularly intensive kinds of cooperation referring to the generation and exchange of innovative knowledge are not very well developed.

From the viewpoint of the regions, the predominance of globally oriented companies produces desired as well as undesired consequences. Global contacts of companies provide at least the chance for a region to have access to external know-how, technological innovations developed elsewhere and foreign markets. How far this chance is really used is dependent on the position a region obtains in the location hierarchy of globalized companies. If the region is just an extended assembly line, conditions are of course not as favourable as if head offices, with strategic core functions such as research and development, are established there. True of both cases is that globally oriented companies remove capacities from a region earlier the less they are integrated in regional networks with other companies. The negative effects for a region with no distinct endogenous networks can be serious.

Global regions

Regions with a close integration in global networks as well as distinct intraregional integration are called 'global regions', referring to the notion of 'global city'[5]. Successful global regions are those whose networks incorporate an adequate supply of quality knowledge resources, along with the ability and willingness of local firms to make use of external sources of knowledge with a clear focus on innovation (Huggins, 1997). Silicon Valley is an example of this kind of region: it accommodates companies that are globally active and have a worldwide leading position in the information technology and software industries. Intensive and flexible forms of division of labour as well as cooperation between companies and the employees of the region (Saxenian, 1994) may arise simultaneously.

Regions with both distinct regional *and* global ties are predestined to take the part of a worldwide forerunner. Whereas regional ties facilitate competitive production clusters, global ties provide an input of external know-how and access to new markets, and prevent a cluster from becoming inflexible[6]. A combination of regional and global ties therefore offers the most favourable conditions for permanent development capabilities for regional economic systems.

A number of authors emphasize the importance of the combination of regional and global networks. Ernst (1999: 31) concludes from his study on the information technology industry: 'The dynamic coupling of domestic and international knowledge linkages is of critical importance for economic growth in a globalizing world'. Similar comments are found in Storper and Harrison (1991: 411), Freeman (1995: 21), Markusen (1996), Freeman and Soete (1997: 315) and Almeida and Kogut (1997: 102). The literature in general, however, is dominated by analysis focusing only on the study of networks on one specific spatial level. There is little literature that tries to analyze the interlinkages of networks on different levels.

Only a very small number of regions are in the favourable position of being designated as global. It is extremely difficult for other regions to catch up with these forerunner regions. This is most obvious in the discussion of exogenous and endogenous development models. An investigation by Kim and von Tunzelmann (1998) on the Taiwanese information technology industry is very informative in this respect[7]. The dynamic growth of this industry was possible because Taiwan has functioning local and national network structures, and achieved integration in the production networks of transnational information technology companies. According to Kim and von Tunzelmann, the alignment of these different network levels in Taiwan was decisive for success, although it was dependent on the coincidence of a number of favourable conditions, such as the possibility of using connections to the networks of native Taiwanese in the US information technology industry (Saxenian, 1997).

Another example of a successful regional catching-up strategy is the Irish software industry (Fuchs and Wolf, 1998), a process only possible because of numerous favourable conditions (i.e., financial aid from the European Union, an excellent educational level of the population and intensive governmental support for direct foreign investments). For a long time Ireland has been a *branch plant economy*, but during the past few years besides foreign companies (or partly because of them) a respectable endogenous potential has developed in the country's software industry. The strategy to develop a regional economic sector with the help of specific global ties was successful to a very large degree in Taiwan and Ireland. It is very difficult to reproduce these development paths in other regions. Global regions must expect serious problems only in connection with fundamental change, such as technological paradigmatic change.

Regional and global ties in the multimedia core industry

What does the proposed distinction mean for the multimedia sector? First of all, it can be said that at present this sector is at a formative stage so that any analysis of organizational forms can only be preliminary. The assumption regarding the importance of both regional and global ties may be used in principle despite this restriction (see table 3). But the positioning of regions in the four-field table in such a fluid sector is questionable and a shifting of assignments is very well possible, but given the strength of path dependencies also not very likely.

The multimedia sector has a very high number of young, small or even one-man companies in all regions. The fact that newly founded companies have more regional cooperation relations in comparison to older and larger companies (Almeida and Kogut, 1997) makes one expect fewer global ties in the multimedia sector than in other established economic sectors. Nevertheless, there are already significant differences to be observed between the regions developing a multimedia cluster, that allows us to use our four-field distinction in a meaningful manner.

Table 3: Examples of the multimedia core industry

Integration in global networks...	Regional networks .... weak	.... strong
.... weak	North Eastern England (Cornford, 1997)	Wales (Cooke/ Hughes, 1999)
... strong	Guetersloh (Hilbert et al., 1999)	California (Scott, 1998; Egan/Saxenian, 1999)

The generation of multimedia products and services is an economic activity for which clear-cut industrial structures are difficult to ascertain. During the late 1990s, a core group of multimedia producers came into existence, focusing on activities such as generating products and services for multimedia (so-called multimedia agencies, web designers, CD-ROM producers and others). Around this core, companies from numerous related industries (particularly print media, audio-visual media, advertising, software, etc.) have – besides other activities – become multimedia producers, forming the first periphery of the multimedia labour market. The second periphery consists of companies that use multimedia but are not active as producers (see table 4). The arguments in this chapter are concentrated on the multimedia core industry.

The emergence of an innovative economic sector such as multimedia is considered to be a fundamental and radical change, resulting in a combination of fragmentation and isolation (field 1 of table 3) in regions with unfavourable pre-conditions. With regard to Cornford's study (1997), this description is true for the region of Northeastern England. According to his analysis, the possibilities of integration in multimedia-related economic sectors are very unfavourable and there are comparatively few, mainly very small, companies producing multimedia. These firms do not show any intensive kind of cooperation and have only a few distinct contacts with extraregional or global market actors. They particularly lack a *hub firm* making extraregional contacts. Cornford (1997: 9) concludes 'that there is little chance of a substantial multimedia business emerging in the region'.

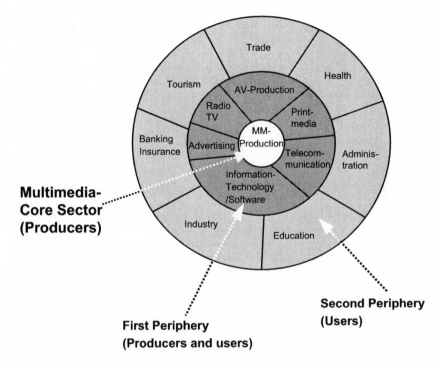

**Multimedia-
Core Sector
(Producers)**

**Second Periphery
(Users)**

**First Periphery
(Producers and users)**

Table 4: Multimedia producers and peripheries

Regions in which a cluster of networking young and small multimedia companies developed, but where there are no globally active multimedia companies, belong to field 2 of our four-field-table. This characterization applies to the region of Cardiff/Wales, for example. According to Cooke and Hughes (1999), a scene of predominantly smaller multimedia companies developed there open to regional cooperation. Until now a strong integration in global networks is obviously not typical for the multimedia industry in Cardiff. Yet another kind of local embeddedness was very fruitful for growth, such as the demand for content in Welsh language. The industry originated largely, though not entirely, in the media sector in spin-off firms from the broadcasting industry. The development of the industry is supported by numerous public initiatives that seem to play an important role for the stabilization of this mini-cluster. There is even a certain degree of multi-level governance offering support from the grass roots, and self-organization, through to the city and regional authorities and up to the European Union level. There are more examples from other regions where a specific demand for regional culture and language supported the development of a multimedia industry (e.g., Finland). On the one hand, these market niches provide favourable conditions for the growth of an industry. On the other hand, however, they also restrict the growth of these industries. Thus multimedia industries of field 2 will only be able to grow beyond a certain level if they succeed in achieving a more intensive integration in global networks.

As mentioned above, the majority of companies of the multimedia core sectors are small or medium-sized. Nevertheless, some regions within the multimedia sector can be identified corresponding to the pattern of 'cathedrals in the desert' (field 3). In this case, global players are large companies of the first periphery of the core multimedia sector and are being engaged in the multimedia core sector nowadays as well. The region around Guetersloh is an example (Hilbert et al., 1999). Bertelsmann, one of the worldwide leading media companies, has its head office there and company units based there are responsible for at least part of the company's multimedia activities. In its home region, Bertelsmann is the biggest employer. The Bertelsmann company units cooperate very intensively – for example in the form of customer-supplier relationships – but there are only limited business relations with other regional firms. Knowledge transfer from Bertelsmann to other companies in the region or personnel moving from Bertelsmann to other regional companies occurs rarely. This is the reason why the company's impact on the development of a regional multimedia cluster remains weak.

California (or more exactly the Bay Area around San Francisco and Southern California around Los Angeles) is a typical example of a multimedia region in field 4. Scott (1998: 161) describes the Californian multimedia sector as 'second to none in size, innovativeness and developmental potential' and claims that the region has assumed the 'position of worldwide supremacy'. Scott also emphasizes the 'double-sided local and global character of the in-dustry': close and intensively used networks of multimedia firms exist as well as a strong global orientation and integration of the sector. The multimedia industry tends to locate in dense-transaction intensive complexes made up of many small- and medium-size producers working together in tightly knit social divisions of labour. At the same time, the commercial reach of the industry is effectively worldwide. Therefore, Scott sees excellent development perspectives for the Californian multimedia industry even if he warns against complacency in view of other regions' efforts to catch up.

In Southern California, the multimedia industry seems to have developed in close con-nection with the Hollywood entertainment complex and the creative design culture existing there. On the other hand, the functional and locational proximity to the high-tech milieu of Silicon Valley could equally be used for the expansion of the industry and access to valuable assets.

The fact must be emphasized that – as shown in fields 2 and 4 of our four-field table – the development of regional production structures in the multimedia core sector seems to resemble to a high degree the characteristics of industrial clusters or industrial districts in general. This is remarkable because the central role of an advanced and network-integrated information and communication technology in this sector might have suggested that spatial proximity is more or less insignificant. Available evidence, however, suggests that spatial proximity to customers and cooperation partners is important for multimedia firms as well (Braczyk et al., 1999).

Conclusion

This chapter has demonstrated that successful economic regions can be characterized by certain constellations of global and regional network integration. The intensity of network integration is, however, different from sector to sector. What applies to the dominant sectors of a particular region might not be valid for other industries at the periphery. Limited capacity to integrate in the dominant structures of a region at any rate makes it difficult for new sectors to achieve visibility and excellence. Catching up with regions already advanced in certain areas is a process difficult to handle, as there are many preconditions for the management of it. Politicians must learn from experience how far they can promote the interaction of regional and global ties in multimedia production and elsewhere so that a region may profit from them.

Notes

1. An industrial cluster is a set of industries related through buyer-supplier and supplier-buyer relationships, or by common technologies, common buyers or distribution channels, or common labour pools. A regional cluster is an industrial cluster in which member firms are in close geographic proximity to each other (Enright, 1996: 191).
2. For the sake of simplicity, a four-field table is used to describe what is actually a combination of two continuous dimensions. Moreover, this depiction should not give the impression that regional and global ties as such are decisive for the potential for economic development of a region. Not taken into consideration are numerous factors that should also be noticed, i.e., exchange rates or basic political conditions.
3. Alternatively, regions in this field could be called, according to Hilbert et al. (1999) 'lonesome rider regions' or according to Markusen (1996) 'satellite platform districts'.
4. Turok (1993, 1997) and McCann (1997) discuss the regional integration of the Scottish 'Silicon Glen'. According to McCann's argumentation about a comparatively high degree of the regional embeddedness of the Scottish electronic industry, the asssignment in the four-field table should be revised.
5. See Sassen (1994). Huggins (1997: 103) uses the concept 'global region' for regions 'which are able to integrate geographically-restricted economies into the global web of industry and commerce'.
6. See the above-quoted argument by Camagni (1991).
7. According to Ernst (1999: 31), the Korean innovation system of information technology developed because of a 'co-evolution of international and domestic knowledge linkages'.

References

Almeida, P. and Kogut, B. (1997) 'The exploration of technological diversity and the geographic localization of innovation', *Small Business Economics*, 9, 21–31.

Amin, A. (1993) 'The globalization of the economy: an erosion of regional networks?' in G. Grabher (ed.), *The Embedded Firm: On the Socioeconomics of Industrial Networks*, London and New York, Routledge, pp. 278–95.

Amin, A. and Thrift, N. (eds) (1995) *Globalization, Institutions, and Regional Development in Europe*, Oxford, Oxford University Press.

Asheim, B. and Gertler, M. (2005) 'The geography of innovation: regional innovation systems' in J. Fagerberg, D. C. Mowery and R. R. Nelson (eds), *The Oxford Handbook of Innovation*, Oxford, Oxford University Press, pp. 291–317.

Aydalot, P. and Keeble, D. (eds) (1988) *High Technology Industry and Innovative Environments: The European Experience*, London, Routledge.

Boekholt, P. and van der Weele, E. (1998) 'Southeast Brabant: a regional innovation system in transition' in H.-J. Braczyk, P. Cooke and M. Heidenreich (eds), *Regional Innovation Systems*, London, UCL Press, pp. 48–71.

Braczyk, H.-J., Cooke, P. and Heidenreich, M. (eds) (1998) *Regional Innovation Systems: The Role of Governances in a Globalized World*, London, UCL Press.

Braczyk, H.-J., Fuchs, G. and Wolf, H.-G. (Hrsg.) (1999) *Multimedia and Regional Economic Restructuring*, London, Routledge.

Bramanti, A. and Maggioni, M. A. (1997) 'The dynamics of milieux: the network analysis approach' in R. Ratti, A. Bramanti and R.Gordon (eds), *The Dynamics of Innovative Regions: The GREMI Approach*, Aldershot, Ashgate, pp. 321–41.

Camagni, R. (1991) 'Introduction: from the local 'milieu' to innovation through cooperation networks' in R. Camagni (ed.), *Innovation Networks: Spatial Perspectives*, London, Belhaven, pp. 1–9.

Cooke, P. and Hughes, G. (1999) 'Creating a multimedia cluster in Cardiff Bay' in H.-J Braczyk, G. Fuchs and H.-G Wolf (eds), *Multimedia and Regional Economic Restructuring*, London, Routledge, pp. 252–68.

Cornford, J. (1997) 'The myth of "the" multimedia industry: evidence from the North East of England (and beyond)', unpublished draft paper, Newcastle upon Tyne.

Dobbin, F. (ed.) (2004) *The New Economic Sociology: A Reader*, Princeton, NJ, Princeton University Press.

Egan, T. and Saxenian, A. (1999) 'Becoming digital: sources of localization in the Bay Area multimedia cluster' in H.-J. Braczyk, G. Fuchs and H.-G. Wolf (eds), *Multimedia and Regional Economic Restructuring*, London, Routledge, pp. 11–29.

Enright, M. J. (1996) 'Regional clusters and economic development: A research agenda' in U. H Staber, N. V. Schaefer and B. Sharma (eds), *Business Networks: Prospects for Regional Development*, Berlin and New York, de Gruyter, pp. 190–213.

Ernst, D. (1999) 'How globalization reshapes the geography of innovation systems: reflections on global production networks in information industries', unpublished paper, prepared for DRUID 1999 Summer Conference on Innovation Systems, Kopenhagen.

Feldman, M. P. (1994) *The Geography of Innovation*, Dordrecht, Boston and London, Kluwer.

Fischer, M. (ed.) (1998) *Clusters and Regional Specialisation: On Geography, Technology and Networks*, London, Pion.

Forrester, V. (1999) *Economic Horror*, Cambridge, Polity Press.

Freeman, C. (1995) 'The "national system of innovation" in historical perspective', *Cambridge Journal of Economics*, 19, 5–24.

Freeman, C. and Soete, L. (1997) *The Economics of Industrial Innovation*, 3rd ed., London and Washington, DC, Pinter.

Fuchs, G. and Wolf, H.-G. (1998) 'The emergence of new industrial clusters – the role of regional governance in multimedia development: a comparison of California, Ireland and Baden-Württemberg', *Current Politics and Economics of Europe*, 8, 225–55.

Fuchs, G. and Wassermann, S. (2005) 'The regional innovation system of Baden-Württemberg' in G. Fuchs and Ph. Shapira (eds), *Rethinking Regional Innovation*, New York, Springer, pp. 113–51.

Gehrke, B. and Legler, H. (1998) 'Regional concentration of innovative potential in Western Germany', *Vierteljahreshefte zur Wirtschaftsforschung*, 67, 99–112.

Glasmeier, A. (1995) 'Flexible districts, flexible regions? The institutional and cultural limits to districts in an era of globalization and technological paradigm shifts' in A. Amin and N. Thrift (eds), *Globalization, Institutions, and Regional Development in Europe*, London and Oxford, University Press, pp. 118–46.

Grabher, G. (1993a) 'Rediscovering the social in the economics of interfirm relations' in G. Grabher (ed.), *The Embedded Firm: On the Socioeconomics of Industrial Networks*, London and New York, Routledge, pp. 1–31.

———. (1993b) 'The weakness of strong ties: the lock-in of regional development in the Ruhr area' in G. Grabher (ed.), *The Embedded Firm: On the Socioeconomics of Industrial Networks*, London and New York, Routledge, pp. 255–77.

———. (1995) 'The disembedded regional economy: the transformation of East German industrial complexes into western enclaves' in A. Amin and N. Thrift (eds), *Globalization, Institutions, and Regional Development in Europe*, London and Oxford, University Press, pp. 177–95.

Granovetter, M. (1973) 'The strength of weak ties', *American Journal of Sociology*, 78, 1360–80.

———. (1985) 'Economic action and social structure: the problem of embeddedness', *American Journal of Sociology*, 91, 481–510.

Hage, J. and Alter, C. (1997) 'A typology of interorganizational relationships and networks' in R. J. Hollingsworth and R. Boyer (eds), *Contemporary Capitalism: The Embeddedness of Institutions*, Cambridge, Cambridge University Press, pp. 94–126.

Hilbert, J., Nordhause-Janz, J. and Rehfeld, D. (1999) 'Between regional networking and lonesome riding: different patterns of regional embeddedness in new media's business in North Rhine Westphalia' in H.-J Braczyk, G. Fuchs and H.-G. Wolf (eds), *Multimedia and Regional Economic Restructuring*, London, Routledge, pp. 131–54.

Huggins, R. (1997) 'Competitiveness and the global region: the role of networking' in J. Simmie (ed.), *Innovation, Networks and Learning Regions?* London and Bristol Penn, Jessica Kingsley, pp. 101–23.

Kim, S.-R. and von Tunzelmann, N. (1998) 'Aligning internal and external networks: Taiwan's specialization', *IT. SPRU Electronic Working Papers Series*, paper no. 17, Brighton, Falmer.

Krugman, P. (1991) *Geography and Trade*, Cambridge, MA, MIT Press.

Markusen, A. (1996) 'Sticky places in slippery space: a typology of industrial districts', *Economic Geography*, 72, 293–313.

McCann, P. (1997) 'How deeply embedded is Silicon Glen? A cautionary note', *Regional Studies*, 31, 695–703.

Molina, A. and Kinder, T. (1999) 'From purposiveness to sustainability in the formation of multimedia clusters: governance and constituency building in Scotland' in H.-J. Braczyk, G. Fuchs and H.-G. Wolf (eds), *Multimedia and Regional Economic Restructuring*, London, Routledge, pp. 269–97.

Piore, M. J. and Sabel, C. F. (1984) *The Second Industrial Divide: Possibilities for Prosperity*, New York, Basic Books.

Porter, M. E. (1990) *The Competitive Advantage of Nations*, New York, Free Press.

Preissl, B. and Solimene, L. (2003) *The Dynamics of Clusters and Innovation: Beyond Systems and Networks*, Heidelberg and New York, Physica.

Pyke, F. and Sengenberger, W. (Hrsg) (1992) *Industrial Districts and Local Economic Regeneration*, Geneva, International Institute for Labour Studies.

Sassen, S. (1994) *Cities in a World Economy*, Thousand Oaks, CA, Pine Forge Press.

Saxenian, A. (1994) *Regional Advantage: Culture and Competition in Silicon Valley and Route 128*, Cambridge, MA, Harvard University Press.

———. (1997) 'Transnational entrepreneurs and regional industrialization: the Silicon Valley-Hsinchu Connection', paper presented at the Conference on Social Structure and Social Change: International Perspectives on Business Firms and Economic Life, Taipei.

Scott, A. J. (1988) *Metropolis: from the Division of Labour to Urban Form*, Berkeley, University of California Press.

———. (1995) 'The geographic foundations of industrial performance', *Competition and Change*, 1, 51–66.

———. (1998) 'From Silicon Valley to Hollywood: growth and development of the multimedia industry in California' in H.-J. Braczyk, P. Cooke and M. Heidenreich (eds), *Regional Innovation Systems*, London, UCL Press, pp. 136–62.

Smith-Doerr, L. and Powell, W. L. (2005) 'Networks and economic life' in N. J. Smelser and R. Swedberg (eds), *The Handbook of Economic Sociology*, 2nd ed., Princeton, NJ, Princeton University Press, pp. 379–402.

Staber, U. H. (1996a) 'Networks and regional development: perspectives and unresolved issues' in U. H Staber, N. V. Schaefer and B. Sharma (eds), *Business Networks: Prospects for Regional Development*, Berlin and New York, de Gruyter, pp. 1–23.

———. (1996b) 'The social embeddedness of industrial district networks' in U. H. Staber, N. V. Schaefer and B. Sharma (eds), *Business Networks: Prospects for Regional Development*, Berlin and New York, de Gruyter, pp. 148–74.

Sternberg, R. (1998) 'Innovative linkages and proximity – empirical results from recent surveys of small and medium-sized enterprises in German regions', Working Paper No. 98-01, University of Cologne, Department of Economic and Social Geography, Köln.

Storper, M. and Harrison, B. (1991) 'Flexibility, hierarchy and regional development: the changing structure of industrial production systems and their forms of governance in the 1990s', *Research Policy*, 20, 407–22.

Thurow, L. C. (1997) *The Future of Capitalism*, London, Nicholas Brealey Publishing.

Turok, I. (1993) 'Inward investment and local linkages: how deeply embedded is Silicon Glen?' *Regional Studies*, 27, 401–17.

———. (1997) 'Linkages in the Scottish electronics industry: further evidence', *Regional Studies*, 31, 705–11.

Uzzi, B. (1996) 'The sources and consequences of embeddedness for the economic performance of organizations: the network effect', *American Sociological Review*, 61, 674–98.

CHAPTER 19

Cyber-states and the 'Sovereignty' of Virtual Communities

Roy Smith

A key dimension of processes of globalization has been a revolutionary advance in telecommunications. The development of the Internet has been influential in numerous ways. It has enhanced the ability to transfer private capital, thereby contributing to the undermining of the fiscal autonomy of governments. It has also allowed greater freedom of personal communications and, as such, has impacted on broader social interactions. To date, the majority of these communications are not intended as a direct challenge to notions of national identity or the legal authority of governments, although some may be contrary to certain national laws on censorship. However, an interesting phenomenon is occurring involving the creation of websites which seek to claim statehood and elements of sovereignty. This chapter explores the legitimacy of these claims and, more importantly, the implications of these sites with regard to conceptions of statehood and sovereignty.

Two types of polities claiming sovereignty are considered. The first, illustrated by the Principality of Sealand, involves a physical space that has been occupied and its inhabitants are seeking recognition as an independent political unit with sovereign jurisdiction over this space. The second, illustrated by the Dominion of Melchizedek (DoM), poses a more complex dilemma having its origins purely in cyberspace. In attempting to enhance its claims to sovereignty, it has also made claims on physical space, some of which is already claimed by existing states. Prior to looking in more detail at these claims, it is necessary to briefly review notions of statehood and sovereignty. These will then be set within a broader context of an evolving global political economy and the manner in which certain aspects of these notions are being challenged.

Statehood and sovereignty

The issue of sovereignty remains a dominant concern within both the practice and study of international relations. Despite numerous challenges to the degree to which the sovereign state should remain the prime focus for the analysis of international relations, it continues to be recognised as a central, if not the only, player in the game. Here the question is not so much the role and/or autonomy of the state: rather, the nature of statehood and, thereby claims to sovereign status, will be considered.

Robert Jackson (1990) has explored the concept of quasi-states with particular reference to developing states. He argues that certain constraints prevent many of these states from claiming what might be regarded as a full set of characteristics for statehood and/or sovereignty. The distinction made here recognizes that statehood in the form of acknowl-edged territorial claim, resident population, flag, national anthem, diplomatic recognition by other members of the international community and so forth are no guarantee of auton-omy to act. Neo-colonial factors which impinge on 'nation-building', under-developed resource bases and disadvantaged positions in the global system of trade all act to undermine the autonomy of numerous states. Other related factors can arguably be said to also under-mine the sovereignty of more developed states. A more recent development in information technologies and communication systems has taken the question of sovereignty a stage further. We are now seeing the emergence of what have been described as 'cyber-states'.

In an interesting reversal of the dilemma Jackson has highlighted, a new form of quasi-state is populating one of the major tools of the process of globalization, virtual 'space'. As opposed to having an acknowledged claim of statehood but with limited sovereignty, the cyber-states have created an element of sovereignty for themselves and now seek the status of statehood from their 'peers' in the 'real' world. Understandably, with a notable exception to be discussed below, such recognition has been slow in coming. The cyber-states are not unique in claiming statehood/sovereignty. Any number of movements for self-determination have presented similar arguments, but with the significant difference of claiming disputed *physical* territory. The cyber-states are in largely uncharted territory where the major dispute is with their basic argument that they can have any claim at all.

Since the Peace of Westphalia (1648), sovereignty has largely been viewed within a legalistic framework regarding legitimate authority over a designated territory. Growing interdependence between states, the free-flow of capital, transboundary pollutants and multi-centred production processes have all contributed to a reassessment of the parameters of sovereignty. Yet despite these challenges, the issue of sovereignty remains a guiding principle for all manner of international relationships. For the cyber-states many of the issues, which are challenges for traditional states, are either non-applicable, such as pollu-tion, or actively enhance their role, for example as conduits for financial services and other network-based transactions. As such, the increased number of such transactions and, to some extent, the broadening of uses made of electronic communications may give greater weight to some of the claims for sovereign status and identity.

Alan James has noted that when considering the various discourses regarding sov-ereignty a 'profusion of concepts is being paraded' (James, 1999: 457). He goes on to identify three key elements of statehood, implicitly given as a prerequisite for claims of sovereignty: territory, people and government. In reverse order, the cyber-states can reasonably claim a degree of government by virtue of the management of their websites and day-to-day running of their affairs. Possibly this may be challenged as a rather tenuous claim given that this type of governance may not be directly comparable with the running of a traditional state. The question of people can be considered within the context of the cyber-states who invite people to apply for 'citizenship'. This usually involves some financial transaction that provides the potential citizen with a passport and similar papers of identification. Again, such docu-mentation will only be of value if it is recognized as having legitimacy by other states, particularly in the case of travel documents. The third attribute, that of territory, is clearly the most contentious as cyberspace is, by definition, singularly lacking in physical territory.

Several of the cyber-states are attempting to cross the virtual boundary to enhance their claims to statehood/sovereignty by staking claims in the 'real world'. A notable example of this is the so-called Dominion of Melchizedek. This particular cyber-state complicates matters still further by claiming several existing territories, including part of the Northern Atolls of the Marshall Islands in Micronesia, Karitane, Clipperton and Malpelo Islands in Polynesia, a section of Antarctica and Jerusalem, which it claims as its original capital. This last claim refers to a religious dimension that gives greater depth than some other claims but, of itself, does not add any legal weight. These claims to existing physical territory are of interest as it suggests that the cyber-states themselves are aware of the need for a physical base. This may be for practical reasons as the hardware and personnel managing these sites do require being located somewhere. Ideally, this would be beyond the legal jurisdiction of any other state.

The claims for physical territory also complicate the broader question of the cyber-states' more far-reaching claims for statehood and sovereignty that are not based on territorial claims. Disputed claims to territory have been an ongoing aspect of the Westphalian system since its formation. At this level, the cyber-states operate in much the same way as other states. Moreover, there is some irony in this desire to claim physical territory while at the same time being at the vanguard of mapping evolving non-territorial community relationships. The dominant trend in the disciplines of geography and international relations in recent years has been to downplay physical characteristics of territories in favour of factors related to time and space compression, often associated with the use of the Internet. Strategic issues are still relevant in terms of availability of resources, distance from markets and as a factor in the conduct of armed conflict, although technological advantage may prove to be of growing relevance (Gray, 1999). Despite these caveats, the issue of 'place' is argued to have undergone a radical transformation in our increasingly globalized world.

Place and chips

The communication revolution associated with micro-chip processor technology highlighted a debate which had already commenced. One might argue that the development of nuclear weapons and superpower doctrine of mutually assured destruction would forever alter the relevance of place and related localized factors. However, during the latter half of the twentieth century, two distinct but related trends have emerged. First, technological developments have reduced the significance of physical location in many important areas of human activity. For example, multi-centred sourcing of resources for the production of goods has led to the growth of multinational business enterprises that draw on both material and labour resources from across the globe. Some of the transport costs of these resources are passed on to the consumer of the resulting manufactured product. However, apart from the very small percentage of economic activity that can be described as 'fair trade', the cost of resource depletion and environmental degradation tends to remain at the local level. As such, there is a growing separation between how resources are consumed, on a global scale, and the specificity of exactly where the related environmental impacts of this consumption are most keenly felt (Robbins, 2004: 37). Second, as economies develop, a growing number of workers are performing tasks that are based on the processing of digitalised information, This type of work is only constrained by access to relevant computing facilities (CSTB, 2001: 23). As such, local environmental factors are secondary considerations.

A common response to a degraded environment is to migrate to somewhere perceived to be offering better life opportunities. Overwhelmingly this has involved a shift from rural to urban living. This can also exacerbate degradation as rural areas continue to be exploited in order to serve the demands of growing urban populations. Attachment to place may also be a factor in this as the decline in self-sufficient subsistence lifestyles can result in a lowering of reliance on, and therefore appreciation of, one's natural environment. This does not mean that there cannot be an appreciation of an urban environment and lifestyle. However, such an environment is more likely to be subject to a greater degree of transformation and discontinuity. Connecting place with a sense of identity and allegiance is a fundamental aspect of the significance of locality, identity and issues of self-determination (Godkin, 1980).

The consequences of where one lives derive from more than physical environment. A class-based analysis would focus on social stratification and resulting positions of power and opportunity. This again highlights the complexity of attempting to distinguish physical factors from the more ambiguous issues of social position and identity. The cyber-states have simply taken this a step further by reducing the physical element to the minimum. Greater emphasis is placed on access to the necessary technology to participate in cyberspace, the means to invest relevant currency (in whatever form it might take) and the willingness to accept the norms and values of a given cyber-society. This may appear to be a relatively simplistic reduction of existing societies. Where governments are most challenged by the cyber-states is in their ability to circumvent existing state operations. This may be, for example, via e-commerce and the avoidance of paying tax on goods and services that would normally become government revenue. Such operations already exist and do not rely on any claims to statehood or sovereignty. An even greater concern for governments arises from the possibility that these cyber-states will be perceived as offering a deeper sense of identification for people than that associated with their current system of authority.

Post-territoriality and turbulence theory

Just as geography and international relations have debated the issues of place and space in recent years, this has been accompanied by various reassessments of the role and limitations of government authority. In particular, both governments and their citizens have had to acknowledge that the ability to act autonomously has declined. More accurately, the consequences of actions have become increasingly part of a broader scenario. Globalization has had the double effect of both developing a complex range of interconnections between states, yet also 'distancing' many citizens from their governments. This refers to a sense that governments can become perceived as having lost the ability to act on behalf of their citizens. Such feelings will be enhanced for those who are not benefiting from global economic trends.

Under such circumstances, it is not surprising that there is scope for other actors to jockey for position in the new world disorder. The post–Cold War period has seen a variety of theses suggesting the 'end of history' (Fukuyama, 1989) or the 'end of geography' (O'Brien, 1992). Certainly there is some credence in acknowledging that evolving technologies and an altered global strategic environment do suggest some sense of alteration. DiMuccio and Rosenau offer one of the more convincing formulations of an approach to make some sense of the current period of change. They describe a 'turbulence theory' with a particular emphasis on a relocation of loyalties. Drawing on neo-functionalist approaches, they argue that we are witnessing 'the simultaneity of integration and disintegration, fragmentation and aggregation, centralisation and decentralisation' (DiMuccio and Rosenau, 1992: 73). Undoubtedly this is an unsettling experience, and one that may fuel feelings of alienation, again depending on one's position in various relationships.

Ideas of turbulence can be seen as an internal dynamic of the Westphalian system. But DiMuccio and Rosenau argue that this system itself is under unprecedented strain. Although the cyber-states appear to be attempting to be accepted as a part of this system, they are actually an example of how far removed many governments have become in working effectively in an evolving global environment. Giddens (1990: 71) has discussed the dimensions of globalization in the familiar terms of the nation-state system, world capitalist economy, world military order and the international division of labour. He attempts to approach the individual experience of modernity by 'disembedding' it from the immediate local experience and explicitly acknowledge the global forces that shape this experience. This theme is explored in earlier work by Marshall Berman (1982), who also stresses the relationship between individuals, institutions and processes that are global in scale.

Cyber-states, regardless of their motives, can be seen as representing the latest development of the turbulence explicit within a yet to be determined post–Cold War order. The Internet has been instrumental in the evolution of a tri-polar global political economy based around the US, Europe and the Asia-Pacific region. 'Regionalisation' has been argued to be a more relevant term than 'globalization' when looking at how the international economy has developed in a very uneven manner (Jilberto and Mommen, 1998). Africa, the Middle East and the former Soviet Union are noticeable in having a lower rate of Internet connectivity than the three economically dominant regions mentioned above (see www.internetworldstats.com/stats). Castells (1996: 135) argues that for these latter regions it is not their statehood or even sovereignty that is under threat. Rather it is that within this emerging economic order they are becoming structurally irrelevant. At the turn of the millennium, it is undeniable that the dynamics of economies, and other forms of power, are shifting in new and diverse ways. This applies at both the state and non-state levels. The use of cyberspace is one 'terrain' upon, or within, which this spectacle is unfolding.

Increased use of the Internet could be argued to increase the power bases of some states, especially if one takes into account where many of the world's largest multinational corporations originate from and the revenue this generates for the home government through taxation and other indirect benefits. Others, as noted above, have found this process to increasingly marginalize them within the global economy. Cyber-states, whatever legal standing one wishes to perceive them as having, illustrate one of the key processes by which an emerging political and economic 'landscape' is developing. The next two sections looks at two types of cyber-state and consider the significance of their existence and the manner in which they are playing a role in this process.

The principality of Sealand

The first type of cyber-state is one that has a clear physical location, about six miles off the Suffolk coast. As such, it is, arguably, within the jurisdiction of the UK. Here is the first point of contention regarding sovereignty. The origins of Sealand date back to the Second World War and the creation of air and sea defences in the English Channel and the North Sea. Sealand, or Roughs Tower as it was originally named, was one such platform built and later abandoned by the military and subsequently claimed by the self-proclaimed Prince Roy of Sealand under the law of salvage on the high seas. At that time, 1967, Sealand was beyond the UK's three-mile limit of jurisdiction. Despite this, forces of the Royal Navy attempted to reclaim the base, prompting warning shots to be fired against them. This led to a High Court ruling that determined that Sealand was, indeed, beyond the jurisdiction of the court.

Having seemingly established that Sealand was an independent principality, Prince Roy continued to renovate the structure and live there with his family. Further controversy arose when, under the Law of the Sea Convention, the UK extended its territorial waters to the extent that Sealand fell within the redrawn boundary. Sealand countered by extending its own claims. However, this potential conflict has yet to be legally ruled upon. The UK government has given ambiguous messages regarding its view of Sealand, with the Foreign and Home Offices having their own dispute over who should deal with the matter. Until recently, the consequences of the establishment of Sealand were minimal. However, the expansion of Internet-based businesses and the growth of online financial transactions have altered this.

Sealand gained renewed publicity following investment from HavenCo, a company specializing in online financial services (McCullagh, 2000). HavenCo pre-empted concerns that they might be accused of conducting illegal activities by providing a list of services they would not be offering (www.havenco.com/law). The desire for confidentiality may be a matter for further speculation, but the central point here is that it was hoped investors would perceive Sealand as having a tradable resource – independence from a higher authority. In terms of territoriality and physical resources, it is difficult to imagine a political entity with fewer resources. Yet in the evolving 'Neteconomy', such independence has greater relative value, for some, than vast tracts of extractable minerals. The type of business being proposed on Sealand was similar to that occurring in numerous tax havens and off-shore banking locations around the world. All are less dependent on the characteristics of their physical location than on the rules and regulations relating to financial transactions. Again, this illustrates the relative decline in importance of geographical factors.

Despite the clear existence of Sealand in physical space, albeit a contested one, it has increased its significance and impact as an international actor by non-physical means. There has been no conquest of physical space, no territorial aggrandizement, yet Sealand has attracted what amounts to considerable foreign direct investment and subsequently raised its international profile. This question of profile is interesting as it may form another basis by which Sealand's legitimacy as an actor can be judged. Here, perhaps, a distinction needs to be made between actors claiming sovereignty and other non-state actors. For example, multinationals such as Exxon, IBM or McDonalds have high international profiles, yet they do not appear to aspire to claims of sovereignty or statehood. Similarly, campaigning groups such as Greenpeace or Amnesty International, who have also taken advantage of opportunities offered by the Internet, have significant international profiles. Sealand's claims are of a different order in that it strives for recognition of legitimacy from its potential peer group.

Governments generally recognize multinationals working for profit, or campaign groups working for humanitarian or environmental ends. If not in a formal sense at least their existence is not denied. Some governments may be critical or supportive of their actions depending on particular circumstances. They may be blocked or encouraged to operate within host states. Their profile and the way in which they interact with governments may be contentious should conflicts arise. Sealand and other states only acknowledged in cyberspace would appear to face a more difficult task in establishing themselves on the international stage. Even Sealand's apparent advantage in occupying an undeniable physical space does not guarantee acknowledgement of sovereign status. Despite this apparent disadvantage, Sealand has demonstrated characteristics of statehood by attracting investment, managing its affairs and operating separately from any higher authority. Of course, these operations could still be subject to challenge, most likely by the UK. Should the UK, perhaps in conjunction with other states wishing to monitor and regulate international financial transactions, insist upon imposing its authority on Sealand, further conflict over the legality of such a move seems inevitable. The stakes for pursuing such claims were raised with the relocation of HavenCo's operations to Sealand. Although the level and extent of investment in HavenCo was less than initially anticipated, to the point that one of the prime movers in this venture left the company within two years of moving to Sealand, it continues to maintain its claim as an independent political entity. When a fire broke out on the platform in June 2006, this reinforced the physical nature of the principality. For a very short period, the platform had to be abandoned. Despite this set-back, the 'royal' family are determined to maintain their claim to this territory.

In looking at Sealand, it appears that we are witnessing two levels of actorness in the international system. One is at the level of international recognition of legal entities acknowledged by other states to share their characteristics of statehood. The other has more in common with the operations of multinationals that are accepted as actors. With many multinationals now having annual turnovers well in excess of the gross domestic product of many states, there is a blurring of the hierarchies of the public and private realms.

The ability to act in a meaningful way in the evolving global economy will vary by issue area and over time dependent on a myriad of factors and circumstances. However, if one accepts that economic issues are increasingly dominating world politics, then it follows, at least in terms of the practicalities of autonomous action, that actors with stronger economies would appear to have greater freedom to act. Here actors could mean both state and nonstate. Yet there are numerous examples where the apparent dominance of a particular power has not always led to their successful pursuit of their agendas. The classic example is the United States' inability to win the Vietnam War. Here there was clearly much more at play than a simplistic equation of which side could mobilize the greater number of forces or level of technology applied to warfare. The US felt restrained in using the full capability of its military arsenal; it also had domestic political considerations in terms of a vocal and well-organized anti-war protest movement. Such are the political considerations that are enmeshed with a government's economic power. Arguably multinationals, other non-state actors and, perhaps, cyber-states are freer to act than governments.

Given that there appear to be constraints in the public realm of state governance, why should such status be deemed attractive? Sealand, Melchizedek and others with aspirations to statehood could continue to operate as a conduit for financial services, promote religious-orientated statements to the world and remain free of the more negative aspects of government office, from maintenance of infrastructure to welfare provision. In the case of Sealand, the physical proximity to the UK has meant that the issue of legal jurisdiction had to be addressed.

Having considered the situation of a very specific cyber-state that has an undeniable presence in reality, I now turn to those states that have created themselves from virtually nothing – those that have arisen without an obvious claim to physical territory.

Dominion of Melchizedek

Many websites exist claiming to be representing aspiring states. Some are more fanciful than others. The technology to set up such a site is now widely available and can be applied by simply creating a homepage and making exaggerated claims. Some relate to physical territory, others simply ask people to join a particular virtual community. The issue of statehood appears to become a problem once recognition from existing states is claimed or your operations are deemed illegal or unacceptable in some other manner.

The Dominion of Melchizedek (DoM) is one of the more established cyber-states. It has been in existence since 1990 and developed an extensive website with detailed arguments for why it should be considered a sovereign entity (www.melchizedek.com). Its claims to existing territories have in themselves ensured a degree of conflict and notoriety. Numerous financial dealings have led to the US Office of the Comptroller of the Currency issuing a statement warning people against doing business with banks claiming to be based in DoM. Such a reputation would appear to diminish any hope of DoM achieving legitimacy in the eyes of the international community. A rare exception to this is cited by DoM in the form of a 1993 letter from the President of the Central African Republic that formally recognizes the Dominion, adding an invitation to open a mission in CAR. A spokesman for the US State Department commented on this, suggesting that some states 'would recognise the State of Denial if it had a letterhead' (Leiby and Lileks, 1995).

How close does DoM come to meeting widely recognised criteria for statehood? A government structure is not only in place but appears quite extensive including an executive branch with a president, vice president, cabinet members and ambassadors. There is a legislative branch known as the House of Elders and a judiciary branch with a Supreme Court. Formally, the apparatus of government appears to be in place, even though it is fundamentally lacking credibility if other states will not acknowledge and interact with it. Such an arrangement may still be dismissed on the grounds of scale and the fact that there appears to be a marked lack of both territory and population to rule over. Yet other states are acknowledged despite relative smallness. There has been no international ruling on minimum size for a state to be viable. All that is lacking at the level of government is acceptance by more established states.

The issue of population is difficult to analyse, as DoM does not make accurate demographic data publicly available. What is known is that citizenship is offered. Significantly, one is not required to relinquish one's current citizenship status. Therefore, there is no loss and a potential gain in adopting citizenship. What exactly is gained is far from clear. There is anecdotal evidence that DoM passports have been accepted at some customs and immigration points, but these examples are sporadic. Again, this hinges on recognition and the according of legitimacy by other states. Sealand has issued similar documentation and extended this practice to issuing stamps and producing its own currency. Such symbolic gestures appear to be undertaken to establish a greater sense of 'presence'. All states are social constructions and the use of such symbols are indicative of how a state continually attempts to reinforce both its own identity and an image of itself which it presents to other states.

Citizenship of a cyber-state seems to have a very specialized role or meaning. On one hand, it might add to the claim to statehood. Sheer scale of numbers could mean that other states would have to, at least, acknowledge that something was occurring. Of course, many people do join international groupings, such as religious orders, but this does not mean that they are necessarily recognized as having a status other than their original nationality. For example, the Catholic Church could fall into this category where there is a sense of dual or coinciding identities. Members may hold particular convictions, but they are still subject to the laws of their home state. To have real meaning, those wishing to adopt cyber-citizenship would need to relinquish previous rights under their former citizenship. For many this would make the prospect much less appealing. DoM has explicitly made reference to groups that have either been marginalized in their home states or are involved in moves towards secession and self-determination. Its homepage identifies a broad range of such groups, including Basques, Kurds, Sikhs and Tamils. Again, this is controversial within the various states these groups are located.

Realistically each of these groups is more likely to continue to promote their own cause of self-determination within currently disputed territory. What advantage would be gained for them by showing some allegiance to DoM or any other cyber-state? The DoM homepage discusses 'new forms of international organisation and co-operation as a step towards an internationally united planet'. At one level, this may appear to reflect an idealized view of some form of global governance. The tone of much of the writing on this site is heavy in spiritual symbolism, biblical references and a sense of 'mission'. DoM has taken a step back from calling for statehood as it is commonly understood and now refers to itself as an 'ecclesiastical sovereignty'. The claims on territory and the desire for independent autonomy remain as strong as ever. The emphasis on the religious dimension may be to set itself apart from other cyber-states, or simply to widen its appeal to those of a religious bent.

DoM is interesting in terms of the manner in which it promotes itself as a political entity. Despite almost universal non-recognition from other states, it continues to act as though it is part of the community of states. For example, it has previously issued a declaration of war against France in protest at the latter's nuclear test programme. It has called for the bringing to justice of war criminals following the conflicts in former Yugoslavia and it has written to the UN Secretary General informing him of its willingness to accede to various international treaties. None of these actions have any formal weight without recognition from other states. Such acts offer engagement and clearly crave recognition and signs of legitimacy. To date, such appeals have largely fallen on deaf ears. There is little to suggest that this situation will change in the near future. On 3 September 2004, DoM claimed to have entered into a Treaty of Peace and Recognition with the government of Burkina Faso. Despite such rare examples of recognition of political legitimacy, DoM appears to be more widely thought of as being a cynical front for financial dealings that are deliberately withheld from international scrutiny and accountability.

Parallel polities?

Whilst exhibiting some elements of sovereignty and potential statehood, neither Sealand nor DoM have succeeded in convincing the vast majority of the world's governments that they should be considered as legitimate states. Yet it is impossible to deny their existence. In the case of Sealand, it is clearly a physical entity with a presence and significance via the financial transactions for which it is a conduit. Similarly, DoM's presence cannot be denied while it attempts to claim physical territory. Are governments hoping that the phenomenon of cyber-states will go away if ignored?

The extent to which cyber-states are expanding their presence on the Internet suggests that this is a trend likely to continue. This does not mean that they will necessarily challenge the role of traditional states and governments. Rather, they seem to symbolize increased usage of the Internet both in the realm of commerce and extending to involve aspects of identity and community building. As such, certain aspects of this might further undermine the level of control state governments have over their economies and their populations. Again this is a trend already identified regardless of the emergence of cyber-states. From a postmodern perspective, there does not have to be an oppositional relationship between states and cyber-states. Everard (2000: 125) makes this point when he says the polities in virtual space can be seen as 'an extension, rather than a different order of existence. . . post-modernists prefer the term "alterity" rather than difference, that is, an interplay among a matrix of alternatives, rather than the more hierarchical binary dichotomies that charac-terised modernist thought'. From this analysis the cyber-states are simply a logical progres-sion arising from the processes made possible by advanced communication systems.

Much of the debate surrounding cyber-states is missing their broader significance. It tends to focus on contested territorial claims and the possibility of fraudulent financial transactions. These are serious issues, but it is the manner in which these entities are oper-ating and what has become possible via Internet technology that is of even greater signifi-cance. This is what challenges the position of existing governments far more than the claims of Sealand or DoM. As more people become connected to Internet sites, they are entering a world of possibilities ranging from consumer choices to being subject to any number of political and ideological statements. It remains difficult to judge the extent to which this will have a direct impact on issues of social control for governments. There is an alternative argument that governments themselves are using the Internet, CCTV surveillance and related technologies to monitor their populations even more closely. While most commen-tators highlight the rise of civil society's engagement with communication technologies, it is often overlooked that governments are also embracing these technologies for their own purposes. For example, the monitoring of individuals has increased dramatically post-9/11. Security checks at international airports now routinely include retina identification scanning and such screening is likely to be extended to more personal information regarding religious or political affiliation and even sexual orientation (Hadley, 2004). Again this raises question regarding civil liberties and the relationship between governments and citizens.

Cyber-states are an example of the use of technologies that are connected to the under-mining of 'traditional' government autonomy rather than a direct challenge to such governments' authority, other than where there is a direct territorial dispute. Existing governments may deny the legitimacy of cyber-states, but they cannot deny the processes that cyber-states represent. As the global political economy evolves, it is these processes of Internet technology, the free flow of capital and, probably to a lesser extent, aspects of ideology, which will shape the political, economic and social landscape of the coming years. Cyber-states have played a role in further highlighting the possibilities of the Internet. How these are taken forward will be determined at both the level of government and also, crucially, in the ways an increasingly networked population chooses to make use of these possibilities.

It's life – but as you want to know it

The above examples have highlighted how individuals might, at least partially, attempt to circumvent dealing with their 'home' states by identifying with 'parallel' cyber-states. This phenomenon has been taken still further with the expansion of sites such as 'Second Life' developed by Linden Lab, where it is possible to buy an alternative identity, or even multiple identities, represented by computer graphics known as avatars. To some extent this might be seen as an extension of well-known role-playing games such as Dungeons and Dragons. Yet, the world of Second Life has now become so sophisticated that it is possible to buy 'land' on which to develop properties or businesses. Most intriguingly, the Second Life currency of Linden Dollars can now be exchanged for actual US dollar currency at the LindeX currency exchange (Knowledge@Wharton, 2005). This development, perhaps more than any other yet to evolve, demonstrates a clear interface between the virtual and the real. Ironically, as virtual worlds evolve to impact in more meaningful ways on the 'real' world, there are also concerns that the rise of cyber-interactivity may become a distraction, or possible avoidance technique, for real-world issues.

Rob Shields (2003) has produced some of the most wide-ranging and insightful writings on the implications of emerging virtual activity. This work goes beyond the issue of political sovereignty and questions of statehood. Rather, the emphasis is at the level of the individual and how patterns of work and entertainment activities are evolving. With reference to the latter, questions can be raised in respect of when apparently superficial activities, such as creating an imagined alternative identity in a virtual world, become an activity of greater significance. The scale of Second Life is worth noting. By November 2007, the number of Second Life 'residents' exceeded eleven million. Given this community was only launched in 2003, this represents a significant number. Moreover, there is every indication that as more people become aware of this phenomenon, and Internet connectivity also increases globally, membership is likely to continue to expand. October 2006 was the date when it was calculated that humans were officially 'overdrawn' in terms of eating into the capital of Earth's resources at a non-sustainable rate. A report published jointly by the Worldwide Fund for Nature and the Global Footprint Network identified this date as the tipping point for an environmental crisis that could only be redressed by radical remedial action (WWF/ GFN, 2006). Although some might say there is only a tenuous connection to be made between the two above events, it is worth noting that the rise of virtual activity is taking place within the context of the degradation of our physical environment.

The relationship between the virtual and the real has been explored here mainly in terms of political sovereignty. Both Sealand and DoM have utilized Internet technology to promote themselves as political entities. Neither has been successful in achieving widespread recognition as legitimate international actors. The Second Life phenomenon is different in that it is not attempting to be seen as an international actor. Rather it allows participants to interact with each other outside of their formal national identity. At a more extreme level, it also allows the creation of a preferred identity. In some respects, this may be a relatively harmless and benign activity. However, if an emphasis on vituality comes at the expense of awareness, interest and action to maintain the real world, this is clearly a cause for concern.

References

Berman, M. (1982) *All That Is Solid Melts into Air: The Experience of Modernity*, New York, Simon and Schuster.

Castells, M. (1996) *The Rise of the Network Society*, London, Blackwell.

Computer Science and Telecommunication Board (2001) *Building a Workforce for the Information Economy*, Washington, DC, National Academy Press.

DiMuccio, R. and Rosenau, J. (1992) 'Turbulence and sovereignty in world politics: explaining the relocation of legitimacy in the 1990s and beyond' in Z. Mlinar (ed.), *Globalization and Territorial Identities*, Aldershot, Avebury, pp. 60–76.

Everard, J. (2000) *Virtual States: The Internet and the Boundaries of the Nation-State*, London, Routledge.

Fukuyama, F. (1989) 'The end of history?', *The National Interest*, Summer, 3–18.

Giddens, A. (1990) *The Consequences of Modernity*, Cambridge, Polity.

Godkin, M. (1980) 'Identity and place: clinical applications based on notions of rootedness and up-rootedness' in A. Buttimer and D. Seamon (eds), *The Human Experience of Space and Place*, London, Croom Helm, pp. 73–85.

Gray, C. (1999) 'Clausewitz rules, OK?', *Review of International Studies*, 25, 161–82.

Hadley, C. (2004) 'Your personal passport', European Molecular Biology Organization Reports, 5 (2), 124–26.

Jackson, R. (1990) *Quasi-States: Sovereignty, International Relations and the Third World*, Cambridge, Cambridge University Press.

James, A. (1999) 'The practice of sovereign statehood in contemporary international society', *Political Studies*, 47, 457–73.

Jilberto, A. and Mommen, A. (eds) (1998) *Regionalization and Globalization in the Modern World Economy*, London, Routledge.

Knowledge@Wharton (2005) 'The new new economy: earning real money in the virtual world', online at www.knowledge.wharton.upenn.edu/article.cfm?articleid+1302.

Leiby, R. and Lileks, J. (1995) 'The ruse that roared', *Washington Post*, November 5.

McCullough, D. (2000) 'A data sanctuary is born', online at www.wired.com/techbiz/media/news/2000/06/36749.

O'Brien, R. (1992) *Global Financial Integration: The End of Geography*, London, Pinter.

Robbins, R. (2004) *Global Problems and the Culture of Capitalism*, Boston, Allyn and Bacon.

Shields, R. (2003) *The Virtual*, London, Routledge.

Worldwide Fund for Nature and the Global Footprint Network (2006) *Living Planet Report 2006*, Gland Switzerland WWF International. www.internetworldstats.com/stats.htm; www.footprintnetwork.org; www.havenco.com/law.html; www.secondlife.com.

CHAPTER 20

The Nuclear Condition and the Soft-Shell of Territoriality[*]

Richard J. Harknett

How should we ponder state security in the globalizing conditions of the early twenty-first century? In our current era, it is the possession, pursuit or lack of nuclear weapons capability that frames much of the dynamics associated with international security. While much attention in security studies and policy after 2001 has focused on the tactic of terrorism, it is the nuclear condition that overlays security competition. We live in a nuclear prominent world. Despite the fact that millions have died since 1946 due to non-nuclear conflict, it is the potential of nuclear use that drives much security-related diplomacy. Relations between states with nuclear forces differ from security competition between non-nuclear states (consider India and Pakistan, pre- and post-nuclear tests or the difference in US policy towards nuclear North Korea and non-nuclear Iraq). The pursuit of nuclear weapons as opposed to conventional military technology engenders distinct state and international reactions, ranging from sanctions (Iran in 2007), coercive threats (Libya in 2000s) and preventive military strikes (Israel against the Iraqi Osirak nuclear facility in 1981). Even the suspicion of pursuit can serve as a basis for preventive war, as non-nuclear Iraq experienced in 2003 (Harknett, 2003a). When considering the significance of terrorist threats since 2001, in fact, much of the focus on combating terrorism rests on a fear of non-state actors acquiring a nuclear device. Whether such a fear is overblown, as some have argued (Mueller, 2006), it is a driving planning principle, for example, of American homeland security efforts.

A framework of nuclear prominence requires book-length exposition to develop (Harknett, manuscript), so this chapter will focus more narrowly on a key fundamental flaw in thinking about the nuclear era – a misconception concerning the basic relationship between the state's pursuit of security and today's dominant military technology. This chapter offers a particular conceptualization of territoriality that points to a future international system in which state security competition will remain potent. This will hold despite the emergence of serious non-state threats.

Although inexorably tied to the Cold War superpower competition, nuclear weaponry must be understood as an underlying feature of contemporary world politics. The end of the Cold War did not end the parallel nuclear era. September 11, 2001, did not displace it either. The emergence of a capacity instantaneously to inflict societal-wide devastation represents an essential break with international political history.

This chapter assesses the extent to which the most significant military capability of the twentieth and early twenty-first century shapes how we think about the fundamental rationale for the territorial state – that is, its ability to afford protection to its population. I argue that the nuclear era requires a re-conceptualization of territoriality within the dimension of state security competition in which state territorial integrity is fundamentally supported, not through organizing for defence, but through reliance on nuclear deterrence. States, of course, pursue a range of security strategies including such things as homeland defence, but the underlying condition of the nuclear era places a premium on strategies that focus on preventing use, rather than absorbing, containing and minimizing costs. Rather than overwhelm the state's ability to afford protection, nuclear possession can reinforce territoriality. Such a conceptualization has serious implications for both theory and practice.

This is not a static analysis, but one that recognizes that the emergence of this particular weapon technology parallels a global dynamic that serves to reinforce and expand the nuclear condition. *Lethal* globalization is the accelerating trend in the diffusion of information, financial capital, goods, services and people that supports disruption and destruction. This dangerous subset of globalization is creating a condition in which decreasing amounts of effort are required to produce acts of increasing harm. The dimension of security competition between states – a dangerous dimension that has caused millions of deaths in the past century alone – remains the most serious because states retain the most capacity for *sustained* efforts of disruption and destruction. Lethal globalization promises to make non-state actors potent security threats as well, but their ability to sustain wide-scale conflict is not clear and the distinctions between chemical, biological and nuclear weapons, despite their grouping under the label of weapons of mass destruction (WMD), are important and require more study. This chapter focuses on the increasingly overlooked underlying shift that nuclear weapons have brought to state relations and concludes with an observation of how the frame of territoriality can help in thinking about non-state security dimensions as well.

The second phase of the nuclear era

The Treaty of Westphalia (1648) is considered a traditional demarcation for the emergence of the modern international system, defined by the central status accorded the territorial state. It is an international system that has been dominated by the dynamics and logic of power politics (Vasquez, 1993). The basic unit of the current international system is the territorially defined, mutually exclusive state (Mellor, 1989; Gottmann, 1973). It is this system of rule that, in modern times, has been considered best for fulfilling the twin objectives of physical protection and promotion of a general population's welfare (Ruggie, 1993). The fact that thirty new territorial states became members of the United Nations just as recently as the 1990s speaks to this system of rule's continued prevalence (United Nations, 2000).

The essence of the territorial state is its territoriality – that is, its defensibility against hostile outside forces. Although the stability of the state rests on other factors, such as internal and external legitimacy (Herz, 1973: 31) as well as relations with other states (Gulick, 1955; Morgenthau, 1985), the fundamental rationale for organizing within the territorial state unit is its potential ability to protect a specific population. The establishment of a basic level of security serves as the foundation for all other political-social activities.

In the context of international relations, territoriality consists of the set of state policies and organizations constructed to deny the extension of direct political control over one's territory to hostile external forces, and to constrain indirect political influence. In this sense, territoriality supports the modern manifestation of sovereignty, in which political authority structures are territorially bounded (Hinsley, 1986). Sovereignty and territoriality reinforce each other. The undermining of territoriality, therefore, would strike at the foundations of national sovereignty as we conceive of it today. To the extent that the protective power of the state is enhanced, it can be argued that territorially bounded authority structures are supported. Since the sovereign territorial state is the central unit of the international system, the state's enhancement or detraction directly affects the potential for systemic change.

Whether the territorial state will continue to be considered the most efficacious political-social structure has been a central topic of debate in the literature on international economics and research into the technological revolutions in communications and transportation (Krasner and Thomson, 1996; Toffler and Toffler, 1993). Globalization debates over issues such as population growth, pollution, ozone depletion, migration and health have centred on questions concerning the appropriateness and limitations of the territorially bounded state international system (Wijkman, 1996; Matthews, 1996; Simon, 1996). Interestingly, the debate over the future of the state has received less attention from traditional security studies specialists. The emergence and history of the modern state has been tied closely in security studies literature to the development of military capabilities and organizations that have enhanced territorial defence (McNeill, 1982). This chapter directs attention towards the relationship between recent advancements in military capabilities (i.e., nuclear weapons) and the modern state structure. The question is whether the nuclear era has changed the function and power of the state to afford protection to its populace.

In examining the relationship between state territoriality and nuclear weapons, it becomes clear that the Cold War may be understood best as a transition period in which state approaches to security lagged behind strategic reality (Harknett, 1998). Mutual superpower possession of nuclear weapons eliminated military assault against their respective homelands and major allies as a rational option for challenging the status quo. Objectively, such a move would have led to catastrophic costs that would have outweighed any potential benefit. Yet, both main Cold War protagonists remained mired in a focus on the ability to project and use military power to advance national interests. The Cold War followed the pattern of traditional power politics, which assumes, given anarchy, the constant potential for conflict and, thus, promotes a self-help approach to security (Vasquez, 1993; Waltz, 2000). Both the US and the Soviet Union pursued nuclear strategies that, at times, included the possibility of limited use, counter-force first strikes and pre-emption (Freedman, 1989, 2004); all of which seem absurd in the face of a strategic environment dominated by assured destruction capabilities. In retrospect, it is a testament to the robust nature of mutual assured destruction (MAD) that despite heavy investment in modernization and war planning, neither superpower could find a sustainable escape from the condition (and implications) of assured destruction.

This is not the first time in modern history that state approaches to security seem to have been at odds with new strategic conditions brought about by technological innovation. In the early-1900s prior to the First World War, the political and military doctrines of all the great powers placed great emphasis on maintaining the military offensive. This focus on offensive capability and tactics endured despite available evidence, which included the recently fought American Civil War and the Russo-Japanese conflict, suggesting that defensive innovations had made such offensively oriented doctrines problematic (Miller et al., 1991). This strategic reality, in which the advantage had shifted from offence to defence, did not come into full view until fighting began. It was a reality confirmed by the devastating losses incurred on both sides of the Great War.

Not unlike the generals and military analysts of the early twentieth century, post–Second World War strategists noted the potential impact of technological and military innovation, but hesitated to conclude that it required a fundamental alteration in state security behaviour. However, simply because change is not acted upon does not mean that in reality it has not occurred. In historical terms, therefore, the Cold War might be considered the first phase of a broader and novel international context that also began in 1945 – a period that can be differentiated as the nuclear era. The severe competition (Cold War) between the US and the Soviet Union overshadowed a more subtle and underlying change in the method by which states should organize themselves for protection (nuclear era). A shift in strategic reality – this time from a defence to a deterrence-dominated territorial security environment – has been occurring since 1945. This is the case despite the superpowers' hesitancy to change fully their military doctrines during the first phase of the nuclear era to reflect the shift (Mlyn, 1994). Fortunately to date, the world has avoided the type of confirmatory action the strategists of the early twentieth century experienced.

The changes wrought in state security relations by the emergence of nuclear weapons have been relatively obscured from vision, first by the Cold War edifice, then by the 'peace dividend' and 'end of history' notions that followed its collapse, and currently by a focus on terrorism. Critical to re-conceptualizing the territorial state in the nuclear era is the recognition that the mass destruction potential of nuclear weapons holds out the prospect of altering, in significant ways, how states perceive their security interests. Despite other real security challenges, it is the impact of nuclear weapons on territoriality that is key.

Territoriality and the universalist solution

John Gerard Ruggie (1993: 143) considers the work of John Herz in the 1950s and 1960s the only 'serious' attempt by an international security specialist to address territoriality in the context of the nuclear era. In a series of articles, John Herz argued that the basic rationale behind the organization of state policies and structures was to provide for protection against external aggression. The maintenance of a state's territorial integrity was a prerequisite for the establishment of internal social order and the promotion of a population's general welfare. The state, according to Herz, attempted to fulfil its protective function through the construction of a relatively impermeable territorially demarcated hard-shell of defence. This hard-shell could be enhanced, of course, through appropriate application of military strategies, which would guide the technical development, the tactical use and the operational deployment of military capabilities. In some cases, offensively oriented doctrines that advocated holding the initiative to put at risk the assets of opposing states were perceived as the best defence. However fulfilled, the protective function of the state became a central issue for all modern states. The degree to which states differed in their ability to carry out this function was reflected in the distribution of power across the international system. The major states of the international system tended to be those with the base capabilities to protect themselves against external interference. John Herz argued that the advent of nuclear weapons called the protective function of the territorial state into question. Because of nuclear weapons, the most powerful units in the international system had become vulnerable to utter devastation in an instant. The hard-shell of defence had been overwhelmed by a technical advance, which had ushered in a new 'condition of permeability' (Herz, 1973: 121).

The possession of a relatively small number of these weapons can put at risk an entire society. Possession of an assured destruction capability by all parties involved in a dispute creates a unique strategic environment. Continued survival depends not on one's own actions, but on the continued sanity of one's opponents. For Herz, state territoriality in a nuclear context becomes a misnomer. The destructive potential of nuclear weapons means that states no longer have principal control over their own protection. This new condition of absolute permeability, for Herz, means a loss of protective power at the state level.

According to Herz, this loss of protective power creates incentives and pressures to move away from the modern state system. The desire and need for protection continues to exist even if the territorial state can no longer provide it. Some new authority structures must be created to fulfil this function. The pressure will only increase as nuclear weapons spread to more countries. As more states acquire the destructive potential associated with these weapons, more state security relations will have to function under a condition of permeability. Hard-shell territoriality will begin to disappear on a broader scale. In a proliferated world, the continued survival of individual societies will be linked and connected on a daily basis. Herz concludes that since security in the nuclear era may no longer rest at the state level, it must become a global concern. Nuclear weapons pressure territoriality and, thus, create the incentive to move towards an alternative universalist system of global order. The universalist solution to a nuclear world flows from a theoretical analysis of the impact nuclear weapons have had on state territoriality. Herz sees this analysis flowing from a realistic assessment of the security problems facing states in the nuclear era. He proposes a global response to the nuclear predicament. Post-1991 policy debates moved in the opposite direction, however. The pressures created by nuclear weapons on state territoriality led, particularly in the United States, to policies that essentially have sought to restore pre-nuclear territoriality.

Herz's universalist solution rests on a recognition of the current security reality, accepts it and suggests that it must be dealt with under new structures. The basic desire for security is the driving force. What might be distinguished as the restorative solution, however, posits an ideal situation in which, through technical solutions and greater trust, both the technology and knowledge associated with nuclear weapons can be forsaken and we can return to the days in which conventional capabilities held sway.

Territoriality and the restorative alternative

The superpowers and their great-power allies made nuclear weapons central to their state security during the Cold War. They also pursued a co-ordinated policy, which breached ideological lines, to stop the spread of nuclear weaponry to other states in the system. With the end of the Cold War, the spread of nuclear weapons became recognised as a primary international security threat. Major efforts were begun to strengthen and broaden the trade practices, technology transfer agreements and international treaties that encompass the nuclear non-proliferation regime (Clinton, 1994). The prevailing wisdom supporting nuclear non-proliferation policy promoted a simultaneous reduction in the role to be played by nuclear weapons in great-power politics (Harknett, 1994). The US and Russia presented the disarmament begun under the Strategic Arms Reduction Treaties (Start I and Start II) and the Moscow Treaty of 2002 as fulfilment of pledges made in the Non-Proliferation Treaty to link non-nuclear weapons states' rejection of nuclear weapons with sustained reductions by nuclear weapon states. Thus, non-proliferation in the 1990s became intertwined with a broader consensus on moving away from a nuclear weapon-dominated international security environment (Nye, 1992; Clinton, 1999). Taking the lead in 1993, the United States initiated a national security strategy that it hoped would: (1) reverse the spread of nuclear weapons to rogue countries through counter-proliferation (identified at the time as Iran, Iraq, Libya and North Korea); (2) strengthen existing denial tools through non-proliferation; and (3) reduce the role of nuclear weapons through disarmament and greater reliance on extended conventional deterrence (Clinton, 1994). Although domestic politics led to a US Senate rejection of the Comprehensive Test Ban Treaty (CTBT), the consensus against nuclear weapons remained strong, with 135 countries completing ratification through 2006. The Bush administration continued along the restorative path, applying counter-proliferation strategies through the creation of the Proliferation Security Initiative and deploying Ballistic Missile Defence capabilities (Bush, 2006: 18). Despite rhetoric to the contrary, American strategists view missile defences as supporting power projection potential that can be applied during regional crises against weaker states that might possess a small missile force armed with WMD warheads. Missile defence is a capacity meant to restore the relevancy of conventional force balances (Harknett, 2001a).

In terms of territoriality, non-proliferation, nuclear disarmament and missile defence, policies can be viewed as responses to the loss of protective power at the state level that seek to restore a form of pre-nuclear-era defensibility to the state. What is so intriguing about this approach is that it accepts the Herz analysis of the impact of nuclear weapons on state territoriality, yet rejects his solution. Non-proliferation and disarmament policies are driven by an underlying recognition that protective power has been lost at the state level. However, rather than advocate a global transformation of political organization and authority to deal with the condition of permeability, non-proliferation and disarmament policies taken to their logical end promise to reverse that condition. In a nuclear-disarmed world, defensibility is attainable again; the hard-shell is relevant. With territoriality restored, the rationale for the state system remains secure.

The reasons for the US and other great powers to seek this solution to the nuclear era are clear. A return to an international system of relatively impermeable territorial states would mean that varying abilities to provide protection would again be a basis for distinguishing state power internationally. Where the traditional relationship between military capabilities and defensibility exists, basic power politics dominates. The restoration of such a system obviously favours those states possessing heavy concentrations of traditional measures of power and, not surprisingly, these same states take the lead in non-proliferation efforts. Recommending in favour of American ratification of the Comprehensive Test Ban Treaty, an American official put it bluntly: 'given our overwhelming conventional superiority, assigning a broader role to nuclear weapons would cause far more problems than it would solve' (Shalikashvili, 2001: A21).

Both universalist and restorative solutions to the nuclear era assume the following: that the protective function of the state has been overwhelmed by nuclear weapons; that the loss of protective power undermines state territorial integrity; and that the undermining of state territoriality threatens the stability of the territorial state system. The universalist solution assumes that the new condition of permeability produced by nuclear weapons is permanent and thus requires systemic change. The restorative solution sees this condition as reversible, requiring only state behavioural and capability changes.

The universalist solution has typically been critiqued as a utopian vision. The restorative solution, however, also rests on a set of idealistic principles (Carr, 1946). Successful non-proliferation and eventual disarmament require a high degree of state co-ordination and trust. The movement to reduce the role played by nuclear weapons short of disarmament runs against traditional balance of power dynamics in which existing capabilities rather than professed intentions drive state assessments of one other. Giving conventional forces an enhanced role in one's defence posture does not change the fact that nuclear weapons exist. Imagine a regional crisis in which an ally of the US is threatened by a state possessing a small nuclear arsenal. In order to deter potential aggression against the ally, the US might threaten the regional adversary with retaliation by precision-guided conventional weaponry. Because of the US dominance in high-tech conventional weapons, it might be believed that the punishment that could be inflicted would be of such a high level as to make an attack on the American ally worthless. However, relying on conventional deterrents to dissuade a nuclear-armed regional actor does not transform the environment into a pure conventional military situation. Would the US have attacked Iraq in January 1991 or March 2003 with a conventional air assault if Saddam Hussein had possessed a nuclear weapon? Would the crisis dynamics have been different had Baghdad attempted to deter a US offensive with the threat of nuclear retaliation on Israel and Saudi Arabia, even if in reality it turned out to be a bluff? (Harknett, 2003c). While greater emphasis on conventional weapons might support non-proliferation efforts, in the end, hard-shell territoriality can only be restored through total nuclear disarmament. This, of course, would require not only the dismantling of existing arsenals, but intensive verification regimes as well. One of the paradoxical twists associated with nuclear weapons is that the likelihood of their use increases as their numbers decrease. Nuclear use becomes *thinkable* again below the assured destruction level of possession unless trust and cooperation become such international norms that no state considers cheating (that is, retaining a nuclear capacity despite disarmament). Current non-proliferation policy's restorative path requires a level of trust unattained to date in international political history.

In terms of the universalist solution, although moving beyond the current state system is unlikely, it is based, ironically, on a more realistic assessment of the contemporary security environment and how self-preservation drives people to organize politically.

Soft-shell territoriality

Although a number of questions can be raised regarding the two solutions to the nuclear era offered above, it is the basic analysis concerning the impact of nuclear weapons on territoriality that is critical. Both conclude that nuclear weapons have overwhelmed the protective function of the state and thus promise to undermine the integrity of each territorial unit and the territorial state system. The brief history of the nuclear era, however, suggests that such an assessment is inaccurate (or at least debatable). Although the time period is too short and the number of relevant states too small to support a sophisticated correlative analysis, the empirical record to date is clear. Nuclear weapon states have not engaged in sustained war with each other. When military crises between nuclear states have arisen, in every case the direction of the confrontation has been towards de-escalation and a non-military resolution. Although the empirical record is constrained by the above-mentioned limitations, it is of some significance. During the first sixty years of the nuclear era, wars have been fought between states when at least one side did not possess nuclear weapons (US-PRC in Korea, India-Pakistan, India-PRC) but not after mutual possession. The absence of war between nuclear powers cannot be explained away by a lack of dispute. During the Cold War, the two superpowers engaged in a number of military crises that in every instance led to de-escalation rather than war. The same is true with the 1969 Sino-Soviet border confrontation and the several post-1987 Pakistani-Indian crises. Although the cause of a non-event is difficult to establish, the unmistakable trend in security relations between nuclear-weapon states has been towards crisis de-escalation as threats increase and, ultimately, to war avoidance.

One possible explanation for this trend can be drawn from a different look at the relationship between nuclear weapons and territoriality. Rather than viewing the impact of nuclear weapons as stripping away the protective function of the state, it is possible to conceptualize their impact as an enhancement to territorial integrity. It is true that the destructive potential of nuclear weapons has made every country vulnerable to rapid annihilation. The pre-nuclear conceptualization of territoriality as a hard-shell of defence in which protection was achieved by planning to repulse an offensive attack has indeed been undermined by nuclear weapons. The traditional relationship between offensive and defensive strategies no longer makes sense in the nuclear context. However, Herz made a fundamental error in his otherwise thoughtful analysis (the same is true of restorative analysis that accepts the Herzian view of territoriality). Herz narrowly defined the means of protection that can be associated with the function of protection. Conceptually, he made no distinction between defensibility (that is the ability to defend oneself) and the role of the state as protector. Prior to the end of the Second World War, indeed, protection of state territorial integrity rested on the ability to repel an attack. That this was the primary manner by which states fulfilled their protective function should not mean that it is the only way to fulfil that function, however. The undermining of a particular means does not necessarily imply abandonment of the function.

Within the dimension of state security competition, the protective function is fulfilled by the ability to dissuade an attacker. Rather than attempt to resist attacking forces physically, protection rests on the attempt to convince a potential opponent not to initiate an offensive in the first place. Territoriality in the nuclear era can be conceptualized not as a hard-shell of defence, but rather as a *soft-shell of deterrence*. The territorial state retains its protective function in the nuclear era through the dissuasive power of nuclear possession.

What is the consequence of soft-shell territoriality on international security relations? In a security environment dominated by conventional weapons, the ability to project and use force depends on a variety of factors: the size of a military force, the sophistication of the weapons, industrial base, soldier training, geography and weather. Traditionally this ability has been used to measure how power is distributed across the international system. Great powers are distinguished by their military prowess, particularly in their relations with smaller powers (Mearsheimer, 2001). The variation in defensibility impacts significantly on great-power/small-power dynamics and on the range of behaviour in which each type of state can engage. The classic case of the Melian dialogue as told by Thucydides captures this relationship well. As the generals of ancient Athens prepared to invade the tiny island of Melos, they explained away their actions by noting that 'the strong do what they have the power to do and the weak accept what they have to accept' (Thucydides, 1985 [1954]: 402; Harknett, 2001b; Harknett, 2002). In a world of hard-shell territoriality in which offence and defence are highly relevant, differences in military capability (even subtle ones) will impact on state security relations.

The world of soft-shell territoriality, however, potentially alters the dynamics associated with traditional power politics. This alteration holds not only for great power relations constrained by a condition of mutual assured destruction, but, given further proliferation, for great-power/weak-state relations as well (Preston, 1994). The traditional realist view has held that the independence of small or weak states depends on the balance of power, a great power benefactor and/or 'their lack of attractiveness for imperialistic' exploitation (Morgenthau, 1985: 196). According to this view, the independence of small powers is exogenously dependent. This is what differentiates them from great powers, which, on a rising scale, possess the internal ability to protect themselves. Soft-shell territoriality supported by nuclear possession challenges this fundamental distinction. In the world of soft-shell territoriality, all states become dependent, to a certain degree, on decisions made outside their borders. Ultimate security rests on restructuring the decision-making of potential opponents so that war is no longer considered an option. While that dissuasive influence requires possession of a particular capability, whether security is actually gained is more directly tied to the decision-making of the opponent.

The lack of an effective hard-shell, which is critical in distinguishing states in a conventionally dominated security environment, may become less consequential if a robust soft-shell is in place. Since nuclear weapons simplify greatly a state's ability to inflict destruction on an opponent at a relatively low level of nuclear possession, differences in conventional force structures will become less relevant. The weakness in defensive power typical of small states may be compensated by the possession of nuclear deterrent power. While small nuclear-armed states will remain defensively weak, and thus permeable, the soft-shell of deterrence may be effective in constraining the willingness of great powers to project military capability abroad. Although *able*, great power states may be *unwilling* to use force when faced with the risk of nuclear retaliation. This may hold even if the levels of retaliation between the great and weak powers are disproportionate. Would the US use conventional force in the Middle East/Persian Gulf against a country that threatened to retaliate with nuclear weapons against Israel and one American city? Can the US in such an instance assume that the country attempting to deter its action would be 'self-deterred' because of the larger US nuclear arsenal? Why should a leadership facing defeat differentiate between loss of leadership as a result of conventional military victory or nuclear bombing when, in either event, power and the lives of the leaders are likely lost? The mere fact that these questions would have to be asked implies that such a context for dispute is already different from one in which conventional military force is the defining factor. Although the

US, in the above example, would be capable of producing a conventional military victory, the question becomes whether it would be willing to make the attempt in an environment of heightened risk. Although deterrence is not guaranteed, nuclear use can insure greater cost in the event of war.

In this sense, the impact of nuclear weapons on territoriality may be to enhance individual state territorial integrity despite continued variance in the traditional sources of power. Rather than undermine the territorial state system as Herz suggested, deterrence power may stabilize it. While conflicts of interest will still exist, a world of soft-shell territoriality increases the incentives for states to co-operate in avoiding war even while they try to gain advantages over one another. This last point is important. Organizing state territoriality around the soft-shell of nuclear deterrence does not mean an elimination of competition in the pursuit of power and influence, but rather a re-direction of that competition away from direct military challenges to state territorial integrity. The distribution of power would remain significant. It would, however, be measured through greater attention to such variables as economic disparities, natural resource endowment and political stability. The ability to affect state behaviour beyond one's borders would have to emphasize these non-military sources of power. The struggle for power and the contest over influence would increasingly take place in a realm in which direct military challenge to territorial integrity would no longer serve as arbiter.

The promise of soft-shell territoriality

The end of the Cold War signalled the cessation of a particular competition, not the conclusion of an era. The superpower rivalry overshadowed the true transformation in state security relations begun in 1945, and to some extent 11 September 2001 has proven a distraction to it. The change wrought by the nuclear era is one of adaptation in the means by which states protect themselves. Territoriality – the ability to protect and support a state's territorial integrity – had traditionally been perceived in terms of defence. The level of vulnerability produced by the threat of nuclear attack is such that territoriality must be rethought. Rather than promote a forward movement beyond state sovereignty or a reversal of the vulnerability altogether, the possession of nuclear weapons by more countries will tend to enhance the territorial integrity of states across the distribution of traditional power within the state system.

The emergence of non-state actors through lethal globalization as serious security threats does not undermine a focus on state consolidation and territoriality. The potential of individuals or small groups to use WMD is in line with Herz's notion of permeability. While other security options (homeland security) are being added to deal with this condition, the primary strategic response to the non-state dimension of security competition, counterintuitively, is intriguingly to push security back towards the state dimension, where deterrence dominates (Harknett, 2003b). Ultimately, the response to non-state actor threats, since 11 September 2001 has been an increased emphasis on state accountability and threats of military responses (even preemptive raids) against states that give sanctuary or indirect support to non-state actors (Bush, 2002, 2006). Of course, the main military actions taken in response to the attack were against countries – Afghanistan and Iraq.

Coercive threats against states will remain a central feature of security competition even as other options are added to deal with the non-state dimension of security. The territorial state and its system will seek to remain alive and well behind a soft-shell of nuclear deterrence. Nuclear states may venture out preventively and preemptively against non-nuclear states, but such a dynamic will only reinforce the prominence of nuclear capacity. Soft-shell territoriality and the nuclear condition is an essential frame for understanding twenty-first-century international security.

Notes

* The author wishes to thank the Charles Phelps Taft Research Center at the University of Cincinnati for its generous support.

References

Bush, G. W. (2002) Remarks by the President on the six-month anniversary of the 11 September attacks, online at http://www.whitehouse.gov/news/releases/2002/03/20020311-1.html.
———. (2006) *National Security Strategy of the United States*, Official US policy document, online at http://www.whitehouse.gov/nsc/nss/2006/.
Carr, E. H. (1946) *The Twenty Years' Crisis, 1919–1939*, New York, Harper Torchbooks.
Clinton, W. (1994) *A National Security Strategy of Engagement and Enlargement*, July, Washington, DC, Government Printing Office.
———. (1999) *A National Security Strategy for a New Century*, December, Washington, DC, Government Printing Office.
Freedman, L. (1989) *The Evolution of Nuclear Strategy*, New York, St. Martin's Press.
———. (2004) *Deterrence*, Cambridge, Polity Press.
Gottmann, J. (1973) *The Significance of Territory*, Charlotiesville, VA: University Press of Virginia.
Gulick, E. (1955) *Europe's Classical Balance of Power*, New York, Norton and Company.
Harknett, R. (1994) 'The logic of conventional deterrence and the end of the cold war', *Security Studies*, 4, 86–114.
———. (1998) 'State preferences, systemic constraints, and the absolute weapon' in T. V. Paul, R. Harknett and J. Wirtz (eds), *The Absolute Weapon Revisited: Nuclear Arms and the Emerging International Order*, Ann Arbor, University of Michigan Press, pp. 65–100.
———. (2001a) 'Global stability in a changing defense environment' in J. Larsen and J. Wirtz (eds), *Rockets Red Glare: Missile Defense and the Future of World Politics*, Boulder, CO: Westview Press, pp. 156–81.
———. (2001b) 'The fate of Melos', *Norton's IRWebSource*, New York, Norton and Company.
———. (2002) *Lenses of Analysis: A Visual Framework for the Study of International Relations*, New York, Norton and Company.
———. (2003a) 'Fear, opportunity, and preventive war: the American rationale for conflict with Iraq' in E. Reiter (ed.), *Jahrbuch fur internationale Sicherheitspolitk*, Berlin, Verlag E.S. Mittler and Sohn GmbH, pp. 101–19.
———. (2003b) 'Integrated security: a strategic response to anonymity and the problem of the few', *Contemporary Security Policy*, 24, 13–45.
———. (2003c) 'Brace yourself for a showdown with Saddam', *Toronto Globe and Mail*, February 13, A27.
———. (manuscript) *Nuclear Prominence: Security and the Contestability of Costs.*
Herz, J. (1973) *The Nation-State and the Crisis of World Politics*, New York, David McKay Co.

Hinsley, F. H. (1986) *Sovereignty*, 2nd ed., Cambridge, Cambridge University Press.

Krasner, S. and Thomson, J. (1996) 'Global transactions and the consolidation of sovereignty' in R. Art and R. Jervis (eds), *International Politics: Enduring Concepts and Contemporary Issues*, 4th ed., New York, HarperCollins, pp. 319–39.

Matthews, J. T. (1996) 'Redefining security' in R. Art and R. Jervis (eds), *International Politics: Enduring Concepts and Contemporary Issues*, 4th ed., New York, HarperCollins, pp. 486–98.

McNeill, W. (1982) *The Pursuit of Power*, Chicago, University of Chicago Press.

Mearsheimer, J. (2001) *The Tragedy of Great Power Politics*, New York, Norton and Company.

Mellor, R. (1989) *Nation, State, and Territory*, London, Routledge.

Miller, S., Lynn-Jones, S. and Van Evera, S. (eds) (1991) *Military Strategy and the Origins of the First World War*, Princeton, NJ, Princeton University Press.

Mlyn, E. (1994) *The State, Society, and Limited Nuclear War*, New York, State University of New York Press.

Morgenthau, H. (1985) *Politics Among Nations*, 6th ed., New York, Knopf.

Mueller, J. (2006) *Overblown: How Politicians and the Terrorism Industry Inflate National Security Threats, and Why We Believe Them*, New York, Free Press.

Nye, J. S. (1992) 'New approaches to proliferation policy', *Science*, 256, 293–297.

Preston, T. (1994) 'The challenge of nuclear proliferation in the post-cold war era', unpublished manuscript, Department of Political Science, Washington State University.

Ruggie, J. G. (1993) 'Territoriality and beyond: problematizing modernity in international relations', *International Organization*, 47, 139–74.

Shalikashvili, J. (2001) 'The test ban solution', *The Washington Post*, 6 January, A21.

Simon, J. (1996) 'The infinite supply of natural resources' in R. Art and R. Jervis (eds), *International Politics: Enduring Concepts and Contemporary Issues*, 4th ed., New York, HarperCollins, pp. 498–505.

Thucydides (1985) [1954] *The Peloponnesian War*, New York, Penguin Classics.

Toffler, A. and Toffler, H. (1993) *War and Anti-War: Survival at the Dawn of the 21st Century*, Boston, Little Brown.

United Nations (2000) *Growth in UN Membership: Basic Facts about the UN*, New York, Department of Public Information.

Vasquez, J. (1993) *The War Puzzle*, Cambridge, Cambridge University Press.

Waltz, K. (2000) 'Structural realism after the cold war', *International Security*, 25, 5–41.

Wijkman, P. M. (1996) 'Managing the global commons' in R. Art and R. Jervis (eds), *International Politics: Enduring Concepts and Contemporary Issues*, 4th ed., New York, HarperCollins, pp. 466–85.

Index